Exceptionalism in Crisis

CIVIL WAR AMERICA

Caroline E. Janney and Aaron Sheehan-Dean, *editors*

This landmark series interprets broadly the history and culture of the Civil War era through the long nineteenth century and beyond. Drawing on diverse approaches and methods, the series publishes historical works that explore all aspects of the war, biographies of leading commanders, and tactical and campaign studies, along with select editions of primary sources. Together, these books shed new light on an era that remains central to our understanding of American and world history.

A complete list of books published in Civil War America is available at https://uncpress.org/series/civil-war-america.

ALYS D. BEVERTON

Exceptionalism in Crisis

Faction, Anarchy, and Mexico in the US Imagination during the Civil War Era

The University of North Carolina Press *Chapel Hill*

This book was published with the assistance of the Authors Fund of the University of North Carolina Press.

Set in Arno Pro by Westchester Publishing Services
Manufactured in the United States of America

Library of Congress Cataloging-in-Publication Data
Names: Beverton, Alys D., author.
Title: Exceptionalism in crisis : faction, anarchy, and Mexico in the US imagination during the Civil War era / Alys D. Beverton.
Other titles: Civil War America (Series)
Description: Chapel Hill : University of North Carolina Press, [2025] | Series: Civil War America | Includes bibliographical references and index.
Identifiers: LCCN 2024045012 | ISBN 9781469685205 (cloth) | ISBN 9781469685212 (paperback) | ISBN 9781469685229 (epub) | ISBN 9781469687537 (pdf)
Subjects: LCSH: Exceptionalism—United States—History—19th century. | Exceptionalism—Confederate States of America. | United States—History—Civil War, 1861–1865—Influence. | Mexico—Politics and government—Foreign public opinion. | United States—Relations—Mexico. | Mexico—Relations—United States. | BISAC: HISTORY / United States / Civil War Period (1850–1877) | SOCIAL SCIENCE / Ethnic Studies / Caribbean & Latin American Studies
Classification: LCC E468.9 .B49 2025 | DDC 973.7/13—dc23/eng/20241118
LC record available at https://lccn.loc.gov/2024045012

Cover art: *Map of the United States of America* by George Woolworth Colton, 1857. Courtesy of the Library of Congress Geography and Map Division.

To my Year 9 history teacher, Mr. John Bell,

who made the past crackle and spark.

Contents

Acknowledgments

This book began as a PhD thesis. It has therefore been the touchstone of my academic identity as I moved from PhD student to early career scholar. In traversing this path, I have accumulated many debts. Indeed, if left to my own devices I doubt I would have got much further than scribbling down a few preliminary research questions before I became discouraged or overwhelmed and gave up. Developing this project from an idea into a thesis and then into a book required support of various kinds from many different people. What follows is my attempt to acknowledge some of those helping hands, though their contributions are more meaningful to me than I have been able to express in words here.

Those who had the first and most profound influence on this project were my PhD supervisors at University College London (UCL), Professor Adam I. P. Smith and Dr. David Sim. For four years they tested my assumptions, challenged my conclusions, and showed me how to be a better researcher and communicator of history. Both Adam and David are the best kind of PhD supervisors—knowledgeable and wise, they are also generous and kind. I consider it very fortunate that I not only had their guidance during my PhD studies, but that they remain my friends to this day. I doubt I will ever stop needing their advice and am grateful that, so far, they have not cut me off.

The intellectual environment at UCL gave me inspiration and motivation during the critical early stages of this project. Here I must thank my fellow PhD students Matt Griffin, David Tiedemann, Mark Power Smith, Gareth Davies, Eilish Gregory, Misha Ewen, Cat Beck, and Marjolein van Bavel for their companionship and camaraderie. I will always look back fondly on our time well spent together in Birkbeck Bar. The wider Americanist community at the University of London also kept me stimulated and focused. I'm grateful to every member of the North American History Seminar Series at the Institute of Historical Research for this, and especially to Dr. Alex Goodall and Dr. Dan Peart, who were both good enough to read early draft portions of my thesis.

During my PhD studies I was fortunate to receive institutional support, which enabled me to undertake two research trips to the United States.

Grants from the British Association of American Studies (BAAS), British American Nineteenth Century Historians (BrANCH), and the Royal Historical Society (RHS) enabled me to visit first the New York Public Library and then the Library of Congress in Washington, DC. The value of these trips derived only partially from the materials they enabled me to access. As anyone who studies a country they do not live in knows, such trips nourish one's connection to the place one spends so much time reading, thinking, and writing about.

Once the PhD was done, transforming it into a book manuscript was another Herculean task that required the help of many people. My first thanks here go my two excellent PhD examiners, Professor Robert Cook and Professor Nicola Miller. Their questions put me through my paces and made clear to me those aspects of my project that needed work. At this stage I also benefitted from presenting my work to the wider Americanist community, both in the United Kingdom and the United States. The European Association of American Studies, BAAS, BrANCH, Institute of Historical Research, Oxford Early American Republic Series, Society for Historians of American Foreign Relations, and Southern Historical Association were all good enough to allow me to present my work to their members. Testing one's ideas before an audience—especially an audience more expert on the topic at hand than oneself—provides a powerful (albeit terrifying) kind of motivation, and I always returned to my work after these experiences with renewed energy and determination. Thanks also to my colleagues at Oxford Brookes University—a fantastic team of scholars who have cheered me along the way and reminded me to protect my research time even during grading season. My particular gratitude goes to Dr. Thomas Robb, my fellow US historian at Brookes, who generously read a full draft of this manuscript and asked for nothing in return.

I owe a big debt of gratitude to the editorial team at the University of North Carolina Press. First to Mark Simpson-Vos for standing by the project from start to finish. Also and especially to Debbie Gershenowitz and Alexis Dumain for their unflagging support throughout; thank you for patiently steering this first-time author through the twists and turns of the publication process. Two anonymous readers of the draft manuscript were the absolute best of their kind: professional, thorough, and constructive. Each read the manuscript with an open mind, judging it on its own terms and offering feedback that came from a genuine wish to make the manuscript stronger. Anything that is lacking in the final analysis is entirely due to my own limited ability to execute their excellent advice. A special thanks must also go to

Aaron Sheehan-Dean, who more than once went out of his way to offer his time and advice to me when he did not have to.

And finally, to my friends and family, and especially to my parents Sue and Alan and my husband Nathan. To thank you all properly for the many ways that you've helped me throughout this process would require writing another book. Since I don't have the energy for that, this will have to do.

Exceptionalism in Crisis

Introduction

For its first eighty-five years, the United States republic seemed to be, on the whole, functioning as designed. During that time the nation witnessed forty-two cohorts of congressmen in the House of Representatives, fourteen rounds of Senate elections, and twenty-one presidents in office. At each presidential election, the same process had played out: voters cast their ballots, a winner was decided, and the losing candidates conceded their loss. This is not to say that there hadn't been disruptions. Occasionally allegations of fraud and other forms of electoral malpractice surfaced or bouts of violence broke out on election days. Still, typically such abuses were eventually rooted out, popular passions cooled, and transfers of power occurred peacefully. The US republican experiment, it appeared, was a success—that is, until the presidential election of 1860.

The nation's mood in the run-up to the twentieth presidential election had been fractious. Four candidates stood, each representing a fragment of the shattered two-party system that had ordered national politics for the past thirty years. The campaign rhetoric was fiery. Republicans joined abolitionists in warning of a "Slave Power" conspiracy. Meanwhile across the South, Fire-Eaters, proslavery Southern separatists, threatened to pull their states out of the Union if Northern voters dared thrust upon them an antislavery president. These were ominous signs. And yet few were prepared for what came next. On November 6, 1861, US voters elected Republican Abraham Lincoln as their next president. The result electrified the Southern states. Within six weeks, South Carolina had announced its secession from the Union. Over the following four months, six more states did the same. By February 1861 they had formed their own nation: the Confederate States of America. The conflict between the free North and the slaveholding South, for generations contained by compromise and negotiation, had finally burst beyond the confines of the constitutional system. Two republics now stood where there had previously been one. A military standoff followed, shots were fired, and by April 1861 these republics were at war.

These were exhilarating, terrifying, and bewildering times to live through. It is understandable, therefore, that people in both the Union and the Confederacy searched for examples of other civil wars to better understand the conflict unfolding before them and predict what might come of it. US history offered no useful precedents, and so Northerners and Southerners looked beyond their borders. There were plenty of examples to choose from, particularly if one was willing to reach far back into the past. After all, internecine conflicts had long been the bane of democratic republics both ancient and modern. During the Secession Winter of 1860 to 1861, however, the experiences of one country above all others were on the minds of many. "The history of Mexico," the *Weekly Wisconsin Patriot* noted that February, offered numerous "gory examples" of the damage that the "sweeping hurricane of a war among neighbors, fathers and brothers" could inflict upon a self-governing people.[1] These examples were not encouraging. Indeed, the newspaper continued, judging by Mexico's past it would be less painful for North Americans "to declare [war] against all Europe—yea, against all the world combined, than for us to engage in a bloody strife, with our own line of consanguinity."[2]

The *Patriot* was not alone in turning to Mexico to think through what civil war would mean for the United States. From the conflict's beginning, people in both the North and South trawled Mexican history in search of clues that would explain the causes and consequences of their own domestic crisis. As they did so they acknowledged, whether explicitly or tacitly, that the US crisis bore many of the hallmarks of the type of domestic discord that, until that point, most North Americans had believed only occurred south of the Rio Grande. For much of the first half of the nineteenth century, civil conflicts of one kind or another had been rumbling throughout the Spanish American republics, devastating their economies and leaving their political systems in tatters. Antebellum US Americans had contrasted this chaotic picture against the relative tranquility of their own republican experiment, which had been humming along without major disruptions for eighty-five years—a sign, perhaps, that God had marked out the United States as the New World's exceptional republic.

This book is a study of how the US Civil War upended this comforting myth. After April 1861, no one could claim that Providence had exempted the United States from the scourge of fratricidal strife. Whether they welcomed the war or not, this was an extraordinary realization for people in the Union and the Confederacy to come to, and one that forced them to revisit certain long-held assumptions about their country's identity and global purpose. This study follows this soul-searching process as it manifested in public discourse, primarily the print media. Here Northern and Southern editors, journalists, politicians, and orators grappled with the fact that their civil war was following the same pattern that Mexico and the other Spanish American republics had been locked in for decades: the breakdown of the electoral system, a turn to arms, and the exchange of bullets to settle a political dispute.[3]

Though prompted by the Civil War, this national identity crisis was not resolved by the ending of the conflict. Mexican history showed that fratricidal contests tended not to be singular events, but instead created conditions of deep and persistent division in public life, which would periodically erupt into domestic violence for many years to come. As US Americans witnessed factionalism, contested elections, and paramilitary political violence plague their postwar republic, many of them wondered if this would be their fate too. This is, in essence, a book about how US Americans lost their faith in their nation's exceptionalism and the long, difficult journey they went on to regain it.

Mexico and US Exceptionalism

It was easy for people in the antebellum United States to believe that Providence had written two very different fates for the US and Mexican republics. At the dawn of the nineteenth century, independence movements broke out across Spanish America. By 1825, most of the region's colonies had re-formed into a string of eighteen self-governing nations running from southwestern North America to the horn of South America. Each of them resembled the United States insofar as they were constitutional democratic republics. However, it would soon transpire that similarity in form did not guarantee parity in outcome. Throughout the late 1820s and into the 1830s, US newspapers carried reports from Mexico and Central and South America that painted a tumultuous picture of corrupted elections, strongmen vying for power, and communities devolving into rebellion. The Spanish American republican experiment was off to a rocky start.[4]

Watching these events, observers in the United States became exasperated. Initially, many of them had been beguiled by the Spanish American revolutionaries—Bolívar, Ribas, Mariño—who spoke the language of Washington and Jefferson in Spanish accents. They had also been pleased with the thought that the Spanish American colonists' drive for independence had been inspired by US Americans' own war against the British Empire and their success in maintaining a republic thereafter. Throughout the late 1820s and 1830s, however, as they read about the convulsions below their border, US Americans' hopes that Spanish America would be the world's second bastion of democracy faded. The fact that many of these new republics sought to curtail or end slavery within their borders troubled citizens in the slaveholding portions of the United States even further. The result was that, over the course of the second quarter of the nineteenth century, US Americans' view of the Spanish American republics darkened. The common opinion became that these countries were inherently shaky constructions administered by narrow-minded, swarthy men who were more interested in personal gain than in governing and who were incapable of controlling their unruly multiracial populations.[5]

Mexico, more than any other Spanish American republic, became the target of US Americans' criticism. Originally born an empire in 1821, independent Mexico was rechristened a republic in 1824 and soon thereafter became one of the hemisphere's most unstable self-governing nations. The country's break with the Spanish colonial system had been traumatic. The Iberian political traditions that had governed New Spain placed authority in the monarch, who in turn managed certain powerful corporate groups including the Church, the military, and the owners of landed estates. Upon separation from Spain in 1821, Mexicans had struggled to agree on what source of political legitimacy would replace kingly authority as the basis of their new government. Pre-independence elites pushed for the same institutions that had ordered the colonial regime—slavery, caste hierarchy, established ecclesiastical power, and the land-owning classes—to be maintained. Arrayed against them were various shades of reformers who, inspired by Enlightenment notions of rational liberalism, wished to sweep away the relics of Spanish colonialism and create a centralized democratic state that would break up economic and social monopolies and safeguard individual rights.[6]

Antebellum US newspapers tended to portray Mexican politics as defined by a sharp split between liberalism and conservatism. While these neat categories do not capture the complexities of political thought in nineteenth-century Mexico, it is true that the country's political leaders generally sorted into one of these two broad camps, each representing opposing views on central questions of governance relating to federalism, secularism, and economic modernization. The depth of their disagreements was such that, during Mexico's first few decades of independence, political contests between Liberals and Conservatives frequently escalated into existential fights to determine the very form and nature of the country's system of government. Conflict between the factions intensified in the mid-1850s, when the dictatorial president Antonio Santa Anna was deposed by Liberal leader Benito Juárez and then replaced by Juan Álvarez. The event precipitated a full-blown civil war, known as the War of Reform (*Guerra de Reforma*), which lasted from February 1857 until December 1860. Added to this were numerous ethnic, regional, and class divisions that further cut Mexican society into fragments and were themselves the source of periodic uprisings, most notably in areas such as Yucatán where Native and peasant populations were large, impoverished, and deeply embittered against government authorities.[7]

Even in times of notional peace, there was an unsettled air to Mexican politics. Between 1825 and 1855 the republic saw forty-eight turnovers in the presidency, none of them legitimated by a lawful democratic election. The professional military class exercised greater influence over civilian politics in Mexico than in any other Spanish American republic, and it was common for military strongmen (*caudillos*) to gather followings of loyal soldiers to help them stage coups to overturn the results of an election or oust a sitting president, governor, or other executive from office. Once in power new incumbents usually took certain antidemocratic measures, such as pushing through legislation to extend their terms in office, to protect themselves from similar usurpations.[8]

The Catholic Church also exercised considerable power over Mexico's political system. This was largely due to its extensive landholdings as well as certain privileges that it received from the national government, an arrangement established during the colonial era that continued into the republican period. In addition to its economic clout, the Church played an important role in the everyday lives of Mexican citizens, especially in terms of education and in the administration of birth, death, and marriage records. Clerical leaders frequently wielded this power against politicians who attempted to curb the Church's influence in Mexican society. Pro-secularization Liberals, for example, often complained that Church leaders riled up their peasant congregants, encouraging them to rebel against any local, state, or federal legislator who threatened clerical interests.[9] Taken together, the outsized power of both the military and the Church undercut the authority of elections in deciding the leaders of government in Mexico, which in turn eroded citizens' faith in and engagement with the country's democratic system.

During the 1810s and 1820s, most US Americans had been relatively uninterested in the part played by the colonists of New Spain (later to become Mexico) in the revolutionary tumult then unfolding across Spanish America. The country was vast and barren, they believed, and its population largely composed of Native and mestizo peasants. Other stages of the revolutionary drama were far more appealing. In the urban centers of Argentina, for example, events moved faster and their principal actors looked and behaved in ways more recognizably European. This lack of interest continued after Mexico gained independence in 1821. Though contiguous, the United States and

Mexico were in practical terms distant from one another. Their shared border, which no one had yet clearly defined, cut across desert plains dominated by largely autonomous Native tribes that recognized allegiance to neither country. Few Mexican or US citizens lived in these borderlands, meaning that the two populations rarely encountered one another.

Over time, however, US Americans' eyes were drawn to their closest neighboring republic. Throughout the 1820s and 1830s US settlers pushed south and west across the continent. When the government in Mexico City opened up portions of its northeastern territory to foreign settlement, US Americans flooded in. By 1830 around 16,000 of them lived in the Mexican state of Texas. Meanwhile other travelers from the United States—mostly explorers, anthropologists, and scientists—trekked deeper into the Mexican interior to observe its unfamiliar environs and cultures. The result was a steady stream of scholarship on the subject of Mexico entering US literary markets throughout the 1830s and 1840s, most famously William Prescott's *The History of the Conquest of Mexico*. Through Prescott's words, US readers could marvel at the fallen civilization of the ancient Aztecs, shake their heads at the cruel avarice of the Spanish conquistadors, and lament Mexico's Indigenous population's ongoing slide into indolence.[10]

Along with new opportunities for immigration and exploration, growing interest in Mexico was fueled by conflict. In 1835, English-speaking Anglo settlers who had moved to Texas (Texians) and their Spanish-speaking allies (Tejanos), rebelled against Mexican rule. By 1836 they had claimed independence and established their own republic. While many US Americans cheered on their revolutionary kin south of the border, some worried that Texan independence would cause trouble between the United States and Mexico. These concerns were vindicated in 1845 after the US Congress admitted Texas into the union. The act was an affront to Mexico City, which still claimed sovereignty over the state. War between the United States and Mexico was the result. The conflict lasted for two years, during which roughly 80,000 US troops, along with all manner of camp followers, flooded into Mexico. Veterans of the war later produced a wealth of literature on the sights and sounds that they had encountered while fighting below the border.[11]

Conflict between the two nations continued even after the war had ended. The 1848 treaty that closed the US-Mexican War transferred 525,000 square miles of Mexican territory, inhabited by roughly 80,000 Mexicans and Native Americans, to the United States. The treaty also established a new US-Mexican border running roughly 2,000 miles, from San Diego on the Pacific Coast to Brownsville, Texas, on the Mexican Gulf. The loss of territory coupled with the humiliation of defeat dealt a serious blow to Mexico's finances and national self-confidence. In the decades that followed, political turmoil grew as its leaders fought over how best to revive their country's fortunes. One consequence of this instability—which would ultimately culminate in full-blown civil war in 1857—was that successive national governments struggled to establish authority over Mexico's distant frontier regions. This in turn created tensions between Mexico City and Washington, DC, which throughout the 1850s argued over security, smuggling, and contested land claims in the borderlands. This perennial wrangling ensured that Mexico was rarely absent from the pages of antebellum US dailies, usually appearing as a poorly managed country unable to fulfill its diplomatic responsibilities.[12]

All of this meant that by midcentury Mexico had become the Spanish American republic with which people in the United States were probably most familiar. This does not mean that their perceptions of the country were accurate, however. Most literature on Mexico that circulated through US literary markets during this time—the vast majority of which was written by US Americans or Europeans—centered around two related themes: the country's extraordinary natural riches and its seemingly endless political turmoil. The causes of the latter were the subject of extensive discussion. Some writers pointed to the legacies of Spanish colonialism, which had supposedly left Mexicans unprepared for independence by neglecting to educate them in the practices of responsible self-government while simultaneously draining their country of its natural resources.[13] Others accused the Catholic Church of weakening the nation by hoarding its wealth and keeping its inhabitants in a state of superstitious ignorance.[14] Most often, though, US Americans contended that Mexico's political woes had something to do with the racial composition of its population. In the late eighteenth-century, many in the United States had still subscribed to the Enlightenment-inspired notion that all people, regardless of physical characteristics, had the capacity to achieve comparable levels of so-called civilization if given the necessary time and instruction. As the first half of the nineteenth century progressed, however, Western theorists—primarily pseudoscientists, but also philosophers, historians, and other academics—became captivated with the idea of classification. Rather than emphasizing mankind's shared humanity, such thinkers postulated the existence of distinct races, each with their own physical, mental, and emotional traits that were more or less fixed in nature and meant that individual races could be ranked in hierarchical order. The common theory was that Europeans were most capable of rational thought and emotional regulation, while those races that occupied the bottom rungs of the ladder—typically thought to include Africans and the Indigenous peoples of Australia and the Americas—were of low intelligence, irrational, and emotionally immature. Such notions found a particularly receptive audience among white US Americans who, as Reginald Horsman explains, were "anxious to justify" the ongoing "enslavement of blacks and the . . . possible extermination of the Indians" within their nation's borders.[15]

US Americans also projected these theories outward, using them as a lens through which to interpret the wider world. When it came to Mexico, for example, racial science offered an explanation as to why that country had struggled to sustain a functioning democracy. The popular assumption in the United States was that Mexico's population was comprised of three distinct races: Spanish Europeans, Native Americans, and Black Africans. Native and African heritage was thought to be predominant among the peasant classes, whom US travelers typically characterized as childlike and tribal, and therefore unable to think beyond their own interests or form connections outside of their immediate communities. This narrow-mindedness apparently disposed these portions of Mexican society to making war on perceived enemies, whether these be state or federal authorities or rival ethnic or sectional groups. Meanwhile US authors described Mexico's elites, who supposedly possessed higher proportions of Spanish ancestry, as fiery and vainglorious, prone to both violence and preening. They also credited Mexico's governing classes with a kind of crude but cunning intellect, which supposedly rendered them incapable of engaging in broad-minded responsible governance but did give them talents in political chicanery. Added to all of this were high numbers of peoples of mixed-race heritage. The term *miscegenation* would not become common in US parlance until the 1860s. Nevertheless, by the antebellum era US Americans were well-versed in those racial science theories that held that unions between members of different races produced children who inherited the worst qualities of each of their forebears and were, moreover, liable to physical weaknesses and mental disorders.[16]

Regardless of which theory they subscribed to, most midcentury US Americans could agree that Mexico contained some fatal flaw that had doomed its republican experiment to chaotic tragedy. In the habit of homogenizing the hemisphere, moreover, many claimed that the same was true of all the Spanish American republics. Indeed, by the 1850s phrases such as "Mexican republicanism" had become pejorative bywords in the US lexicon for the kind of political instability and violence supposedly inherent to Spanish American republicanism writ large. Labeling Mexico a failed republic therefore enabled US Americans to collapse the endless complexities of the wider hemisphere into a single unit while sharpening their sense of their own nation's distinctiveness.

This latter point deserves some elaboration. The precise term *American exceptionalism* would not gain widespread use until the twentieth century. Nevertheless, the idea that the United States somehow existed outside the laws and patterns that governed other countries was widely accepted among every generation of US Americans since the nation's founding. Historically, this notion has had a close relationship to the tradition of isolationism in US foreign policy thinking. To preserve its blessed distinctiveness, to avoid being corrupted by the conflicts and corrosive forces that troubled other nations, so the theory ran, the United States ought to hold itself apart from the routine wranglings of international diplomacy by eschewing alliances, collaborations, and intrigues with other countries. This was the edict that George Washington had issued to his countrymen in his famous Farewell Address as he stepped down from the presidency in 1796. The message resonated among subsequent generations of US Americans, forming the historical touchstone for the isolationism that has become one of several influential traditions in US foreign policymaking.

However, it is important not to exaggerate the hold of isolationism in both US diplomatic circles and society more broadly. There is a notion, still persistent today, that nineteenth-century US Americans, with Washington's warning still ringing in their ears, were especially isolationist. Thus most of them took only a passing interest in events taking place abroad and typically made their political choices based on domestic not foreign policy matters. This characterization does not bear up to scrutiny, however. Indeed, as the last thirty years or so of transnational scholarship has helped to show, US Americans of the nineteenth century in fact cared deeply about foreign affairs. This was not just because their country had international interests that they wished to see preserved and advanced. It was also because these US Americans had built and continually reaffirmed their national identity through watching and making interpretations about the world around them. This was true not despite but because of the concept of exceptionalism and the role that it played in informing this identity. After all, reinforcing the myth of exceptionalism required US Americans to engage in a constant process of comparison with foreign nations in order to identify those characteristics that supposedly made their own country unique.

During the first half of the nineteenth century, Mexico was a particularly common counterpoint in this process, as writings by contemporary US journalists, scientists, and other travelers reveal. Nearly every theory used by such authors to explain Mexico's political woes contained an analog in the US experience that supposedly revealed why the United States had thrived where Mexico had floundered. US Americans compared the history of Spanish colonialism to British rule in the Americas, which had taught colonists the rudiments of common law and allowed them to practice local self-government. They paired their condemnations of the Mexican Catholic Church with celebrations of how Protestantism had encouraged religious toleration and mass education in the United States. And of course, the caricature of Mexico's mongrelized hordes provided a stark contrast to antebellum US society, which, though it certainly contained non-white and mixed-race peoples, had clear racial boundaries policed by both law and social custom and designed to protect the supposed purity of its white population.[17]

In buttressing the mythology of exceptionalism, the notion that some essential law differentiated the United States from Mexico served certain rather more specific purposes for US Americans. Among these was that it provided them with reassurance as they navigated the process of nation-building following independence. Throughout the first half of the nineteenth century, the United States experienced its share of political turbulence, including constitutional crises, nascent separatist movements, and more than a few significant popular rebellions. By the 1850s, moreover, the country's political landscape had become severely polarized, fragmented into sections that were increasingly hostile toward one another.[18] So far, however, each constitutional crisis had been resolved, every separatist movement quashed, and all rebellions put down. And while the tone of antebellum politics was growing more heated, on the whole state and federal elections passed off peacefully, with losing candidates accepting defeat and popular tempers simmering down after election day. US Americans could therefore still read their newspapers for the latest Mexican news and be comforted by the thought that, whatever their own political troubles might be, they were nothing compared to what happened south of the border. There was still something about the US republic that meant that it was not, and could never become, like Mexico.

The Challenge of the US Civil War

The outbreak of the Civil War on April 12, 1861, dealt a profound blow to the myth of US exceptionalism. As they gradually came to terms with the seriousness of the conflict, Southerners and Northerners were forced to reckon with the reality that the United States was in fact not immune to the kind of internal disorders that had plagued Mexico for decades. The point was made even more apparent after the spring of 1862, when war broke out in Mexico. This conflict can be best understood as another round in the generations-long struggle between that country's Liberal and Conservative factions. The Liberals had triumphed in the War of Reform. President Benito Juárez's installation in the Palacio Nacional in January 1861, however, marked only a pause in—rather than an end to—hostilities. Defeated Conservative leaders fled to Europe, where they appealed to various monarchical governments for assistance in mounting a counterassault that would overthrow the Juárez administration. French emperor Louis-Napoleon saw in this an opportunity to fulfil his long-held ambition to expand France's imperial presence in the Americas. By the spring of 1862, France had landed troops on Mexican soil and declared war on the Liberal government.[19]

And so as blue- and gray-clad soldiers met on battlefields from Virginia to Louisiana, south of the border Mexican Liberal troops faced off against the well-trained French Army and its Mexican Conservative allies. North America's two republics were now each engaged in wars that were either partially or wholly rooted in civil conflict, the traditional Achilles heel of self-governing democracies. People in the former United States could therefore see the potential consequences of their civil war not only in Mexico's past, but in regular newspaper coverage of the ongoing Franco-Mexican conflict. Struck by their similarities, editors and journalists in both the North and South made analogies between their situation and that of the people of Mexico. Increasingly they deployed terms such as "Mexicanization," "Mexicanized," and "Mexicanizing" to describe what they saw as the destabilization of the United States' political institutions. This language was not entirely new. Such terms had occasionally appeared in antebellum US discourse to describe any kind of deterioration in the laws, principles, and practices that underpinned US democracy. These instances were rare, however, and often dismissed by others as hyperbolic. Thus in 1858 the *New York Times* mocked its rival newspaper the *New York Tribune* for warning that rapid territorial expansion would foment volatility in United States politics until the country became "debased and Mexicanized."[20] The *Herald* confidently retorted that such a scenario was not possible in "the great nation to which we belong."[21] For this newspaper and many others at the time, Mexicanization was the fever dream of alarmists, not a credible threat to US society.

Following the Secession Crisis of 1860–1861, however, the tone and intent of such language changed. Public voices of various ideological and sectional affiliations began to speak with greater frequency and apparent earnestness of the United States becoming like Mexico. "The evils that have crushed, and oppressed, and broken down the unhappy people of Mexico, are about to be adopted by us," warned Representative Thomas Corwin as he stood before the US House in January 1861.[22] Historically Mexicans had looked to the United States "as a model for stability in the execution of the laws" and "public sentiment."[23] Now, however, that model was compromised and the dynamics between the North American republics were therefore becoming distorted. North Carolina's *Weekly Standard* agreed. "Disunion at this time," the newspaper exclaimed, is "fraught with numerous and great calamities," concluding the article with a condemnation of those Southerners who would "*Mexicanize* this Republic by breaking it up."[24] Meanwhile the *Nashville Union and American* countered that it was the Republicans, with their plans to wield federal power to oppress the slaveholding states, who wished to see the United States employ the same practices "that have reduced Mexico to anarchy."[25]

It is unsurprising that US Americans succumbed to dark thoughts about their country's future while it was gripped in civil war. This book shows, however, that they continued to make fretful analogies between their republic and Mexico long after the conflict had ended. Gregory Downs has shown that the contested presidential election of 1876 sparked an explosion of references in public discourse to the United States' impending Mexicanization.[26] The political crisis then engulfing the nation, he argues, reminded contemporaries of the trauma of secession and caused them to worry that their country was backsliding into internecine turmoil, possibly even another civil war. What Downs presents as a rhetorical phenomenon particular to 1876, however, is better understood as a spike in a trend that had been present in US public political discourse since the Civil War and would continue to be a feature of it until the early 1880s. To be sure, and as this book will show, US Americans did not draw parallels between the state of their politics and that of Mexico with the same frequency and intensity throughout this time period. Rather, as Downs's analysis suggests, certain flashpoints of heightened political turbulence triggered surges in the use of Mexicanization rhetoric. The 1876 election was undoubtedly one of these. Casting a wider chronological net reveals others, including the Secession Winter of 1860–1861, the rollout of congressional Reconstruction in 1866–1867, and the months following the assassination of President Garfield in 1881. This broader view also shows that the language had multiple shifting partisan and sectional iterations. Following the 1866–1867 congressional elections, for instance, many Southern publications warned that the new Republican-controlled Congress would Mexicanize the states of the former Confederacy through military occupation and the imposition of so-called Negro rule. At the same time, Republican-leaning publications were responding to vigilante violence committed by white supremacist groups in the postwar South by warning of the United States' impending Mexicanization at the hands of unreconstructed rebels.

As the above examples suggest, between the mid-1860s and early 1880s it was common for users to weaponize the language of Mexicanization. Indeed, exclamations of the United States' apparent slide into a Mexicanized state were not usually intended as mere lamentations. Far more often they appeared as accusations leveled at one's political opponents—whether these be secessionists or abolitionists, radicals or office-seekers—as a way to blame them for bringing about the apparent demoralization of national politics. Given this, it is reasonable to suggest that those warning of the United States' impending Mexicanization were not giving voice to a genuine concern but were instead seeking to alarm the public with an exaggerated threat in order rouse and rally them behind a particular political party, faction, or movement. In fact, the evidence presented in this study bears this interpretation out to a degree. As will be shown, Mexicanization discourses were most certainly used by political actors in efforts to weaken opponents in electoral campaigns as well as to justify the need for certain policies supposedly designed to return stability to US politics.

That at times users may have deployed the language somewhat cynically does not render this rhetorical phenomenon unworthy of study, however. Indeed, the very fact that so many journalists, politicians, editors, orators, and other public figures from all regions and every major party in the United States utilized this language at some point across the better part of two decades can tell us something important about wider US society at this time. It indicates, for example, that these individuals (who were, we must remember, in the business of persuading in order to harness the collective power of the voting public) believed that the language of Mexicanization would resonate with ordinary US Americans. It is worthwhile to note here that this language did not emerge in a vacuum. April 1865 marked the close of formal military hostilities between the Union and the Confederacy; throughout the late 1860s and 1870s, however, sectional conflict continued, largely through unofficial channels such as the terrorist campaigns of paramilitary groups and other forms of spontaneous popular political violence between former Confederates, freed people, and their Republican allies. For many years following Appomattox, US Americans therefore had reason to believe that their nation still teetered uneasily on the brink of another dissolution. A writer for *Harper's Weekly* aptly summed up this uneasy feeling in late 1867. There had been a time, the author recalled, when US citizens had believed that their "republic was charmed. Other countries had suffered, but we were exceptional."[27] The trials of civil war and reunion, however, "have taught us that even in the United States there is no security against civil trouble."[28] Though "we need not, indeed, imagine that we are already Mexicanized," the writer continued, the "country still trembles with civil war, and peaceful order is not yet restored" and convulsions might yet arise that could "plunge us into very serious difficulty."[29]

It is the contention of this book that the emergence, prevalence, and persistence of the discourse of Mexicanization from the mid-1860s to the early 1880s reflected a very real sense of insecurity that permeated US society during this time. It further argues that political leaders believed that the language of Mexicanization could help them tap into this popular uncertainty and use it to their advantage. This is because Mexicanization narratives not only gave voice to popular concerns about the state of US political culture, but also provided ways to explain and remedy it. Gregory Downs describes phrases such as Mexicanization as "open-ended analogies," which expressed a general concern about the chronicity of violence in US politics.[30] While this certainly was a concern at this time, by conducting a more extensive study of how this language was used throughout the 1860s, 1870s, and into the 1880s, this book shows that US Americans discussed the causes and consequences of Mexicanization in more precise terms than this. At its core was the concept of factionalism, meaning a scenario in which popular politics became tribal, with parties binding their members together through shared hatred of the opposition, whom they viewed as would-be destroyers of the country. When excessive factionalism occurred, the common theory ran, the wheels of government ground to a halt and the institutions and customs that supported it disintegrated. Politicians would view one another as adversaries rather than as colleagues and cease working together for the common weal. Meanwhile voters would countenance all kinds of malpractice—slander, forgery, bribery—on the part of their chosen representatives so long as it kept the despised opposition out of power. And if the enemy did gain office, the use of any means up to and including violence was justified in order to turn them out and so save the country from destruction.

An aversion to factionalism had been part of US political culture since the nation's founding. Even as they witnessed the rise of the two-party system during the 1830s, people in the United States continued to celebrate independent-mindedness and the willingness to cooperate with political opponents as desirable qualities in their representatives. Thus they lauded such feats of negotiation as the Missouri Compromise and the Comprise of 1850 as examples of a proud US tradition, dating back to the writing of the Constitution, wherein the nation's leaders put aside their differences and acted together for the common good.[31] The events immediately following the 1860 presidential election, however, suggested that US lawmakers' compromising ability had reached its limits. The nation's leaders had become so consumed with factionalism, it appeared, that their sectional tensions could no longer be contained within the legal confines of the Constitution. The country's institutions had therefore given way, opening the floodgates to internecine warfare, just as had occurred multiple times throughout Mexican history.

This theory found many subscribers both in the North and South throughout wartime and the postbellum period. Where there was disagreement was in deciding who was to blame for introducing the plague of factionalism into US politics. There are a number of excellent studies dealing with the topic of anti-factionalism (also referred to as anti-partyism) in US political culture in the Civil War era.[32] Using the language of Mexicanization as an index to this phenomenon, however, is a novel approach that yields certain useful insights. First, it provides a way to nimbly track popular concerns regarding factionalism across region and party, enabling one study to examine its multiple iterations as they emerged in different sectional and partisan contexts. Second, following the language of Mexicanization leads one across certain temporal boundaries that scholars have erected in their efforts to segment the nineteenth century into manageable portions. By the mid-1870s, for example, those characters who throughout the previous decades had been most often blamed for Mexicanizing the republic—abolitionists and slavocrats—had lost much of their relevancy in national politics and therefore their menace in public discourse. As this book will show, however, the language of Mexicanization persisted. By now, however, it centered around new perceived nefarious actors who were apparently perpetuating the wartime culture of partisanship for their own purposes. Historians do not typically include the late 1870s and the early 1880s in their studies of the Civil War era. As this book will show, however, for many contemporaries these years simply continued the pattern that had defined national politics since 1861, when the United States had first succumbed to the sickness of Mexicanization.

The language of Mexicanization also reveals how rather staid concerns about the corrosion of public spirit and civic responsibility—notions drawn from classical republican theories that only the best educated in midcentury US society would have closely studied—could be popularized in public discourse and in this way imbued with the power to shape political narratives, perceptions, and perhaps even behaviors. Comparisons with Mexico could be used to present one's political opponents as un-American, as defilers of the United States' original form and a threat to the country's future survival. Cross-border comparisons also helped writers and orators tap into popular anxieties about the integrity of the US republic, specifically regarding the destabilizing effects of factionalism. By doing this, those deploying this language could then make the case that a certain piece of legislation, policy, or program of reform would reverse the United States' slide into Mexican chaos. Indeed, throughout the period studied here, numerous and often conflicting agendas were sold to US voters in this way; secession, emancipation, Black enfranchisement, and territorial and commercial expansion were all presented as panaceas that would in different ways bridge partisan and sectional divides in the public sphere. By promising to avert the nightmare scenario of Mexican chaos, advocates of these measures endowed them with conservative connotations, presenting them as methods to purge the United States of the disease of factionalism and so restore it to its original condition of domestic tranquility. Comparisons with Mexico, in short, could make revolutionary policies palatable to even the most cautious members of the public.

Finally, studying Mexico's place in US public discourse during the Civil War era offers unique insight into certain complexities and contradictions that ran through US political culture at this time. Those studies that examine popular anti-factionalism in the midcentury United States typically present us with a picture of a fearful society that felt itself to be under siege from malignant internal forces. To an extent, this study reaffirms this view. However, the language of Mexicanization reveals how US Americans' sense of vulnerability existed alongside sentiments of national confidence and even hubris. Certainly the language centered on the idea of the possible ultimate ruination of US politics. And yet the specter of total Mexicanization only had the power to rouse the people of the United States because everything they had been taught about their country's global significance told them that they must fight against this outcome with all their power. As has been discussed, comparisons with Mexico were most often used as rallying cries urging people to gather behind one course of action or another. This strategy could only be effective if those who heard the cry retained some fragment of hope that the demoralization of the US republic might yet be reversed, its complete Mexicanization averted, and thus its status as the Western Hemisphere's exceptional republic restored. In this way, the discourse played as much upon US Americans' national pride as their insecurities and shows us how intimately connected these two sentiments were in the United States' political culture.

The Hemispheric Perspective in Civil War Scholarship

Among the many myths that shroud the history of the US Civil War, one of the most enduring has been that it was a constructive rather than a destructive conflict. From the moment of their victory, Unionists began to speak of the war as a moment of national rebirth. The country, they proclaimed, had not only survived its civil strife, but had been strengthened by it. The postwar US economy was an expansive, rapidly industrializing behemoth, and its financial systems were more complex and deeply enmeshed in global banking structures than ever before. More than this, US Americans had seemingly vanquished the insidious doctrines of states' rights and secession and erected in their place a robust central government that could intervene in nearly all aspects of national life. And perhaps most importantly, Unionists claimed, the United States had purged itself of the slaveholding aristocracy and was therefore ready to reconstitute its national creed on the basis of true democracy. Such claims endowed the United States' internecine conflict with special significance. They suggested that the war had been necessary—a rite of passage, as it were, through which the United States had to pass in order to be cleansed of the lingering vestiges of colonialism, namely the institution of slavery, and to progress to the next stage of its providential destiny.

Over the years, this interpretation of the Civil War's salutary nature has shown remarkable staying power in US popular culture, and it is not difficult to see why. After all, the idea that the Civil War was an essential (perhaps even inevitable) part of the United States' development gave meaning to otherwise senseless suffering and turned national tragedy into national triumph. It also invited its subscribers to believe that the Civil War had not been caused by weaknesses in the US system of government, but rather was a byproduct of that system's natural evolution. The US Civil War could therefore be viewed as distinct from comparable internecine conflicts in world history; other nations' civil wars were ruinous, it suggested, while that of the United States had been regenerative. Throughout the nineteenth and into the twentieth century, historians helped to develop and legitimize this reading of the Civil War's significance. They achieved this in part by framing the war as a watershed, the critical point at which certain core aspects of US society underwent profound transformation. The most obvious of these was the transition from Black enslavement to Black freedom. However, historians used the Civil War to mark a host of other metamorphoses, such as the shift from a pre-industrial to an industrializing economy or from a politics of sectionalism to a politics of class conflict.[33] Diplomatic historians similarly used the Civil War to explain the apparent transition from antebellum territorial expansionism to postwar commercial aggrandizement, which by the mid-twentieth century would culminate in the United States' emergence as a global superpower.[34] By using the Civil War to demarcate these phases of national development, scholars satisfied their impulse to compartmentalize the past, placing history's endless complexities into neat units and sequencing them in such a way as to create a straightforward narrative in which the United States moved seamlessly from one stage of nation-building to the next.[35]

Such Whiggish readings of Civil War history have largely fallen out of favor in contemporary scholarship. Historians today tend to embrace rather than avoid the conflict's messy elements, wrestling with its murky beginnings and ambivalent endings head-on while acknowledging both its progressive and regressive consequences. And yet glimpses of the old teleological narrative occasionally still reappear. Some can be found, for example, in the body of scholarship that examines the Civil War's international dimensions. As previously discussed, the assumption still persists that the nineteenth-century United States was a nation largely isolated from and unconcerned by the world around it. However, this notion has become increasingly difficult to maintain thanks to the explosion of international and transnational studies over the last three decades or so. This research has shown us how deeply immersed the nineteenth-century United States was in global currents of finance, commerce, and ideas, and the extent to which US Americans at the time were both informed about and interested in events taking place beyond their borders. While much needed, however, collectively these studies have inadvertently perpetuated certain other assumptions, which this book now seeks to address. Specifically, there is a tendency among transnational analyses in particular to re-center the Civil War as a critical turning point not only in the United States' past but also in the history of the wider Atlantic world. This is partly due to the simple fact that many of these studies make extensive use of materials produced by Unionist and Confederate publicists, which were aimed at global and especially European audiences. Historians have shown how both the Union and Confederacy launched energetic public relations campaigns that aimed to win over European governments and citizens to their respective causes. Confederate spokesmen invoked the language of Atlantic nationalism to claim that rebel Southerners were like Hungarians, Poles, or the Irish in that they too had suffered under the heel of a despotic power and yearned for self-determination.[36] Northerners, meanwhile, drew upon these same transatlantic discourses by insisting that their aim was to save the Union, and that the Union was worth saving because it was the world's best example of a functioning democratic republic. If the United States was torn apart by a slaveholding aristocracy, they argued, its power as a symbol of hope for democratic nationalists around the world would be destroyed.[37] Both Unionists and Confederates, in short, used the language of nineteenth-century Atlantic nationalism to emphasize the global import of their respective war efforts. Scholars who have studied them have in turn amplified their message that the Civil War was no parochial squabble over transitory sectional interests, but rather an existential battle to determine the fate of liberalism, democracy, and self-government the world over.

These historians have also shown that such messages were eagerly consumed by interested audiences around the world. Don H. Doyle's excellent *The Cause of All Nations* provides persuasive evidence of this. Though purportedly a global history, this study is principally concerned with how the US Civil War was perceived in Europe. There, Doyle suggests, many observers spoke of the contest as the continuation of a higher struggle "between the forces of *popular* versus *hereditary* sovereignty, *democracy* versus *aristocracy*, *free* versus *slave* labor," which had been playing out across the world for decades.[38] To underscore the Civil War's international significance, Doyle argues that Union victory inspired self-styled champions of liberty across the Atlantic world with new energy by pointing to a wave of liberal nationalist victories that followed in its wake—the passage of the 1867 British Reform Act, the completion of Italian unification, and the Canadian confederation being just a few of the most notable. Viewed in this way, the US Civil War emerges as a decisive factor in moving the world on from the age of empires and slavery and toward a new era of modernity defined by self-governance and free labor.[39]

While it does not deny their existence or import, this study does contend that focusing solely on transatlantic connections only reveals one aspect of how US Americans understood their civil war's international meaning. Indeed, this book situates itself within an emerging scholarly trend that is pushing against the US-European paradigm in transnational Civil War studies by adopting alternative geographic lenses through which to analyze the conflict. For example, historians including Patrick Kelly, Gregory Downs, Evan Rothera, and others have, in different ways, examined the US Civil War within the context of the wider Americas, and specifically in relation to certain contemporaneous hemispheric conflicts such as Mexico's War of Reform, the Ten Years' War in Cuba, and the Argentine Wars of Unification.[40] These studies have shown that the countries engaged in these wars, including the United States, were navigating similar challenges that were particular to them as colonial or postcolonial New World societies. These challenges included, but were not limited to, dealing with the legacies of chattel slavery, managing relations with Indigenous populations, establishing national sovereignty over unsettled borderlands, and determining the proper balance of power between the branches of their governments. By using a hemispheric lens, these studies highlight how these issues, held in common with many other nations in the region, were central to the US Civil War's causes and consequences, demonstrating that the conflict can be viewed as part of a wider *American* story in which the people of the New World struggled together through the trials of colonialism, independence, and nation-building.

In both its approach and conclusions, this book offers a unique contribution to this evolving body of scholarship. First, many of the studies mentioned above follow the activities of individuals who, in various ways, forged or reinforced connections between the US Civil War and comparable conflicts happening elsewhere across the midcentury Americas. These include itinerant soldiers who traveled from Uruguay to the United States to Mexico fighting various manifestations Old World reactionism and well as intellectuals from Buenos Aires to Boston who corresponded on matters of postwar and postcolonial state-building. Rather than examine ties between the United States and its hemispheric neighbors by following these small groups of highly motivated transnational actors, this book examines how these hemispheric connections were understood by those US Americans who remained at home. It is therefore not a typical transnational study in the sense that it does not prioritize tracing objects, people, or ideas moving back and forth across borders. Rather, it is a study first and foremost of US society, and the place that the wider hemisphere held in US Americans' collective imagination.

To achieve this, this book turns to the realm of public discourse in the United States as expressed in printed materials such as pamphlets, published speeches, and newspapers. Newspapers constitute by far the largest portion of its source base. By the mid-nineteenth century, the US printed press was an extraordinarily large and dynamic industry, with advances in printing technology and transportation meaning that most localities had at least one newspaper if not more, and enabling certain metropolitan publications such as the *New York Herald*, the *New York Tribune*, and the *Chicago Tribune* to achieve nationwide circulation. To be sure, the expansion of print media was not felt evenly across the country. The 1850 census revealed that the entire number of periodicals published in the slave states amounted to just over 700, compared to just over 1,800 in the free states. Rates of literacy were also lower in the South. The same census revealed that in some areas of the slaveholding South, illiteracy among white adults reached as high as one in seven persons, while illiteracy among adults in the Northern states never reached above one in seventeen. These numbers do not include the antebellum South's Black population, which, due to the fact that most slaveholding states by this time had laws on the books that prohibited teaching enslaved people to read and write, likely only ever attained around 10 percent literacy, though precise numbers are difficult to determine.[41]

Still, these numbers do not detract from the fact that there was a growing print culture in the slaveholding states during the first half of the nineteenth century. As Beth Barton Schweiger points out, the combined literacy rate in 1850 among white adults across these states was roughly 80 percent. While not as impressive as the free North's 93 percent, this was still "one of the highest literacy rates in the world."[42] Moreover, by 1861 around 800 newspapers were in existence in the eleven states that would form the Confederacy, some of which commanded a sizable readership that extended well beyond their local communities.[43] This was especially true of the Richmond papers. The *Richmond Enquirer*, for example, had a circulation of around 8,000, while the *Richmond Daily Dispatch* boasted one of around 18,000.[44] Though this was dwarfed by the circulation rates of the New York dailies (the *New York Tribune*'s was around 77,000), articles from the *Enquirer*, *Daily Dispatch*, and the other Richmond organs were frequently reprinted by editors across the South and indeed the nation, giving them an influence over the agenda and tone of both regional and national public discourse that was far greater than their readership numbers would suggest.[45]

All of this meant that by the antebellum era, the press had become the principal means by which US citizens from all regions learned about events happening in other parts of their country and indeed the wider world. This included Mexico. As has been alluded to, throughout the 1840s and 1850s a steady stream of writings by soldiers, explorers, scientists, and historians on the subject of Mexico entered US literary markets. Collectively, such materials created a popular understanding among US Americans about Mexican history, demographics, and culture. Layered onto this was the regular news from south of the border, which US readers received through their newspapers. There were only two principal channels by which news could pass from Mexico into the United States at this time: a British-run steamship line that connected Veracruz to New York via Havana, and overland trails cutting across the US-Mexican borderlands that could be traversed by horse or wagon. Both of these routes were vulnerable to disruption and delay. Moreover, as will be discussed more fully in the following chapters, the information that did eventually reach the United States was often refashioned or altered by individuals seeking to push certain political agendas. Still, the fact remains that almost all major newspapers in the United States during this time could and did regularly report on current affairs in Mexico. Some had their own journalists stationed in the country while others reprinted dispatches communicated through the Associated Press. Many supplemented these sources with information gleaned from the European press, which reached the United States via transatlantic steamship or, after 1866, the transatlantic telegraph cable.

As this summary suggests, much of the news about Mexico that circulated in the United States during this time was written by US Americans or, to a lesser extent, Europeans whose texts had been translated into English. But it is important to point out that Mexicans did have a hand in determining what information about their country US readers received. Each government in Mexico City during the period studied here understood that US Americans held their country in low regard and was determined to rectify this. Their chief means of doing so was through their minister to the United States, supported by a group of subordinate diplomats who comprised the Mexican Legation. As we shall see, two such ministers—Matías Romero between 1859 and 1867 and Manuel de Zamacona from 1877 onward—were especially adept at charming influential US editors, journalists, and politicians. Both oversaw a period of marked improvement in popular opinion of Mexico across US society. Still, these ministers were fighting an uphill battle, for they had to contend with two formidable opponents—US Americans' prejudices and their fickleness—which meant that surges in pro-Mexican feeling in the United States were usually transitory. While many US Americans cheered for the Mexican republic while it was being invaded by French imperialists during the 1860s, for example, their affection dissipated soon after the conflict was over. Indeed, for much of the 1870s, as Mexican politics seemed to return to its usual rhythm of *pronunciamientos* and rebellions, old tropes reemerged in US press coverage, which bemoaned Mexico's supposedly incurable instability and the hopelessness of its republican experiment.

Successive administrations in Mexico City also had to contend with the fact that their domestic political opponents sought to present US audiences with their own interpretation of current affairs in Mexico. As has been mentioned, US publications frequently clipped pieces from foreign newspapers. On occasion, this included publications from Mexico. Indeed, a perusal of the midcentury US press reveals repurposed articles from Mexican organs representing a variety of ideological and partisan affiliations, including the

Liberal newspapers *La Rabia* and *La Sombra* and Conservative publications such as the *Mexican Extraordinary*, *El Siglo Diez y Nueve*, and *La Voz de Mexico*. Depending on their political affiliations, such newspapers could be either positive or condemnatory about the administration in Mexico City at that time and the state of the country more broadly. Aware of this, editors in the United States tended to trust only those reports that came from Mexican newspapers that aligned with their own preexisting assumptions or interests. Mexicans' ability to inform US perceptions of their country, in short, was always limited by the extent to which US newspapermen were inclined to believe them. What all of this means is that most of the images of Mexico that appeared in US newspapers were to some degree influenced by US Americans' assumptions, interests, and agendas. Studying them can therefore yield valuable insights into the public mood in the United States at any given time—or, at least, insight into what those editors, journalists, and others at the helm of US public discourse interpreted the public mood to be.[46]

As has been alluded to, some historians who have examined the hemispheric dimensions of the US Civil War have identified parallels between the causation and consequences of this conflict and contemporaneous wars elsewhere in the Americas. Many of these studies have also devoted at least part of their analyses to exploring if and how such cross-hemispheric comparisons were perceived by contemporaries at the time. In doing so, most have concluded that the 1860s and 1870s was a notable period of Pan-American unity. This has been perhaps most forcefully argued by Evan Rothera, who posits that the outbreak of comparable conflicts in the United States, Mexico, and Argentina between the 1850s and 1870s inspired feelings of sympathy and alliance among the people of these nations, which helped to wash away the prejudices that they had long held toward one another. Focusing in particular on US soldiers, intellectuals, and reformers who either traveled to or else corresponded with counterparts in Mexico and Argentina during this time, Rothera asserts that "new understandings emerged," and that "many people favored cooperation because they understood that they were not going it alone; their wars were part of a much broader struggle."[47]

This book agrees that the period from the 1860s to the early 1880s witnessed some remarkable shifts in US Americans' perceptions of Mexico, and that at certain times this manifested in widespread professions of fraternity with the United States' sister republic. It also argues, however, that these warm expressions of Pan-American unity had a darker underside. Before the US Civil War, people in the United States had predicated their national identity on the notion that their country was essentially different from, and superior to, Mexico. After 1860, many of them were therefore unsettled to find their country in what they considered to be a Mexican-style condition of civil strife. Their unease comes into view once the focus of analysis extends from the minority of transnational individuals who forged, strengthened, and glorified their connections with Mexican Liberals and other likeminded peoples south of the border to include the US population more broadly. Certainly, many US newspapers expressed sympathy for the Mexican republic in its struggle against the French and spoke of the French Intervention and the Southern rebellion as being part of the same reactionary assault against American free government. However, this did not stop these same publications from simultaneously using cross-border analogies as a way to express their dismay over the disintegration of the once mighty US republic and their horror that it might now become like Mexico.

In making this analysis, this book also engages with a long scholarly tradition that examines popular US perceptions of Mexico, and the relationship between these perceptions and US national identity. Historians have long been interested in how US Americans viewed their southern neighbors, especially in the prejudices that distorted these opinions.[48] Such studies usually focus on periods of conflict between the United States and neighboring countries such as Mexico. This is understandable. After all, these were periods when hemispheric relations were at the top of the political agenda in the United States and so at the forefront of public discourse. They were also usually times when imperialistic ambitions were running high among US Americans and talk of gaining land and resources from or exacting punishment upon one of their weaker neighbors dominated public conversations. Unsurprisingly, then, scholars examining the US press at such times see evidence of Mexico and other regional countries being disparaged and belittled, while the United States is heralded as honorable, capable, and strong.

Turning the lens of analysis away from periods of imperialistic hubris and toward times of national crisis, however, reveals a rather different picture. Certainly, as discussed earlier, even during the tumult of their civil war US Americans clung to the notion of their exceptionalism as best they could; such an elemental part of their national self-identity could not be dispensed with easily. And yet this study reveals the severe strain that the sectional war and its aftermath put this faith under. While generations since have characterized the US Civil War as an exceptional contest, unique from other internecine conflagrations in its healing and perfecting effects, this study reveals that public faith in this notion was not unwavering from the outset. Although some at the time insisted that the war would have an ultimately uplifting effect on US society, such professions existed alongside others of deep worry that it might be the ruination of their country. According to these voices, the US Civil War might ultimately prove to be unexceptional and so, they feared, might their nation. In this way, this study alerts us to the fact that although by the end of the nineteenth century the United States had achieved hemispheric commercial, financial, and military supremacy, for contemporaries the journey to this destination was punctuated with moments of hesitation and doubt.

Concern for the nation's survival was just one of the many sentiments that manifested in Northern and Southern public discourse during the Civil War era. One way to examine these is to consider the various international discourses contemporaries had at their disposal, each of which were layered with certain concerns and ambitions that people in the United States experienced at different times during wartime and the postwar period. The language of Atlantic liberal nationalism, for example, helped them to remember the Civil War's higher purpose and celebrate the extraordinary changes that it had wrought on their society. There were times, however, when there seemed to be little to celebrate, when it appeared as though the country might never find respite from the tumult of violence and factionalism. At such times, US Americans turned to discourses of Mexicanization to vent their anxieties. At first glance it may appear contradictory that Civil War–era US Americans could be filled with both hope and dread about the future of their republic, that they could imagine its ascendency to the uppermost heights of global power one moment and the next be consumed with worries about its decline into Mexican chaos. We must always remember, however, that contemporaries in the United States, unlike historians since, had no way of knowing which future lay ahead of them. The Civil War, moreover, had disabused them of the notion that their country was protected from the dangers that had historically brought down republics. In the postbellum era in particular, both confidence and uncertainty therefore ran through the bloodstream of the United States, its citizens buoyed by the triumph of having survived the Civil War while haunted by the possibility that the conflict had exposed the fallacy of US exceptionalism.

Chapters

US Americans had made occasional analogies between their republic and Mexico prior to the 1860s. With the advent of the Civil War, however, these comparisons become a staple feature of their political public discourse. This book therefore takes as its starting point the Secession Crisis of 1860–1861. Chapter 1 tracks the emergence of analogies with Mexico in Northern public discourse, specifically in the pro-Union press and other widely read literature produced by wartime patriotic organizations. These organs crafted a narrative that castigated rebel Southerners as antidemocratic Mexicanizers of the US republic who had deliberately fomented the sectional conflict in a bid to override the nation's lawful democratic processes. This narrative took on new life after the spring of 1862, when France invaded Mexico in collaboration with a minority of Mexican Conservative and clerical forces. Unionist spokesmen seized on this event to draw cross-border connections between Southern rebels, French imperialists, and Mexican priests—all alleged collaborators in a plot to bring down North American republicanism. The chapter explores how this framing was designed to emphasize to the Northern people the un-American nature of the Confederates' bid for independence, highlight the continental stakes of the Civil War, and position the Union war effort as a redemptive fight to preserve the essence of US exceptionalism. It also shows how this narrative succeeded in helping to hold together a politically diverse coalition behind the Union war effort, a task made especially challenging after January 1863 when President Lincoln's Emancipation Proclamation expanded the purpose of that effort from just reunion to also include emancipation.

Unionists were not alone in placing the Civil War into a continental framework. Chapter 2 explores how Confederate spokesmen also used Mexico to craft a narrative that positioned their own war cause as an effort to defend the essence of US exceptionalism, albeit by transferring this essence to an independent South. Confederate writers mirrored their Unionist counterparts in drawing cross-border parallels, although their connections depicted Northern abolitionists and Juarist Liberals as co-conspirators seeking to destroy social and political order in their respective republics. After 1862, Southern publicists used this narrative to justify the decision by the administration of President Jefferson Davis to support Emperor Louis-Napoleon's effort to depose the Juárez government. They also deployed it to sustain popular support for the Confederate cause—a fight, they said, to restore to the South the kind of domestic tranquility it had enjoyed before the old United States had been infiltrated by abolitionists. Though this narrative would be tested throughout the Civil War, most Confederate organs clung to it all the way to the conflict's bitter end. Thus in April 1865, now facing reentry into the Union, rebel organs lamented that the Confederacy's fall had extinguished the last bastion of true republicanism in North America, and with it any hope white Southerners had for future domestic peace.

The Civil War ended in 1865. The French Intervention in Mexico, however, raged on for two more years. Following Appomattox there was a groundswell of popular support in the United States for an invasion to push French forces off the continent. Chapter 3 explores how certain US politicians and editors attempted to harness this interventionist enthusiasm to mold public opinion on the issue of postwar Reconstruction. Republican leaders, for example, warned their countrymen that the rebel foe was not yet fully subdued and that a rigorous Reconstruction program was necessary to eradicate all vestiges of the slavocracy from the nation. When this was done, they claimed, the United States' symbolic influence as the world's exemplary republic would be restored and soon inspire Juaristas to victory over their French invaders. This message held together a diverse coalition behind Radical Reconstruction; it did not, however, go uncontested. The Southern press, along with many Northern Democratic publications, warned that Radical Reconstruction would drive the South into a condition of "Mexican anarchy." They too attempted to manipulate popular interventionist enthusiasm, campaigning for a US invasion of Mexico as a means to reunify the United States without the need for meddling in the South's social order. They also insisted that a US intervention south of the border would demonstrate to the world the postwar United States' strength and virility. Indeed, for these and many other US Americans, the continuation of the French invasion after 1865 was a worrying sign that the Civil War had done serious damage to the United States' global image and that the international community viewed their postwar nation as weak, fractured, and unable to fulfil its role as the defender of New World republicanism.

Chapter 4 moves deeper into the postwar period, bridging the late Reconstruction era and the early 1880s. In 1881 President Garfield's assassination at the hands of a disappointed office seeker reignited the discourse of Mexicanization in the United States. This version, however, differed from those that had preceded it. During and immediately after the Civil War, US Americans had blamed either Northern radicals or Southern aristocrats for Mexicanizing their republic. By the early 1880s, however, their accusations were more commonly leveled at political operatives in both the Republican and Democratic parties who, they believed, exacerbated societal divisions as a way to lever themselves into office. Chapter 4 traces the origins of this narrative to the early 1870s, when several influential conservative Republican organs began to worry that unscrupulous politicians were using Reconstruction to perpetuate sectional tensions in US society. During the 1872 presidential campaign, these organs coalesced behind the Liberal Republican Party and called for an end to Reconstruction lest factionalism be permanently ingrained into US political culture. The Liberals' bid for the presidency failed; their particular narrative of Mexicanization, however, lived on. Over the course of the 1870s, a growing number of Democratic and Republican voices, concerned by the unsettled state of the postwar South, used this interpretation of Mexicanization to insist that Reconstruction must end if the United States was ever to harmonize and return to its proper standing as the world's model of stable democracy. In this sense, US Americans' retreat from Reconstruction was in fact a shift in tactics to combat the same problem they had been battling since 1861: the scourge of factionalism and all the misery that it caused.

This book's final chapter focuses on the late 1870s and early 1880s. Having identified excessive partisanship and office-seeking as the latest blight on US politics, opinion makers in the United States searched for innovative ways to combat this ill. In 1876 Mexico's new president Porfirio Díaz inaugurated an ambitious program of economic regeneration south of the border. To finance his plans, Díaz courted US capital by flattering US Americans that his program to stabilize and modernize his country was inspired by the United States' own postwar project of internal improvements. Díaz's message fell on fertile ground. In the early 1870s, boosters in the US South were calling for federal investment in their region's infrastructure to facilitate trade south of the Rio Grande. Over the course of the decade publications from across the United States seized on this idea, advocating US commercial and financial expansion into Mexico. This would be, they declared, a form of Manifest Destiny refashioned for the postwar era, whereby the United States would pursue its interests south of the border by seeking out business and trade opportunities rather than land. They also insisted that relaunching the Manifest Destiny mission would distract US Americans from the controversies of Reconstruction and so finish the still incomplete task of postwar national harmonization. In 1876 President Díaz opened Mexico's doors to US trade and investment. In doing so he gave people in the United States the opportunity to carry out this new form of reconciliation. By the 1880s, US Americans no longer invoked Mexico as an ominous portent of their own future, but instead imagined the country as a protégé that under their tutelage was moving steadily toward modernity. Anxieties about the fragility of the US republic, once a source of sectional antagonism, had created new cross-sectional alliances based on a collective rejection of Reconstruction and an embrace of a new era of continental commercial and economic expansion.

CHAPTER ONE

The Continental Union Cause, 1861–1865

If nothing else, members of the New York Union League could throw a good banquet. After all, they had hosted many since their organization's founding in 1863, each one attended by brilliant, wealthy, or otherwise influential guests who were treated to rich food and expensive wines in luxuriant surroundings. These events had become opportunities for New York City's most powerful citizens to rub shoulders—and in the name of a worthy cause to boot. The League was a patriotic association with the self-proclaimed mission of boosting popular morale in the North for the ongoing fight to put down the Confederate rebellion. Among its many activities, the League held dinners so that New York City's literary, business, and political elites could publicly reaffirm their loyalty to the Union. The toasts (To Lincoln! To the Union! To liberty!) and accompanying speeches that were delivered during these evenings were often recorded and then disseminated to the public. Sometimes they appeared on the pages of the city's newspapers; occasionally the League itself published and sold them as pamphlets so that readers might take heart from the rousing patriotic sentiments contained within.[1]

The banquet that the New York League hosted on March 29, 1864, was a little different from those that had come before it, however. This time, attendees gathered to celebrate not the Union's war effort, but that of the Mexican republic, which at that time was fighting off an invasion by France. The venue was the famous Delmonico's restaurant, and the guest of honor was Señor Matías Romero, Mexico's minister to the United States.

Having traveled from his residence in Washington, DC, to attend the occasion, Romero was hit with a wave of light, warmth, and music as he stepped into the restaurant that evening. The League had reserved four saloons, each one decorated with exotic flowers "festooned from arch to arch" or hanging as pendants from the "fretted ceilings."[2] One room housed a small orchestra playing *La Jaroba*, *La Sinolita*, and other Mexican marches. Through a doorway "arrayed in fragrant wreathes and garlands" was the main dining room.[3] Here Mexican and US flags hung from the walls, entwined and heavy with symbolic grandeur. Occupying pride of place in the center of the banquet table was a magnificent *pièce montée* composed of "pyramids of sugar," each puffed ball "inscribed with the names of Juarez, and other statesmen of

Mexico" and the entire structure flanked by "the palm and the cactus, types of the flora of Mexico."[4]

Guests began to arrive at seven o'clock. There were twenty-seven of them in total, mostly Union politicians and businessmen along with a handful of Mexican diplomats. After initial greetings in the reception rooms, the guests were ushered into the main apartment, where they sat down to a lavish dinner consisting of half a dozen courses. At around nine o'clock the plates were cleared and James W. Beekman rose to his feet. The wealthy New Yorker and former state legislator had been appointed Chairman of Proceedings for the evening, and it was his duty to lead the first toast: "To Don Benito Juarez, Constitutional President of the Mexican Republic."[5] The room echoed his call with "great enthusiasm."[6] Six more rounds of toasts followed, each honoring a different aspect of the Mexican nation, from its statesmen and lawyers to its artists and poets. For each toast, a guest from among the US Americans in attendance was called upon to deliver a short speech on the chosen theme. On the eighth round, Beekman raised his glass to the historians of Mexico and invited Frederic de Peyster, president of the New York Historical Society, to respond.

"I came to express, by my presence, the sympathy which I feel toward a sister republic," de Peyster began, adding that his feelings were especially profound because Mexico's war against the French imperialists so closely resembled the United States' ongoing fight against the Southern rebels.[7] Though challenged by these twin assaults, de Peyster was confident that neither Mexicans nor Unionists would allow free government on their continent to be destroyed. If each "will rally round their national standard" with "determined courage and undaunted decision," he asserted, they would triumph.[8] Then, purged of monarchists, clerics, and slaveholders, "the republics of North America will shake hands in brotherly sentiment and alliance" and together look forward to a future of undisturbed peace.[9]

Such expressions of sympathy toward Mexico had by this time become commonplace in Unionist public discourse. Following the onset of fighting between French and Mexican forces in the spring of 1862, Northern popular opinion had steadily moved to favor Mexico's side in the dispute. By 1863, people at all levels of Union society were finding ways to demonstrate their support for the country they now affectionately called their "sister republic," from the wealthy financiers who attended League dinners to the factory workers who cheered at public rallies when a speaker issued the call *Viva México*! That they cared so deeply about another country's war while fighting one of their own is, perhaps, curious. And yet it was precisely because of their contemporaneous fight against the Confederacy that Unionists took such an interest in the Franco-Mexican conflict. Historian Patrick Kelly describes a spirit of "continental fraternity" engulfing Northern society after 1862 that was fueled by the idea that the US Civil War and the French Intervention in Mexico were fundamentally connected.[10] Both US Republicans and defenders of the Juárez government in Mexico championed broadly similar liberal values of individual rights, constitutional government, and free labor capitalism. Each, moreover, were fighting enemies—monarchists and clerics south of the border, slaveholding aristocrats to the north—who were supposedly devoted to Old World systems of government based on social hierarchy and hereditary privilege.

The spirit of continental fraternity that Kelly describes was not a spontaneous phenomenon. Historians have documented how Matías Romero worked tirelessly to promote the Mexican cause to the Northern public throughout the years of the French Intervention.[11] Yet few of these scholars have asked why Unionists—and particularly editors, journalists, and other influential contributors to Northern public discourse—were so receptive to the minister's messaging and embraced the Mexican cause with such fervency. This chapter shows that the answer lies in the fact that promoting this spirit of "continental fraternity" was beneficial not only for Romero's purposes, but also for certain Unionist leaders seeking to advance political agendas of their own.

Citizens of the mid-nineteenth-century United States had been taught to believe that theirs was an exceptional republic impervious to the domestic convulsions that plagued the self-governing nations of Spanish America. The outbreak of the Civil War in April 1861, however, shattered this illusion. When Mexico came under siege from a part-domestic, part-foreign assault the following year, Unionists were struck by the similarities in the crises then engulfing the two North American republics. For them, these similarities were a painful reminder of how far their once mighty republic had fallen. As de Peyster confessed at the conclusion of his toast that night in Delmonico's, the "sad position of Mexico" both echoed and magnified the "like sad realities which press upon my country."[12] The professions of continental fraternity that came to suffuse Union public discourse from 1862 onwards ostensibly expressed Northerners' determination to see North America's antidemocratic assailants defeated. Beneath this strident language, however, ran a current of uneasiness that stemmed from Northerners' recognition that the United States had descended into a condition of Mexican-like instability, and their fear that their country might share with Mexico a future of unending domestic chaos.

Fear is a powerful motivator—or, at least, this is what many of the major voices in Union public discourse seemed to believe. This chapter demonstrates that Union editors, journalists, and politicians attempted to use their countrymen's anxieties about the United States' supposed slide into Mexican-like chaos for their own political purposes. The strategy was most apparent during the second half of the Civil War in the wake of President Lincoln's 1863 Emancipation Proclamation, which expanded the war to save the Union into a fight to also end slavery. Some Unionists celebrated the Proclamation as a triumph for humanitarianism.[13] Others, however, were nervous about this enlargement of war aims.[14] Pro-administration editors, orators, and writers therefore sought to explain the Proclamation in ways that spoke to the concerns of these more skeptical portions of Northern society. The Mexican Question offered them one means of doing this. First, these individuals compared the rebel Slave Power to the priesthood in Mexico, which at that time was conspiring with French imperialists to bring down the country's republican government. Once they had established this connection in the public mind, they were able to then make the case that if the Union militarily defeated the Confederacy but allowed the slaveholding class to reenter the nation, the United States' future would resemble Mexico's past—a never-ending struggle against an antidemocratic faction within the body politic that was determined to either dominate the republic or destroy it. In short, Unionist writers and orators deployed the specter of Mexico in order to present Northerners with an ultimatum: either embrace emancipation or condemn the United States to join the long list of failed New World republics.

Early Responses to the French Intervention in Mexico

When Señor Romero first assumed his position as Mexico's *chargé d'affaires* to the United States in December 1859, he knew that a challenge lay ahead of him. Since its founding in 1824, the Mexican republic had been roiled by civil conflicts between various factions—republicans versus monarchists, landowners versus peasants, government authorities versus Indigenous communities—which Romero understood had damaged the country's reputation in the United States. "The causes of our past turmoil," he wrote to his government's Secretary of Foreign Affairs in January 1861, have "already become proverbial here and were considered by many to be without remedy."[15]

Still, Romero was hopeful that US Americans' opinion of Mexico could yet be improved. The start of his tenure in the United States coincided with a critical juncture in Mexican history. In December 1860 Conservative forces surrendered to the Liberal army, ending four years of bitter civil war. Romero had been sent to the United States by the newly reestablished Liberal government, headed by President Benito Juárez, which viewed its victory as a mandate to inaugurate its party's long-held plans to untether Mexico from the legacies of Spanish colonialism. The Liberals' agenda centered on breaking up three institutions that had held disproportionate power over Mexican society and politics since the colonial era: the military, *hacendados* (large landowners), and the Catholic Church. In doing so, President Juárez and his allies hoped to transform Mexico's downtrodden masses into upwardly mobile citizens of a stable and rapidly modernizing society.[16]

Following the US presidential election in November 1860, Romero moved quickly to inform President-elect Abraham Lincoln of the new Liberal era dawning south of the Rio Grande. In January 1861 he boarded a train in Washington, DC, bound for Springfield, Illinois. Upon his arrival Romero managed to secure a meeting with Lincoln, who was preparing for his own journey back to the nation's capital. Having welcomed Romero into his home, Lincoln invited the minister to provide him with a summary of recent Mexican history, of which the president-elect professed to be ignorant. Romero was happy to oblige, regaling Lincoln with a version of his country's past that he would come to tell many times over during his sojourn in the United States. Contrary to popular US opinion, he began, Mexico's rocky experience with self-government was not due to the racial composition of its population. Rather, "the machinations of the clergy and the army" were "entirely responsible for the constant revolutions that had devastated Mexico since its independence."[17] Thanks to the Liberals' victory in the War of Reform, however, "these groups had now been completely conquered" and would be "unable to raise the standard of rebellion again."[18]

Romero then noted how fortunate it was that the Liberal triumph in Mexico had coincided with Lincoln's own election victory. The Liberals had long believed that Mexico and the United States ought to cultivate a close commercial and financial relationship, he explained, and had therefore been disappointed with the series of Democratic presidents who throughout the 1850s had seemed more interested in finding ways to absorb portions of Mexico's territory.[19] Now that the federal government was in the hands of the Republicans, however, an amicable relationship between the United States and Mexico might yet flourish. As Romero pointed out, not only did Republicans share the Liberals' commitment to representative democracy, social mobility, and free labor, many of them had been critical of the territorial expansionism of previous Democratic administrations. In reality, both Romero and the government he represented were fully aware that the Republican coalition contained its share of imperialists who, if it weren't for the issue of slavery, would likely endorse extending the US border into Mexico. As Romero took care to emphasize to Lincoln, however, the Juárez government was nonetheless hopeful that the incoming administration in Washington, DC, would seek to develop a relationship with Mexico that would "be truly fraternal and not guided by the egotistic and antihumanitarian principles which the Democratic administrations had pursued."[20]

Having listened to this discourse, Lincoln asserted his sincere desire for the "peace and prosperity of Mexico" and the two men parted with a pledge to work toward creating "the most intimate and friendly relations" between their nations.[21] It was an encouraging start to Romero's mission. Even then, however, storm clouds were gathering that would darken the skies of this new era in continental relations, for though Mexico was emerging from its civil war, the United States was teetering on the precipice of its own. The month before Romero's visit to Springfield, South Carolina had voted to secede from the United States. By the time he met with Lincoln, Mississippi, Florida, and Alabama had done the same. Soon after Romero's return to Washington, DC, he learned that Louisiana had become the sixth state to leave the Union. In February 1861 the Montgomery Convention announced that the seceded Southern states had formed a new nation—the Confederate States of America (CSA).

War broke out between the Union and the Confederacy on April 12, 1861. Soon after, the Juárez administration announced neutrality toward the conflict. This did not mean that Mexico City was ambivalent to the war unfolding north of its border, however. As Romero had already made clear to Lincoln, Mexico's Liberal leaders felt an ideological affinity with the Republican government in Washington, DC. They also understood that the most enthusiastic imperialists of the antebellum United States were now gathered in the leadership of the CSA, and that if this putative republic won independence, it would be a constant menace to Mexican sovereignty and security. The Juárez government therefore refused to formally receive Confederate envoy John T. Pickett when he arrived in Mexico City in the spring of 1861, meanwhile pointedly maintaining official diplomatic relations with the United States. By the summer, Mexico City had agreed to allow Union troops to land at the Mexican port of Guaymas and cross northwestern Mexico in order to enter New Mexico Territory from the south. Though officially neutral, Mexico City had made it clear which side of the North-South contest it favored.[22]

Romero's plan to inaugurate an era of peaceful collaboration in US-Mexican relations was also disrupted by events in Mexico. For decades successive governments in Mexico City had struggled to secure a steady source of revenue to underwrite the country's administration. An inefficient tax system coupled with periodic costly domestic wars meant that by 1861 Mexico was deeply in debt to foreign creditors. In July, with the national coffers practically empty, President Juárez declared a two-year moratorium on his country's international debt payments. Mexico's principal creditors—Great Britain, France, and Spain—responded swiftly. Convening in London in October, they agreed to launch a tripartite expedition to occupy Mexican customs houses in order to collect the duties owed to them. Spanish troops landed at Veracruz in December; British and French forces arrived the following month.[23]

Though not unprecedented in world history, the Tripartite Powers' use of naval and military intimidation to settle a financial dispute was the kind of high-handed response that imperial powers typically only meted out to weaker nations. Certainly this was Romero's view of the situation. That the expedition was insulting to his country, however, was only part of his concern. As the diplomat intimated to President Lincoln in another meeting, which took place in the White House in August 1861, certain Mexican Conservative leaders had for the last year or so been reaching out to various European heads of state hoping to persuade one of them to help Conservatives overthrow the Juárez administration and replace it with "an aristocratic and monarchical form of government."[24] Apparently their preferred candidate was French emperor Louis-Napoleon, whom Conservatives had long admired as a supposedly enlightened autocrat who blended firm central authority with industrial modernization and commercial expansion.[25] According to Romero, the fact that France had entered into the London Convention in October 1861 suggested that Louis-Napoleon had accepted the Conservatives' invitation.

Convinced that his country was facing an existential crisis, Romero appealed to the Lincoln administration for assistance. In an early example of an argument he would repeatedly return to over the coming years, Romero invoked the United States' self-proclaimed role as the defender of free government in the Americas. US Americans had been the first in the New World to establish republican institutions, he noted in a letter to Secretary Seward in November 1861, and had since then "manifested most zeal for their preservation and propagation."[26] It was therefore impossible to imagine that they would now "look with indifference upon the storm which is brewing . . .

against the Mexican nation," for clearly this was not a war upon Mexico alone but also "against republican institutions in America and the autonomy of this continent."[27]

In his effort to propel the Lincoln administration into action, Romero had some help. From Mexico, US Minister Thomas Corwin was sending dispatches to the State Department, which echoed Romero's warning that one or more of the European powers was plotting to ally with Conservative forces to mount an insurrection against the Juárez government.[28] Secretary Seward was sufficiently concerned by both these and Romero's communications that he authorized Corwin to negotiate a loan with the Juárez administration to enable it to recommence its debt payments and thereby avert a conflict with its European creditors. When the treaty was brought before the US Senate in December 1861, however, it was rejected.[29]

In making this decision, senators were acting in accordance with the majority of public opinion in the Union at that time, at least insofar as it can be gauged in the national press. Indeed, there was a definite coolness in the initial response of many Union newspapers to Mexico's predicament. By late 1861 many Northerners were coming to the realization that the fight to put down the Southern rebellion would be a long and difficult grind. Few were therefore inclined to expend time and monies rescuing Mexico from its entanglement with the Europeans. In fact, a good many newspapers expressed the opinion that the Tripartite Expedition was a perfectly legitimate mode of recourse for creditor nations to adopt against a recalcitrant debtor. The *Philadelphia Inquirer*, for example, pointed out that the London Convention explicitly denied any intention on the part of its signatories to meddle in Mexico's domestic politics, reassuring readers that "so far as the purposes of the expedition have been made public, they are literally to enforce a settlement of long pending accounts between the turbulent and rapidly changing governments of Mexico and their defrauded and outraged creditors in Europe."[30] The *New York Times,* also relying on European sources, reprinted a long article from the *London Times* that noted that it was not unusual for Mexico to find itself at odds with foreign creditors. For decades that "decaying republic" had been ruled by a "succession of factions" composed of "insolent underlings" who were incapable of managing their country's financial and diplomatic affairs, the newspaper explained.[31] As such, the European powers had every right to demand payments owed to them, and the United States had no right to object to their doing so. Apparently forgetting that during the 1837 depression a number of US states had defaulted on their international debt payments, these newspapers implied that Mexico's dilemma was a consequence of some pathological weakness in that nation's character. The "fiscally irresponsible Mexican republic," the *New York Times* sniffed in a later article, had brought its present dilemma upon itself.[32]

At this time only a handful of the Union's major newspapers unequivocally took Mexico's side in the dispute. Prominent among these was the *Liberator*, a Boston-based newspaper that enjoyed a paid circulation of around 3,000, although its actual readership was likely far higher.[33] In January 1862 the *Liberator* warned its readers that the Tripartite Expedition would "furnish the fulcrum for further aggression" and possibly even an "invasion of Mexico."[34] The newspaper was especially suspicious of the "Parisian bandit" Louis-Napoleon, toward whom it harbored a long-standing hatred.[35] The *Liberator*'s editor was William Lloyd Garrison, an immediatist abolitionist who had grown his newspaper into the most influential antislavery organ in the mid-nineteenth-century United States.[36] Garrison saw the US abolition movement as part of a global struggle against all forms of oppression and hierarchy.[37] In his view, slaveholders in the United States were just one part of a wider network of reactionaries, despots, and aristocrats that kept peoples around the world underfoot. Thus, when French revolutionaries had forced the abdication of King Louis-Philippe in 1848, the *Liberator* had celebrated it as a triumph for the global cause of liberty.[38] But Garrison's hopes for France had later been dashed when, following the violence of the June Days, French voters elected Charles Louis-Napoleon Bonaparte as their president, persuaded by his pledge to restore order in their country. Once in office, Louis-Napoleon fulfilled his promise by banning political associations, disenfranchising large swathes of the electorate, and executing a coup d'état in 1851 that established the Second Empire and made him emperor in perpetuity. During the years that followed, the *Liberator* repeatedly condemned Louis-Napoleon for having subverted the promise of the French Revolution and called on the people of France to unite "in arising to cast off such a yoke!"[39]

When Louis-Napoleon signed the London Convention, Garrison surmised that the French emperor, already known for his foreign exploits, had set his imperial gaze on Mexico. Events would soon prove the editor correct. Upon their arrival at Veracruz, the Tripartite Powers' representatives entered into talks with Mexico's minister of foreign affairs, Manuel Doblado. After discussions, Great Britain and Spain announced that their claims had been satisfied, and by April 24, 1862, both had withdrawn their troops from the country. The French, however, remained. Declaring that he could not trust any promises made by President Juárez, Louis-Napoleon sent a man-of-war to blockade the port of Mazatlán on Mexico's Pacific Coast. Meanwhile

French forces marched westward from Veracruz into the Mexican interior. On May 5, 1862, they clashed with Mexican forces under the command of General Ignacio Zaragoza at the city of Puebla. War had broken out south of the border.

The Battle of Puebla was a resounding victory for the armies of the Mexican republic (also known as the Juarists or *Juaristas*). Soon after, however, the military tide turned against them. French troops counterattacked and contained Mexican forces at Orizaba, Veracruz, on June 14. Strengthened by reinforcements from Europe, Louis-Napoleon's troops then made a series of advances, taking the port of Tampico in October and Xalapa, the state capital of Veracruz, in December 1862. Meanwhile the *Liberator*, along with a handful of other abolitionist Union organs including the *North Star* and the *Burlington Free Press*, kept readers abreast of these events while continuing to emphasize the Mexican conflict's larger international context.[40] As the *Liberator* put it, "the Emperor had already slain" liberty in France "and the same thirst for republican blood and life urged the death of sick Mexico."[41]

The French emperor was not the only villain in this drama. The *Liberator* took care to point out that Mexico's "Catholic priests" had welcomed French troops into their country and were currently assisting the invasion.[42] It is true that the French Intervention enjoyed support from a large portion of the Mexican priesthood, which hoped that Louis-Napoleon would derail the Liberals' plan to disestablish the Catholic Church. Clerical support for the Intervention was by no means universal, however. It is also worth noting that the French invasion was backed by a significant number of Conservatives, some disaffected Liberals, and certain politicians with personal grudges against the Juárez administration.[43] Nevertheless, the *Liberator* emphasized bishops and priests as the chief traitors aiding in their own republic's destruction. This emphasis was likely an outgrowth of the strain of anti-Catholicism that ran through the US abolitionist movement and that viewed the Church hierarchy as another of the world's oppressive forces.[44] Over the course of the French invasion, such beliefs would frequently lead the *Liberator* and other Northern abolitionist organs to gloss over the complexities of pro-Intervention sentiment within Mexican society, presenting Union readers with a simplified picture in which traitorous Mexican clergymen had sold out their republic in return for favors from French imperialists.

During the initial months of fighting between French and Mexican forces, the view across the rest of the Union press was ambivalent; while few newspapers wholeheartedly approved of France's actions, nor did many enthusiastically rally to Mexico's defense. Press opinion shifted over the course of 1862, however, partly due to changes in the nature of information about the Mexican conflict that was available to Northern newspapermen. There was a long-standing precedent in the United States by which Congress could request official documents from the executive branch pertaining to foreign policy-making, including State Department correspondence with foreign governments. Traditionally, this had been done on an ad hoc basis; Congress would submit a request for documents relating to a specific diplomatic issue and the president would comply, assuming that in his judgement doing so would not jeopardize national interests. In December 1861, however, the Lincoln administration took the unprecedented step of responding to three such requests from Congress by releasing an entire volume of documents, which did not pertain to a single foreign policy issue, but instead was comprised of the State Department's communications with multiple countries including the principal European powers.[45]

The act was met with widespread approval in Congress, which quickly ordered "tens of copies to be printed" and made available to the public.[46] This in turn gave the Union press—which so far had been largely reliant on European sources when following the events of the French Intervention—new insight into the situation below the border. The impact was not immediate; the first volume of what would become known as the *Foreign Relations of the United States (FRUS)* series was huge, and it took reporters some time to trawl through its contents. At the time of its publication, moreover, other foreign policy matters, namely the dispute with Great Britain over the seizure of the *Trent,* dominated Union press coverage of foreign affairs. It was therefore not until the spring of 1862 that articles appeared from Union journalists describing what they had learned about the war in Mexico from reading State Department correspondence. In May, for example, a writer for Joseph Medill's antislavery *Chicago Tribune* confessed to being impressed by the "honorable and straightforward" conduct of Mexico's representatives in their dealings with the European officials who had disembarked at Veracruz the year before.[47] Dispatches showed that Mexican foreign relations secretary Manuel de Zamacona had explained to the Europeans that his government's decision to *temporarily* suspend its debt payments was not the consequence of reckless spending, but was instead due to the fact that money was needed to put down various antigovernment rebellions taking place at the time, which had been instigated by treasonous Conservatives. Letters further showed that this request had been met with an extraordinarily insulting reply from French military commanders, who had denounced "Signor Zamacona, President Juarez, and the whole Government of Mexico, as banditti and a pest among civilized nations."[48] "No one can read these documents," the *Tribune*'s journalist concluded, "without gaining a higher opinion than is commonly entertained of the intelligence and rectitude of the present Government of Mexico."[49] A reporter for the *New York Tribune* came to a similar conclusion. The French officials' efforts to aggravate rather than settle the dispute with the Juárez government had "all the disagreeable features of part of a conspiracy," the journalist surmised, adding that in his view a "quarrel was—above all things—desired by France."[50]

It is no coincidence that the *New York Tribune* and the *Chicago Tribune* were, like the *Liberator,* firm opponents of slavocrats, monarchists, and any other supposed enemies of liberal self-government; already disposed to take the side of any American republic that found itself in a dispute with a European emperor, they were happy finally to have evidence that would allow them to unreservedly back the Juárez government in its war with France. It would take the occurrence of a series of significant events in Mexico during the spring and summer of 1863 to definitively move the remainder of the Union press into Mexico's column, however. On May 17, 1863, the city of Puebla fell to French forces commanded by General François Achille Bazaine. President Juárez and his cabinet, which had been operating from the city, were forced to flee northward to Paso del Norte. The following month, French troops entered Mexico City. From there French officials convened an assembly of 215 Mexicans and tasked them with deciding what form of government would replace the Juárez administration. This so-called Assembly of Notables was comprised of powerful Conservative landowners, businessmen, lawyers, and priests. The body's executive committee included former Mexican president General José Mariano Salas, the bishop of Puebla Pelagio Antonio Labastida, and Juan Almonte, one of the Conservative leaders who had helped to convince Louis-Napoleon to launch the Intervention. The Assembly's members were, almost to a man, well-known antirepublicans; the outcome of their deliberations was therefore predictable. On July 10 the body announced that the "Mexican Nation, through its organ, the Assembly of Notables" had chosen a hereditary monarchy as its new form of government.[51] The Assembly then offered the crown of what it called the Mexican Empire to Archduke Ferdinand Maximilian I of Austria.[52]

The announcement inflamed public opinion in the Union like no other event of the French Intervention so far. As the *New York Tribune* explained, for months Louis-Napoleon's ultimate intentions regarding Mexico had been open to speculation. Now, however, there could be no doubt that his goal was the "abolition of a republican form of Government in Mexico."[53] Outrage spread far beyond abolitionist and antislavery organs, however. Back in December 1861, the *Philadelphia Inquirer* had dismissed warnings from Romero, Corwin, and others that an invasion of Mexico was afoot.[54] By the summer of 1863, however, the newspaper was compelled to admit that the recent actions of the "packed Junta of the Notables of the city of Mexico" amounted to a "contemptible trick" being played against "a sister republic, torn by internal strife, laid prostrate at the feet of the great military despot of Europe."[55] Iowa's *Charles City Republican Intelligencer* was equally appalled by the turn of events south of the border. "The disguise of Napoleon is at length cast off," the newspaper thundered, "and we now clearly behold his plans for propagating monarchical institutions and the Catholic religion upon this continent" with the aid of "the bigoted, retrogressive, monarchical priest party of Mexico."[56] The Democratic-leaning *New York Herald* similarly announced that France's talk "about debts and outrages" committed by the Juárez government had been mere pretense; no matter what wrongs Mexico had committed, these were no justification for "invading her soil, robbing her mines and degrading her sons and daughters."[57] It was now clear to Union newspapers across the ideological spectrum that this was no ordinary dispute over unpaid debts; rather, it was a monarchical-imperial assault against a New World republic and the free government ideals for which it stood.

Slaveholders, Priests, and Emperors

As the ideological dimensions of the French Intervention came into sharper focus, so too did the Union press's awareness of certain similarities between that conflict and their own fight against the Southern rebels. To an extent, Northern commentators had been first encouraged to draw such parallels by Matías Romero. As Don Doyle explains, Romero was determined to convince Unionists that their national interests were bound up with those of the Mexican republic, and from 1862 onward had therefore "carried out a vigorous public diplomacy campaign" in the North centered on the notion that there "existed an integral link between the slaveholders' rebellion in the United States and the 'Church party' rebellion in Mexico."[58] Both factions, the minister argued, were "in rebellion against popularly elected republican governments" and "sought foreign intervention to defeat the popular will," and both "must be crushed before either republic could live in peace."[59]

As the French Intervention unfolded, Union organs were increasingly receptive to Romero's argument. Most Northerners at the time were familiar with the concept of the Slave Power. First popularized by abolitionists in the

1840s before entering mainstream Republican discourse during the following decade, the notion hinged on an image of the Southern slaveholding class as a grasping aristocracy, which, accustomed to exercising unchecked mastery over enslaved people, had developed a taste for domination in all other realms of society. The theory ran that in the political sphere, these so-called slavocrats were determined to control all three branches of the federal government in order to wield their power in the service of Southern interests. Antebellum antislavery propagandists had warned that the Slave Power would use any means necessary to realize this ambition, including subverting the United States' democratic system of government.[60] The fallout of the 1860 presidential contest, which saw eleven slaveholding states leave the Union rather than abide by the outcome of a free election, appeared to prove this point. As the *Liberator* put it, Southern secession was driven by a "hatred of a Republican form of government" and the Confederate rebellion therefore constituted "treason against Republicanism."[61] According to this interpretation, the Civil War was not a conflict over territory, tariffs, or even slavery per se, but between the theories of democratic and oligarchical government.

Based on this view, it was no great stretch for Unionists to see how the Southern rebellion shared certain features in common with the French Intervention in Mexico. As the *New York Tribune* pointed out in July 1863, both Louis-Napoleon and the Confederate leadership possessed an "intense hatred of democratic institutions" and a "desire to substitute [them] for the rule of aristocracy, or even monarchy."[62] This accusation was a direct retort to Confederate propagandists attempting to place their independence movement within the US revolutionary tradition by comparing themselves to the North American colonists who had risen up to throw off the British imperial yoke in 1776.[63] Indeed, drawing parallels between the slavocracy and French imperialists turned this narrative on its head. As the *Tribune* explained, Southern rebels were not patriots but traitors who, like the French in Mexico, wished to "re-introduce the European theory of government upon this Continent."[64] The fact that the Richmond government had publicly declared its support for the French Intervention was taken as further proof that the leaders of these assaults on North American republicanism were cooperating with one another.

As these ideas circulated in the Union press, the scale of this imagined conspiracy grew. Since the start of the Civil War, a substantial minority of Northerners had objected to the Lincoln administration's use of military force to put down the Southern rebellion. This sentiment was particularly strong in the Midwestern states of Ohio, Indiana, and Illinois, where many communities had close familial and trading connections with the South. Dissent also came from among some Catholic immigrant groups in northeastern cities who did not view the Civil War as their fight and who were also wary of the nativist elements in Lincoln's Republican Party. Throughout 1862, antiwar sentiment increased as it became clear that the South would not be easily trounced and that Unionists must therefore prepare for a long and grueling fight. In response, the Lincoln administration enacted a series of controversial measures, including the suspension of habeas corpus, designed to clamp down on any disloyal elements in the North that might undermine the war effort. Paradoxically, these measures fueled the fires of the antiwar movement by enabling its leaders, including Horatio Seymour, Fernando Wood, and Clement L. Vallandigham, to add tyrannical tendencies to their list of grievances against the Lincoln administration. The 1862 midterm elections saw antiwar Democrats (otherwise known as Peace Democrats or Copperheads) win in Ohio, Indiana, and Pennsylvania. Meanwhile clandestine antiwar organizations such as the Knights of the Golden Circle stepped up their activities aimed at sabotaging the Union Army's recruitment efforts and giving assistance to its deserters.[65]

Much as they compared Confederates to French imperialists, Union publications also claimed to see resemblances between antiwar Northerners and those Mexican Catholic leaders who were aiding the French Intervention. Mexico's priests, the *Chicago Tribune* declared, were "the copperheads of that country" who, like their Northern counterparts, had betrayed their republic by entering into an "unholy alliance . . . for the purpose of crushing out the principles of free government."[66] The prevalence of Catholics in the Northern antiwar movement provided fodder for such accusations. For example, one Indiana newspaper predicted that, should France intervene in the Civil War against the Union, Copperheads would "take sides with Maximilian, Louis Napoleon, the House of Hapsburg, and the Jesuit propaganda" because they wished to see not only monarchism but also Catholicism ascendant in North America—a "blind, medieval faith" that was fundamentally "anti-progressive" and un-American.[67] In a speech later published by Wheeling's *Daily Intelligencer*, General Franz Sigel went beyond hypotheticals to insist that Copperhead collusion with the French invasion was already well underway:

> Look at England—look at France—look at Mexico—look at Jeff. Davis—look at the Copperheads in our midst. All are working to the same end; all are in unison to destroy this great and good government. . . . The Copperheads are the re-actionists who are the allies of the enemy within

> our lines. . . . All the odds and ends of these mean and sordid elements will flock around the standard of Maximilian in opposition to the proud flag above me—the symbol of protection to the weak and elevation to the oppressed.[68]

By enabling them to place the Slave Power within a global antirepublican network, the Mexican Question had given Union newspapers a way to reveal to their readers new international dimensions of the United States' domestic conflict. As the Copperhead movement in the North grew throughout 1862 and 1863, these newspapers warned their readers that this network now extended from Paris to Rome, Mexico City to Richmond, and into the very heart of the Union.

The Union Press Embraces "Our Sister Republicans"

While the French Intervention revealed to Unionists certain international enemies, it also illuminated some previously undervalued allies. During the antebellum period, most US editors and journalists had subscribed to the idea that Mexico's seemingly chronic political turbulence was caused by some innate, incurable flaw in the nation's character. As France's invasion of Mexico progressed, however, some of them revisited these assumptions. They were prompted to do so in part by the propaganda efforts of the Juárez administration, which was acutely aware that French officials were working hard to convince foreign audiences that most Mexicans, supposedly lacking any true affection for democratic republicanism or sense of patriotic pride, welcomed Louis-Napoleon's plan to replace their republic with a monarchy. Understanding that foreign powers could later use this narrative to justify granting recognition to Louis-Napoleon's puppet regime, Mexican officials utilized various channels to counter it. In December 1862, for example, the Mexican Congress issued a public manifesto, later printed in the *New York Times*, which praised the manner in which "the Mexican Republic has accepted the ravaging war which the Emperor of the French has sent against it" and insisted that the war effort would be carried on "for as long as may be necessary, and with all the vigor and perseverance which wars of that nature demand."[69] Indeed, the manifesto continued, rather than exposing the weakness of Mexican nationalism, the French invasion had given it new life. In fighting for their republic Mexicans had found "firmness in the object . . . perseverance in action, and the union of all hearts, cooperating all and in all possible ways, each one according to his means, to obtain the result we aim at."[70]

The Mexican government's effort to reach Union audiences was aided by the fact that, from December 1861, the previously described publication of an edited volume of all US diplomatic correspondence became an annual practice in the United States. As such, many of the Juárez administration's letters describing the condition of its war effort, sent to the State Department via Romero, eventually found their way into the public sphere.[71] Romero augmented this process by periodically passing such communications directly to friendly newspapers. "By the latest advices from the city of Mexico to the Mexican Minister, Senor Romero," read one *New York Herald* article based on information that had been obtained in this way, "it appears that the aspect of affairs is encouraging. . . . The Mexicans have three armies in the field . . . so that they are confident of repulsing attacks."[72] Finally, US journalists stationed in Mexico who were following Juarist forces often came to hold a favorable view of these soldiers' fighting ability and their prospects for ultimate success. One such correspondent for the *New York Times*, who was attached to a Juarist company based near Queretaro, explained in October 1863 that, contrary to "French fabrications," the Juarists "are full of courage and hope" and were "exerting themselves with great energy and wisdom in organizing a force to resist the French."[73] "It is a great mistake to believe that even a fractional part of the Mexican people, outside of the City of Mexico, hold any sympathy with the French," the journalist continued. "On the contrary, there is a *deep and deadly hatred felt toward the invaders in all the outlying States*."[74]

Over the course of 1863 the combined efforts of the Mexican government, Juarist agents, and sympathetic Union journalists in the field bore fruit. While Northern newspapers occasionally suspected that their Mexican sources were exaggerating the size and skill of the Juarist military, few denied that the French were encountering serious resistance south of the border. In the parlance of nineteenth-century nationalism, martial skill translated into patriotic devotion. As articles circulated describing the courage of Juarist fighters, therefore, some Union newspapers began to question those stereotypes, so widely accepted in US society, regarding Mexicans' supposed lack of national spirit and vitality. As DC's *Washington Chronicle* remarked in May 1863, Louis-Napoleon had believed he would easily "conquer a distracted, broken priest ridden people . . . who were tired of their government, or rather their political chaos, and who had gained an unenviable reputation for cowardice and lack of military ability."[75] To the emperor's surprise, however, this "wretched nation" had held its own against the "trained soldiers" of France, for whom "not only war, but victory was traditional."[76] The *Boston Daily Advertiser*, meanwhile, admitted that the strength of the Juarist war effort had surprised not only Louis-Napoleon, but many Unionists as well. "Mexico, as a nation, has been deemed effete," the newspaper acknowledged in June 1863, "her people being unable to maintain steady self-government" and "unable to defend their independence."[77] Yet the determination with which Mexicans were currently fighting the French invasion ought to persuade all reasonable people to rethink such views. "The Mexicans have demonstrated the existence . . . of a much nobler side of their character than they have heretofore had the credit of," the newspaper continued. "They have shown that a nation, torn by internal dissensions . . . may still unite, in the presence of external danger, and fight with devotion and heroism against an invader."[78]

On the pages of Union newspapers, then, Juarists were increasingly depicted as brave fighters animated by a simple yet earnest love of their republic. This suggests that there was a degree of malleability in Northerners' racialized views of their Mexican neighbors. Certainly, racial science had been gaining ground in both scholarly and lay circles in the United States throughout the antebellum era.[79] Yet the influence of these theories should not be overstated—though biological classifications were coming into vogue, older definitions of race as a blend of blood, culture, and environment still retained some traction in midcentury US society. Indeed, well into the 1850s US editors, journalists, and other commentators continued to refer to the so-called Mexican race as a bundle of biological, societal, and cultural elements and debated the relative importance of each of these factors in shaping Mexico's character.[80] The persistence of at least some ambiguity in racial thinking meant that, by the time of the French Intervention, Unionists still had the flexibility to redefine which characteristics they associated with the Mexican people. A good example comes to us from an August 1863 *New York Times* article that described Mexico's "priests, generals and officers" as a "creole aristocracy" that had inherited their Spanish forbearers' predilection for cruelty, domination, and hierarchy.[81] By contrast, the article continued, the "five-sixths of the Mexican nation" who were "Indians, or mainly of Indian blood" were untainted by these Old World inheritances.[82] The *Times* went so far as to suggest that the Native American portions of the Mexican population possessed a uniquely *American* love of liberty, which was best exemplified by President Benito Juárez, "a native Indian" and "representative of the real people of Mexico" who wished "for a real republic, and a real nationality."[83] In making this claim, the *Times* turned traditional anti-Mexican racial prejudices on their head, transforming the prevalence of Native bloodlines among that population from a vice into a virtue, and even suggesting that it explained the courage Juarists had shown in their fight against the French.

Few Union publications were as emphatic as the *Times* in their praise of the so-called Mexican race. Still, most were willing—at least rhetorically—to accept Mexicans as valued allies in the defense of North American republicanism. It is reasonable to assume that, in part, the rapidity with which some Northern publications changed their view of Mexicans was due to expediency; finding themselves facing similar assaults from enemies who seemed to be in collusion, it would have been unwise of Unionists to spurn the friendship of their Mexican neighbors, who could offer them both geostrategic cooperation and moral vindication. This latter factor was especially important. Indeed, most articles in the Northern press that spoke positively about the Juarist war effort contained some reference to the notion that Mexican republicans and Unionists were fighting on the same side of a single war. As the *Chicago Tribune* put it, the Civil War was just one part of a "quadrilateral fight" playing out across the continent "between the French and rebels on the one side, and the Mexican and Federal forces on the other."[84] "The Mexican republicans understand that their interests are identified with the preservation of . . . the Union party," and vice versa.[85] An important factor behind the willingness of Union newspapers to rethink their low opinion of Mexicans, in short, was that they believed themselves to be tied to them in a single crisis fighting a common enemy.

The twin wars of North America—rebellion above the border, invasion below—inspired many of the Union's foremost newspapers to identify certain ideological connections stretching across the Rio Grande. As they did so, they placed the Union war effort in an *American* transnational narrative that emphasized Mexico and the United States' shared experiences in colonialism, revolution, and republicanism. This narrative contained a pronounced anti-European edge, casting the Slave Power as a vestige of European colonialism, the Southern rebellion as Old World reactionism, and both Unionists and Mexican Liberals as the standard-bearers of the New World's revolutionary tradition. The power of this narrative therefore lay in its ability to place the roots of the Union cause in the United States' revolutionary birth, while extending its branches to the far reaches of the North American continent. As we shall see, while this framing aimed to bolster popular enthusiasm for the Union war effort in general, certain parts of the press would harness its power to engender public support for some of the Lincoln administration's more controversial war measures.

A New Monroe Doctrine

By the summer of 1863, the Union press understood that Louis-Napoleon aimed to erect a monarchy in Mexico. This then raised the question of what the US government's response to this assault on American republicanism ought to be. The Lincoln administration favored neutrality. As Secretary Seward had explained in dispatches to Union diplomats stationed abroad, which later appeared in the Northern press, Washington, DC, had "neither a right nor a disposition to intervene by force in the internal affairs of Mexico, whether to establish and maintain a Republic . . . or to overthrow an imperial or a foreign one."[86] Members of the Juárez administration were disappointed by this cautiousness. Ideally, they would have welcomed a Union military intervention to put a halt to the French invasion, though they also understood that this was likely too much to expect of Northerners while they were fighting their own war for national survival. Juarist representatives therefore concentrated on pressuring the Lincoln administration to lift its 1861 ban on the exportation of arms out of the Union in order to allow undersupplied Mexican forces access to much-needed war matériel. Juarist agents also funneled US capital into their war effort by selling Mexican republican bonds on Northern financial markets. Finally, they orchestrated the covert movement of arms and munitions from Union ports into Mexico to the tune of hundreds of thousands of dollars.[87]

Romero was involved in all of these activities to varying degrees. He also augmented them by writing a steady stream of letters to the US State Department from 1862 onward, putting forward various arguments as to why the Lincoln administration ought to abandon neutrality toward the French Intervention. Among these was that the policy betrayed the United States' responsibilities as the supposed defender of free government in the New World. As Romero put it to Secretary Seward in June 1862, this God-given role had found formal articulation in the "wise and forecasting policy" of President James Monroe.[88] Here Romero was referring to Monroe's 1823 message to Congress in which the president, reflecting on the recent Spanish American revolutions, had insisted that the world was now divided into two blocs, each defined by distinct forms of government: monarchical Europe and republican America. Given that this division was natural, even providential, Monroe had asserted, the self-governing nations of the Americas were "henceforth not to be considered as subjects for future colonization by any European power."[89] To enforce this dictum, Monroe had promised that the United States, the foremost of the New World republics, would "consider any attempt [by the European powers] to extend their system to any portion of this hemisphere, as dangerous to our peace and safety."[90]

In making this pledge, Monroe had not committed the United States to any particular course of action should a European power encroach upon the hemisphere.[91] What Monroe's doctrine (later the Monroe Doctrine) did do, however, was irrevocably tie US Americans' sense of national honor to the maintenance of an imaginary wall between the European and American Continents. Romero understood this. Indeed, by invoking the Monroe Doctrine he was appealing not only to Northerners' sense of duty, but also their pride; the French invasion of Mexico, he suggested, was an insult to the United States and its self-claimed standing as the foremost power in the Western Hemisphere. Even as he did so, however, Romero was aware that some US Americans interpreted the Monroe Doctrine as a possessive as well as a protective declaration, a way to ward off would-be European rivals to ensure that the United States enjoyed primary control over the New World's land, markets, and resources. In his communications with Union officials, Romero was therefore always clear that US aid ought to be extended to his government in the spirit of fraternal brotherhood between two equal allies, and that the United States should not expect any territory from or special influence over the Mexican republic in return for this assistance.[92]

In his campaign to persuade the Lincoln administration to abandon neutrality, Romero was facing some serious headwinds. The problem was not only that Secretary Seward and the president were both committed to the policy, but that large portions of the Union press supported them in this position. Certain newspapers did occasionally endorse the idea of a US loan to Mexico, or else suggested the easing of the arms embargo to allow Mexican agents to legally procure weapons within the United States. But even in these cases, such support was tempered by the concern that even these relatively modest measures could push Louis-Napoleon toward a closer relationship with the Confederacy.[93] While pro-Juarist sentiments were widespread in the wartime North, therefore, they were not enough to challenge the consensus opinion that the Union could not offer substantial material aid to Mexico without fatally jeopardizing its own war effort.

Still, while they acknowledged its necessity, few Union editors or journalists relished neutrality; many openly struggled to reconcile the policy with their understanding of the United States' historic role as the model and protector of free government in the New World. In this way, neutrality magnified a concern that had earlier appeared in the Northern press during the Secession Winter of 1860–1861 regarding the damage the sectional conflict was doing to the United States' global reputation. In February 1861, with seven states out of the Union, the *Weekly Wisconsin Patriot* had pleaded with the nation's leaders to find an "honorable means for reconciliation."[94] Failure to do so would mean civil war between the North and South, likely to be followed by further separations, which would throw the country into "perpetual commotion and bloody strife."[95] If this came to pass, the United States would be doomed to reenact the "history of Mexico" and its "gory examples" of endless internal unrest.[96] Once the Civil War began, newspapers across the Union repeated these gloomy predictions. As the *Milwaukee Daily Sentinel* foretold in 1862, continual domestic convulsions of the kind that had "made Mexico a shame and a reproach among republics" now threatened to "reduce our own favored land to the same misery."[97]

Viewed from this perspective, Louis-Napoleon's invasion of Mexico suggested that the European powers had recognized that the United States was going the way of the failed Spanish American republics and had resolved to use this to their advantage. "It cannot be doubted," Washington, DC's, *National Intelligencer* sighed, "that if there had been no civil war here . . . the Mexican expedition would have been an impossibility."[98] The *New York Tribune* agreed: "The virtual degradation of Mexico into a French satrapy is a direct result of the Slaveholders' Rebellion. . . . Our extremity is Napoleon's opportunity."[99] Clearly the French emperor had calculated that the Union would be unable to protect Mexico while fighting the Confederacy. More troubling still was the thought that Louis-Napoleon would not have dared attempt a revival of monarchism in Mexico had he not believed that, thanks to the Civil War, the very idea of democratic self-government was losing its appeal among the people of the New World. As the *New York Tribune* explained, for decades the United States' symbolic power had exerted a "controlling influence over the deliberations of European cabinets," who knew that they could not reimpose their institutions upon the hemisphere's independent nations so long as their populations had the US model to aspire to. In this way, the United States had kept its independent neighbors "safe from [European] intrigues purely through the force of its example."[100] Now that the US republic had been overcome by internal weaknesses, however, it no longer offered the world an example of the blessings of democratic self-government. "Nobody imagines that [the French Intervention] would or could have been effected had this republic been united . . . as it was ten or even five years ago," the *Tribune* concluded.[101] The real rub of the French assault on Mexico, then, was that it made the United States' own fall from grace so painfully apparent.

In their most pessimistic moments, some newspapers worried that the United States' diminished standing on the world stage made it too vulnerable to foreign interference, perhaps even recolonization. Since gaining independence, US Americans had been wary of suspected plots by the European powers to corrupt and disrupt their republic. This popular fear had receded somewhat over the first half of the nineteenth century as the United States consolidated its position on the North American continent. Still, paranoia about European intrigues had never entirely lost its grip over US society, peaking episodically in response to perceived threats lurking on the nation's borders. For much of the 1830s and 1840s, for example, white Southern leaders had warned that Britain was conspiring to convert the Republic of Texas to abolitionism and then to use the country as a base from which to infiltrate the United States with antislavery influences. The Secession Crisis of 1860–1861 precipitated another spike in public discussions about possible outside infiltration, maybe even invasion. As then-senator William Seward told his congressional colleagues in January 1861, "the Union has, thus far, proved itself an almost perfect shield against" foreign war.[102] Unity had enhanced each individual state's commercial value, geopolitical reach, and military strength—all qualities that had made hostile foreign actors think twice before picking a fight with the United States. The separation of North and South, Seward asserted, would shatter this power. Moreover, he noted that "We know, from the sad experience of other nations, that disintegration once begun, inevitably continues" and argued that further separations would follow in the wake of Southern secession, until the United States had disintegrated into a string of petty confederacies.[103] "Jealousies" would soon spring up among them, Seward predicted, "which in turn would bring on frequent and retaliatory wars."[104] The European powers would take advantage of the chaos, offering military protection to one confederacy or another in return for land, or else simply sending in armies to conquer the region wholesale. "And thus," Seward ended, "our country, having expelled all European Powers from the continent, would relapse into an aggregated form of its colonial experience, and . . . become the theatre of transatlantic intervention and rapacity."[105]

Throughout the Civil War, Union newspapers continually fretted about possible foreign intervention in their fight with the Confederates, which in the worst-case scenario could end with the United States being carved up between the European empires. During the war's initial months, Northern organs typically pointed to Great Britain as the most likely of the European powers to attempt something of this kind. As one Iowa newspaper reminded its readers in early 1862, for the last eighty years Britain had been watching its former North American colonies "like a hawk who fixes her piercing glance upon the prey she will grasp in her talons."[106] Reflecting on the recent *Trent* Affair, the newspaper warned that the British were looking for an excuse to intervene in the Civil War on the side of the South in order to "see forever this prosperous and blessed land disappear amidst the convulsions of anarchy."[107] With the advent of the French Intervention in Mexico, however, Unionists' calculations regarding the source and nature of foreign threats to their nation gradually changed. In late 1863, for example, the *Ohio Democrat* acknowledged that the British still believed that they had a historical score to settle with the United States ("let us not forget that we were once her *Colonies*").[108] Nevertheless, the newspaper was now convinced that France posed a far greater and more immediate danger to the Union. From his vantage point in Mexico, the *Democrat* warned, Louis-Napoleon would inevitably look to the US Southwest as another "inviting field" for colonization and begin plotting how to bring the "golden fruits" of "California and New Mexico" into his "imperial clutch."[109] It is worth noting here that the *Democrat*'s assessment of the French emperor's wider continental ambitions was not far off the mark; Louis-Napoleon viewed not only Mexico but both the US Southwest and parts of Central America as potential fields into which France's commerce, political influence, and (if necessary) troops might be extended.[110] Such ambitions filtered down through the French imperial military and diplomatic apparatuses, and help to explain why the Union press periodically picked up rumors about French officials feeling out opportunities to expand the emperor's reach beyond Mexico. In June 1864, for example, the Paris correspondent for Boston's *Saturday Evening Gazette* reported that French agents were currently in California warning residents of the "darkness of the future which awaits them" if they remained "united with the Federal States," which apparently would be subjected to "ceaseless agitation" in the future as more separatist movements followed Southern secession.[111] Allegedly the French agents then contrasted this gloomy forecast with the "peace" and "security" Californians would enjoy if they became part of the new government that French imperialists were constructing in Mexico.[112] The *Gazette*'s reporter ended by warning that there was good "reason to believe that these whispers have not found listless or incredulous ears in Californians," whose loyalty to the Union was known to be tenuous.[113]

Such feelings of national vulnerability were compounded by US neutrality on the Mexican Question—a necessary but deeply frustrating position for those US Americans who believed that the French invasion not only endangered Mexican republicanism, but also posed a symbolic challenge and possible physical threat to the United States itself. For them, the Union's inability to address this danger amplified their insecurities about the integrity of their republic, which had been first thrown up by the outbreak of the Civil War. It was in this way that the issue of the Franco-Mexican War began to generate its own particular power in Union politics; while few seriously argued against neutrality toward the conflict, Northern political leaders and editors came to see that they could harness the vexation the wider public felt regarding their nation's inability to decisively act on the Mexican Question to advance certain domestic political agendas.

Among the first to do this were members of the nation's patriotic organizations, in particular the Union Leagues. The first Union League was established in 1862 in New York City. By the following year, Leagues had appeared in Philadelphia, Boston, and Cincinnati. Drawn from the upper echelons of the urban North's political, business, and intellectual communities, League members engaged in various activities aimed at boosting popular support for the Union war effort, including holding public rallies, organizing recruitment drives, and publishing patriotic literature for mass consumption. This last endeavor was primarily accomplished through the Loyal Publication Society (LPS), the literary arm of the New York League, which published thousands of pamphlets and distributed them to both Union troops in the field and the wider public. The form and content of the pamphlets varied; often they consisted of reprinted speeches delivered by orators at public events, others were essays lifted from journals, and some had been written by League members themselves. Taken together, however, the LPS pamphlets all sought to explain the causes and meaning of the Civil War in ways that would resonate with as many Northern readers as possible.

This task became more challenging after January 1863. That month, President Lincoln issued the Emancipation Proclamation and thereby made the liberation of enslaved peoples in the rebel states a formal Union war aim. Some Northerners cheered the measure as a triumph for humanitarianism.[114] Others, however, were nervous. While they distrusted the Slave Power, a substantial portion of the Northern population had no love for the enslaved. Furthermore, many of them had serious doubts regarding the constitutionality of federally mandated emancipation and worried over the social and economic implications of millions of Black Southerners transitioning en masse from slavery to freedom.[115]

League members recognized that the Emancipation Proclamation had been met with wariness among certain portions of Northern society. In response, they sought to explain the necessity of freeing the enslaved in ways that spoke to these Northerners in particular. One strategy was to justify emancipation not as a moral measure, but as a tool for national reunion and subsequent stabilization. At the first meeting of the Philadelphia Union League in May 1863, for example, the new organization's president Nathaniel B. Browne informed his audience that the genius of the Framers of the US Constitution had been their ability to put aside the "jealousies and jarring interests of the States and sections."[116] They had done this, he continued, because they had understood that "state pride and sectional attachments," which placed "self, neighborhood, section or party" above the "country and its welfare," led to "lawlessness and anarchy."[117] That same month Colonel Charles Anderson made a similar point when speaking to the Union Club in Xenia, Ohio. He elaborated on the theme by adding that, since the ratification of the Constitution, the growth of slavery in the United States had seen a self-interested faction emerge within the body politic of the kind that the Framers had warned against. For decades the "domineering" Slave Power had demanded "special privileges" from its countrymen, Anderson thundered, and Northern legislators had acceded for the sake of national peace.[118] The Southern rebellion proved that the slavocracy would live "by these compromises only so long as they served their purposes," however, at which point "they discarded them and demanded new ones."[119] The Slave Power's thirst for domination, Anderson insisted, could never be sated.

Anderson used this reasoning to argue that, even if the Union Army defeated Confederate forces, any attempt to bring the South back into the national fold with slavery intact would fail to resolve the original causes of disunion. Over time the Slave Power would recover its strength, until it was once again able to hold the nation to ransom over the threat of another rebellion. To guarantee lasting peace, therefore, it was necessary to destroy the slavocracy, and this was only possible by destroying slavery itself. "They say it is an Abolition war," Anderson observed in reference to Northern critics of the Emancipation Proclamation, "a war carried on for the purpose of abolishing slavery. But, as I look at it, there is nothing in it but a simple contest between two great principles, which are utterly irreconcilable, which can no more exist together than fire and water. These principles are those of the free institutions of Republican Government and those of Absolutism."[120]

Anderson's message was clear: radical though it may seem, emancipation was a restorative measure that would purge the United States of the disruptive elements that had infiltrated its society over recent decades. This would return that spirit of cooperation to national politics that the Framers had so cherished, and that had blessed the United States with unparalleled tranquility in those halcyon years immediately following its founding.

The promise of an end to domestic discord was no doubt appealing to a population currently in the throes of civil war. Still, certain LPS publications found a way to enhance this message by connecting the prospect of reunion and lasting domestic peace to the attainment of even more ambitious national goals. In late 1863 the organization published a pamphlet titled "The Monroe Doctrine." Its author was congregationalist minister and abolitionist Joshua Leavitt, who had originally written the piece for the *New Englander and Yale Review*. Leavitt began by noting that the 1823 Monroe Doctrine had been born out of a "golden period of our political history" when US citizens and their representatives had been guided by a common "devotion to public interests."[121] As Leavitt described it, "Party spirit had not eaten out the keen sense of what becomes the honor of the country. And slavery had not yet extinguished patriotism in half the States of the union. It was the lull of party strife called 'the era of good feelings.' It was the transition period between the patriotic inexperience of our infant government and the dominant selfishness of later years."[122]

According to Leavitt, domestic harmony had enhanced the country's international clout. Thus, when in 1823 the United States, "the first of American republics," had announced that the Western Hemisphere was henceforth reserved for free institutions, the world had taken note.[123] "This declaration, so plain, so explicit, and so firm," Leavitt enthused, had "electrified Europe."[124] The Holy Alliance, which had been drawing up plans to reconquer the Americas, abandoned their intrigues—out of fear not of the United States' military might, Leavitt emphasized, but of the strength of its institutions. The monarchs of Europe had understood that the success of the US republic would make it impossible to compel populations living within its sphere of influence to tolerate anything but republicanism for themselves.

Turning to the present, Leavitt explained that since that time, slavery and sectionalism had seeped into US politics; national unity had weakened, undermining the country's symbolic power and prestige overseas. All of this was apparent, he argued, in the fiasco that was the French Intervention in Mexico. Leavitt believed that the Lincoln government ought to have made a "frank and explicit" public condemnation of the actions of the Tripartite Powers when they had first moved against Mexico in late 1861.[125] This would have indicated to the world that, even when "at the lowest point of our disasters," the United States could still carry out its duties as "the leading republic of the New World, and the ready representative of the Political System of America, with which European politics had no business to interfere."[126] Such a declaration "might have caused a hitch in the progress" of the Europeans' designs against Mexico by giving "proof to the world of our continued confidence in the stability of our institutions, and in the inherent strength of our government to maintain itself" despite its civil troubles.[127] "The world would have seen," Leavitt continued, warming to the topic, "that the spirit of the republic was wholly unbroken, and that we exacted from other nations the same respect and deference, which they were ready enough to pay us in the glorious days of President Monroe."[128] Of course, the Lincoln administration had failed to issue any such condemnation, or at least one "frank and explicit" enough to satisfy Leavitt.[129] The world had therefore been left to infer that the Civil War had shaken US Americans' self-confidence to the point where they had relinquished their role as the hemisphere's defender of free government.

Leavitt's pamphlet was a hit. Ohio's *Cleveland Morning Leader* gave it an unequivocal endorsement, predicting that it would give "a right direction to the public mind in regard to the Monroe Doctrine."[130] An Iowa newspaper similarly praised the pamphlet as "an able review" that correctly presented the French Intervention and the Civil War as twin fronts of a single contest between "the two systems of Government, in Europe and America."[131] No doubt Leavitt's essay was so popular in part because it neatly articulated the already widely accepted view that there was a connection between the Union and Mexican republican causes. More than this, however, "The Monroe Doctrine" showed Northerners a way to aid Mexico without imperiling their own war effort against the Confederacy. Leavitt had argued that the United States' former ability to shield the Western Hemisphere from European predators had derived from the self-evident strength of its domestic political institutions. From this reasoning, certain prominent newspapers concluded that Unionists could best help the Mexican republicans by concentrating on the restoration of the US republic to its original exemplary stature—a goal that could only be accomplished by defeating the Confederates and, crucially, eradicating the institution of slavery. As the *New York Tribune* explained, although the United States could not spare troops to send over the border, "a speedy triumph over the rebels" would see the power of the US example flow southwards and compel "France to quit Mexico."[132] The *Chicago Tribune* agreed. The "surest way to lend aid to Mexico," the newspaper argued, was to "defeat the Southern rebel," not just militarily but also by taking apart the social and economic apparatuses of Southern slaveholding society.[133] By connecting the destruction of the Slave Power to the survival of the Mexican republic, these writers aimed to redirect the energy created by Northerners' desire to act on the Mexican Question back into the Union war effort. At the same time, they raised the stakes of annihilating the Slave Power to continental proportions; ending slavery would not only save the US republic but the whole of North America from aristo-monarchical subversion.

More than this, the above framing also enabled pro-administration organs to argue that eliminating the Slave Power could profoundly reshape the United States' future relationship with Mexico and indeed the wider hemisphere. Some publications, such as the *Milwaukee Daily Sentinel*, put forward the possibility of territorial expansion. As the newspaper explained, once the French had been expelled from Mexico, that country's population, "torn and weakened . . . by long years of political distraction," would "gladly avail themselves of the protection and alliance of the great American nation," handing over their country to the benign control of the United States.[134] Such views were in the minority, however; most organs, particularly those aligned with the Republican Party, leaned closer to the *New York Tribune*'s opinion that any plans to acquire land from Mexico smacked of the aggressive imperialism of the antebellum Slave Power. As the *Tribune* reminded its readers, "the indecent rapacity wherewith Texas was seized and Mexico invaded, and Spain bullied to surrender Cuba" had all been "inspired and fomented by the slaveholding oligarchy of the South."[135] Each instance had undermined the United States' influence with the Spanish American republics, which had come to look upon the so-called model republic with distrust and fear.

Here the *New York Tribune* was echoing Matías Romero's call to Northerners to put aside schemes to acquire land from Mexico. For Romero, this was an essential step toward reconstituting the US-Mexican relationship as a partnership of equals. For the *Tribune*, by contrast, it was a means to usher in a new era of US hegemony in the Western Hemisphere. As the newspaper explained, destroying the Slave Power would rejuvenate the US republic's moral influence. The country could then win hemispheric allies by the sheer force of its example, thereby proving that "there are arguments more powerful than those of the sword."[136] The *Tribune* was far from alone in voicing such ambitions. In a second essay that appeared in *The New Englander* in July 1864, Joshua Leavitt echoed the *Tribune*'s hope that a post-emancipation United States—"redeemed and disenthralled"—would use pacific means to advance its interests on the continent and throughout the wider hemisphere.[137] Once Spanish Americans' trust in the United States had been restored, he predicted, they would open their markets, resources, and trade routes to US Americans, allowing the latter to reap the benefits of territorial expansion without taking on its burdens. "Possessing such advantages of wealth, and intelligence, and free political institutions," Leavitt foretold, the United States would extend its influence "from ocean to ocean" and "preclude for many ages the idea of any successful competition in the race for national greatness" in the New World.[138]

Agents of the Juárez administration had hoped to invoke the Monroe Doctrine in a way that would secure Northerners' assistance without encouraging their imperialistic ambitions. The above discussion demonstrates that they failed on both counts. First, Union editors, journalists, and orators rather ingeniously found a way to present neutrality toward the Franco-Mexican conflict as a roundabout means of fulfilling the United States' self-claimed role as defender of New World republicanism. Second, this narrative was predicated on the promise of restoring US hegemony over Mexico and the other Spanish American republics. Certainly, most Union publications would have agreed with Romero that, if it survived its civil war, the United States must eschew the territorial expansionism of the antebellum era. Indeed, their plans to instead spread US ideologies, technologies, and manpower into Mexico appeared benign when contrasted against Southern slaveholding imperialism or France's ongoing assault on Mexican sovereignty. Still, even these pacific ambitions pivoted on the establishment of an unequal relationship in which the reunified United States would remodel Mexico in its own image and open its markets and resources to US interests, a process that would then be repeated across the southern portions of the hemisphere. Such visions suggest that nothing less than the promise of hemispheric supremacy could convince enough Northerners to accept the necessity of emancipation.

Pro-administration organs took care to present this narrative in nonpartisan terms; their invocations of *national* security, identity, and destiny were consciously designed to draw together as wide a swathe of the Northern population as possible behind the Emancipation Proclamation specifically and the Lincoln government's conduct of the war effort in general. As we shall see, though initially somewhat successful, their efforts eventually ran aground on the rocky shores of Northern party politics. The ship first began to swerve as the 1864 presidential election approached.

The Mexican Question and Northern Party Politics

In mid-1863, Romero resigned as Mexico's *chargés d'affaires* to the United States and returned home, ostensibly in order to play a more hands-on role in the fight against the French by enlisting in the Juarist army. However, Romero had also grown frustrated by the lack of financial support he received from his government, which he claimed inhibited his ability to conduct an effective propaganda campaign in the United States.[139] Still, his sojourn in Mexico proved to be short-lived. By the fall of 1863 he was back in the United States, this time with a promotion to the rank of minister and promises from Minister of Foreign Relations Sebastián Lerdo de Tejada of the henceforth timely payment of his now increased salary. Judging by newspaper coverage of his arrival in New York City that October, Romero returned to his post with renewed energy. According to a *Philadelphia Reporter* journalist who followed the minister while he spent a few days in the city before heading to Washington, DC, Romero spent much of his time in "free conversation with some of our citizens on the present condition of affairs in Mexico."[140] During these conversations, the minister openly expressed his intention to redouble his efforts "to persuade this Government to enter into an alliance offensive and defensive with the JUAREZ administration, with a view of a common defense against European encroachments on this continent."[141]

The journalist correctly noted that it was unusual for a minister "to unbosom himself" in such a way to the press before having been formally received by his host government.[142] That Romero did so was an indication of a shift in strategy that would characterize the second leg of his tenure in the United States. Between 1859 and his departure in 1863, the diplomat had poured much of his energy into lobbying the Lincoln administration via the State Department. Over time, however, Romero had come to realize that Secretary Seward's commitment to neutrality was unwavering. As such, during his second stint in the United States Romero concentrated on expanding his propaganda activities beyond the cabinet. In addition to continuing to grow his network of contacts among Northern newspapermen, for example, the minister made more efforts to communicate directly to the public by giving interviews to journalists, attending high-profile dinners, and occasionally delivering speeches at public rallies. Romero also placed increased emphasis on cultivating allies within Congress. Though the creation of the *FRUS* was a great help to him, its publication came only once a year. If he had friends in Congress, however, Romero could ask them to submit resolutions requesting the executive branch to share documents pertaining to specific foreign policy issues at more regular intervals, thereby enhancing the minister's ability to feed information to the Union public regarding events in Mexico as they took place. Such resolutions would have the added benefit of prompting debates in Congress on the Mexican Question, which would in turn help to keep the issue toward the top of Northern political discourse.

One of Romero's first congressional contacts would also prove to be among his most useful: California senator James McDougall. The two men had first met in early January 1863, just prior to Romero's temporary departure from the United States. McDougall had reached out to Romero to express his concern that Louis-Napoleon was plotting to "acquire territory on the Pacific," specifically Southern California.[143] The congressman then showed Romero a resolution that he had drafted that called on the Lincoln administration to "lend such aid to the Republic of Mexico, as is or may be required to prevent the forcible interposition of any of the States of Europe in the political affairs of that Republic."[144] Romero had approved the resolution, and on January 19 McDougall presented it to the Senate. "Our difficulties do not change the rule of our duty," McDougall impressed upon his colleagues in the speech accompanying his resolution, "nor relieve us from resisting, to the extremity of most sanguinary war, the overthrow of a republic on our borders by the arms of a European potentate, and the establishment in its place of a European monarchy."[145] Both honor and principle demanded that the Union take action on the Mexican Question.

McDougall insisted that there was more than national pride to be gained from intervening in Mexico. As he asked his colleagues, supposing the Lincoln administration sent forces across the border, "How would the truly democratic masses of the South care to band with the Emperor of the French against the United States?"[146] McDougall argued that although some portions of the Confederate leadership had monarchist sympathies, the rank and file of the rebel army were devout democrats. Given this, the sight of Northern soldiers fighting against French monarchists would "detach from the rebellion many true republicans," who would flood into Mexico to take up arms alongside the Union troops.[147] Not only would this fatally weaken the Confederate military effort, but the experience of joining "hand in hand" for "the maintenance of free institutions" would do much to engender forgiveness and goodwill between the Northern and Southern people.[148] In this way, the South might be safely returned to the Union without the need for stringent measures, such as emancipation, to ensure its obedience. In sum, the senator argued, the surest way to reunite the sections was a righteous war against a foreign foe.

McDougall had put forward an intriguing proposal. It failed to win over the majority of his fellow senators, however, who voted thirty-four to ten to table his resolution. Nevertheless, the idea of a US intervention in Mexico was now in the air, and although the Senate had been unreceptive to the idea, it did begin to gain traction among certain portions of the press. The *New York Herald*'s Washington correspondent, for instance, believed that the California senator had given "an able exposition of the views, intentions and acts of the French Emperor" and that his plan for an intervention in Mexico had merit.[149] Still, the reporter reasoned, given its current military position, the Union could not afford to risk provoking a war with France at this time. This article was published in early 1863. At this time there was still some uncertainty in the Union press regarding Louis-Napoleon's ultimate intentions regarding Mexico. At the same time, Confederate and Union troops had been scrapping back and forth in Virginia for months without decisive victories for either side. The stalemate was draining morale, both among Northern troops and the wider population, a situation worsened by a recent series of changes in Union Army leadership due to President Lincoln's dissatisfaction with his commanding generals. For all of these reasons, the *Herald*'s correspondent concluded, military action on the Mexican Question was at this time "not at all probable, nor indeed would it be wise."[150]

Several months later, the formation of the Assembly of Notables in Mexico, coupled with improvements in the Union's military fortunes, prompted the *New York Herald* to revisit McDougall's proposal. On July 3 Major General George Meade's Army of the Potomac repelled attacks by Confederate General Robert E. Lee over a three-day campaign at Gettysburg, Pennsylvania. The battle involved huge losses for both sides; between 46,000 and 51,000 troops died in total. Still, the Union Army had warded off a potentially disastrous Confederate invasion of the North.[151] For the *Herald*, it was a momentous victory, which marked an effective end to the rebels' hope of winning independence on the battlefield. "The work of putting down the armed forces of the rebellion may be considered substantially accomplished," the newspaper jubilantly announced.[152] This being the case, "The question recurs, what is the line of policy that should be pursued in view of a speedy and harmonious restoration of the Union?"[153] As the *Herald* saw it, President Lincoln had two options: he could either offer an armistice to the Confederacy and negotiate the "restoration of the Union under our existing federal constitution," or continue to prosecute the war until the South was completely destroyed, at which point he could impose upon it "reconstruction based upon the extinguishment of Southern slavery."[154]

The *Herald* believed that both humanity and national security obliged Lincoln to choose the former option, and that McDougall's Mexico plan could facilitate its execution. "With internal peace and the Union fully reestablished," the newspaper explained, the United States would be in possession of "a million veteran soldiers and a hundred thousand experienced, warlike sailors."[155] Sending these men—who would include both Union and Confederate veterans—across the Rio Grande to bring about "a final and decisive settlement with . . . France in regard to American affairs" would encourage them to view one another as brothers-in-arms rather than as enemy combatants.[156] This would ease the transition of former rebel soldiers back into civilian life in the US national fold while also binding Northerners and Southerners together in patriotic pride as they watched their troops chase French imperialists off the continent.[157]

Apparently President Lincoln did not read the *Herald*; at least, he did not heed the newspaper's advice. After the Battle of Gettysburg, Union troops pressed on and the Civil War entered its third winter. Disappointed, the *Herald* abandoned its efforts to persuade the president to renounce emancipation as a precondition for reunion and instead placed its hopes on seeing Lincoln turned out of office in the upcoming 1864 presidential election. While proudly independent, the *New York Herald* generally aligned with the War Democrats, especially on matters relating to the conduct of the Union war effort. Though adamant that the "traitors of the South" must be crushed, for example, the newspaper shared many pro-war Northern Democrats' opposition to abolition and their belief that the "foolish and nearsighted abolitionists and negro-worshippers of our land" were at least partially to blame for having provoked Southerners into secession.[158] The *Herald* was also hopeful that a Democratic president would ensure that Lincoln's unconstitutional war measures—emancipation, the draft, the suspension of habeas corpus—"will be swept into oblivion," thereby clearing the way for negotiations with the Confederacy to restore the Union "as it was," meaning *with* the South and *without* emancipation.[159]

The *Herald* argued that a military intervention in Mexico would aid in the consummation of this particular method of reunion. "France has trampled upon the Monroe doctrine by forcibly establishing a monarchy in Mexico," the newspaper reminded its readers in late 1863.[160] If the United States turned its attention to redressing this insult "as soon as the rebellion is over," it would provide its recently reunited citizens with a common enemy against which to rally.[161] The resultant surge in popular patriotic fervor would "avoid all criminations and recriminations between the North and South," which might otherwise bedevil national politics in the postwar period.[162] A foreign war, in short, would steer the United States through the difficult process of reconstruction without the need for drastic federally mandated political or social reform in the South. "Policy and justice alike incite us to this course," the *Herald* insisted, "which will again make our country feared and respected abroad, united, prosperous and peaceful at home."[163]

By early 1864, the *Herald*'s calls were beginning to make inroads in the Northern Democratic press.[164] Unfortunately from the newspaper's point of view, at the same time Senator McDougall's efficacy as an advocate of intervention in Mexico was rapidly diminishing. This was due in part to

McDougall's growing unpopularity with his California constituents, many of whom were dissatisfied with the senator's conservative Democratic politics and unsparing criticism of the Lincoln administration's management of the war effort. In February 1864 the California State Legislature even passed a resolution censuring McDougall for having misrepresented the wishes and opinions of the people of California.[165] The senator's personal conduct was also a matter of concern; McDougall was an alcoholic, and his frequent bouts of public inebriation had begun to damage his standing among his fellow congressmen. As one California newspaper reported in May 1864, McDougall "has only been in the Senate a few times this Winter, then drunk, booted like a dragoon and spurred like a Spanish vaquero. He falls drunk from his horse on Pennsylvania Avenue. In a word, he is the first drunkard in Washington."[166]

McDougall's declining reputation was also a problem for Minister Romero, who relied on the senator as one of his most vocal allies in national government. Still, all was not lost. In late 1863 the House of Representatives gained a new Foreign Relations Committee chairman—Representative Henry Winter Davis—who was openly sympathetic to the Mexican republicans' plight. More than this, the Maryland representative saw certain domestic political advantages to be gained from criticizing the Lincoln administration's handling of Mexican affairs. In December 1863 President Lincoln had announced a plan to readmit Louisiana, by then back under Union control, into the nation. Representative Davis opposed the plan on the grounds that the provisions for reunion that it required of Louisiana, such as that 10 percent of its citizens take a loyalty oath to the Union, were too lax. What was needed, Davis believed, was a wholesale reformation of each rebel state before it was permitted to reenter the Union. Together with fellow Radical Republican Senator Benjamin Wade, the congressman wrote an alternative, more stringent plan for reunion that required, among other provisions, 50 percent of the white male population of each rebel state to take an oath of loyalty before it was allowed back into the Union. The Wade-Davis Bill was submitted to Congress in February 1864; Lincoln pocket-vetoed it by allowing the bill to expire without his signature when the congressional session ended in July.

His frustration with the executive branch growing, Davis saw the Mexican Question as a way to potentially weaken the president politically.[167] Between January and March 1864, the congressman met with Romero several times to discuss the matter. The product of their meetings was a resolution drafted under Davis's direction by the House Foreign Relations Committee, which reached the House floor for a vote in April. Given that it would later become the subject of extensive public discussion, House Resolution (H.R.) 58 is worth quoting in full: "*Resolved*: That the Congress of the United States are unwilling by silence to have the nations of the world under the impression that they are indifferent spectators of the deplorable events now transpiring in the Republic of Mexico, and that they think fit to declare that it does not accord with the policy of the United States to acknowledge any monarchical government erected on the ruins of any republican government in America under the auspices of any European power."[168]

In terms of policy prescription, the resolution was rather toothless; unlike McDougall's proposals, it did not call on the Lincoln administration to send any form of aid to the Juarists. In fact, Davis proposed no change to the government's neutral position toward the Franco-Mexican conflict. What his resolution did do, however, was articulate the antipathy with which allegedly all Unionists viewed the French Intervention, the implication being that the Lincoln administration had failed to adequately represent this popular sentiment in its past dealings with Louis-Napoleon's government. Loudly condemning the French Intervention without questioning US neutrality toward the conflict proved to be a popular position in Congress. On April 4, 1864, the resolution passed the House by a unanimous vote—a rare example of cross-party unity in a Congress otherwise marked by deep partisan divisions.[169]

Congress's intervention on the Mexican Question prompted a range of responses in the national press. The *Boston Daily Advertiser* sympathized with the sentiments expressed in the April 4 resolution but regretted its timing. "Mr. Davis and his committee" had exposed the Lincoln government to the "painful suspicion of internal dissensions at Washington," the newspaper complained, which would in turn weaken the government's position when dealing with France in the future.[170] The *Albany Evening Journal* was even more forceful in its criticism. "By opening up an irritating issue," the newspaper warned, Congress would "invite, aye, provoke a quarrel which France (in other respects disembarrassed) is too ready to accept."[171]

Other publications were more positive. Though generally supportive of the administration's handling of the Mexican Question, the *Chicago Tribune* was nonetheless pleased that Congress had given voice to the "sentiment of the immense majority of the American people" on the matter of the French Intervention.[172] The *Philadelphia Inquirer* also thought it proper that "the greatest Power on the Western Continent, should speak out the sentiments of the people."[173] *Harper's New Monthly*, meanwhile, praised the resolution as a cheering example of wartime bipartisanship. "In the midst of our own war," the magazine marveled, "every member of our House of Representatives, of every party, who is present when the vote is taken, records his name against the French scheme. . . . This unanimity undoubtedly represents that of the country."[174] Satisfying a widespread desire to make it clear to the international community where the people of the United States stood on the matter of Mexico, without risking a conflict with France in the process, the resolution found substantial support across the national press.

As it happened, *Harper's* satisfaction with this moment of apparent cross-party consensus was misplaced. Although Davis's resolution passed the House by a unanimous bipartisan vote, Northern politicians belonging to different political factions had endorsed it in the hopes of advancing competing domestic agendas. This became increasingly clear as the 1864 presidential election drew closer. Six days after the House voted on Davis's resolution, Austrian archduke Maximilian I signed the Treaty of Miramar, thereby formally accepting the crown of the Mexican Empire. Maximilian then set sail from Austria for Mexico, stopping en route first in Paris and then Rome to receive the Pope's blessing for his new government. The emperor arrived in Mexico in May 1864, by which time French forces had advanced deep into the country's central and western regions. A series of significant victories followed Maximilian's arrival, particularly in the north, where French and Imperial (as Emperor Maximilian's forces were known) troops took possession of the city of Durango on July 3 and the states of Sinaloa and Jalisco in November.[175]

As Maximilian settled into the Palacio Nacional, the 1864 US presidential election race was heating up. By this time, Minister Romero was convinced that Lincoln's reelection was both unlikely and, if it did occur, the worst outcome possible for the Juarists. Early on, therefore, he reached out to the other likely presidential contenders. In April 1864, Romero secured a meeting with General John C. Frémont, who would go on to head the ticket for a breakaway faction from the Republican coalition known as the Radicals. Romero was pleased to find Frémont "very favorably disposed toward our cause. Bitterly censuring the administration's policy in the Mexican Question, he is disposed to adopt a bold attitude if he should be elected."[176] Once again demonstrating his willingness to cultivate friends of any partisan affiliation, Romero also made contact with General George B. McClellan, one of the potential nominees of the Democratic Party, who according to the minister also "highly disapproves of the administration's policy . . . and favors the Monroe Doctrine, although apparently he will not go as far in this respect as Fremont."[177] Though he preferred a Radical victory over a Democratic one, throughout the summer of 1864 Romero worked to shore up the friendship of leaders from both parties, convinced that any change of administration in Washington would be positive news for the Juárez government.[178]

Thanks in part to Romero's efforts, the Mexican Question permeated, though it did not dominate, the presidential campaign over the coming months. There was little debate over the substance of Mexican policy; all three parties with candidates in the running essentially agreed on maintaining neutrality, at least for the duration of the Civil War. Rather, the Mexican Question functioned as a subsidiary to debates taking place over other issues that were ultimately more central to the election. These included the question of a ceasefire with the Confederacy, the wisdom and practicality of emancipation, and the use of extraordinary executive powers during wartime. For both Democrats and Radical Republicans, for example, making enthusiastic endorsements of the Monroe Doctrine was a way to burnish their pro-Mexican—and therefore pro-republican and anti-authoritarian—credentials while bringing into question the Republicans' willingness to defend these quintessential US values both at home and abroad. Indeed, a favorite joke among Democratic newspapers at this time was that "Lincoln's view of the Monroe doctrine is like that of a Yankee candidate for Governor of Maine. He favored the temperance law, but was opposed to its enforcement."[179] The Radical organ the *New York New Nation*, meanwhile, believed that the president's "cowardice in dealing with Louis Napoleon" echoed his subservient approach to both the Southern Slave Power and slaveholders in the border states, which had resulted in his administration's "half measures" on emancipation and its foolish faith in "compromise as a possible solution of the struggle" between North and South.[180]

As it happened, the Radical campaign would come to a premature end. Following Frémont's nomination, President Lincoln engaged him in negotiations in an effort to bridge the schism between the Radical and moderate factions of the Republican coalition. The president's efforts bore fruit in September 1864 when Frémont withdrew his candidacy in return for the removal from Lincoln's cabinet of Postmaster General Montgomery Blair, an old enemy of Frémont's. And so, for the remaining months of the campaign, Republicans would only have the Democrats to tussle with over Mexican policy. Often, Republican newspapers charged that Democrats' calls for a bolder approach to the Mexican Question were in fact designed to start a conflict with France, which would undermine the Union war effort. Noting that many Democrats opposed the continued prosecution of military hostilities against the Confederacy and were therefore calling for a ceasefire, the *Chicago Tribune* asked why those "who think we are too weak to put down the rebellion believe that we could more successfully fight both the rebellion and France?"[181] Diverting troops into Mexico at this time would guarantee the collapse of the Union war effort, the newspaper continued, especially if it also prompted France to intervene in the Civil War on the side of the South. "All rebeldom would howl with exultation at such an assertion of the Monroe doctrine as [Democrats] pretend to urge," the *Tribune* asserted.[182] The only explanation for this irrational proposal was that the Democratic Party was under the thumb of "the copperheads" who "are seeking to bring up France to the help of Jeff Davis, thereby driving back the Union armies in defeat and slaughter."[183]

On November 8 the majority of voters in the Union chose to reelect Abraham Lincoln as their president. Though the Mexican Question had gained attention over the course of the campaign, it was by no means the deciding factor in the election's outcome. Throughout the first half of 1864, the Union's military prospects had looked dim. In the spring General Grant had mounted a massive campaign in Virginia, but after sustaining significant losses at the battles of the Wilderness, Spotsylvania, and Cold Harbor, he had found himself bogged down near Petersburg. By the fall, Union General William T. Sherman was similarly stalled outside Atlanta and unable to take the city. Lincoln himself had worried that war-weariness would make the Democrats' offer of an immediate ceasefire tempting to Northern soldiers and citizens alike. Beginning in late summer, however, a series of Union victories—including the capture of Mobile Bay in August, Sherman's occupation of Atlanta in September, and General Philip Sheridan's takeover of the Shenandoah Valley the following month—dramatically improved the Union's military standing. Revitalized, Northerners endorsed the Republicans' plan to push ahead with the war effort, with every state except Kentucky, New Jersey, and Delaware giving Lincoln its electoral votes.[184]

Military events were therefore highly significant in swaying voters at the ballot box. In light of this, Lincoln's reelection should not be read as a ringing popular endorsement of his administration's neutrality toward the Franco-Mexican conflict. Nevertheless, the 1864 result did suggest that most Northern voters were prepared to tolerate the continuation of neutrality, at least for the present. Certainly, this was Minister Romero's interpretation of the election's outcome. When Frémont dropped out, the minister had swung his support to McClellan. When in November Northerners then returned Lincoln to the White House, Romero understood that only one of two extraordinary events could now alter US Mexican policy: Confederate surrender or a change of president. As it turned out, both events would take place within the next five months.

One War Ends, the Other Continues

On July 19, 1865, residents of New York City gathered at the Cooper Institute for an event hosted by the United Service Society, one of the many patriotic organizations formed in the North during the Civil War. The popular orator Joshua Leavitt was the final speaker of the day. Less than three months earlier, Confederate general Robert E. Lee had surrendered at Appomattox Court House. Reflecting on this as well as the recent passage of the Thirteenth Amendment, Leavitt felt confident in declaring that the fight against the slavocracy had been won. However, he also warned his fellow citizens that in their moment of victory they must not forget that the second front of the assault on North American republicanism continued to rage south of the Rio Grande. Though US Americans had "happily escaped the blow" of the Franco-Confederate conspiracy, Leavitt reminded the crowd, their "neighbors have felt its full weight."[185] Leavitt insisted that it was not "in the nature of the American people to see this with indifference"; US aid for Mexico, he implied, would soon be forthcoming.[186]

Similar sentiments had been repeated many times over in Northern public discourse throughout the Civil War. Though initially cautious, as the French invasion of Mexico unfolded, Unionist politicians, editors, and other loyal leaders declared their support for the Juarists as fellow defenders of free government. Louis-Napoleon's scheme to overthrow the Mexican republic was anathema to US Americans' long-held belief that the New World must be shielded from the intrigues of European imperialists. But there was more than this to Unionists' embrace of the Mexican cause. As this chapter has shown, leading voices in Northern public discourse associated the Union war effort with that of the Juarists in order to promote to their audiences a particular interpretation of the Civil War's causes and meaning. They had, for example, compared Southern rebels to Mexican clerics and French imperialists in order to emphasize the former's supposedly undemocratic, anti-American nature. Their allegation that these three factions were joined in a conspiracy to bring down free government in North America, meanwhile, framed the Civil War as a continuation of the historic contest between Old and New World theories of government. The North-South conflict therefore had global antecedents, and its outcome would determine the fate of free government not only in the United States, but throughout the hemisphere.

Some contributors to public discourse also attempted to use this narrative to persuade the public to accept the Lincoln administration's more controversial war measures, namely emancipation. They did this by insisting that the Slave Power was a disruptive faction that would continue to foment disharmony within the US body politic if it was permitted to reenter the Union. The administration's supporters hoped that this argument would resonate with a population all too familiar with the deadly consequences of excessive division in the political realm. To make the promise of future domestic peace even more appealing, however, Unionist organs encouraged Northerners to think continentally. While they professed solidarity with the Juarists, the politicians, newspapermen, and orators examined here were uneasy that the United States had devolved into a condition of internal chaos analogous to that of their notoriously anarchic Mexican neighbors. They therefore stressed to the public that, once the Slave Power was destroyed and national harmony restored, the United States would resume its standing as the New World's model of stable self-governance. Emancipation would not only guarantee domestic peace, therefore, but also reconnect the country to its providential destiny as the hemisphere's exceptional republic. Though this message failed to resonate with all factions across the Northern political spectrum, it did help to keep a diverse coalition of voters united behind the administration, especially during the difficult latter years of the Union war effort.

Leavitt's speech that July day in 1865 struck a triumphant tone. With the rebellion defeated and emancipation achieved, he was confident that the United States' exemplary image had been restored to its former glory. Assured that the US republic's symbolic power was already radiating south of the Rio Grande, Leavitt predicted that US Americans would soon hear news of a string of Juarist victories over Imperial forces. With the slavocracy gone, meanwhile, all sources of dissension within the United States had presumably been eradicated and its citizens could now work on reunifying the sundered fragments of their nation. Leavitt's optimism would not last long, however. As later chapters will show, the expectation among Unionists that emancipation would guarantee lasting peace between a reunified North and South were dashed on the rocky shores of Reconstruction politics. Sectionalism, social conflict, and political discord would persist long after the Civil War, as would US Americans' anxieties about the integrity of their so-called exceptional republic.

CHAPTER TWO

Imagining a Franco-Confederate Empire, 1861–1865

The Confederate government's first diplomatic mission to Mexico was a debacle. Problems began when Secretary of State Robert Toombs appointed Colonel John J. Pickett to head the mission. Pickett had an intimate understanding of Mexican trade and tariff laws thanks to the five years he had spent as US consul in Veracruz under the Pierce administration. However, Pickett was also an outspoken racist and longtime advocate of US territorial expansion into Spanish America—qualities unlikely to endear him to the Liberal government in Mexico City. His mission to establish friendly relations between the Confederacy and Mexico was further complicated when, upon his arrival in that country in the spring of 1861, Pickett discovered that the Mexican foreign minister Manuel Doblado had already formally received Union minister Thomas Corwin and engaged him in negotiations to arrange a US loan to Mexico.

Over the following weeks, Pickett struggled to make progress. The Juárez administration refused to give him a formal audience, meaning that he was blocked out of Mexico City's political and diplomatic circles. Frustrated, Pickett penned angry dispatches to the State Department in Richmond disparaging President Juárez, his cabinet, and the Mexican Liberal Party in general. In December, Pickett was involved in a barroom brawl with a traveling Yankee. Mexican authorities arrested and held him for thirty days, after which Secretary Toombs recalled Pickett to Richmond. As the Confederate diplomat departed, another scandal broke; some of the derogatory dispatches Pickett had written about the Mexican administration had been intercepted at New Orleans and sent to the Juárez government.[1]

Recognizing that formal relations with Mexico City were—for the time being, at least—hopeless, Richmond concentrated on sending agents into northern Mexico to cultivate trade relationships with any state officials in the region whose loyalty to the Juárez administration was tenuous. It was not until 1864 that President Jefferson Davis's administration would again attempt to open formal relations with Mexico City. By that time, the government housed in the capital was the newly established Mexican Empire headed by former Austrian archduke Maximilian I. While the Mexican republic had been unreceptive to its overtures, Richmond hoped to make a close ally of Mexico's constitutional monarchy.

Scholars have described the Davis administration's support for the French Intervention and subsequent Maximilian regime as a case study in pragmatic statecraft. As historian Patrick Kelly argues, the policy was primarily driven by "realpolitik strategic" considerations, namely the expectation that, in return for the Confederacy's friendship, Louis-Napoleon would recognize the slaveholding republic as an independent nation.[2] Kelly views Confederate leaders' willingness to build Southern independence upon the ruins of the Mexican republic as a "clear repudiation of the Founders' commitment to the core principles of democratic self-government."[3] Thus Richmond's embrace of the French Intervention "exposes the South's complete indifference to the fight for progressive nationalism in other nations."[4] In short, while Confederates cherished their own independence, they cared little about the fate of self-government beyond their borders.

There is much truth to this interpretation; it is, however, incomplete. President Davis and his cabinet certainly hoped there would be a transactional dimension to the relationship they sought to develop with both Louis-Napoleon and Maximilian. The people of the Confederacy, however, needed reasons beyond sheer expediency to fully embrace the monarchical project in Mexico. Before the Civil War, most editors, journalists, and other contributors to Southern public discourse had not held the Mexican republic in high esteem. To many of them, republican Mexico, forever roiling with rebellions, was the worst example of what befell a multiracial democracy when unfettered by social hierarchies. Despite this, antebellum Southerners, alongside their Northern countrymen, had been taught that Providence had set aside the New World for republicanism. Moreover, following secession proseparatist advocates insisted that the Confederacy had inherited the United States' title as the exceptional republic, and with it its role as champion of free government in the Western Hemisphere. At least in theory, therefore, the attempt by a European empire to overthrow an American republic ought to have insulted Confederates' sense of national honor as much as it did that of their Union counterparts.

From 1862 onward, Confederate editors, journalists, and politicians took it upon themselves to explain how Richmond's support for the French Intervention aligned with popular conceptions of an independent South's future role in the hemisphere. They did this by first arguing that, contrary to Northern popular opinion, the original US mission had never been to convert every hemispheric country into a democratic republic—a preposterous notion, they claimed, given Spanish Americans' incapacity for self-government. Instead, Confederate publicists insisted, it had been the task of the old United States to protect those countries' right to self-determination, and so ensure that all peoples in the New World were free to choose whatever form of government they wished, whether it be republican, monarchical, or otherwise. Adamant that the Maximilian Empire had the support of the Mexican population, Confederate publicists then reasoned that Richmond had upheld this principle in its support for the French Intervention and that the Confederacy was therefore properly discharging its duties as the New World's new exceptional republic.

This conception of the South's hemispheric mission had implications beyond the Mexican Question. Those who crafted it emphasized that, as a model of democracy tempered by racial hierarchy, an independent Confederacy could bring about a political reformation across Spanish America whereby the region's latent conservative elements would rise up, dismantle their unstable republican systems, and replace them with centralized regimes dedicated to law, order, and economic modernization. While inspiring, this vision was paired with an ominous alternative: should the fight for Southern independence fail, Confederate organs warned, Northern radicalism would be unleashed upon the hemisphere. Union troops would overwhelm the South and then march into Mexico, where they would chase out the French and reinstall Juárez in power. Northern hordes would then fan out across Central America, the Caribbean, and eventually South America, conspiring with these regions' worst radicals—socialists, abolitionists, miscegenationists—in a collective effort to plunge the southern portions of the New World into disorder. Thus weakened, the independent Spanish American nations would be powerless to resist the consummation of the final stage of the scheme: permanent military occupation under a hemisphere-wide Yankee empire. Thus, Confederate publicists used the Mexican Question in much the same way as their Unionist counterparts did, to sketch out the larger geopolitical stakes of the North-South conflict and inspire their readers to rally behind the war effort by instilling within them both the hope of hemispheric glory and the terror of hemispheric disaster.

The Confederate Press and the Monroe Doctrine

With no relationship with the Juárez government to speak of, during the first year of the Civil War the Confederate government was left to forge an alternative diplomatic path south of the border. This largely consisted of sending agents into Mexico's northern frontier in search of partners willing to buy Southern cotton in return for war matériel and other articles useful to the wartime Confederacy. By the summer of 1861, some of these agents were cautiously optimistic that, although the Liberals were hostile, there were elements of Mexican society that were either neutral or sympathetic toward the Confederacy. Merchants—both Mexican and foreign—were apparently willing to do business with whoever controlled the northern side of the US-Mexican border. In addition to this, as one August dispatch from Confederate agent José Augustin Quintero explained, the "intelligent and well-to-do Mexicans are familiar with the causes and history of the secession of the Southern States, and they sympathize with the Confederacy."[5] Exactly who comprised these supposed better elements of Mexican society was not made clear; however, it should not be surprising that the Confederacy had some friends south of the border. Mexican Conservatives, for example, prized values of order, stability, and hierarchy similar to those at the heart of Confederate republicanism. The doctrines of states' rights and secession, moreover, had passionate adherents among regional leaders in northern Mexico, many of whom had long been engaged in efforts to separate their states from the Mexican union. A good example was Governor Santiago Vidaurri, who enjoyed near-autonomous control over the border states of Coahuila and Nuevo León and would become one of the Confederacy's most useful partners in the borderlands.[6]

The outbreak of hostilities between French and Mexican forces in the spring of 1862 threatened to disrupt this nascent network of commercial contacts. The initial reaction of most Confederate newspapers to the event was a mix of confusion and suspicion. What was Louis-Napoleon's plan for Mexico? Might it conflict with the Confederacy's wartime interests vis-à-vis the Mexican frontier or with its long-term ambitions on the continent? These concerns peaked that summer when the Confederate press learned that French consuls in Galveston had been quizzing local officials about the strength of Texans' dedication to the Southern cause, an apparent indication that Louis-Napoleon hoped to detach the state from the Confederacy and absorb it into whatever regime he was building in Mexico. Confederate Secretary of State Judah P. Benjamin responded by swiftly expelling the offending consuls from the Confederacy.[7] Following this incident, however, relations between Richmond and Paris improved. Louis-Napoleon's government apologized for the actions of what it insisted were a few rogue consuls. This cleared the way for Southern spokesmen in Europe to express Richmond's support for France in its conflict with the Juarists. In October

Confederate diplomat John Slidell met with Louis-Napoleon in person to assure him of the Davis administration's approval of his Mexican scheme, even suggesting that France enter into an alliance with the Confederacy based on their "mutual interests and common sympathies" regarding affairs in North America.[8]

There were good reasons why the Confederate State Department instructed its representatives to encourage Louis-Napoleon's venture in Mexico during its early stages. Among the most powerful was the logic that the more entangled the emperor became in Mexico, the more likely he would be to recognize Confederate independence.[9] Though it had begun the enterprise with British and Spanish partners, by the spring of 1862 France was alone on the continent. An alliance with the Confederacy would ensure that whatever regime Louis-Napoleon built in Mexico had a friendly nation on its northern boundary, which would double as a buffer against any future efforts by the United States to meddle in its affairs. Viewed solely in light of the South's need for recognition, therefore, Richmond had a strong incentive to offer the French Intervention its full support. Nor was it only members of the Confederate government who made this calculation; from the very beginning of the French Intervention large portions of the Southern press eagerly discussed the possibility of a quid pro quo with Louis-Napoleon's government on exactly these terms.[10]

Still, France's invasion and possible occupation of Mexico did raise certain issues regarding the Confederacy's long-term hemispheric interests. It could complicate future efforts to acquire new land to the south, for example, plans that had been an important factor driving Southern secession. After all, in the run-up to the 1860 presidential election, proslavery advocates had warned that President Lincoln's pledge to prevent slavery's expansion west and south would effectively suffocate the peculiar institution. In the liminal period following the election, furthermore, pro-separatist organs had enticed Southerners into the Confederacy by pledging that an independent South would establish a grand slaveholding empire across the western and southern United States as well as tropical portions of the hemisphere.[11] Nor was this an empty promise. Adrian Brettle shows us that even during the tumult of war, Confederate planners attempted to lay the groundwork for the realization of this imperial ambition by pushing ahead with a range of initiatives, including industrial and infrastructure development and establishing Confederate sovereignty over the southwestern territories.[12]

With that said, when it came to dealing with the outside world Confederate leaders tended to present their future plans for the hemisphere rather differently. Robert E. May has convincingly argued that "once embroiled in war," the administration in Richmond and its diplomats overseas "shrewdly suppressed imperialistic rhetoric and programs rather than project an aggressive image counter-productive to getting international recognition and assistance."[13] An examination of the Confederate press reveals that at least some influential publications endorsed the use of this tactic in regard to the Mexican Question. Certainly, this was the view of the *Charleston Mercury*, which in early 1863 admitted that while it regretted that France's presence on its southern border "hems in the Confederacy," if the "permanent occupation of Mexico by France means ultimate recognition of the Confederacy" then the sacrifice was worth making.[14]

While the *Mercury*'s disavowal of imperial designs on Mexican land was likely born of expediency, other similar proclamations from Confederate organs were seemingly more genuine. Throughout the antebellum period a minority of Southern leaders had warned of the harmful consequences that would come from adding Mexican territory to the United States. As we have seen, in the decades leading up to the Civil War US Americans developed many theories to explain apparent disparities between republicanism above and below the Rio Grande. Racial theories had a particularly strong resonance among Southern commentators who, given the centrality of race-based hierarchy to their own slaveholding society, found the prevalence of racial mixing in Mexico particularly offensive. "We may talk about priestly domination and all that sort of thing," the *Wilmington Journal* asserted in 1860, but "it is race, and not religion or government that is mainly at fault in these old colonies of Spain."[15] Acquiring Mexican territory would introduce into the United States large numbers of mixed-race peasants, commentators had warned, whose religion, language, and character was incompatible with US civilization. Following the formation of the Confederacy, some leading Southern editors expressed a newfound appreciation for this argument. As the *Richmond Examiner*'s John M. Daniel put it, annexing Mexican land in the near- or medium-term future "would bring foreign and conflicting elements" into the Confederacy during its period of national infancy, when consolidating domestic social cohesion would be at a premium.[16] For this reason alone, Daniel concluded, "filibustering, conquest and annexation" ought to have "no part of the policy or practice of the southern Confederacy."[17]

And so, whether because of wartime imperatives or predictions about the Confederacy's postwar priorities, few major Southern newspapers voiced objections to the French Intervention on the grounds that it might interfere with their government's ability to take land from Mexico at some future date.

The question of territorial expansion was not the only issue that the invasion raised for Confederates, however; another was the challenge that it posed to the Monroe Doctrine. By early 1863 Union newspapers were in full voice castigating the Davis administration for having abandoned the Monroe Doctrine through its support for the French Intervention. There was more than a little justification for this accusation. A review of their correspondence suggests that Southern diplomats, presumably acting under the direction of the Richmond State Department, jettisoned all mention of the Monroe Doctrine in their dealings with Louis-Napoleon's government. Indeed, far from condemning the French Intervention, they repeatedly celebrated it as a boon for the people of Mexico. Confederates, Slidell assured French foreign minister Thouvenel, "have no other interest or desire than to see a respectable, responsible, and stable government established in that country," which is exactly what Louis-Napoleon proposed to give it.[18] Nor would Richmond object to the invasion on the grounds that it violated Mexican sovereignty, given that "his Imperial Majesty has no intention of imposing on Mexico any government not in accordance with the wishes of its inhabitants."[19] The Confederate diplomat finished by pointing out how far this position differed from that of Unionists, who, "animated by that spirit of political proselytism," insisted that Mexico and all American nations conform to their particular definition of good republican government.[20]

Certain publications in the Confederate press echoed Slidell's arguments, adding that the Monroe Doctrine, conceived forty years previously, was simply no longer relevant. This was the position of Montgomery's *Weekly Advertiser*. The newspaper reasoned that in the present day, the greatest threat to Southern liberty was not European monarchism but Northern abolitionism. If Richmond could secure Louis-Napoleon's assistance in defeating the Yankees by allowing France "a controlling interest in the affairs of the wretched 'Republic' of Mexico," therefore, the price was worth paying.[21] The "Monroe doctrine belongs to the era of the old Union," the *Advertiser* declared, "and we are perfectly willing that it should perish with it."[22] The *Charleston Mercury* came to much the same conclusion. War between the North and South, the newspaper surmised, meant that "the Monroe doctrine is very dead for all time to come."[23]

Other Southern publications could not dispense with the Monroe Doctrine so easily, however. The capital's largest newspaper, the *Richmond Daily Dispatch*, for example, was disturbed by accusations that the Davis administration had betrayed this tenet of antebellum US foreign policy and felt compelled to answer them. It did so by reinterpreting the Doctrine in such a way as to argue that Richmond's response to the Mexican situation aligned with, rather than ignored, its true original purpose. When that "famous declaration" was first announced, the newspaper explained, the dynamics of global geopolitics were "entirely different from the state of things existing now."[24] The "Spanish colonies of Mexico and South America" had been "fighting for their independence so successfully that, as Mr. Monroe . . . maintained, there no longer existed even a remote possibility to [Spain] of reducing them to obedience."[25] Meanwhile certain European monarchical powers, including Prussia, Austria, and Russia, had convened in the Holy Alliance and "resolved that they had a right to interfere in the domestic concerns of other nations."[26] Having already marshalled their combined military forces to restore the "odious government of Ferdinand VII" in Spain, the Alliance had now turned its gaze to the New World with a view to bringing the "rebellious South American and Mexican subjects" back under the colonial yoke.[27]

So far, this history of the Monroe Doctrine aligned with the version circulating in the Union press at this time. Where the *Dispatch*'s narrative differed from that of its Northern counterparts, however, was in the details. When describing the conflict brewing between the Holy Alliance and the independent Spanish American nations, the newspaper made no mention of opposing ideologies, of a clash between republicanism on the one hand and dynastic rule on the other. Its characterization of the United States' intervention in this transatlantic conflict was similarly apolitical. The *Dispatch* acknowledged that President Monroe had declared that future efforts by Europeans "to introduce their peculiar maxims of government, and to impose them upon the South American States, could not be viewed by us as a friendly act."[28] The newspaper did not explain what these "peculiar maxims of government" were, however. Instead, it emphasized that the Holy Alliance had planned to *impose* such institutions onto self-governing countries. This imposition, the newspaper insisted, was the true crime against which President Monroe had objected. The *Dispatch*'s implication was that the Monroe Doctrine had committed the United States to defending its neighbors' right to choose their own systems of government free from outside interference; it did not pledge US Americans to ensure that the system that each of these countries chose would be republican.

Other Confederate publications echoed this reading. "The Monroe doctrine," the *Fayetteville Semi-Weekly Observer* insisted, "consists of the strongly affirmed determination of the United States Congress, at the suggestion of President Monroe, that no foreign power should be allowed to interfere in any matter with the internal policy or government of any nation on this

Continent."[29] The *Memphis Bulletin* similarly asserted that at the heart of the "Monroe doctrine" was the principle of "popular sovereignty," meaning a peoples' right to decide which system of government they wished to live under.[30] Only a disingenuous student of history would suggest that President Monroe had believed that all New World governments must be republican, the newspaper continued. On the contrary, Monroe and his cabinet had understood that "the races of America . . . are as different in their aptitudes and tastes as in their origin, and the form of government which suits one does not necessarily suit the other."[31] Indeed, Monroe had supposedly expected the Spanish American republics to ultimately flounder and for their populations to seek out more stable (meaning less democratic) forms of government, a process he was adamant the United States must respect.

Using this reading of the Monroe Doctrine to justify Richmond's endorsement of the French Intervention hinged on the supposition that the people of Mexico had chosen to replace their republic with an imported monarchy. Apparently, this was something that most Confederate newspapers could easily believe. As discussed previously, the trope that Mexico was a failed republic was deeply engrained in antebellum US society, and especially in the Southern states. If anything, the experience of separating from the Union had sharpened many Confederates' disdain for the Mexican republic. In the months following the 1860 presidential election certain secessionist leaders had pointed to Mexico's condition to impress upon their fellow Southerners the necessity of cutting ties with the now Republican-controlled United States. "Well, the election is over," began a letter written by Mississippi state senator James Phelan Sr., which appeared in Alabama's *Weekly Advertiser* that November: "*Lincoln is elected,* and we have to meet it, not as something in the future, but as a *present reality*."[32] Under the incoming "Black Republican administration," he continued, "slavery is destined to a slow but *certain destruction in the Union,*" which, according to his interpretation of Lincoln's plans, would be followed by the "debasement and demoralization of negro amalgamation."[33] "A few generations will see a *mulatto race* possess this country, as they now do Mexico and Central America," Phelan continued, "Let the Southern non-slaveholders awake to their danger and strike for disunion."[34]

During the war that followed, Confederate newspapers' opinion of the Mexican republic sank, if possible, even lower. While they disparaged Mexico's political classes in general, publications in the antebellum South had looked upon the Mexican Liberals with particular suspicion, believing that they were, much like Northern abolitionists, radicals determined to uproot established institutions and plunge their societies into social anarchy. Once the Civil War began, the nature of information available to Confederate newspapers about current affairs in Mexico tended to reinforce such perceptions. Without formal relations between Richmond and Mexico City, there was no equivalent to Matías Romero to facilitate the flow of positive news about the Mexican republic into the region. Editors and journalists instead had to rely on alternative sources, principally the small number of Confederate journalists stationed below the border as well as the European and Mexican presses. In their use of the latter, Southern editors could be very selective, choosing to republish articles only from those Mexican organs they deemed reliable, which usually meant anti-Juárez. A January 1862 article from the Conservative *Mexican Extraordinary*, later reprinted in the *Charleston Mercury*, is a typical example of how such sources depicted life in Mexico under Liberal rule:

> The condition of [Mexico] has not improved, nor shows signs of improvement, robbers exist in all the highways and byways of the country.... Mails are robbed nearly every day on all the principal routes. Assassinations, sackages, etc. go on as usual. The government is poor.... Commerce is at a stand. Little is doing, and prospects growing more gloomy.... The disorders and demoralization of the republic, from one extremity to the other, and in nearly every State and Territory throughout its length and breadth, which prevail ... [have led to the] impoverished condition of the national finances.[35]

All of this helps to explain why the revelation in 1863 that Louis-Napoleon planned to overthrow the Juárez administration and replace it with a monarchy failed to produce much outrage across the Confederate press. Indeed, most publications readily accepted that Mexicans—supposedly weary of the Liberals' mismanagement—welcomed this change of government. Both the *Memphis Daily Appeal* and the *Richmond Sentinel*, for example, uncritically republished reports from Veracruz newspaper *El Eco del Comercio* describing scenes in the city of Puebla following its occupation by Imperial troops in May 1863. "Joyful peals of the bells from every steeple in the city solemnized the adhesion of Mexico to the French intervention," the writer enthused, while "the inhabitants flocked by the thousands to sign resolutions to that effect."[36] Confederate press coverage of the formation of the Assembly of Notables the following month was similarly positive. While most Union organs decried this act as an egregious violation of Mexicans' democratic will, major Confederate newspapers accepted it as a valid form of democratic legitimation. Though the Assembly comprised only 215 individuals, the *Richmond*

Sentinel explained, they were all Mexicans—and among the most educated and enlightened in the country to boot. As such they represented the "large and respectable portion of the population," most of whom "favor . . . the French program."[37] When the Assembly proclaimed for a constitutional monarchy on July 10 and invited Maximilian to take the throne, Confederate newspapers carried descriptions of spontaneous popular celebrations breaking out across Mexico. The *Richmond Enquirer*'s account was typical of many others: "The *Te Duem* has been sung in the Cathedral; most of the Mexican cities have notified their adhesion to the new order of things. A government has been inaugurated . . . and we are told this arrangement was received with vehement cheers for France, the Emperor, and the *Mexican monarchy*."[38]

According to such reports, Mexicans were not only celebrating the end of their republican experiment but also its replacement with a French-devised system of constitutional monarchy. The emphasis here on France's role in the undertaking was deliberate, for Confederate publications tended to overlook the contributions—both military and ideological—of Mexican Conservatives to the new regime taking shape south of the border. Certainly, most of them agreed that the Conservatives constituted the best of a bad bunch insofar as Mexican politicians were concerned and that their priorities—order, tradition, hierarchy—were largely correct. Still, Confederate journalists and editors paid scant attention to the party and its leaders throughout the duration of the French Intervention; certainly, there was no rallying around the Mexican Conservatives in a manner comparable to how Union organs celebrated President Juárez and his heroic *Juaristas*. This was likely due in part to a lack of familiarity; after all, there was no official Conservative spokesmen in the Confederacy to coordinate a public relations campaign on behalf of the party. Another probable reason was that deep racial and cultural prejudices inhibited Confederate publications from fully embracing even the Conservative Mexicans as their ideological kin.

Confederate publications were more comfortable crediting France—a European country whose recent political history many of them were familiar with—as the architect of the Mexican monarchical project. Louis-Napoleon came in for particular praise. In fact, admiration for the French emperor among certain portions of the Southern press dated as far back as the 1848 French Revolution. People in the United States had followed that event closely, tracing its trajectory from popular uprising to bloody carnage on the streets of Paris. The violence of the July Days had been particularly displeasing to observers in the antebellum slaveholding class, who were wary of the French radicals' mantra of liberty, equality, and fraternity. Knowing that reform movements in the nineteenth-century Atlantic world often inspired and sustained one another, these Southerners had worried that the rise of radicalism in France would embolden its advocates in the United States, specifically those troublesome abolitionists. They had been pleased, therefore, to see the French people elect Louis-Napoleon as their president in 1848. Historian Jeffery Zvengrowski has shown that this was especially so among old Jacksonian Southern Democrats, who felt certain ideological affinities with the new ruler of France. Louis-Napoleon seemed to share their respect for popular democracy, for example, having been elected by a direct popular vote and, once in power, mandating that all French elections would be held on the basis of universal male suffrage. At the same time, they also appreciated Louis-Napoleon's apparent understanding of the danger of the popular will when left unregulated and the consequent necessity of circumscribing democratic activity and directing it into appropriate channels. Many Jacksonian Democratic leaders had therefore praised Louis-Napoleon's 1852 reforms, which reduced the number of elected legislative bodies in France's national government to a single deliberative chamber while greatly expanding his own executive authority. They also admired how the now-emperor had used these powers to build a muscular central state capable of directing his nation's military and economic development. Finally, Southern Jacksonians approved of Louis-Napoleon's imperialist ventures in places such as Algeria and Cambodia that aimed to subdue nonwhite native populations in order to make room for European settlers. From this they surmised that the French emperor shared their own belief in the need to impose racial order on the world's untamed wildernesses in preparation for their subjugation under white civilization.[39] This admiration went both ways. During the Civil War, Louis-Napoleon on more than one occasion expressed his approval of the Confederates' respect for social order and hierarchy and his sympathy with their wish to separate themselves from the North, which the emperor agreed was a society languishing with social decay and radicalism.[40]

With the advent of the French Intervention in Mexico, the topic of Louis-Napoleon's style of governance shifted from a niche interest among certain Southern Jacksonian leaders into a matter of widespread public discussion in the Confederacy. "Mexico, in her chronic anarchy, was bound to fall under the overmastering influence of either England, the United States, or France," reasoned the *Richmond Enquirer* in July 1863.[41] It was therefore fortunate for Mexicans that France, "the best governed country in Europe," had taken on the role.[42] The newspaper was also pleased to see that the Assembly of Notables had opted to "approximate, as nearly as circumstances permit, to the government system of France itself."[43] Here, the newspaper was referring to the fact that certain hallmarks of Louis-Napoleon's brand of monarchism, which blended centralization with populism, were apparent in the Mexican Empire taking shape below the border. The popular will ostensibly had been consulted through the Assembly of Notables, for example. Moreover, the Assembly had approved a system of government centered on a strong monarch, who was nonetheless bound by a written constitution that would keep him responsive to the people. The fact that Louis-Napoleon had chosen Maximilian to take the throne of the Mexican Empire was also viewed as a good sign, for the archduke was known to be liberal on commercial matters and deeply committed to modernizing the Mexican economy. It was rumored, furthermore, that Maximilian planned to reestablish the Mexican Catholic Church, a move some Confederate publications predicted would have a calming influence on Mexican society.[44] Finally, these portions of the Southern press were optimistic that the incoming regime would restore racial order south of the border. As one writer for *De Bow's Review* pointed out, Louis-Napoleon had already "introduced the Coolie and apprentice system of labor in Algeria."[45] Supposedly both he and Maximilian now planned to do something similar in Mexico by expanding that country's existing system of "peon servitude" and inviting white European immigrants to take up leadership roles in the Mexican economy to oversee the country's industrial development.[46]

A consensus was emerging that Louis-Napoleon was not another Old World reactionary pushing against the advance of liberty and progress in the Americas. "It is only in the most verdant hours of juvenility that any living man now believes in the adaptability of Republican forms to every people," the *Richmond Daily Dispatch* pronounced in November 1863.[47] Furthermore, the newspaper continued, these were not the days of the Holy Alliance when European monarchism was retrograde and repressive; rather, Louis-Napoleon was championing a new form of liberal authoritarianism that was wise, moderate, and especially well-suited to a chronically anarchic society such as Mexico. Matthew Karp has found that many prominent Southern leaders in the antebellum period were especially interested in economic modernization and industrialization, not only for their own region but for all southerly portions of the Americas.[48] This same ambition was expressed by much of the wartime Confederate press, which frequently measured the anticipated positive outcomes of changes to Mexico's system of government in economic terms. As the *Dispatch* explained, "a strong and steady Government" in Mexico would stamp down on the country's continual rebellions and guarantee "security to person and property," enabling businesses and small landholders to expand their enterprises while encouraging the masses to redirect their energies away from uprisings and toward productive economic pursuits.[49] With "order and security" established, moreover, foreign "enterprise, industry, and capital will flock" to the country, so that before long it would "assume a position as a producing and commercial nation that will surpass the largest calculations."[50] The Mexican Empire, in short, was not the enemy of progress in Mexico, but the instrument by which it would finally be achieved. The *Richmond Daily Dispatch* thought likewise. The litmus test of good government in Mexico ought not to be the degree of political liberty it allowed its citizens, the newspaper began, but rather its ability to provide these citizens with stability, security, and economic development. Indeed, it continued, "Mexico, which has always been in a state of anarchy and civil convulsion, cannot be the loser by any change which will ensure her stability and peace. Better a monarchy, with the security of life, property, and such liberty as a people are capable of, than a Republic, with the inevitable conditions of demagogism, social and political degradation, a precarious tenure of all the great interests of society, and the constant perils of anarchy and civil war."[51]

It should be noted here that accepting monarchism for Mexico did not mean that these organs advocated it as a form of government suited to all peoples, and certainly not for citizens of the Confederacy.[52] As the *Richmond Enquirer* put it, the Mexican Empire "is strongly monarchical, and if the Mexicans and their new Protector think that a suitable kind of government for the country, so let it be."[53] "We have such a government as fits ourselves, and mean to keep it," the newspaper added, "let all other people go and do likewise, or otherwise."[54]

At base, these newspapers were repeating the core aspects of the position alluded to earlier, which Slidell and other Confederate diplomats had outlined to the French government soon after the Intervention began—namely, that Richmond only wished for order and stability in Mexico, that an enlightened monarchy was the best means to achieve this, and that the vast majority of Mexicans recognized this truth. What the Confederate press did that was new was to take this straightforward diplomatic position and place it within a wider narrative that envisioned a future Western Hemisphere guided by the principle of political pluralism whereby all nations in the region would choose whatever form of government best suited the interests, needs, and capabilities of their respective populations. By insisting that this vision had been the foundation of the original Monroe Doctrine, these publications presented Richmond's Mexican policy as a demonstration of how an independent Confederacy would fulfill its self-claimed role as the new exceptional republic and therefore protector of liberty in the New World.

Rewriting the Monroe Doctrine in this way did not resolve all of the issues the French Intervention raised for Confederates regarding their place and role in the hemisphere. As we shall see, though some Southern organs were prepared to disavow plans for territorial expansion into Mexico while the French remained in that country, they understood that many of their readers expected the Confederacy to eventually assume a position of commercial, financial, and geopolitical dominance in the Western Hemisphere by one means or another. As they discussed the Mexican Question, therefore, the Southern press took pains to explain how France's potentially permanent presence in North America would not jeopardize the Confederacy's ability to ultimately achieve regional hegemony.

A Plan for Hemispheric Supremacy

In the fall of 1863, a translated version of a French pamphlet entitled *Mexico, France, and the Confederate States* reached North America. The author was Michel Chevalier, a member of Louis-Napoleon's inner circle who had a prominent role in shaping French imperial policy. Though unofficial, Chevalier's pamphlet claimed to put "forth with substantial accuracy the general theory of American affairs in favor at the Tuileries."[55] The pamphlet was read by editors on both sides of the Mason-Dixon Line. Union publications mostly downplayed its significance, questioning its provenance and occasionally speculating that the pamphlet had been penned by a Confederate propagandist.[56] In the Confederate press, meanwhile, the publication caused a sensation. The *Wilmington Journal* urged its readers to obtain a copy, assuring them that its contents were "in perfect harmony with the 'known leanings'" of Louis-Napoleon.[57] The *Richmond Daily Dispatch* similarly insisted that "Chevalier's pamphlet was written at the instigation of the Emperor" and that its proposed plan for Mexico would therefore "be strictly followed" by France.[58]

The reason for this warm reception was clear; in his pamphlet Chevalier had commented at length on the Civil War and offered a full-throated defense of the Confederate cause. For decades, the Frenchman wrote, Northern politicians had treated the Southern states poorly, growing rich from the sale of their cotton while refusing to give them due representation in national policymaking. Chevalier intimated that for this reason alone, Louis-Napoleon sympathized with the Confederate independence project. He added, however, that the emperor also believed that an independent Confederacy would "guarantee [French troops] against attack by the North," which openly opposed Louis-Napoleon's activities in Mexico.[59] This being the case, Chevalier predicted, "the recognition of the Southern States will be the consequence of [France's] intervention [in Mexico] . . . a diplomatic act which will consecrate the final separation and secession of those states from the American Union."[60] This was a significant intervention. While previous dispatches from Southern agents in Paris had suggested that Louis-Napoleon personally favored the Confederate cause, they had also made it clear that this view was not shared by many others inside the imperial government. As Stève Sainlaude has shown, the emperor was surrounded by cabinet ministers who either favored the Union or were adamant that France remain neutral toward the US Civil War. Little wonder, then, that the Confederate press was thrilled by this bold and very public pledge of forthcoming recognition from a French official purporting to speak with the emperor's authorization.

Chevalier also offered thoughts on what a long-term partnership between a French-occupied Mexico and an independent Confederacy might look like. Louis-Napoleon, he explained, envisioned Mexico's political reformation as a way to kick-start a larger process of economic regeneration in that country. This was a project that apparently had extraordinary potential. As Chevalier explained, Mexico was the "only tropic country whose soil abundantly yields the finest grains," while its vast quantities of "precious wood and splendid dies" were, if properly exploited, enough to "furnish the whole word."[61] Furthermore, the country's geographic position, "an equal distance between Asia and Europe," meant that it could become a vital way station for merchant ships traveling between East and West.[62] Chevalier also commented on Mexico's vast mineral reserves. The "general loins of its mountains, rising eight or nine thousand feet above the level of the sea are filled with almost inexhaustible mines," he enthused, most of which "have never yet been adequately worked."[63] All of this economic potential had for years been unrealized thanks to the perennial anarchy that had engulfed Mexican society. By creating "a government which may have some chance of stability," however, France would allow Mexicans to turn their attention from revolutions to industry, agriculture, and internal improvements.[64] This done, Chevalier asserted, Mexico would soon export enough raw materials to "rival the most commercial nations of the new world."[65]

It is still not clear what Chevalier's motivations were for writing this pamphlet. That he penned it under the emperor's direction is possible, though unverified. Alternatively, Chevalier may have written the pamphlet on his own initiative in the hope that its public reception would embolden Louis-Napoleon to override the advice of certain counselors and adopt a more pro-Confederate approach to the ongoing US Civil War. Whatever the truth, most Southern publications chose to believe that the pamphlet represented the views of the French emperor, and as such seriously engaged with its author's proposals for the future of French-Confederate relations in North America. Confederate editors were especially intrigued by Chevalier's plan for Mexico's economic regeneration, for example. Trade between the antebellum South and Mexico had been rather lackluster; the economies of each were primarily agricultural, and neither produced much of what the other needed. After the spring of 1862, however, the existence of war on both sides of the Rio Grande precipitated a lively cross-border trade in munitions, war matériel, and cotton. Exchanges were largely clandestine, conducted by a motley cast of Confederate merchants, French military officials, and renegade Mexican state governors.[66] The *Richmond Daily Dispatch* was hopeful that, when peace eventually returned to the continent, this wartime trade would develop into a full-fledged commercial partnership between the Confederacy and Maximilian's Mexico. "With a strong and steady Government, and security to person and property," the newspaper predicted, Mexico's productive industries would diversify and expand.[67] This would be "detrimental to the North," which, on bad terms with Mexico City, would be shut out of that country's booming economy.[68] Meanwhile the Confederacy would be among the Mexican Empire's closest allies and therefore in a position to negotiate reciprocity treaties to allow its citizens privileged access to Mexico's natural resources, financial markets, and investment opportunities. For these reasons alone, the *Dispatch* concluded, "the South may well exclaim, 'Long live the Mexican Empire!'"[69]

Confederate organs speculated that Mexico's economic regeneration would also open up fresh lands for Southern farmers and planters. In his pamphlet Chevalier had promised that the presence of French troops in Mexico would be temporary. He had added, however, that the departure of these soldiers would be followed by an influx of French immigrants who would make Mexico their permanent home. "Mexico waits for—invites—demands emigration," Chevalier declared, but only emigration of a certain kind.[70] Rather than the "unhealthy foolish emigration which transports . . . creatures without industry or intelligence," Mexico needed entrepreneurs, engineers, miners, and skilled agriculturalists who would bring with them the modern technologies and know-how necessary to efficiently exploit the country's extraordinary natural resources.[71] While Chevalier stated that these immigrants would be drawn from Europe, his description of the opportunities that awaited skilled workers in Mexico likely resonated with readers in the Confederacy. Indeed, from the summer of 1863 onward reports appeared in the

Confederate press describing outfits of Southern men organizing to resettle en masse south of the border, usually in Mexico's northern mining districts. The most famous of these schemes was concocted by former California senator William Gwin, who in early 1864 presented Louis-Napoleon with a plan to establish colonies in Sonora and Chihuahua and people them with emigrants from the US Southwest and, according to certain reports, the Confederacy.[72] Although Gwin's colonization scheme never came to fruition, Confederate newspapers reported that Louis-Napoleon approved of the idea, which they interpreted as confirmation that the incoming Maximilian regime would provide a hospitable environment for Southern settlers.[73]

Confederate publications also speculated that, in addition to welcoming white laborers, the new government in Mexico would be amenable to receiving any Southern planters who arrived south of the border with their human chattel in tow. Chevalier was personally opposed to Southern slavery. At the same time, he acknowledged the supposedly disruptive effects that immediate emancipation would have on Confederate society. "The complete abolition of slavery," he reasoned in his pamphlet, "can only be the work of peace and of time."[74] Chevalier therefore suggested that, once their alliance was cemented, France might persuade the Confederacy to gradually emancipate its enslaved people. This proposal was the only aspect of *France, Mexico, and the Confederate States* that received serious criticism in the Confederate press. "It is as well to put a stop to all calculations of this character at once," the *Hillsborough Recorder* stated firmly. "If Napoleon means to interfere with the question of slavery in any way whatever . . . we can have nothing to do with him."[75] Other newspapers chose to believe that, on the matter of slavery at least, Chevalier spoke only for himself. They also predicted that when faced with the realities of the Mexican climate and domestic labor supply, French imperial officials would forget about their nation's abolitionist dogma. "The French want Mexico for its cotton producing capabilities," the *Yorkville Enquirer* asserted, and upon finding that "cotton cannot be produced by white labor" and that "they can get slaves nowhere else but in Africa" the French would "open the African trade at once."[76] "Emperor Napoleon is no humanitarian," the newspaper concluded; "If he wants negroes to cultivate his cotton lands, he will not stand upon scruples."[77]

Others thought it more likely that France would adjust rather than abandon its abolitionist creed by making use of alternative coercive labor systems already in existence below the Rio Grande. As has been discussed, reports that Louis-Napoleon had imported coolies into Algeria led some Southern publications to speculate that the emperor would do something similar in

Mexico, most likely by expanding that country's system of peonage. While recognizing that peonage was not identical to chattel slavery, these Confederate organs viewed its potential enlargement in Mexico as a boon to the advance of racial order south of the border. Indeed, the differences between peonage and slavery struck one writer for *De Bow's Review* as so small that, should they wish to travel to new pastures, Confederate enslavers would find Mexican peonage "easily convertible, should it be deemed necessary, into the patriarchal institution of slavery."[78] In much the same way as they endorsed the notion of political pluralism, then, certain Confederate publications were apparently willing to embrace diversity in the hemisphere's labor systems, so long as these systems were based on the principles of social order, racial hierarchy, and commercial development.

Confederate publicists were well aware that Louis-Napoleon's plans in the Americas extended beyond Mexico, and that the emperor likely hoped to expand his country's commercial and financial reach deeper into the hemisphere. *De Bow's Review*, for example, gave its readers a detailed outline of the French emperor's scheme to construct an interoceanic canal across the Isthmus of Tehuantepec, which would allow French merchants improved access to Asian markets. French imperial ambition need not be a threat to the Confederacy's own hemispheric interests, however. As *De Bow's* explained, by allying with the Mexican Empire the Confederacy was sure to be granted "free passage of the Isthmus" once construction of the canal was completed.[79] The *Memphis Daily Appeal* similarly believed that Louis-Napoleon had included the Confederacy in his alleged plan to draw Mexico, Central and South America, and France into a close trading alliance. As the newspaper explained, the emperor aimed to "connect the trade of the Mediterranean with the trade of the Chesapeake, and extend continuous water communication from the interior of Europe to the Rocky Mountains, the Gulf of Mexico, all the way to the horn of Brazil."[80] In short, an independent Confederacy would be a nodal point in a broader southern transatlantic commercial system, a position that would give the country primary access to the goods and markets of every other member of the network.

Such discussions implied that a young Confederacy would be the junior partner in any future relationship with France in the hemisphere. Southern newspapers' willingness to accept this prospect was perhaps borne from a certain humility, which they had learned through the trials of warfare. In contrast to antebellum separatists' strident talk of an independent South's glorious global future, wartime Confederate organs were more ready to concede that following the Civil War their republic would need to enter a period of convalescence during which its government would concentrate on repairing infrastructure, reviving domestic industry, and consolidating its authority over the outer reaches of its territory. Given this, why not allow France to expend capital and energy spearheading economic regeneration in Mexico and other portions of the Americas, a process from which the Confederacy would later benefit? However, few Confederate organs proposed that their republic rely on French support in perpetuity. After all, to do so would be to deny that the Confederacy, by virtue of its supposed exceptionalism, was destined to become the leading power of the New World. It would also place faith in France's lasting loyalty to the South—a risk, given Louis-Napoleon's well-known mercurial temperament and self-interested ambition. Even as they contemplated an alliance with France, therefore, Confederate editors and journalists discussed how their republic could eventually overtake its French partners as the hemisphere's dominant nation.

Some suggested that the first step toward this goal ought to be the cultivation of a broad set of foreign allies. Matthew Karp has shown that antebellum Southerners were deeply interested in creating alliances with other "slaveholding regimes across the Americas," such as Brazil and Cuba.[81] During the Civil War, certain Confederate publications expanded this logic to argue that their nation seek out close relations with all so-called conservative powers in the Americas, regardless of whether they were slave societies. The *Atlanta Confederacy*, for example, looked forward to a time when Maximilian's regime would be strong enough to stand without the need for French bayonets to prop it up. At that point "a close bond of fellowship" could develop between Mexico City and Richmond, "a union which we heartily approve, as natural, expedient and right" because it would be based on their shared adherence to the values of "peace, order and social liberty."[82] According to this plan, a multitude of other alliances would then arise from this partnership. As the *Memphis Daily Appeal* noted, Austria wished to guarantee "the possession to Maximilian of the Mexican throne" and would therefore gladly recognize the Confederacy in return for its support for the archduke's new regime.[83] Meanwhile Spain, seeking to guarantee "permanent retention of the islands" of Cuba, Puerto Rico, and Santo Domingo, would also ingratiate itself with the Mexican-Confederate power bloc taking shape in North America.[84] The *Appeal* imagined these relations forming under the impetus of strategic self-interest; other publications believed that ideological and cultural affinities would draw such an alliance together. The "Catholic powers of France, Spain, Italy, Brazil, and Mexico," a contributor to *De Bow's Review* pointed out, all shared Confederates' understanding of the importance of social hierarchies for maintaining stable governments.[85] They also aligned with many Confederates in the belief that the attainment of domestic order was indispensable to the achievement of more lofty objectives such as individual liberty, social mobility, and economic modernization. With their political philosophies so well aligned, the writer continued, these powers would inevitably enter into "closer union" with the Confederacy to create a "religious and commercial league" that would promote their common values across the hemisphere and around the world.[86]

These organs argued that by developing a network of conservative allies, eventually the Confederacy would be able to advance its own interests on the world stage without needing to rely on France. *De Bow's Review* waxed exuberant as it contemplated how these connections would spur the Confederacy to a position of not just hemispheric but global commercial preeminence. "The trade of the South would be no longer confined to Philadelphia, New York, and Boston," the journal explained, "but would be extended to London, Liverpool, Havre, Paris, Lisbon, Madrid, Vienna, Genoa, Florence, Rome, Havana, and Rio Janeiro," enabling the country to "grow to be the richest and most glorious confederate republic the world ever beheld."[87]

This writer imagined the Confederacy's rise to hemispheric supremacy in commercial terms. Others thought more about its ideological dimensions. The *Richmond Daily Dispatch*, for example, anticipated that the success of the Maximilian regime would inspire other independent Spanish American nations, "thoroughly disgusted with chronic revolution and perpetual bloodshed" under republicanism and longing for "secure peace and quiet," to call for more centralized systems of government.[88] Naturally they would appeal to the hemisphere's foremost conservative powers—namely France, Spain, and the Confederacy—to aid them in exchanging "democratic forms for the possession of substantial happiness."[89] Few Southern publications proposed that the Confederacy would directly intervene in the internal politics of neighboring nations, preferring instead to imagine their nation's role as providing a model of slaveholding republicanism that other American countries could learn from, though perhaps never fully replicate. The famous orator and religious leader Benjamin M. Palmer summed up this idea well in a speech he delivered in New Orleans in 1863 that was later republished in the *Richmond Daily Dispatch*. As Palmer told his audience, the mission that Providence had bestowed upon the original United States to uphold the republican system of government had now "been remitted to us. We are to take it up and work it out."[90] To Palmer, this "working out" would be an internal process whereby Confederates would maintain and refine the institutions, systems, and cultures of their slaveholding republican society, rather than being distracted by efforts to erect identical governments in foreign countries. Thus the Confederacy would "constitute a great nation, capable of holding power in the family of nations," but not one inclined to interference or proselytizing on the world stage.[91] In this way an independent South would allow political pluralism to flourish in the New World—a process that, if properly done, would see the region's populations inevitably opt for varying forms of conservative government—while closely guarding the experiment of white slaveholding republicanism within its own borders.

As they sought to justify Richmond's response to the Mexican Question to the public, Confederate publications sketched out a picture of their slaveholding republic's future in the wider hemisphere. In this picture the Confederacy would cultivate a network of allies, both European and American, all dedicated to advancing social order, political stability, and economic modernization in the New World. While France would initially take the lead, they promised that over time the Confederacy would ascend to a position of leadership in this global constellation of conservative powers. From there, it would exercise ideological influence through the force of its republican example, and economic power through its commercial might. No doubt this inspiring vision was intended to motivate Confederate civilians and troops as they struggled through the hardships of war. As we shall see, however, Southern publicists used the promise of hemispheric hegemony in tandem with another vision, or rather a threat: namely, what would befall the hemisphere in the event of Confederate defeat.

The Yankee Empire

During the antebellum era proslavery advocates repeatedly charged that abolitionists' professed concern for the enslaved was mere posturing. As South Carolina's *Yorkville Enquirer* had explained on the eve of the Civil War, while "Christian masters" felt "morally bound to protect and provide for their households," including their enslaved members, abolitionists wished to put "the slave into a condition in which there is no guaranty given by the master that his interests will be promoted, or even cared for."[92] The writer added that forcing white and Black people to live alongside one another in a state of artificial equality would be a cruelty to both races. "The superiority of one, and the acknowledged imbecility and degradation of the other will give the one always an advantage over the other," they reasoned, "and thus the habits and interests of the two would be ever conflicting."[93] While abolitionists ("so called philanthropists") claimed that they wished to "alleviate the supposed miseries of the slaves," in reality their plans would condemn enslaved people to a future "fraught with a thousand incurable evils."[94]

This author insisted that most abolitionists understood the dangerous consequences of emancipation. The only logical explanation for their determination to end slavery, therefore, was because they viewed it as a means to ruin the South. As the author explained, abolitionists knew that emancipation would let loose "an anomalous, repulsive, troublesome, decaying and pestiferous element" upon the Southern states with catastrophic effects on the region's economic productivity, political stability, and social order.[95] With the South plunged into chaos, its leaders would be powerless to resist as Northern legislators imposed free labor doctrines on the Western territories, thereby consolidating their control over the federal government. According to this view, then, abolitionism was merely a tool by which to establish Northern dominion over the South in perpetuity.

The French Intervention in Mexico presented Confederate publicists with an opportunity to add continental dimensions to their description of Northern abolitionists' plot for Southern subjugation. They began by claiming that, although in the past many antislavery politicians had opposed territorial expansion, they had done so only because they wished to avoid adding land, and therefore political power, to the antebellum South. The *Memphis Daily Appeal* insisted that in truth, the imaginations of antislavery politicians had long been "inflated with visions of a splendid empire, embracing the entire continent."[96] This would be an empire of a particularly Yankee kind—one gained not by conquest or purchase, but through the spread of dangerous ideas. It was a style of imperialism supposedly taught to them by the British, who had spent the last three decades pressuring rival empires to give up slavery. Ostensibly this was for humanitarian reasons, but the common assumption among Confederate organs was that the British hoped to persuade their competitors to ruin their colonial economies through emancipation, just as had occurred in the British Caribbean in the 1830s.[97] In a similar manner, Richmond's *Daily Dispatch* argued in April 1864, Union politicians loudly condemned Louis-Napoleon for violating Mexican sovereignty when in reality they objected to the Intervention because "the universal Yankee nation has long fixed its greedy eyes upon Mexico" and had been "looking forward to the day when it might find a pretext for making a meal of it."[98] Northerners wished to see Juárez returned to office, moreover, because they knew that the Liberals' anticlerical leveling agenda would plunge Mexico deeper into anarchy and poverty. Once this was done Mexicans would become so desperate that they would appeal to their "sister republic" for salvation, whereupon "the United States will go to Mexico as its deliverers" and swallow the country "as an anaconda would a goat."[99] The *Wilmington Journal* added that Unionists had reinterpreted the Monroe Doctrine as a pledge to preserve the New World for republican government alone so that they could use their opposition to the French Intervention to posture as the defenders of free government in the Americas and as "the (political) saints of the earth."[100] This apparently resembled the way in which the British used the guise of antislavery humanitarianism to cover their own imperial machinations.

Thankfully the Yankees' scheme had been, in the words of the *Daily Dispatch*, "knocked on the head by the French occupation of Mexico," which had forced the Juárez administration into exile.[101] Moreover, Mexico's "conversion into an empire, under the patronage and protection of the Emperor of the French" would transform it into a peaceful and prosperous nation.[102] Having tasted the blessings of liberal monarchism, Mexicans would have no need to call upon the United States to bring them peace and stability. Nor would they have any desire to return to the miseries of republicanism, whether as an independent nation or through absorption into the United States. The "French occupation of Mexico" had therefore created "an effectual barrier to the ambitious plans, purposes, and territorial and political progress of Yankee Doodle," the *Dispatch* surmised—no doubt the "bitterest pill, next to the secession of the South, that the United States has ever been compelled to swallow."[103] Unionists' disappointment was apparently evident in the abuse their representatives were currently hurling at Louis-Napoleon, Maximilian, and their Mexican collaborators. As the *Fayetteville Observer* argued, the resolution passed by the US House on April 4, 1864, contained "a good deal of bullyism" designed to "deter the powers of Europe from any attempt" to aid and improve Mexico.[104] The *Richmond Enquirer* similarly described the US Congress's effort to scare the French "from interfering in the affairs of the nations of this hemisphere" as a "vulgar pretention" borne from that body's frustration that the French Intervention had interfered with their own imperial ambitions south of the Rio Grande.[105]

Confederate newspapers had certain international audiences in mind when they made these accusations. The governments of Britain, Spain, and especially France, they believed, must be shown that Unionist propagandists were erroneously painting Confederates as aggressive expansionists in order to distract the global community's attention away from the North's own imperial ambitions. At the same time, the narrative of Yankee imperialism was also aimed at readers inside the Confederacy. At its heart was the message that the Civil War was a zero-sum game, and that the winner would become the dominant republic in the New World with all the riches and influence this position entailed. Through the Mexican Question, in short, Confederate publications showed their readers the stakes of the contest they were currently engaged in, impressing them with images of both the hemispheric glory that the Confederacy's victory would bring and of their nation's desolation under Yankee rapacity in the event of its defeat.

The Imagined Franco-Confederate Alliance Crumbles

By the end of 1863, support for the Mexican Empire was almost as strong across the Confederate press as pro-Juarist sentiment was in the Union—almost, but not quite. Voices of dissent did exist. Over the course of 1864 a relatively small but vocal group of newspaper editors developed a critique of the Davis administration's Mexican policy. While they were ostensibly engaging in a debate about foreign policy, their opposition was in fact chiefly borne from domestic political concerns regarding the manner in which the national government was conducting the war effort, specifically its willingness to pass measures such as the suspension of habeas corpus and conscription, which violated state and individual liberties. That domestic politics was driving these publications' intervention in foreign policy discussions became especially clear from late 1864 onward, when a downturn in the Confederacy's military fortunes prompted debates in the press about whether Richmond ought to seek a negotiated peace with the Union and so bring the Civil War to an end. As we shall see, organs in places such as North Carolina where Peace sentiment was strong incorporated the Mexican issue into their larger campaign to discredit President Davis and his effort to continue fighting the rebellion "to the last man and the last dollar."

Glimmers of dissatisfaction with Richmond's approach to the French Intervention first appeared in the Confederate press around the time of the formation of the Assembly of Notables in the summer of 1863. In August, for example, North Carolina's *Weekly Standard* published a sharply worded piece doubting the Assembly's claim to represent the will of the Mexican people. "This Junta has selected three citizens to exercise the executive power," the newspaper pointed out, "Gen. Almonte, the Archbishop of Mexico, and Gen. Scales—*all strong partizans* [*sic*] *of a monarchy*."[106] The whole enterprise had been fixed from the start and constituted, according to the *Standard*, "one of the greatest outrages of modern times."[107] What most concerned the newspaper was not that a trick was being played upon Mexicans, but that in seeking an alliance with France, the Confederacy was making itself vulnerable to a similar deception. As the *Standard* explained in a later article, given the right circumstances Louis-Napoleon would not hesitate to orchestrate a takeover of the Confederacy, just as he had done to Mexico. Southerners could therefore find themselves in a situation where they too were "given a foreigner for a King, and to have established the Catholic religion by law among us."[108] Those who "tell the people there is no hope unless France will soon come to our aid," the newspaper concluded, were therefore encouraging Confederates to play a very risky game.[109]

Criticism of Richmond's Mexican policy may have continued to consist only of occasional expressions of skepticism regarding Louis-Napoleon's trustworthiness such as these. In early 1864, however, a series of events on the international stage tested the foundations of the Davis administration's approach to the French Intervention and so created space in the Confederate press for a wider debate about the government's Mexican policy. In March 1864, Confederate newspapers caught wind of some concerning dispatches that had recently arrived at the State Department from John Slidell in Paris. Referencing what he claimed were reliable sources, Slidell explained that the French emperor had definitively decided that he would *not* recognize the government in Richmond. More worrying still, Louis-Napoleon had advised Maximilian to do the same. Proof that the Austrian had heeded this advice came a few months later when, following his arrival in Mexico, William Preston, the man who Richmond had sent to Mexico City to open talks with the new Mexican Empire, was refused an interview with the emperor.[110]

This was bad news for the Confederacy. By this time Secretary of State Benjamin Judah had largely given up attempting to convince Britain to involve itself in the Civil War, instead hinging his diplomatic strategy almost entirely on securing French recognition and friendship. Now this strategy looked to be doomed, and with it possibly the Confederacy's best hope of gaining independence. The news hit the Confederate press like ice-cold water. "We are isolated from all the world," a stunned *Richmond Enquirer* despaired in June 1864, "No people, struggling for its independence, was ever yet so wholly ignored by the rest of mankind; and we this day stand fronting the most fearful odds, the mightiest armaments by land and sea that were ever combined to crush a people to the earth, in the simple, naked might of our own manhood, without ally or friend, or even the barest acknowledgment of our existence. So far as Europe is concerned, we fight here enclosed within a fatal ring of fire."[111]

Not everyone was so shocked at Louis-Napoleon's betrayal, however. Indeed, some saw it as vindication of their long-standing concerns about a foreign policy strategy that placed the Confederacy's fortunes in the hands of a single duplicitous, self-serving European emperor. This was the view of North Carolina representative James Leach, who spoke on the topic during a speech in his home district in July 1864. Leach told his audience that the recent actions of both Louis-Napoleon and Maximilian were proof that neither felt any affection for the Confederacy, and that "their sympathy for us or others extends not beyond their pecuniary and national aggrandizement."[112] North Carolina newspaper the *Daily Progress* echoed this view. "Does not the snubbing Maximilian gave Slidell . . . drive the nail home?" the newspaper asked in April 1864. "Shall we make fools of ourselves by looking to Maximilian, the Emperor, or 'any other man' longer for succor? If we can whip the Yankees into an acknowledgement of our independence, as we all believe we can, let us do it, but no more of recognition or help from abroad—The country is sick of the cry."[113]

To understand why these particular newspapers and politicians were so critical of Richmond's foreign policy strategy, it is necessary to examine their domestic political agenda. Over the course of the Civil War, the Davis administration assumed control over or placed restrictions upon various aspects of civilian life in the Confederacy, often at the expense of state government authority and individual liberties.[114] Conscription, tithing, and impressment all contributed to what historian Michael Bernath describes as the Confederacy's evolution from "a states' rights confederation" into "a centralized nation-state with powers far exceeding those of the US government before 1861."[115] Such measures were highly controversial. Among the most explosive was the Confederate States Congress's decision in February 1862 to allow President Davis to suspend the writ of habeas corpus. Following this decision, areas of the Confederacy where disloyal activities were rife—most notably western North Carolina, Richmond, and eastern Tennessee—were placed under martial law, allowing the government to detain soldiers and civilians suspected of committing treasonous acts for extended periods without bringing them to trial. Though the Congress would later put certain limits on this presidential power, such as requiring Davis to obtain congressional approval for its renewal, the suspension made its effects felt; over 4,000 individuals were arrested and detained under its mandate over the course of the war.[116]

President Davis and like-minded allies accepted that the necessities of wartime required the executive's use of these and other extraordinary powers. Some even argued that there were benefits to be had from a strong and agile central state, whether in times of war or peace. However, others found Richmond's tilt toward centralization deeply troubling. Among the president's most vocal critics was North Carolina newspaperman William Woods Holden. A mercurial figure, Holden began his political life as a Whig but shifted to the Democrats in the 1840s. During this time he dabbled in politics, serving a term in North Carolina's House of Commons in 1846. His real calling, however, was the newspaper business. After having worked at various state organs, Holden took control of the *North Carolina Standard*, later renamed the *Weekly Standard*, in 1842. Throughout the antebellum period he used the newspaper to advocate for the expansion of slavery and occasionally gave favorable attention to the idea of Southern secession. When it came to the crunch in 1861, however, Holden opposed separation and even voted against it as the representative of Wake County in North Carolina's state convention. Still, when his state voted to leave the Union, Holden dutifully followed it into the Confederacy.[117]

During wartime, Holden would demonstrate that his support for the Confederacy did not extend to blanket approval of the president and his administration. In his criticisms of Davis, the newspaper editor claimed to be representing the views of his fellow North Carolinians, particularly the nonslaveholding yeoman farmers who, broadly speaking, had reservations about the project of Southern independence, which seemed to demand many sacrifices from them for the sake of defending the planter aristocracy's human property. Styling himself as a mouthpiece of the common man, Holden used the *Weekly Standard* to air these grievances, routinely condemning President Davis and his allies in Richmond as power-hungry would-be despots seeking to run roughshod over the rights of both states and citizens. Ever the activist, in 1862 Holden began to draw together North Carolina's discontented voters and political leaders into something approximating a political party, whose associates called themselves the Conservatives. By 1864 this loose organization, which included local politicians such as William A. Graham, Edward Joseph Hale, Thomas Ruffin, James T. Leach, Senator John Pool, and Jonathan Worth, was a formidable force in North Carolina politics and had even succeeded in sending a few of their number to the Confederate Congress.[118]

As the Conservatives' influence grew, so too did the intensity of their public attacks on President Davis and his cabinet. During the summer of 1864, for example, Conservative representative Thomas Charles Fuller spoke at a number of public events in North Carolina, where he described to his constituents what he had observed during his time at the national Congress in Richmond. There was, he alleged, "*an awful squinting towards monarchy by a party*—a powerful party in this land of ours."[119] Measures such as martial law, tithing, and impressment were part of a premeditated plot concocted by this faction to steer the Confederacy "towards centralization and monarchy."[120] While the head of this supposed conspiracy was located in Richmond, its arms reached from Virginia to Texas and it commanded followers at all levels of local, state, and national governments. Their collective aim was to take advantage of the war to convince Confederate citizens to allow the federal government to assume control over the country's judicial, military, and economic apparatuses in the name of national security. "They do not say they are for monarchy," Fuller warned, "but their acts, which speak louder than words, prove that they are."[121]

Holden's *Standard* gave these alarming claims a serious hearing. The newspaper thanked Fuller for alerting the Southern people to the fact that "there is a powerful combination on foot to establish a monarchy over these States" and added that "we have frequently sounded the same warning to our readers."[122] This was true; throughout 1864 the *Standard* made numerous references to a monarchical plot forming, not just in Richmond but in state houses and governor's mansions across the Confederacy. The newspaper's use of such heated rhetoric was perhaps fueled by the fact that its editor William Holden was at this time engaged in a contest against incumbent Zebulon Vance for the North Carolina governorship. In July of that year, for example, the newspaper launched a full-throated attack on Col. Duncan McRae, editor of pro-Vance publication the *Confederate*. The *Standard* accused McRae of being "a monarchist at heart and an enemy to popular government," whose support of "test oaths, of gag laws, of the suspension of the writ of *habeas corpus*" stemmed from his "contempt for the people, and . . . desire to establish a monarchy over them."[123] It was a desire shared by "Gov. Vance" who, guided by the philosophy that "'the King can do no wrong,'' had supposedly used his first term as governor to facilitate President Davis's egregious infringements upon the liberties of the people of North Carolina.[124] Together, the *Standard* finished, these individuals were part of that larger party that was "determined, if at all possible, *to fasten a monarchy on these States*."[125]

Historians have examined many aspects of the tussle between states' rights defenders and the national government in Confederate politics, a fight that played out not only in North Carolina but in pockets across the wartime republic. Missing from many of these analyses, however, is an examination of how this conflict intersected with the realm of foreign policy. The oversight is a missed opportunity, as self-styled Conservative Confederates were acutely aware that their fight with suspected monarchists at home was taking place within a wider North American context. Many of them, for example, pointed out similarities between their predicament and that of the Liberals in Mexico, who had also been betrayed by traitorous fellow citizens wishing to turn their republic into a monarchy. "Miserable Mexico!" the *Semi-Weekly Standard* pronounced in July 1864, "after years of civil war the masses of her people are to be governed by an Emperor, forced upon them by the foreign bayonets and the aristocracy of their own county."[126] "The people of the North American States are tending in the same direction," the newspaper continued, for "we know that the aristocracy of the Confederate States are longing for strong government and imperial rule."[127]

It is worth pausing here to consider the nature of these publications' opinions of the Mexican republic. Much like other Confederate organs, the *Standard* maintained that Mexicans had a right to self-determination. Where it differed from many of its contemporaries, however, was in its insistence that Mexicans had long since decided that the government they preferred was a democratic republic, and that as such Louis-Napoleon's venture was a violation of Mexican sovereignty. "Mexicans alone have a right to rule Mexico," the newspaper stoutly proclaimed in August 1863, "but the Emperor Napoleon has, by the strong hand, beaten down the Democratic principle in that country, and forced a distant people, whom he has no right to control, to accept his laws and his Emperor."[128] The *Standard*'s sympathies for republican Mexico did not extend much beyond this point, however. A review of both the *Standard* and other self-styled Conservative newspapers between 1863 and 1864 reveals no editorials praising President Juárez or extolling the Mexican Liberal cause. Indeed, these newspapers rarely discussed events taking place below the Rio Grande in any detail. Articles that did comment on the progress of the Franco-Mexican conflict typically portrayed what the *Standard* termed "the poor decaying republic of Mexico" as a rather one-dimensional character, the pitiable victim of more crafty international actors.[129]

These newspapers' lack of affection for—or even interest in—the Mexican republicans is an indication that, their views regarding the legitimacy of the French Intervention notwithstanding, they subscribed to the same anti-Mexican prejudices common among Confederate newspapers at this time. Though moderate on questions of secession and independence, Holden and like-minded Conservative editors were nevertheless supporters of slavery and the racial social order that it underpinned. They would have therefore struggled to celebrate a mixed-race self-governing republic such as Mexico with the same enthusiasm demonstrated by publications in the Union. Indeed, their interest in Mexico was driven less by a concern for Mexicans than a belief that the Confederacy was at risk of falling victim to Louis-Napoleon's imperial intrigues. As the *Daily Progress* explained in July 1864, the monarchical cabal in Richmond believed that it needed outside assistance to consummate its scheme to subvert the Confederate republic into a monarchy, and had therefore developed a plan for "selling out these States to France and Mexicanizing them *a la* Maximilian" in which they would hand over the South "to the tender mercies of Despotic rule with a foreigner for our master."[130]

What all of this shows us is that public opinion in the Confederacy regarding the Mexican Question was not uniform. To be sure, the majority of newspapers accepted the prospect of forging alliances with autocratic regimes so long as these regimes shared the Confederacy's values of social order, established hierarchy, and liberal commerce. There was, however, a portion of the Confederate press that prized other virtues as the essence of Southern slaveholding republicanism. For these publications, states' rights, individual liberties, and a highly circumscribed executive were the qualities that would ensure the success of an independent South and must therefore guide not only its domestic politics but also its approach to world affairs. Such publications spurned an alliance with the French emperor, viewing this policy as a worrying manifestation of the perceived slide toward monarchism taking place within the Confederacy at this time.

That said, it is important not to overstate the significance of this clash over Mexican policy, at least throughout the first two years of the French Intervention. During this time, criticism of Richmond's handling of the issue was largely confined to a particularly energized and well-organized faction within North Carolina politics. These politicians and newspapermen, moreover, primarily used the Mexican issue as a rhetorical device in state election campaigns to paint their opponents as would-be monarchists. Toward the end of 1864 and into 1865, however, the narrative of a monarchical conspiracy between Richmond and Mexico City became interwoven with a much larger debate Confederates across the South were engaged in over the existential question of whether to continue the military fight for independence.

Mexican Policy and Peace

In March 1864, as Maximilian was making his farewell tour around Europe, President Lincoln appointed Ulysses S. Grant general-in-chief of the Armies of the United States. The announcement was a boost to Union morale; Northerners anticipated that "Unconditional Surrender" Grant would prosecute the war effort with such vigor that the conflict would soon be over. In the months that followed, Grant seemed likely to fulfil these expectations, launching multiple simultaneous offensives in the eastern, western, and trans-

Mississippi theaters. But the fighting was tough going. Beginning in May, Grant's campaign in Virginia was marked by exceptionally bloody battles, most notably those of Wilderness, Spotsylvania, and Cold Harbor. By mid-June, Grant's men were locked into what was effectively trench warfare at Petersburg, unable to take Richmond just 25 miles away. Meanwhile General Sherman's troops were similarly entrenched outside Atlanta, Georgia.

As discussed in the previous chapter, lack of progress on the battlefield coupled with the war's rapidly mounting body count precipitated a rise in antiwar sentiment across the Union. Desertions rose, rumors of Copperhead conspiracies increased, and leaders of the peace faction of the Northern Democracy grew more strident in their attacks on the president. All of this was monitored closely by the Confederate press. William Holden's *Weekly Standard* followed these events with particular interest. By this time, the newspaper had become one of the leading organs of the so-called "Peace Men" in Confederate politics. Members of this movement were diverse. Some were Unionists who wished to see North and South reunited. Others, such as Holden, publicly supported independence but argued that Southerners should not be forced to fight to the "last man and the last dollar" to achieve it. Doing so, they argued, would only further decimate the region's economy, infrastructure, and the civil liberties of its citizens. Holden, for one, advocated ending the war through a ceasefire followed by peace talks with Washington, DC, ideally at a time when the Confederacy was in a strong enough position to negotiate terms favorable to its interests.

While the Peace movement's strongest base of support was in North Carolina, it had adherents throughout the Confederacy. The congressional elections of 1863 saw peace candidates elected in multiple states, including Virginia, Tennessee, Alabama, and Georgia. By 1864, these individuals could point to growing antiwar sentiment in the North to insist that a negotiated peace was not only humane but feasible. In March 1864, for example, Governor Joseph E. Brown told the Georgia State Legislature that the Union, much like the Confederacy, was mutating into a "military despotism; placing all civil rights in a state of subordination to military power, and putting the personal freedom of each individual, in civil life, at the will of the chief of the military power."[131] The growth of the antiwar movement within the Union indicated that the "intelligent Northern Conservative man" recognized this and had begun to ask whether defeating the rebellion was worthwhile if in the process "we must lose our own liberties and rivet upon ourselves and our posterity the chains of military despotism."[132] A Georgia newspaper speculated that these supposedly conservative Northerners were now ready to "accept terms of peace" that would recognize Southern independence in the belief that peaceful separation was preferable to prolonging the ruinous civil war.[133] It acknowledged that such an outcome was impossible so long as President Lincoln, who was determined to fight until the point of Southern surrender, occupied the White House. Still, there was cause for optimism. As the newspaper pointed out, the current public mood in the Union indicated that in the upcoming 1864 presidential election "the conservative men of the North of all parties" would unite to replace the current administration with one that would be open to working with the Confederacy to find a peaceful end to their conflict.[134]

Advocates of this plan insisted that in order for it to work, Richmond would need to signal to Unionists that it genuinely desired to enter into peace talks. This could not be done, they argued, without first revising its current foreign policy strategy. Specifically, the Confederacy would need to call an end to its effort to obtain European recognition. The logic behind this was explained by Alabama newspaper the *Selma Daily Reporter*, which asked its readers to consider the absurdity of Richmond sending agents to "court the favor of monarchies of Europe, who desire nothing better than the failure of republican government, and who have no sentiment or sympathy in common with us," while turning "the cold shoulder upon" potential conservative allies in the Northern states "who really sympathize with us in our struggle for liberty" and "who desire to maintain free government for themselves and are willing to aid us in maintaining ours!"[135] The *Weekly Mississippian* thought likewise. The people of the Confederacy were at a crossroads, the newspaper explained. They could continue to seek recognition from France, which, in the now unlikely event that it occurred, would probably see Louis-Napoleon demanding repayment in the form of some kind of treaty that would "strip us of half our best territory."[136] In the process, Richmond would have also signaled to voters in the Union that it was not open to peace negotiations, thereby encouraging them to elect "another administration in the North . . . upon the war platform."[137] This would guarantee the continuation of the Civil War until both the North and South had succumbed to either "anarchy, empire, or military despotism."[138] Alternatively, Confederates could renounce Louis-Napoleon, Maximilian, and their monarchical plot in Mexico and declare their desire to work with the Union toward a peaceful, possibly even amicable end to the war. This would strengthen the hand of the "Northern 'copperheads'" who "are contending for State rights as well as we" and who in their current efforts "to make the Northern government yield us our rights . . . naturally look for sympathy and encouragement from us."[139] Northern voters would then bring this party into power in the upcoming presidential election; a ceasefire would follow, and after that a peace treaty ending the Civil War that would halt the slide toward despotism on both sides of the Mason-Dixon Line.

Some Peace advocates went further, imagining how this shift in Confederate foreign policy could open the way for the evolution of a broader partnership between the Union and Confederacy in the Western Hemisphere. In early November 1864, Tennessee representative and long-time critic of the Davis administration Henry S. Foote wrote a public letter that formed the basis of a resolution that he would later submit to the Confederate House.[140] Confident that Union voters would elect McClellan as their next president, he predicted that soon after election day a convention of the Northern and Southern states would be called and peace negotiated on the "basis of Southern independence."[141] In addition to settling the question of disunion, the convention would determine the nature of the US-Confederate relationship going forward. Foote's own preference was for "a league offensive or defensive" resembling the Articles of Confederation of 1781, which would consist of a "permanent body of Commissioners" from each country who would coordinate on matters of trade, defense, and foreign affairs.[142] Foote anticipated close and effective collaboration between these commissioners because the international outlook of Northern Democrats so closely aligned with that of all right-thinking Confederates. They would have no trouble, for example, agreeing to the creation of "a new Monroe doctrine" that would pledge to roll back the recent encroachment of European powers in North America and secure "exclusive dominion of the two allied republics over every part of this continent."[143]

Foote's plan made no mention of the Juarists or indeed the people of any of the Spanish American republics. Whether he thought these countries ought to remain independent or be swallowed up by the "two allied republics" is therefore an open question. Instead, Foote's "new Monroe doctrine" was focused on the expulsion of European powers from the New World. As he put it, a Union-Confederate alliance would see to it that "British authority would be swept out of Canada, and French dominion in Mexico would be overturned . . . and thus visit a just retribution on the cold-blooded monarchies concerned, who are now attempting to surround the two republics and limit their growth."[144]

As a committed states' rights advocate, Foote disliked autocrats wherever he found them, whether in Richmond; Washington, DC; Paris; or Mexico City. His suggestion that a US-Confederate partnership would rid North

America of European usurpers was predicated on his assumption that most Unionists shared in this sentiment. Certainly, he had grounds for believing this. After all, the Confederate press regularly reprinted or commented on articles from Northern Democratic organs such as the *New York Herald* proposing a North-South invasion into Mexico to oust the French.[145] What Foote apparently either ignored or did not recognize, however, was that the *Herald* and most likeminded Northern newspapers insisted that any such cross-sectional venture would be a prelude to the North and South's reunion. Foote, by contrast, though a reluctant secessionist, saw it as a means to facilitate their permanent separation.

The hopes of Foote and other Confederate Peace advocates were dealt a serious blow on November 8, 1864, when Northern voters reelected Abraham Lincoln to the presidency. Evidently Unionists believed that they could win the war, and so wished to continue fighting it. Interestingly, however, the notion among Confederate leaders that the war's end might be brought about through a joint North-South invasion of Mexico did not disappear. In January 1865, the Confederate press caught wind of a meeting that had taken place between President Davis and Unionist Maryland politician Francis P. Blair, who had been given permission by President Lincoln to travel to Richmond to propose an immediate ceasefire between the Union and Confederate armies to be followed by the reunion of the states. During their meeting Blair had explained to the president that once this was accomplished, Davis would be invited to lead a body of Confederate veterans into Mexico to help the Juarists throw out their French invaders. This done, Blair continued, Davis would then be permitted to take possession of a portion of Mexican territory for the purposes of establishing a colony there for diehard elements of the by then defunct Confederacy. Nothing definitive was agreed between Davis and Blair that day in January. And yet the scheme apparently caught Davis's interest because the following month he directed Confederate Vice President Alexander Stephens to raise the idea of a North-South invasion against imperial Mexico during the Hampton Roads Peace Conference, which Stephens was due to attend, as was President Lincoln and Secretary Seward. This Stephens dutifully did. He framed the venture as a means to bring about the separation of the sections rather than their reunion, however, and the plan was therefore immediately dismissed by both Seward and Lincoln.[146]

There is still some debate among historians as to why President Davis allowed Stephens to raise the Mexican invasion idea at these peace talks. Some argue that, with the noose tightening around the Confederacy's neck, the president was running out of options and was desperately reaching for any scheme that might yet secure Southern independence, including one that involved sending Southerners to fight alongside Northern troops in Mexico.[147] Another theory is that Davis had no intention of entering into such an alliance with the Union, and that he had merely allowed Stephens to raise the proposal in order for it to be rejected by President Lincoln. This, Davis had apparently hoped, would silence certain peace-minded critics in the Confederate Congress who still looked upon a Mexican invasion as a way to facilitate a ceasefire, thereby allowing Davis freer rein to continue prosecuting the Southern war effort as was his true wish.

Whatever Davis's motivations, any plan for a North-South invasion of Mexico, whether as a means to achieve reunion or independence, would have faced stiff resistance from among the Confederate population more broadly—that is, if the reaction of many major Southern newspapers to the idea is any guide. Indeed, even in the dying weeks of the rebellion anti-Juárez and pro–Mexican Empire sentiment across much of the Confederate press remained steady. Richmond's *Daily Dispatch*, for example, though bitterly disappointed that the Confederacy's warm embrace of Emperor Maximilian had not been repaid with recognition, maintained that it would be "better for [Mexicans] that any nation of Europe—France, England, Austria, even Russia—should hold possession of their country" than the "Yankee land-stealers."[148] In February the *Fayetteville Weekly Observer* similarly pointed out the absurdity of Southerners allying with their Yankee foes against Louis-Napoleon and Maximilian, who "if they have not been alive with sympathy and assistance for us in our sufferings, at least have not inflicted harm nor persecuted us with oppressions."[149] What honor would there be, the newspaper asked, in entering into an "alliance with the hated foeman who has so ruthlessly invaded the hearthstones of our land?"[150]

Many publications maintained this position even as they were forced to acknowledge that their bid for independence had failed. In February 1865, for example, Mississippi's *Weekly Conservative* addressed an article recently published in the *New York Herald* that had declared that Union victory was now a *fait accompli*, and that when their inevitable reunion commenced "a point upon which the people of both sections could unite without any compromise . . . is the Monroe doctrine."[151] The *Confederate* countered that even if defeated, former Confederates would never willingly fight a war with US troops against the Mexican Empire. To do so would only help the US government as it established a military occupation over the postwar

South, which would hold the region in permanent subjugation. The newspaper explained:

> Who doubts that our ports would be blockaded by the great fleets of these European nations, and heavy taxes, an inflated currency, high prices, hard times, and homely living would again be the order of the day? Who doubts that the privilege of the writ of habeas corpus would be suspended. . . . And all this we would have to endure, *not* then as now, of our own free will, to save ourselves, our wives and our little ones, from degradation and bondage, to maintain our own honor, to secure our own independence . . . but in obedience to the behests of our masters, to consolidate our fetters and to rivet our chains.[152]

Cooperation with "our present enemy upon the Monroe doctrine, at this time or at any time," the newspaper concluded, would contradict the "rights, civil and political, for which we are battling. . . . I hate the idea of going to Mexico. No Monroe doctrine is mine."[153]

Throughout 1863 and most of 1864, Confederate publications had confidently planned their slaveholding republic's future in the hemisphere. By early 1865, however, as the Union Army moved deeper into their territory and took possession of key railroads, ports, and cities, it became difficult to maintain faith in such visions. As the Confederacy's military standing deteriorated and its prospects on the international stage turned bleak, space opened up in Confederate public discourse for the consideration of alternative approaches to Richmond's conduct of foreign relations. Some leading Peace advocates proposed joining forces with the Union in an invasion of Mexico in return for either Southern independence or, in the event of defeat, lenient treatment in the process of reunion. While it gained some support throughout January and February 1865, however, this position never became the dominant one among the Confederacy's major publications and leading politicians. Indeed, even as they saw their hopes for an independent republic disintegrate, most declared that they would not compromise the integrity of the Southern slaveholding republican cause by advocating for its soldiers to fight alongside Yankee abolitionists in defense of the mixed-race Mexican Liberals.

The Confederates' Hemispheric Visions Collapse

Four days after General Lee's surrender at Appomattox Court House in April 1865, the *Daily Dispatch* wondered what would become of North America now that the fight for Confederate independence was over. For white

Southerners, the newspaper concluded, the future looked grim. After all, President Lincoln had never wished simply "to conquer the South," but to upend the institutions upon which it was based.[154] Having crushed Confederates on the battlefield, therefore, Republicans would now liberate enslaved Southerners, set them on an equal footing with their former masters, and watch as anarchy consumed the South. The *Dispatch* believed that former Confederates were only the first on Lincoln's list of targets. "The people of the United States have always coveted Mexico," it reminded its readers, though in the antebellum era their jealousy of the South had prevented them from pursuing a "wholesale plunder" of that country.[155] The Confederacy's fall, however, had removed "the only breakwater which now keeps back the tide of Northern aggression."[156] Buoyed by their victory over the South, moreover, Yankees were "no longer unconscious of [their] own power."[157] In possession of "a disposable army of at least three hundred thousand men for the invasion of Mexico" and "a navy which can blockade every Mexican port," the Union would soon "sweep every French merchantman from the ocean" and "within six months after the conquest of the Southern Confederacy, Mexico will become part and parcel of the United States."[158]

For the past four years, the Confederate press had provided readers with inspiring prophecies of hemispheric glory that would follow the consummation of Southern independence. The Confederacy, they insisted, was fated to inherit from the United States the title of the New World's exceptional republic, along with the duties and benefits this station entailed. The advent of the French Intervention in Mexico, however, raised serious questions about if and how the Confederacy would fulfil this supposedly providential destiny. Confederate newspapers therefore created a new hemispheric agenda, one that blended ideology and ambition with a realistic assessment of the young Confederacy's likely military and economic capacities. In this vision, the independent South would form a vital link in a chain of conservative powers stretching across the southern portions of the American and European Continents. This alliance would hold back the tide of Yankee imperialism and oversee the gradual conversion of the Spanish American republics into orderly, centralized regimes. At the height of their ambition, Confederate newspapers insisted that their republic would eventually become the leader of this international alliance, and that the success of the country's slaveholding republican society would be a model that would guide other hemispheric nations' transition from radical republicanism to conservative centralization.

Alongside this promising vision, Southern publicists impressed upon the public what would befall the New World if Confederates lost the Civil War. In this scenario, they warned, the Southern bulwark against Yankee imperialism would be gone. Northern militarism and radicalism would quickly engulf the South before spilling over the Rio Grande and consuming Mexico, the Caribbean, Central America, and eventually the entire hemisphere. In April 1865, as the Confederate military effort collapsed, many publications expressed their fear that this scenario was about to be realized. The fight for Confederate independence had failed, and so now the South would be the first in a long line of victims to be swallowed up by the post-emancipation Yankee empire.

CHAPTER THREE

Reconstructing the Model Republic, 1865–1867

The ending of the Civil War was a protracted process. Confederate general Robert E. Lee surrendered the Army of Northern Virginia on April 9, 1865. General Joseph E. Johnston followed suit in North Carolina on April 26, and then General Richard Taylor surrendered the Department of Alabama, Mississippi, and East Louisiana on May 4. West of the Mississippi River, meanwhile, Confederate general Edmund Kirby-Smith remained in command of approximately 150,000 men who were spread across a vast area that included Louisiana, Texas, Arkansas, and parts of Indian Territory. Though it was strategically significant, most battles fought in the Trans-Mississippi Department (or "Kirby-Smithdom," as it was also called) had been smaller in scale than those in the east, and less deadly too. Confederate troops in the region therefore had not been chastened by the grim defeats of Richmond, Atlanta, and Charleston. And so, when they learned that hero of the Confederate Army General Lee had relinquished his sword to General Grant, many rebel soldiers in the Trans-Mississippi Department were stunned.[1]

General Kirby-Smith, for one, refused to accept defeat. Learning that President Jefferson Davis had fled Richmond and was moving westward, the general prepared to receive the man he still called president. Precisely what Davis was planning, Kirby-Smith could not be sure. Most likely the president was heading for the Trans-Mississippi Department headquarters at Shreveport, Louisiana, from where he could rally the remaining vestiges of the Confederate Army to mount a last stand against the Union. If their showing was strong enough, they might even convince Emperor Louis-Napoleon to reconsider his abandonment of the Confederacy and send troops across the Rio Grande to support the resurrection of the rebellion in the Southwest. Alternatively, Davis and the remnants of the Confederate Army could fall back into Mexico and regroup under the protective shield of the Maximilian government. In either scenario, Kirby-Smith understood, the Texas-Mexican border would play a central role in any effort to keep alive the hope of Confederate independence. The general therefore instructed Southern agents operating in the borderlands to reach out to Mexican imperial officials to prepare for a potential Confederate retreat into Mexico.

Days passed without news that Davis had crossed the Mississippi River. Kirby-Smith's men grew restless. Desertions began to deplete his forces—a trickle at first, then whole groups departing at once, often slipping away at night and melting into the darkness. Kirby-Smith was fast becoming a general without an army. Then on May 10, 1865, Davis was captured in Georgia. Upon hearing the news, Kirby-Smith was forced to accept the hopelessness of his situation. On June 2 on board the Union steamer *Fort Jackson* docked at Galveston harbor, the general agreed to the terms of surrender with Union commander General Edward R.S. Canby. Kirby-Smith did not hang around for long after that. By June 26 he had crossed the border at Eagle Pass into Mexico. From there he traveled across 800 miles of desert plains to Monterrey, where he encountered roughly 100 Confederate exiles including soldiers of varying ranks, former Georgia governor Thomas C. Reynolds, and a handful of other rebel politicians. After weighing his options, Kirby-Smith headed to Veracruz, where he boarded a ship to Havana. Most of his fellow Confederate exiles remained in Mexico. On July 5, Reynolds, accompanied by General Cadmus Wilcox and a few others, boarded a stagecoach. Eleven days later they arrived in Mexico City, where Emperor Maximilian received them at the Palacio Nacional.[2]

Kirby-Smith's experience illustrates the fragmented nature of Confederate defeat as it played out in a series of surrenders throughout the spring and summer of 1865. The last battles of the Civil War were fought in Indian Territory as late as June. Some historians date the war's end even later than that. Gregory Downs reminds us that, in the months following Appomattox, Washington legislators came to recognize that their hard-won wartime gains were fragile. A tentative withdrawal of federal troops from the South had been met with a surge of anti-Black activity as reformed Southern state legislatures drafted Black Codes and disbanded Confederate veterans donned white hoods. Formal hostilities may have ended, but it was clear that many ex-rebels were not reconciled to reunion.[3]

This unsettled climate spurred the Republican-controlled Congress to action. Instead of officially declaring the Civil War over, the body utilized its war powers to erect what Downs describes as a "boldly extra-constitutional occupation" over the former Confederacy.[4] In 1866 there had been 10,000 US troops in the South; a year later, the number had doubled to 20,000 and remained at that level for the next four years. The US government was still committed to demobilization; 20,000 men represented around only one-tenth of its wartime army. It was also a relatively small force given that it was tasked with occupying the entirety of the former Confederacy, a region of roughly 750,000 square miles. Still, the federal government had chosen to maintain a military presence in the South. It had also expanded the US Army's responsibilities in the region. Congressional legislation endowed army officers in the South with a raft of powers over civilian life, such as the ability to arbitrate and void labor contracts, try civilians in courts-martial and military commissions, and monitor local newspapers. Congress instructed that, in order to end this occupation, each former Confederate state must adopt the Fifteenth Amendment into its constitution, among certain other requirements. Georgia was the last state to complete this process in February 1871, which in Downs's view finally brought the Civil War to a definitive end.

Republican congressmen and their allies in the press understood that in order for US citizens, and white Northerners in particular, to accept the continued use of extraordinary federal powers after Confederate surrender, they must be convinced that their country remained on a war footing. Civil convulsions in the postbellum South, which indicated that at least some ex-rebels remained unpacified, provided Republican leaders with some of the evidence they needed to make this claim. Another useful strategy was to point to the wider North American context. Kirby-Smith was just one of roughly 5,000 Confederate veterans who fled to Mexico between 1865 and the early 1870s. To be sure, this was not as many as the estimated 10,000 to 20,000 who fled to the Empire of Brazil during the same period, though Mexico remained more popular among migratory ex-Confederates than other destinations such as Cuba, British Honduras, or Europe.[5] Moreover, the emigration to Mexico had a special resonance in the US press because it seemed to be flowing directly into the Mexican Empire. Some Republicans claimed that fleeing Southerners hoped to convince Emperor Maximilian to launch an invasion of the US Southwest as the opening salvo of a second Southern rebellion. Others charged that the Confederate exiles intended to infiltrate the Maximilian government and then transform the regime into what they had once imagined an independent South would be: a bulwark of conservative rule in North America that would curb the influence and tamper with the interests of the post-emancipation United States. For these reasons, Republicans insisted, the Civil War would never be truly over so long as the Mexican Empire remained standing.

While these claims had some truth to them, they were exaggerated. Initially, Kirby-Smith and some other diehard Confederate generals did indeed hope to convince Maximilian to assist them in launching an assault on the United States. Such hopes had largely dissipated by the fall of 1865, however, when it became clear that the Mexican emperor had no intention of involving his still-fragile regime in a foreign war. Moreover, the majority of former Confederates who traveled south of the border after April 1865 were apparently more interested in peacefully integrating into civilian life. Some established small farming communities in Mexico's unsettled lands, for example, such as the Carlota colony, which began as a 500,000 acre stretch of land located 70 miles west of Veracruz. And while certain ex-rebels did obtain administrative roles in Maximilian's government, these were almost all positions related to facilitating the Confederate migration. One of the most prominent of these individuals, Admiral Matthew Fontaine Maury, was employed by the Mexican Empire as an agent of colonization tasked with selling off Mexico's vacant lands to ex-Confederate settlers.[6]

For Republican leaders in the United States, however, perception mattered more than reality. In the months immediately following Appomattox, they pointed to both the ongoing Franco-Mexican conflict and the stream of ex-rebels crossing the Rio Grande to remind people in the United States that their country was still vulnerable to attack from aristocratic-monarchical-clerical enemies below its border. As months passed and no second rebellion materialized, these claims became less plausible. Indeed, by 1866 news had begun to reach the United States that some of the Confederate colonies in Mexico were floundering due to insufficient funds and attacks by hostile Juarist fighters. Nevertheless, both the Confederate migrants and the Maximilian regime that housed them remained a feature of Republican public discourse into the late 1860s. This was because, while the Mexican Empire no longer constituted a serious physical threat to the United States, it still represented a symbolic challenge to the nation. As a bastion of hierarchy and authoritarianism that opposed everything the post-emancipation Union stood for, Republicans claimed, the Mexican Empire still had the power to galvanize anti-republican elements across North America and even within the United States itself.

This claim was designed to play upon the anxieties of US Americans as they entered the early post–Civil War era. Republican-leaning editors, journalists, and politicians pushed the notion that ex-Confederates were conspiring with imperialists in Mexico as a way of emphasizing to the public that traitorous rebels were still active, both abroad and at home, and were capable of derailing the process of reunion then tentatively underway in the United States. Furthermore, the continued existence of a monarchy in Mexico was held up as a reminder that the United States had a long way to go before it could claim to have regained command of its sphere of influence in the southern portions of the Americas. Just as during the Civil War, domestic political concerns fueled these public discussions over the Mexican Question; the only way to clear North America of all enemies and thus make Union victory secure, Republicans insisted, was to enact a Radical program of social and political reform in the South. Also as in wartime, popular support for the Mexican Liberal cause remained high, especially in the Northern states, largely because it was in the interests of influential Republican politicians and newspapermen to keep it that way.

The Limits of Continental Fraternity

By the spring of 1865, the Juárez administration was operating from the northeastern Mexican state of Chihuahua, which shared its northern boundary with Texas. From there, the government-in-exile watched as the Confederate Army's Trans-Mississippi Department disintegrated and hundreds of rebel veterans passed through the border town of Paso del Norte into Mexico. Juarist officials forwarded details about this migration to Minister Matías Romero in the United States, who immediately saw how he might use it to his advantage. When Lincoln was assassinated in April 1865, Romero had dutifully expressed his government's grief over the passing of a global icon in the "cause of nationality and freedom."[7] In terms of the Juárez government's particular interests, however, the minister understood that the tragedy contained some rays of hope. Lincoln had been unwilling to shift from the neutral position toward the French Intervention first adopted by his administration in 1862. While on the campaign trail in 1864, however, the Republicans' vice presidential nominee Andrew Johnson had delivered some rousing speeches on the Mexican Question in which he had hinted that, once the Confederate rebellion was crushed, US troops would be sent southward to deal with the French.[8] When Johnson succeeded Lincoln as president, Romero was therefore optimistic that US foreign policymaking was now in the hands of someone willing to give the Juarists meaningful material assistance.

Romero's first interview with President Johnson took place on April 22. The minister opened the conversation by referring to the president's speeches on Mexico, remarking that he "rejoiced with all my heart" to have a true friend of the Mexican republic in the White House.[9] Romero later wrote to his government that Johnson had been visibly pleased by this praise. Sensing his advantage, the minister then raised the topic of the former rebels who were currently spilling into Mexico. These were not transient veterans wandering directionless across the continent, Romero insisted; rather, they were part of a coordinated movement. "Jefferson Davis and the other chiefs of the rebellion" were directing the migration, the minister explained, partly with the help of French general François Achille Bazaine, who was stationed just south of the border and who had apparently agreed "to receive fleeing Confederates."[10] Johnson listened to this information with interest, though he declined to commit to any action on the matter at that time. Nevertheless, when Romero left the White House that day he was optimistic that a robust US response to the situation would be forthcoming.

Romero was not the only one in Washington hoping that the president would inaugurate a new approach to the Mexican Question. A few days after his meeting with Johnson, the Mexican minister visited General Ulysses S. Grant, who was in the nation's capital to participate in the Union victory celebrations. The two men were already familiar with one another and had a good rapport, largely based on their aligned views regarding the Mexican issue. Grant shared Romero's uneasiness about the number of ex-Confederates crossing the border, for example. Indeed, his concern was such that in May he sent General Philip Sheridan to command US forces west of the Mississippi with instructions to monitor the migration. One telegraph from Sheridan, written in June, offers insight into the picture he painted for Grant regarding the border situation at that time. The surrenders of generals Kirby-Smith and Canby had been, in Sheridan's assessment, "for the most part a swindle."[11] Many of their forces had been disbanded before US commissioners had arrived, meaning that instead of being handed over to the US Army, much of their military equipment—arms, ammunition, horses, mules—had "been run over into Mexico."[12] At the same time, Sheridan added, "large and small bands of rebel soldiers and some citizens amounting to about two thousand have crossed the Rio Grande into Mexico."[13]

Certainly, Grant was irked that CSA weapons and munitions—property that now legally belonged to the United States—was being spirited across the border. What truly worried him, however, was Sheridan's assessment that all of this was being done in coordination with "representatives of the Imperial Government along the Rio Grande."[14] To both Sheridan and Grant, this indicated a broader conspiracy existing between the leaders of the now defunct Confederacy and the Maximilian authorities along with their French allies. As commander of the Union Army, Grant was able to take certain measures to address this issue. By early 1866, for example, he had increased Sheridan's Army of Observation to around 52,000 troops. Grant also allowed his generals in the Southwest to turn a blind eye to any war matériel leaving the United States that was destined for the Juarist army.[15]

Still, Grant knew that his power to prevent former rebels from crossing the border or to aid the Juarist war effort was limited. He therefore determined to work with Romero to lobby the Washington government to act on the matter.

Throughout the spring of 1865 the two men met with President Johnson numerous times, both together and separately. They also sent the president multiple letters explaining why the Confederate migration into Mexico constituted a national security issue. In June 1865, for example, Grant wrote to the president, warning him that the "large and organized bodies of rebels" then making their way to Mexico intended to use Maximilian's regime as the staging ground for a "long, expensive and bloody" guerilla campaign against US authorities in the Southwest.[16] Grant argued that maintaining "strict neutrality" toward the ongoing Franco-Mexican war would give these ex-Confederates time to gather men and munitions in preparation for this assault.[17] It was therefore imperative that the president engage in "open resistance to the establishment of Maximilian's Government in Mexico," thereby depriving ex-Confederates of a base from which to harass the United States.[18] Grant did not explicitly advocate an all-out invasion, but neither did he reject the eventual possibility of a war between the United States and the Mexican Empire.[19] At the very least, Grant recommended, the US government should grant "equal belligerent rights" to France and the Juarists, thereby allowing "either party to buy Arms or anything we have to sell and interpose no obsticle [*sic*] to their transit."[20] He also suggested that the US government "interpose no obsticle [*sic*] to the passage into Mexico of emigrants," by which he meant the movement of US volunteers into the Juarist army.[21]

In their meetings, President Johnson more than once told Grant and Romero that he sympathized with their position. At the same time, he admitted his reluctance to take any action that might provoke a conflict with France. This being the case, Johnson suggested that while it would maintain neutrality toward the Mexican situation, his government would not go out of its way to prevent any *un*official efforts launched from the United States to aid the Juarists. This was encouragement enough for Romero and Grant. Beginning in May, they put together a plan to march a body of US troops—between 50,000 and 60,000 in total—to southern Texas and muster them out. These men would then cross the border as private citizens and be absorbed into Mexican republican army units stationed in Chihuahua, Sinaloa, and other Juarist strongholds across northern Mexico.

Romero and Grant decided that they needed a figurehead who would both attract US volunteers into this expedition and ensure that these soldiers remained disciplined during its execution. Eventually they settled on General Schofield, who accepted their invitation in late June.[22] On July 19 more good news came; Grant informed Romero that he had briefed Johnson on their plan, and that the president had "authorized [Grant], if he judged it desirable, to proceed on his own account without consulting or arranging prior approval for his actions" from the White House.[23] Both Grant and Romero interpreted this as permission from the president to follow through with their scheme, so long as they were careful not to implicate the US federal government. On July 25 Grant wrote to Secretary of War Edwin Stanton to request that General Schofield be given a leave of absence for twelve months.[24] That same day he penned a letter to General Sheridan instructing him to prepare for Schofield's arrival at the border.[25]

In certain respects, Romero and Grant were aiming to bring order to an informal movement of US citizens into the Juarist army, which by the spring of 1865 was already well underway. This movement was largely composed of Union Army veterans, though not exclusively; a handful of articles appeared in newspapers from this time that described small bands of ex-Confederate soldiers also heading southward to join the Mexican republican military.[26] Such reports piqued the interest of Northern editors in particular, who wondered how these individuals could break with what they assumed was the universal anti-Juarist, pro-Maximilian sentiment in the former rebel states. It is possible that some of these Confederate veterans simply needed employment and, caring little which side of the Mexican conflict they fought for, found it most straightforward to enlist in the Juarist army. However, newspapers in the United States tended to offer more exciting explanations than this. The *St. Louis Republican*, for example, claimed to have letters from a US Army official based in Texas who had apparently conversed with some of these Confederate veterans and found that they resented "Louis Napoleon, who so grievously disappointed their hopes of intervention against the United States in the contest from which they have just emerged" and now intended to inflict a "partial revenge" upon him by "expelling his protégé from Mexican soil."[27] The *Republican*'s source added that a smaller number of these men had "expressed a willingness to go out of pure regard for the principle of the Monroe doctrine, and thought that all interlopers upon American soil ought to be driven off."[28] This explanation is plausible given that, as we have seen, there were segments of the Confederate population that had never abandoned the traditional reading of the Monroe Doctrine as an anti-European, anti-monarchical proclamation.

While the spectacle of ex-Confederates joining the Juarist army was intriguing, the far greater proportion of US Americans flocking to the Juarist ranks were veterans of the Union Army. In fact, the Juárez administration had been courting enlistees from the Northern states for some time. In August 1864, it had passed a law offering Mexican citizenship to all foreigners who joined the Liberal army in addition to a land bounty valued at $1,000 for private soldiers, $1,500 for officers from lieutenant to captain, and $2,000 for field grade officers.[29] The Juárez government had also dispatched agents who set up clandestine organizations to facilitate the recruitment and transportation of US volunteers to Mexico. Most were established in large port cities across the Union and Union-occupied territories, including the Mexican Club of New York, the Monroe League in San Francisco, and New Orleans's Defenders of the Monroe Doctrine.[30]

Following Appomattox, the Juarist recruitment business in the United States boomed; agents from California to Pennsylvania reported that dozens of Union veterans were queuing outside their offices each day or else were milling around docks hoping to catch the next ship heading south.[31] This surge in recruitment activity was soon making national headlines. In May the *Philadelphia Press* reported that "several organizations are being perfected in this city" for the purpose of transporting recruits to Mexico.[32] Meanwhile "over 5000 in the city of New York alone have already enrolled themselves" and "it is also hinted that vessels are being or will be fitted out at Baltimore and manned by hardy crews" destined to join the ranks of the Juarist army.[33] The *New York Tribune* even worried that the sheer number of US Americans seeking to "volunteer their services to the republican cause in Mexico" would soon "complicate our foreign relations" with France by compelling the French minister in Washington, DC, to submit a formal complaint to the State Department.[34]

While Romero was pleased by this spontaneous movement, he believed that it needed to be controlled. Juarist recruitment agents typically worked in isolation, leading to confusion and sometimes competition among them when it came to procuring US volunteers and arranging for their transportation to Mexico.[35] In addition to this, the minister had reservations about allowing into his country large numbers of US veterans who were not answerable to any particular military commander or government. The minister therefore hoped that his plan with Grant would channel US Americans' evident enthusiasm to fight in the Franco-Mexican conflict into a coordinated and well-managed expedition.[36]

Though President Johnson had instructed them to keep their plan covert, Romero and Grant had good reason to believe that many people in the United States would approve of it should it ever become public. After all, it was not just Union veterans who were showing their support for the Juarists; in the heady months following Union victory, people across the Northern states in particular attended rallies in public squares and city halls to celebrate the Mexican republican cause.[37] Many of these occasions were arranged by the same Unionist patriotic organizations that had hosted pro-Juarist events during the Civil War. A July meeting at the Cooper Institute in New York, for example, was organized by the city's Union League to express "sympathy and respect" for the "Mexican Patriot Club," an association of Juarist politicians, diplomats, and military officers who had fled to the United States to escape Imperial forces.[38] Among the speakers at this occasion was Joshua Leavitt, the reverend whose 1863 pamphlet "The Monroe Doctrine" had made him something of an authority on the Mexican Question on the Northern speaking circuit. Leavitt began his speech by reminding his audience that, in their moment of victory, they must not forget their brothers-in-arms still fighting below the border. "The blow which struck down the Republic of Mexico was aimed at the life of the Imperial Republic of the North," Leavitt pronounced. "We ourselves have happily escaped the blow. A wonderful providence has rescued us from the threatened destruction. But our neighbors have felt its full weight. They stand in our place. They are suffering on our account far more than for their own. It is not in the nature of the American people to see this with indifference."[39]

Leavitt called on the Johnson administration to "go to the extreme that law, wisdom, and justice allowed, to strengthen, restore, and advance the Republic of Mexico."[40] These were bold words, but their meaning was ambiguous; Leavitt did not specify what just and wise assistance to Mexico might consist of, nor when it should be offered. Other commentators were more forthright on such matters, however. Conspicuous among the participants at these public events were high-ranking US Army officials, who in the months following Appomattox constituted a new and forceful voice calling for the United States to adopt a more decisively pro-Juarist Mexican policy. In July, for example, the commander of the Department of the Pacific, Major-General G. W. Wright, presided over "a tremendous popular meeting" in San Francisco at which "great enthusiasm prevailed, and strong resolutions were adopted urging the endorsement of the Monroe doctrine."[41] In New York the following month a crowd that had gathered outside the residence of Liberal general Jesús González Ortega cheered at the reading of a letter written by General Sheridan that insisted that the United States join the fight to bring down the Mexican Empire on the grounds that "our work in crushing rebellion will not be done until this takes place."[42]

Much like General Grant, these military officials emphasized both ideological and national security considerations when arguing the case for assisting the Juarists. As General Nathaniel P. Banks put it during a Fourth of July speech in New Orleans, France's attempt to take "advantage of our domestic troubles" to gain a "foothold" in North America had demonstrated that the security of each New World republic was dependent on that of its neighbors, and that an invasion of one was a threat to them all. In recognizing this, Banks claimed to have finally fully understood President Monroe's injunction forty years earlier that US Americans would consider any "new European successes on this continent" as "destructive to our liberties."[43] "The future of the American continent is for Americans," Banks proclaimed, and whenever a "strange, if not hostile, flag is on our borders . . . it must be—will be driven away."[44]

Other voices adding to this pro-Juarist clamor came from among the nation's political classes. During the months immediately following the Confederate surrender, there was a surge in congressional interest in the Mexican Question, particularly among Republicans. "Yesterday John Conness, senator from California, saw me," Romero wrote to his government in late May.[45] Conness had been "among those who believed that while the Civil War lasted the United States should not even speak of Mexican affairs," the minister continued, but with the rebellion now terminated the congressman had told Romero that he finally felt "at full liberty to express his sympathies" for the Juarists and to take up their cause in Congress.[46] Romero explained that "Conness's change is very significant" because it reflected a wider trend: "many people of no less influence have experienced similar changes since the war ended in this country."[47]

Those congressmen who like Conness underwent these "changes" likely felt some genuine ideological affinity with the Juarist cause. It is also probable that many of them shared the concerns of certain US military leaders regarding the security threat the Franco-Mexican conflict posed to the still-reunifying United States. However, these politicians' sudden decision to take up the Mexican Question must also be examined in light of their domestic political interests. In the spring and summer of 1865, President Johnson took advantage of the congressional recess to push ahead with his plan to readmit the former rebel states into the Union. His terms for reentry were minimal and aimed at facilitating a speedy reunion. For example, the president only required that the Southern states' new constitutions endorse the Thirteenth Amendment; all other matters relating to race relations would be left to their legislatures to decide. Johnson also offered amnesty to all ex-rebels who pledged loyalty to the Union, except for the military and political leadership of the former Confederacy, who would have to personally appeal to the president. A presidential pardon entitled a former rebel to all land that had been confiscated from them during the war, including any that had been distributed to formerly enslaved people by the Freedmen's Bureau.

Republican legislators in Washington, DC, saw trouble lurking in the president's path to reunion. There was nothing in Johnson's terms to prevent the original leaders of the rebellion from regaining control of their state legislatures, for instance, or to stop them from using this power to ensnare freed people in new coercive labor systems that sidestepped the Thirteenth Amendment. Determined to derail the president's Reconstruction policy, leading Republicans looked for ways to discredit Johnson in the eyes of the public. Critiquing the administration's Mexican policy became one of the methods they utilized to achieve this—a minor but nonetheless useful rhetorical weapon in their political arsenal.

Beginning in the fall of 1865, congressional Republicans launched a volley of resolutions relating to the Mexican Question, many of them written in consultation with Minister Romero. Few offered much in the way of concrete policy prescriptions. In December, for example, Representative Robert T. van Horn requested more "information" from the administration on the condition of the Maximilian government to enable Congress to consider "what measures might be taken to restore free government in Mexico."[48] That same month, Senator Benjamin Wade and Representative Robert C. Schenk of Ohio introduced a vaguely worded joint resolution suggesting "that the President of the United States . . . take such steps concerning [the situation in Mexico] as will vindicate the recognized policy and protect the honor and interests of our Government."[49] In short, in terms of substance these resolutions were pretty toothless. However, their value lay in providing Republican congressmen with opportunities to deliver speeches on the floor of Congress condemning President Johnson for neglecting the United States' so-called "Sister Republic."

Had the Romero-Grant plan to transport US troops to Mexico been executed, these Republicans would have been forced to outline precisely what action they believed the United States ought to take on the Mexican Question. After all, news that thousands of US veterans had been absorbed en masse into the Juarist army would have required a response, approving or otherwise, from Congress. As it turned out, however, the scheme never came to fruition, thanks in large part to the intervention of Secretary of State William Seward. The secretary had been absent from the State Department for much of the spring of 1865. Initially he had been convalescing following the attack on his life by would-be assassin Lewis Powell, a co-conspirator of John Wilkes Booth. Then in June, Seward's wife Frances died, and the secretary temporarily stepped back from his cabinet duties to enter a period of mourning.

Seward returned to the State Department in July, whereupon he learned of Romero and Grant's plan. Determined that nothing should undermine US neutrality toward the war in Mexico and thereby complicate relations with France, Seward arranged a meeting with General Schofield, the man who Grant had tapped to lead US volunteers across the border. Seward suggested to Schofield that, before he undertook this expedition, he should first travel to France "as a confidential agent of this government."[50] Once in Paris, Schofield would secure an audience with Louis-Napoleon to warn him of an impending "rupture between France and the United States" unless the emperor immediately withdrew his troops from Mexico.[51] An incensed Romero would later tell his government that, "by flattering Schofield with a mission to France," Seward aimed to "separate Schofield from the undertaking" in Mexico.[52] This is precisely what happened. Schofield boarded a ship for France in November; the following January the general wrote to the US State Department from Paris to explain that, despite having met Louis-Napoleon at several balls, he had been unable to obtain a private audience with the emperor. Seward allowed Schofield to linger a few months longer, waiting until May 1866 to instruct the general to return to Washington, DC. By this time, the Romero-Grant scheme had fallen apart.

Meanwhile events abroad helped Seward to persuade President Johnson against military involvement by the United States in the Mexican imbroglio. Throughout the spring and summer of 1865, French liberal leaders such as Jules Favre and Victor Hugo intensified their calls on Louis-Napoleon to end his Mexican venture. "In Mexico," read one Liberal amendment submitted to the *Corps Legislatif*, "we more than ever deplore the blood shed for a foreign prince, the national sovereignty unrecognized, and our future policy badly entangled."[53] What Louis-Napoleon had promised would be a quick, decisive conquest, French liberals argued, had become a grinding war of dubious morality and unclear benefits for France. In addition to this, trouble was brewing on the European Continent, where the Prussian chancellor Otto von Bismarck had signaled his intention to unify all German-speaking regions, including those held by France. The French military, it seemed, might soon be needed closer to home. For these reasons, Seward assured Johnson, Louis-Napoleon was looking to wash his hands of Mexico and leave Maximilian to stand or fall without the aid of French bayonets. However, if the United States chose this moment to send troops over the border, the French emperor would be compelled to keep his forces in Mexico to defend both Maximilian's government and French honor against US aggression. Apparently, the president was swayed by Seward's reasoning; for the remainder of his term,

Johnson did not entertain any more plans, official or otherwise, to offer US military aid to Mexico. In their meetings with the president, both Grant and Romero found Johnson increasingly inclined to echo Seward's argument that the Mexican Empire would come to a natural end on its own without the need for US interference.[54]

While Seward had thwarted Romero's attempt to funnel US troops south of the border, events on the ground in Mexico hampered the minister's ability to sustain popular enthusiasm in the United States for a more actively pro-Juarist foreign policy. Early 1865 had seen Mexican republican troops win a series of important battles along Mexico's northwest coast and northern frontier. In April, for example, Liberal forces under General Miguel Negrete captured Saltillo and Monterrey from the Imperialists. Negrete then headed toward Matamoros, seizing a string of towns along the Rio Grande on the way. Meanwhile Liberal colonel Pedro José Méndez took Ciudad Victoria and Ciudad Tula in April and June, respectively. However, by late summer it seemed that the Juarists' good fortune had run out. Imperial forces under General Bazaine staged a counteroffensive that reversed many of Negrete's advances and culminated in August with Imperialists taking Chihuahua. The Juárez government, which had been using Chihuahua as its provisional capital, was forced to flee northward. Then in October, Imperial colonel Ramón Méndez took Amatlán. From there, the fighting grew messy. Juárez returned to Chihuahua on November 20, but was driven out again in early December. Meanwhile General Escobedo finally captured Matamoros for the Liberals, only to be ousted by troops under General Pierre on November 25.

This back-and-forth created some confusion in the United States. For his part, Romero fed information to the US public through various channels—sympathetic politicians, military officials, newspaper editors—that highlighted Juarist victories and emphasized these troops' unwavering fighting spirit.[55] These encouraging assessments were contradicted by reports that arrived in the United States from other sources, however. Ohio's *Dayton Daily Empire*, for example, summarized a letter from a "distinguished officer of the late Confederate army," who presumably had fled to Mexico after the Civil War, which described "the 'Liberal' cause as perfectly hopeless, and the Empire firmly established."[56] It is unsurprising that ex-Confederates ensconced in the bosom of Maximilian's empire would wish to present a positive image of the condition and future prospects of their host government. Yet discouraging updates about the state of the Juarist war effort were also coming from more neutral and even some pro-Liberal news sources. In August, for example, the *Detroit Free Press*, a publication largely sympathetic to the Juarist cause, reprinted a letter penned by the *London Times*'s Paris correspondent that gave an ambiguous assessment of the situation in Mexico. "Often beaten, repeatedly, as we have been told, utterly scattered and dispersed, the Juarists still manage to keep to the field and give a great deal of trouble," the correspondent explained.[57] Two months later the Mexico City correspondent for the *New York Tribune*, an organ consistently in the Juarist camp, painted an even more dispiriting picture. The Juarist military was now comprised of no more than "a few homeless and wandering squads of guerillas, amounting, perhaps, to 7,000 men in all," the writer explained, most of whom were "scattered all over the country in detachments of 100 to 1,000" and could do little more than stage "the capture of a few mules and horses, the burning and assassination of a few Imperialists, the arrest of diligences and deeds of a few highway robbers."[58]

Along with growing uncertainty over the state of the Juarist war effort there was a fresh wave of confusion about Louis-Napoleon's long-term intentions toward Mexico. Throughout late 1865, US newspapers carried reports indicating that Louis-Napoleon was sending boatloads of munitions and soldiers across the Atlantic to reinforce Imperial forces.[59] Then, in January 1866, the emperor made the stunning announcement that he would withdraw French troops from Mexico in three stages, with the final contingent slated to depart in November 1867. The news was met with great celebration among pro-Juarist organs in the United States.[60] Before long, however, rumors began to circulate that cast doubt on the sincerity of Louis-Napoleon's pledge. In June 1866, for example, the *Georgia Weekly Telegraph* relayed information provided by a US diplomat in Mexico that suggested that "the withdrawal of the French troops will make no difference as regards the military force of the Empire."[61] The newspaper explained that "the greater part of the French troops are to remain for more than a year" in Mexico and "in the meantime ample arrangements have been made, to keep the Mexican army up to the present standard of efficiency, by occasional reinforcements of Austrian and Belgian troops."[62] Furthermore, "hundreds of the French soldiers, whose term of service has expired, instead of returning to France" planned to "remain in Mexico."[63] Though ostensibly residing there as civilian settlers, these veterans would in fact serve as a dormant cell of the Imperial Army, which, "in case of need . . . would of course enter the Mexican army, of which they would form a powerful veteran corps."[64] With ambiguity growing around Louis-Napoleon's long-term plans, some organs in the United States began to rethink their advocacy for US action in Mexico. Was France really preparing to withdraw? If so, US involvement could prompt Louis-Napoleon to backtrack and redouble his military presence in Mexico. Or was Louis-Napoleon's pledge to withdraw only a ruse? In either case, an intervention to support what now appeared to be a flailing Juarist military might end with the United States fighting a fortified Imperial force south of the border single-handed.[65]

Throughout the Civil War various public figures in the Union, not to mention large swathes of the national press, had promised that once the rebellion was defeated the United States would come to Mexico's aid. As we have seen, however, when the time came events conspired against such an outcome. Secretary Seward skillfully maneuvered to ensure that the Johnson administration stayed on the track of neutrality, for example, while Louis-Napoleon's 1866 announcement of the intended withdrawal of French troops from Mexico undermined arguments in favor of US intervention by making such a venture appear unnecessary. Still, these were not the only reasons why the United States failed to pursue a more forthrightly pro-Juarez policy following Appomattox. A closer look at how the US press discussed the Mexican Question in the months following Confederate surrender reveals that another important factor was the growing complexity of the Reconstruction issue in US politics.

The Mexican Question and Early Reconstruction Politics

During the Civil War, certain portions of the Confederate press had loudly condemned what they saw as the abuse of federal power by President Davis and his allies in government. At their most heated, they had warned of a monarchist cabal taking over Richmond in secret alliance with the priests, imperialists, and monarchists then conspiring to overthrow Mexico. After Appomattox, these same publications pointed to the movement of ex-Confederate military leaders and politicians into Maximilian's Mexico to insist that their allegations had been accurate. "The rear guard of the Confederacy . . . will retreat toward its old, but never before open friends," North Carolina's *Daily Progress* foretold in May 1865, "and do its last fighting as a two-fold work in support of its new ally and against the old authority of the government they would have destroyed."[66]

These Southern newspapers shared General Grant's concern that self-exiled rebels would use Maximilian's regime as a base from which to launch guerilla warfare against the United States. They were somewhat vague regarding what Washington, DC's response to this apparent danger ought to be, however. Certainly, some of them were comfortable enough deploying the language of the Monroe Doctrine. In North Carolina, for example, references to the Doctrine appeared frequently in the summer of 1865 during the campaign to elect delegates to the state's upcoming constitutional convention. This was particularly so among politicians and newspaper editors formerly associated with the state's wartime Conservative faction. Historian Andrew L. Slap explains that after Appomattox, these Conservatives "distanced themselves from the [Confederate] war effort," including the doctrine of secession, while signaling their willingness to accede to some of the federal government's demands in the hopes that President Johnson would deal with them leniently, perhaps offering them speedy amnesties and the return of their lost property.[67] No doubt aware of how the Monroe Doctrine had become associated with notions of patriotism in the wartime Union, these political leaders used this language as a way to signal their loyalty to the restored United States. In September, for example, the *New Berne Times* published the platform of two convention candidates, Charles C. Clark and Ulysses H. Ritch, which called on Southerners to embrace "loyalty and devotion to the Union," "the death of slavery," and a willingness to stand up "boldly for the Monroe Doctrine."[68] That same month a meeting of "Union men" in New Berne nominated Clark and Ritch to the state convention and issued a series of resolutions that included, among other things, an affirmation of "the wisdom and sound policy of the "Monroe Doctrine," which the meeting defined as resistance to "native-born or foreign imported emperors or kings" who attempted "to sway their insulting scepters on the soil of North America."[69]

Invoking the Monroe Doctrine in the heat of a political campaign was one thing; endorsing US intervention in the ongoing Franco-Mexican war was another. Indeed, William Holden's *Daily Standard*, previously a leading voice in the Confederate Peace movement and now a standard-bearer of reconciliation, was deeply troubled by rumors circulating in the summer of 1865 that "North Carolina has been called upon to furnish thirty-five thousand men to the United States government, for the purpose of invading Mexico."[70] Such a measure, the newspaper insisted, was unnecessary because "Maximilian's throne is fast crumbling. . . . Without more material aid from France at an early moment, he will most probably be forced to flee that country."[71] When pushed on the question of policy, other like-minded publications chose to endorse nonmilitary assistance to the Juarists rather than outright intervention. "The Mexican republicans want money rather than men," North Carolina's *Daily Progress* explained in September 1865, "and the friends of the Monroe doctrine would, no doubt, contribute cheerfully to assist them. . . . In this way, and by this means, the Emperor Maximilian would very soon find out that he grasps a barren scepter, without giving our government any further trouble."[72]

A similar pattern played out in other portions of Southern public discourse, especially among former Peace or Unionist publications. In Tennessee, for example, the *Nashville Daily Union* insisted in November 1865 that "it has not yet been made to appear, in any form, that the people of Mexico prefer a monarchical form of government, and still less that they prefer the Archduke Maximilian for their own monarch."[73] "He is not there because the will of the people placed him there," the newspaper continued, "he was put there by force—a force *foreign* to the Mexican nation."[74] Nevertheless, the *Daily Union* was clear that the United States should not involve itself in the Mexican embroglio. Assuming that the unpopularity of the Intervention among the French people would eventually compel Louis-Napoleon to withdraw his troops, the newspaper predicted that soon Maximilian would be left to stand or fall on his own. At that point Mexicans would be able "to decide freely what form of government they may prefer, and their decision thus given will be entitled to respect."[75] Alabama's *Montgomery Daily Mail* thought likewise. "Maximilian is in Mexico," the newspaper explained, even though "we wish he were not."[76] Given this reality, the most practical course open to the United States was to "let Mexico henceforth alone."[77] If Mexicans truly desired to keep their republic, the newspaper suggested, then they would fight for it.

In part, these newspapers' refusal to support US military action in Mexico was due to their low opinion of the Mexican republic itself. During the Civil War, Southern Peace advocates had condemned France's violation of Mexican sovereignty without evincing much faith in the Mexican people themselves. This remained true after Appomattox. In one article published in May 1865, for example, the *Daily Progress* lambasted France's criminal invasion of Mexico before acknowledging that the latter had made itself easy prey for ambitious imperial powers by presenting to the world a chaotic "scene of interminable strife" and arguing that Mexico was inhabited by a race cursed with "the darkness of ignorance."[78] The *Daily Standard* was only a little more generous. "President Juarez bears himself most nobly," the newspaper conceded in September 1865, "in adversity he has displayed good and great qualities, and there is scarcely an American heart that does not sympathize with him in his struggle against foreign intervention and despotism."[79] Still, a respectable showing on the battlefield did not translate into a capacity for responsible self-government. "We must recollect that Mexico has failed to govern herself for many long years, and has been cursed by the fell spirit of discord and faction," the newspaper continued, and so while "to all human appearances Juarez and his party are the defenders of enlightened, progressive, republican principles," this was no guarantee that they could maintain a functioning government if and when they regained control of their country.[80] The *Nashville Daily Union* similarly praised those Juarists who were "making hopeful resistance to the foreign usurpation" while reminding readers that "the word Mexico means anarchy" and arguing that even if they succeeded in defending their republic, Mexicans would likely struggle to maintain it once the French invasion was over.[81] With their faith in their so-called Sister Republic lukewarm at best, it was little wonder that these publications were reluctant to call for US soldiers to risk their lives for its defense.

Another reason for these newspapers' coolness toward a US intervention was their assessment of the Mexican Question's relative importance compared to the issue of Reconstruction. In the spring and summer of 1865 these Southern publications, most of which had been Unionist or Peace organs during the Civil War, were, on the whole, encouraged by President Johnson's plans for a speedy reunion and anxious that no other issue enter the national political agenda that might derail its consummation. This included the Mexican Question. As the *Nashville Daily Union* explained, it would be most unwise of the "President to allow this country to drift into war with France about Mexico" when his first responsibility was to "do all within his power to repair the damages of our civil war, and establish throughout the land the conditions of peace which are the guarantees of liberty and Union."[82] The *Daily Standard* elaborated on this theme in August 1865. "The administration has two great burdens upon it at present," the newspaper explained: "the reorganization of the Southern States, and a permanent and healthy regulation of our finances. When these things are satisfactorily disposed of, then Maximilian will be attended to, if, in the meantime, he is not forced to leave Mexico, as he most probably will be."[83] The *Daily Progress* agreed: "With all our prowess, actual and supposed, hostile relations with France would be to us a great calamity" because they would distract the government and people of the United States from the vital task of reunion.[84]

Only a year before the *Daily Progress* had—at least rhetorically—contemplated a North-South invasion of Mexico as a means of ending the Civil War and paving the way for the development of an amicable relationship between the Union and Confederacy as independent republics. Now, however, the question of the day was not separation, but reunion. In these new circumstances, the newspaper surmised that a venture into Mexico might derail what could be a relatively quick and painless reconciliation of the Northern and Southern states. "The real danger of the hour to us are not from Maximilian or his protector, the Emperor of the French," the newspaper explained, "but that in watching where there is at least small danger, we shall forget our immediate concerns."[85] In short, having now calculated that an invasion south of the border would distract from rather than advance sectional reconciliation, this and likeminded newspapers jettisoned the plan altogether.

Unfortunately for these Southern organs, the push for a speedy reunion was about to run into serious difficulties. The summer and fall of 1865 saw the former rebel states reform their governments. Under President Johnson's Reconstruction plan, the new state legislatures were able to pass what became known as Black Codes, which were state laws that severely restricted the economic and civil liberties of freed people. On December 13, 1865, Congress created the Joint Committee on Reconstruction to inquire into the nature of these new Southern state governments. The committee heard from a total of 144 witnesses, most of whom were US Army officers stationed in the South. Collectively, their testimony painted a troubling picture. "Many of the old politicians" who had spearheaded secession were now "engaged in promoting dissatisfaction with the Government," Secretary of the Commonwealth Charles H. Lewis said of Virginia.[86] Meanwhile General Benjamin Henry Grierson informed the Committee that in Alabama, Mississippi, and Tennessee, white people felt no remorse for the part they had played in the rebellion; rather, "their only regret seemed to be that they had not the means to carry out their designs."[87] General Charles H. Howard similarly reported that a "great many persons" in South Carolina "exhibited ill-feeling" toward the federal government and "a disposition to get around" the Thirteenth Amendment "in any way they could."[88] "If the military forces were withdrawn from South Carolina," the general warned, "it would be a source of great injury to the freedmen throughout the State."[89] Thanks in part to such testimony, concern among Northerners regarding the persistence of rebellious sentiments in the South grew, and with it their uneasiness at President Johnson's efforts to welcome white Southerners back into the national fold with their former political rights intact.

As Reconstruction became more fraught, publications such as the *Daily Progress* and the *Weekly Standard* almost completely ceased reporting on Mexican affairs. A survey of these newspapers between late 1865 and the end of the decade turns up only a handful of perfunctory summaries regarding current events in that country, many of which were reprinted from other newspapers. These portions of the Southern press had apparently lost interest in the Confederate migration, the ongoing war against Maximilian's regime, and the debate over the definition and implications of the Monroe

Doctrine. There are a number of possible explanations for this. Among the most plausible is that, as has already been discussed, these publications saw domestic and foreign policy as existing in separate realms. As the Reconstruction Question became more challenging, they therefore scaled down their coverage of foreign issues in order to concentrate their readers' attention on more pressing domestic matters. It is also possible that, unnerved by Northerners' rising suspicion of unreconstructed Southerners, the editors of these newspapers were reluctant to do anything that would breed more distrust between the sections of the Union. If there was still any hope of an amicable reunion between North and South, they may have surmised, it would be best to refrain from reminding Northerners of the unreconciled rebels currently lodged in the bosom of the Mexican Empire.

Interestingly, the notion that Reconstruction and the Mexican Question inhabited distinct spheres both in policymaking and public discourse was not the typical view among US newspapers at this time. For large portions of the Northern Republican press, for example, the two issues were intimately intertwined. A useful illustration of this can be found in the way that such publications responded to certain decrees issued by Maximilian in September 1865. The Mexican emperor was keen to encourage white Southerners to settle in the more remote territories then under his control in order to prevent these lands from falling into the hands of the Juarist army. With this in mind, Maximilian announced a decree that mandated that all Black immigrants who entered Mexico from the United States must be contracted to a patron for a period of five years. The Mexican republic had outlawed slavery in 1837. By this measure, however, Maximilian signaled to Southerners in the United States that if they pledged loyalty to the Mexican Empire, they could come to Mexico with what remained of their human property and attempt to reestablish south of the border the plantations they had lost during the Civil War.[90]

Minister Romero first learned of the decree from dispatches sent to him by his home government. He immediately forwarded copies of the document to friendly newspaper editors, including those at the *New York Herald* and the *Washington National Intelligencer*.[91] The minister also drafted several resolutions condemning the decree, which he then passed on to allies in Congress. One resolution, ultimately submitted to the House by Ohio congressman James Garfield, "called for the correspondence on . . . the so-called decree that attempts to reestablish slavery in the [Mexican] Republic."[92] With Romero's help, news of the decree spread fast. The reaction among certain Black-run newspapers that had been formed in the wake of the Civil War was particularly intense. "Not satisfied with offending the United States by overthrowing the republicanism of Mexico," the *South Carolina Leader* fumed in November 1865, "Maximilian has added to his impertinence . . . slavery under the name of serfdom or peonage" in an effort to "persuade persons whom he calls 'emigrants' to settle in the country."[93] More well-established Northern organs were equally incensed. "The difference between this 'patronage' and undisguised slavery," Connecticut newspaper the *Hartford Daily Courant* declared, "is too small to be appreciated."[94] The *New York Tribune* likewise denounced the "heinous innovation" as a clear invitation to "implacable slaveholders" to spirit their human property across the Rio Grande.[95]

By this time, reports that self-exiled Confederates planned to stage an attack on the United States were appearing with less frequency in the US press than during the months immediately following Appomattox. The slavery decree, however, was taken by some Northern publications as a sign that the migrant Southerners had no intention of quietly retiring to private life in Mexico. A lengthy article published in the *New York Herald* in January 1866, for example, acknowledged that "Confederates are no longer soldiers in arms to whom the French can lend some assistance in their campaigns against our troops."[96] Recent efforts to resurrect slavery in Mexico, however, pointed to a larger project now being developed by rebels below the border that constituted "a deliberately cogitated threat" to the United States.[97] Their aim, the *Herald* explained, was to reconstitute themselves as a slavocracy, exercising all of the economic, social, and political influence in Mexico that they had once enjoyed as slaveholders in the United States. These ex-Confederates would then take control of the domestic and, more importantly, foreign policies of the Mexican Empire, which under their direction would become "a source of uneasiness to the United States" by blocking its efforts to spread liberal democracy throughout the Americas and promoting instead the insidious doctrines of slavery, hierarchy, and monarchism.[98]

Other newspapers added that the emergence of slave-based colonies in Mexico would provide inspiration and encouragement to Southerners in the United States who were currently resisting the post-emancipation order taking shape around them. As the *New York Tribune* pointed out, Maximilian's slavery decree did "not essentially differ from the . . . slave laws and new apprenticeship forms" recently passed by the reformed Southern state legislatures.[99] Indeed, the newspaper continued, ex-Confederates in Mexico and those remaining in the United States were evidently conspiring in a joint effort to "conserve all the despotism of Slavery" both above and below the border "while rendering its legal aspect more plausible."[100]

Even by 1866, then, certain portions of the Republican press were still adamant that the Mexican Empire posed a very real threat to the peace and stability of the reunifying United States. This did not lead them to call for the Johnson administration to reconsider neutrality toward the Franco-Mexican war, however. As previously discussed, multiple factors contributed to this moderation. Another, yet to be explored, was their concern regarding the persistence of disloyalty in the Southern states. During the congressional hearings on Reconstruction in March 1866, one witness testified that "a great many [in Virginia] . . . would be very glad to see the [United States] involved in a foreign war, in hopes that they could again get up a secession party in the South."[101] Major General George Henry Thomas similarly warned that ex-rebel leaders in Georgia, Alabama, and Mississippi anticipated that "in case the government should become involved in foreign war" they would "watch their opportunities to strike for independence of the States lately in rebellion."[102] At that time, there was more than one foreign power that the United States could conceivably find itself at war with. Tensions were running high with Great Britain over the unsettled *Alabama* claims and other issues relating to the Canadian border, for example.[103] However, according to General Benjamin Grierson, unrepentant ex-rebels viewed a conflict between the United States and France over Mexico to be more likely and, from their perspective, more advantageous. As the general explained, "in such an event . . . the enemies of the Government throughout the South" would declare their support for France, rise up in insurrection against the United States, and "attempt again its destruction."[104] Such reports suggested that US military action in Mexico would expose how little had yet been accomplished in the work of reconciliation in the postwar United States, and possibly even roll back the small amount that had been achieved so far.

In the weeks immediately following the close of the Civil War, buoyed by Union victory and convinced that the republic's domestic enemies had been vanquished, some major newspapers in the North had called on their government to settle scores with certain foreign rivals, beginning with the French in Mexico. "A few months ago 'intervention' was our bug-bear, with the constant threat of European despots and their mercenary subjects," the *Chicago Tribune* had pronounced, "but today 'intervention' is our threat and their terror."[105] A year on, however, this confidence in the totality of Union victory—and therefore in the United States' ability to wage war on foes beyond its borders—had faded. For those Southern publications that had never fully embraced the Mexican republican cause, it was easy to simply ignore the wider continental context and focus on the work of reunion at home. For portions of the Northern press, however, goings-on in Mexico remained relevant not despite of but due to the growing complexities of Reconstruction. The Confederate exodus to Mexico, for example, showed that rebel elements within the United States still possessed global connections. Meanwhile apparent efforts to recreate the peculiar institution inside the Maximilian regime was proof that Union victory had not ushered in a new era of liberty in the New World, and that bastions of conservative antirepublicanism could thrive both within the post-emancipation United States and on its borders.

It is tempting to think that, following Appomattox, most US Americans simply lost interest in the Mexican Question and foreign policy more broadly. The above discussion, however, indicates that it is perhaps more accurate to attribute their declining enthusiasm for action in Mexico at least in part to a creeping sense of national fragility that gripped US society toward the end of 1865 and into 1866. During this time the growing controversy around Reconstruction showed that the US republic was not yet ready to assert its former position as the chief power of the Western Hemisphere. As we shall see, as 1866 and 1867 progressed certain political leaders would make use of the uncertainty this realization created to generate popular support for certain aspects of the Radical Republicans' Reconstruction agenda.

Non-Intervention and Radical Reconstruction

Throughout the first half of 1866 the congressional Joint Committee on Reconstruction continued to gather testimony from generals, politicians, and formerly enslaved persons in the South. This done, the Committee issued a report that concluded that the former rebel states were "disorganized communities, without civil government, and without constitutions" and accused Southern legislators of writing laws designed to effectively re-enslave Black Southerners.[106] In response the Committee introduced the Fourteenth Amendment to provide legal protection of freed people's civil rights. President Johnson's efforts to obstruct the amendment only strengthened congressional Republicans' resolve to wrest control over Reconstruction policy from the executive branch. On June 8, its galleries overflowing with spectators, the Senate voted for the Fourteenth Amendment by a count of 33 to 11. Five days later it was approved by the House. Although it would take another two years for the states to ratify the amendment, this was a landmark moment in the advance of Black rights following emancipation.

Spurred on by these gains, the popular tide against presidential Reconstruction grew. Midterm elections that took place between September 1866 and April 1867 led to Republicans taking control of both houses of Congress with majorities large enough to overrule a presidential veto. The new Congress immediately began to pass legislation aimed at effecting a root-and-branch transformation of the South's political and social order. Among these was the First Reconstruction Act of March 1867, also known as the Military Reconstruction Act, which divided the former rebel states into five districts and placed each one under martial law; the districts were to be governed by a military general with the support of federal troops. Later that month the Second Reconstruction Act put these troops in charge of registering voters and overseeing elections in the Southern territories. It also required all voters to recite the registration oath pledging their obedience to the Constitution and laws of the United States. Finally, Congress announced that, in order to be readmitted into the Union with all of their former rights and privileges in place, the ex-rebel states must redraft their state constitutions to include ratification of the Fourteenth Amendment.

For Radical Republicans this was the beginning of a long-cherished plan to reform the United States into a truly democratic nation. Still, some of them understood that not all of their countrymen shared their willingness to demolish and rebuild Southern society. Certainly this was the view of Henry Winter Davis, who had spent time during the Civil War as chairman of the House Foreign Relations Committee but in 1864 had decided against running for reelection to Congress. Davis remained a keen and vocal commentator on contemporary politics, however. For example, in 1865, while speaking at a Fourth of July celebration in Chicago, he saw fit to caution his fellow Republicans against "always talking of justice and humanity to the negro" when explaining their plans for Southern Reconstruction to the public.[107] Instead, Davis advised them to emphasize how their measures were vital to "our safety" as a republic.[108]

This advice aligned with an attempt then underway by certain Republican-leaning newspapers to portray the recent raft of congressional Reconstruction legislation as designed to advance national security, rather than social revolution. For example, the *New York Times* defended the fact that the Reconstruction Acts disenfranchised large swathes of the white Southern male population on the grounds that temporary exclusion from public life would give these ex-Confederates time to adjust to the new "laws of our national existence."[109] This would ensure that, once they were brought back into the national fold, these former rebels would no longer pose a threat to the "harmonious working of the national machinery."[110] The *Chicago Tribune* used the same logic to argue the case for Black male suffrage, which would later become another key component of congressional Reconstruction in the form of the Fifteenth Amendment. The newspaper argued that Black voters would "counteract the treason of the late rebels" by diluting the power of the white Southern vote.[111] In this way, the enfranchisement of Black men would prevent the old Slave Power from reestablishing a monopoly over Southern politics. The subtext of these arguments was that, properly understood, Radical Reconstruction was nothing more than a continuation of the wartime effort to eliminate the Slave Power and so ensure the reunified US republic lasting domestic peace.[112]

Those who presented Radical Reconstruction as a guarantee against future civil discord likely hoped that the message would resonate with those in the postwar United States who still worried about their country's internal cohesion. Still, the pledge invoked rather sedate images of domestic tranquility that, however appealing to a population emerging from civil war, would do little to excite more energizing popular sentiments of national pride or ambition. It was perhaps for this reason that some leading Republican organs emphasized that internal stability was the key to something larger—specifically, that only by steadying its political institutions and culture in this way could the United States regain its former status as the global model of functioning self-governance and with it preeminence among the New World republics.

To make this case, these organs pointed to the way in which the Franco-Mexican conflict had supposedly followed the rhythms of Reconstruction in the United States. Back in May 1865, the *New York Herald*'s Mexico City correspondent had excitedly reported that "the news of the [Union Army's] triumph afforded vast encouragement to the adherents of President Juarez."[113] On April 11, just two days after Lee's surrender at Appomattox, Juarist troops had won a significant victory at Tacámbaro in Michoacán. The following months had seen Liberal forces strengthen their hold over the states of Sinaloa and Chihuahua and occupy almost every significant town along the Rio Grande. "A short time ago," the *Herald*'s reporter remarked, the Juarist war effort "was thought almost hopeless," but thanks to Union victory "new spirits" had been "infused into the Republican armies" south of the border and "nearly the whole of Northern Mexico" was now under "the authority of Juarez."[114]

As has been discussed, it was not long before this Juarist pushback faltered. Beginning in late summer, Imperial troops mounted a successful counterassault, which by the end of the year saw them in control of several key northern cities including Chihuahua and Matamoros. In the United States, Republican-sympathizing newspapers pointed to these setbacks to impress upon their readers that the settlement of the Reconstruction Question had continental ramifications. In February 1866, for example, the *Chicago Tribune* claimed that the "distracted condition into which our domestic politics are again thrown by [President Johnson's] proceedings" had given Maximilian fresh hope.[115] Apparently inspired by the defiance shown by ex-rebels in the US South, the emperor had stepped up his own military efforts and had even called on his native Austria for additional troops. The *Hartford Daily Courant* similarly emphasized to readers how the condition of the Juarist war effort trailed the trajectory of Reconstruction in the United States. Thus, the newspaper explained, a thoroughgoing Reconstruction program to expunge rebellious elements from the South was necessary to rejuvenate the United States' "moral force" in the minds of Mexican Liberals and embolden them to press ahead in their war effort.[116] Should this take place, the *Courant* asserted, then the United States' symbolic power would be "of the greatest importance" in bringing the French Intervention to an end.[117]

Other publications insisted that restoring the US republic's symbolic power would have effects well beyond Mexico. *Harper's Weekly* made no secret of its distaste for the style of foreign policy followed by Democratic politicians during the antebellum era. Their "swagger and bluster," allegedly fueled by slaveholders' insatiable lust for land, had "disgusted every decent nation in the world," the journal recalled.[118] For *Harper's New Monthly Magazine,* the advent of Radical Reconstruction meant that the United States could fully disenthrall itself of the Slave Power and so chart a new course in its hemispheric relations. As the magazine explained, the time was close at hand when "party-spirit and sectional jealousy" in US politics "are to be kept in check" and when the bonds of patriotic devotion would "keep our many people and States as one."[119] Harmony "among our States and races" would regenerate the United States' "vital power" as the world's standard-bearer of stable self-governance, thereby enabling US Americans to "act on foreign nations rather by our example of freedom and prosperity than by meddlesome intervention."[120] Awed by the United States' success, for instance, neighboring countries would seek to imitate its political institutions. This would simultaneously bring these nations the blessings of liberal self-government and enhance US power overseas. After all, political alignment would come hand in hand with economic integration. With their trust in and admiration for the United States growing, the Spanish American republics would naturally open up their economies to US interests, welcoming in the country's technologies, products, and capital. In short, by purifying and unifying the US body politic, Radical Reconstruction would enable the United States to "dominate the continent" by the force of its "own prosperity and intelligence, its liberty and order."[121]

Utilizing a continental framework enabled the early advocates of congressional Reconstruction to link their plans for the South to the return of US grandeur in the wider hemisphere. They did this by arguing that this method of Reconstruction was at base an effort to remove sources of discord from the US body politic and so restore harmony to national politics. In this way, Radical Reconstruction would reconnect the United States to its original role as the most successful of the New World republics, a title that since the outbreak of the Civil War many Northerners had worried might be lost to the nation forever. In many ways this message, which echoed the logic of the case made for emancipation during the Civil War, aimed to gather behind congressional Reconstruction those diverse factions that had constituted the wartime Union coalition. As we shall see, in this endeavor the Radicals and their supporters in the press would be only partially successful.

Northern Democrats Turn on Mexican Policy

In the months following General Lee's surrender, anti-French sentiment was running high in the states of the former Confederacy. This was true not only among Peace publications that had long derided the French emperor, but also among those organs that had once endorsed the Davis administration's efforts to forge an alliance with Louis-Napoleon and his protégé Maximilian. "We have no sympathy for England or France," one such newspaper, North Carolina's *Western Democrat,* announced in August 1865, for "both treated the South villainously during the late war."[122] If the Johnson administration decided to militarily intervene in Mexico, therefore, "we do not believe that the Southern people care how much [the French] are whipped."[123] For all its antipathy toward Louis-Napoleon, however, the *Democrat* did not wish to see Southern men sent into this fight. The South was exhausted, the publication explained, and it would therefore "regret to see this country again involved in war."[124] On the Mexican Question, the *Democrat* therefore proclaimed itself "emphatically for peace."[125] The *Staunton Spectator* agreed. "The South wants war with nobody," the newspaper asserted in November 1865; the section was "much too engrossed with her own sorrows . . . to think about, or care about, either Mexico or the Monroe doctrine, Maximilian or Napoleon."[126]

While general war-weariness was one factor, newspapers in the region also resisted the idea of US action in Mexico on the grounds that Southern lives should not be sacrificed for a cause as unworthy as Mexican republicanism.

"There is not a single honest, intelligent man who believes that Mexico is fit for a republican government," the *Memphis Daily Appeal* insisted in December 1865.[127] So long as it brought stability to that chaotic country, therefore, "it is absurd to haggle about the name" of whatever government ruled Mexico, whether it be republican, monarchical, or otherwise.[128] The *Times-Picayune* agreed. Though bitter toward Louis-Napoleon and Maximilian for their treatment of the Confederacy, the newspaper still believed that these emperors were offering Mexico its best chance at salvation. Referring to reports provided by French imperial officials in late 1865, the newspaper noted that the Juarist army was rapidly dwindling due to its inability to procure new recruits. Clearly this was a sign that "Mexicans are heartily sick of their endless wars and quarrels" under republican governance and wished to try liberal monarchism instead.[129] "Maximilian himself is devoted to his Empire," the newspaper finished, and "believes that it is in his power to make Mexico a great and powerful nation, and to make her people happy and prosperous."[130] Any action by the United States to prevent the consolidation of the Maximilian regime therefore would be against the interests and wishes of the majority of the Mexican population.

Much as with their Republican counterparts, these Southern newspapers' position on the Mexican Question was designed in part to advance certain domestic political aims. Specifically, they used their anti-intervention stance to paint a broader image of the postwar South as humbled, peaceful, and no longer a threat to national security. To emphasize this point, these organs contrasted their position with the warlike attitude adopted by leading Northern publicists, politicians, and US military personnel in the initial months following the end of the Civil War. "Thus far it would appear that the military chieftains are a unit in favor of enforcing the Monroe doctrine," the New Orleans *Times-Picayune* observed in August 1865.[131] For evidence the newspaper referred to a letter written by General Sheridan and recently read to "a meeting of the friends of the Juarez or Liberal party, held in New York city, which was little short of a notice to Maximilian and his backer, Louis Napoleon, to quit Mexico."[132] The newspaper also reminded its readers of "a reported speech of Gen. Grant, at Elmira, New York, to the same effect," another instance of a military general weighing in on national foreign policy.[133] For the *Times-Picayune* this was all part of a larger shift toward the militarization of civic life in the postwar United States, which, if left unchecked, would eventually see "martial law . . . in force throughout the country."[134]

Some of these Southern publications recognized that the movement of ex-rebels into Mexico might undermine their efforts to portray their region as fully pacified. As discussed earlier, certain former Peace organs derided these self-exiled Confederates as incurable monarchists in an effort to emphasize their own patriotism and trustworthiness. A larger portion of the Southern press showed no inclination to castigate these migrants, however; rather, they tended to sympathize with them as fellow mourners of a now-lost republic. At the same time, they attempted to push back against the vilification of these migrants in the wider US press. Atlanta's *Daily Intelligencer*, for example, took umbrage with the accusation made by certain Northern publications that the migration was part of a plot to relaunch the rebellion, or slavery, or both. The newspaper countered that fleeing ex-Confederates were in fact political refugees who regarded the Maximilian regime as an "asylum from Yankee rule."[135] Their aim was simply to find "peace and stability" by putting distance between themselves and a federal government run by vengeful Republicans.[136] The *Western Democrat* likewise argued that the exodus was fueled by ex-Confederates' fear of being "crushed" under "Negro rule."[137] While making a similar point in October 1865, the *Times-Picayune* added that President Johnson could therefore stem the Southern migration by showing that his administration intended to treat former rebels with mercy. "Wise and equal laws," the newspaper advised, would encourage self-exiled Southerners to return to the United States and, "gratified by the proofs that they can have a home and a country where they were born and raised," entice them to join in the work of rebuilding the nation.[138] The message to the president was clear: the former rebel South was, if not repentant, certainly defeated; as such, no overbearing federal oversight was needed to make the region obedient.

These newspapers' treatment of the Mexican Question underwent a change following the 1866 midterm elections when the now Republican-controlled Congress moved to assume direction over Reconstruction policy. Instead of using discussions about the Mexican situation to emphasize the pacified condition of the postwar South, these organs utilized them to highlight the destructive agenda of the now-ascendant Radical Republicans in Washington, DC. During the Secession Crisis, pro-separatist publications had invoked the specter of Mexican anarchy to warn white Southerners of the dangers of remaining in a Republican-controlled Union. From early 1866 onward, premonitions of impending Mexicanization reemerged in Southern discourse. One Alabama newspaper warned in April, for instance, that congressional Republicans' "abrogation of the Constitution, to the exclusion of eleven States from the Union," would be followed by the imposition of equality between the Black and white races in the South.[139] "To submit to a special association perfectly revolting to all sensible persons," the newspaper shuddered, would condemn the Southern states "to a National future like that of Mexico, or of the mongrel South American republics."[140] In May, a Louisiana newspaper likewise derided Republicans for keeping the former Confederate states "out of the Union until they consent to amalgamate with their negroes."[141] The maneuver was clearly designed to see "the once proud, untainted, and noble American people collapse into hordes of emasculated mongrels, meaner and more hopeless than those of Mexico."[142] The New Orleans *Times-Democrat*'s extensive use of the Mexican analogy six months later deserves to be quoted at length:

> From the history of Mexico, since she ceased to be a dependency on the Crown of Spain, instructive lessons may be drawn by our own people. Republicanism in that country failed, because its inhabitants had no respect for their laws, either statutory or fundamental, and because of the mongrel mixture of races of which the great masses of this people were composed, all of whom stood on the same political level. . . . The Radical chiefs of the North . . . are now following the Mexican example . . . and are striving to Mexicanize the South by breaking down the barriers which Nature has established between superior and inferior races.[143]

Some publications moved beyond analogies; under Republican rule, they insisted, the South's fate would be literally entwined with that of Mexico. According to this view, it was no coincidence that many of the Republicans leading the charge on congressional Reconstruction were also vocal champions of the Juarists—a position these newspapers equated with advocacy of US military intervention in the Mexican conflict. In January 1866, for example, New Orleans's *Times-Picayune* described a public event held at the Cooper Institute in New York, which had been organized by prominent Republicans who were supposedly "in favor of expelling Maximilian from Mexico 'immediately, if not sooner.'"[144] The newspaper explained that these Republicans wished to see Mexico repossessed by Juárez Liberals, "of whose management of Mexican affairs we heard such doleful accounts in the current history of the times and the reports of our diplomatic agents there up to the period of the arrival of Maximilian."[145] Their aim, apparently, was to orchestrate the return of Liberal rule in Mexico in order to weaken the country and so prepare it for the same process of US federal occupation the Southern states were currently undergoing. The *Richmond Daily Dispatch* suspected the same; once the Juarists had regained power and then driven their country into a state of disarray, Washington, DC, would pronounce its "obligation to establish order in Mexico . . . by loans and by extending the national protection over the Mexicans."[146] Soon the US government would insist that "protection will . . . not at all answer to restore order to Mexico" and that "positive rule or annexation will probably alone accomplish that."[147] The *Times-Picayune* offered readers a picture of what a Republican-run protectorate over Mexico would look like:

> We judge that the Freedmen's Bureau will be quite as necessary in Mexico as it is in the United States, and that the duty of providing for people who cannot provide for themselves, will devolve, as naturally and necessarily on those who put men into a political condition they are not fitted for, as in favor of blacks who know not how to act or take care of themselves intelligently, in a state of freedom they did not ask for. . . . A freedom's bureau for Mexicans is a necessary part of the "Monroe" doctrine, as it has come to be expounded in the filibustering talk of the day.[148]

Apparently, the Radicals' ambitions did not stop there. Having gained a foothold south of the Rio Grande, fanatical Republican militarism would run roughshod over the hemisphere. "We are bound to interpose in South as well as in North America, for Chili [*sic*] as well as for Mexico . . . and Brazil also," the *Picayune* darkly predicted.[149] And should any foreign power attempt to do for these countries what France was now doing for Mexico by setting up a government "which we do not think to be 'republican' according to our rule, we must fight."[150]

The dynamics of public debate over the Mexican Question following Appomattox largely echoed the positions taken by Confederate and Unionist publications during the Civil War. In the North, editors and journalists condemned the Maximilian regime and discussed plans for the United States to help in his ouster. In the South, meanwhile, most newspapers argued that US interference in Mexico would disrupt that country's stabilization under the benign guidance of a constitutional monarchy. Just as during the war, moreover, these public conversations were not purely about foreign policy. Rather, they touched on what US Americans' believed ought to be the core principles guiding their postwar republic's reunion at home and its future conduct abroad. After the midterm elections of 1866, however, the alliances in the press that had defined the debate over Mexican policy during wartime began to shift. In particular, former War Democrat organs that during the Civil War had enthusiastically supported the Juarist cause increasingly turned their backs on both the Mexican republican project and, crucially, the Republicans' broader plan to recover the United States' exceptional standing in the New World.

James Gordon Bennett, editor of the *New York Herald*, had been among the most vocal opponents of the French Intervention in the wartime Union press. The newspaperman despised concentration of power in all its forms; bankers, slavocrats, monarchs, and the Pope had all been the target of his vitriolic editorials since the *Herald*'s founding in 1835.[151] When Louis-Napoleon made war on the Mexican republic, therefore, Bennett was outraged. "France had no right to intervene in Mexico," he fumed in an 1863 editorial, and "she has still less right to attempt the overthrow of republican institutions in that country, the extinguishment of its sovereignty, and its conquest as a colony of her own."[152] What most angered Bennett was that the French emperor's monarchical pretensions toward Mexico were also an insult to the United States. As one article in the *Herald* put it, "Napoleon is engaged in Mexico combatting the spread of our influence and power on this continent and he is fully determined to conquer [Mexico] for the purpose of erecting it into a barrier against our future aggrandizement."[153] "The American people cannot allow Napoleon to insult the majesty of this government with impunity," the newspaper later declared, "and they will not, as he will find to his cost, unless he retires from Mexico at his first opportunity."[154]

As these fiery denunciations suggest, Bennett was adamant that this affront to US honor must not be allowed to stand. During the latter half of the Civil War the *New York Herald* had therefore given Senator James McDougall's proposals for a US military intervention in Mexico serious airing. Occasionally the newspaper even came out in full support of the idea. Still, these flashes of interventionist enthusiasm, which usually flared after a Union victory on the battlefield, tended to be short-lived.[155] Unlike certain Copperhead organs, the *Herald* maintained that Confederate surrender must be secured before the United States could safely send forces into Mexico. In March 1865, therefore, with the Confederacy on the verge of collapse, the *Herald* announced that the time was finally right to put the proposal for US intervention in Mexico before the public. "The masses of the people and of the armies of the rebellious States are not only ready but anxious to end the war on the simple basis of submission," the newspaper stated.[156] Although the Confederacy's leadership was comprised of slavocrats, it continued, most of its rank and file were liberty-loving democrats who had been duped into participating in rebellion. This being the case, once the Confederacy had fallen, most white Southerners would "be eager to enter upon . . . a crusade" to rout the French from Mexico.[157] After all, the *Herald* argued, these Southerners shared with their erstwhile Northern countrymen an instinctive antipathy toward Old World monarchism, and though "confusion and conflicting sentiment" had ruptured other bonds between them, this tie remained strong.[158] The Monroe Doctrine, the newspaper surmised in a later article, was the "one thing upon which all [Americans] agree."[159]

Other Democratic-leaning newspapers expressed similar thoughts on the Mexican Question around this time. "The South has now and again said something about the balance of power, and about an alliance with Maximilian and France," the *Houston Telegraph* acknowledged in June 1865, before noting that this had been done "under the pressure of self-preservation."[160] Indeed, most white Southerners were republicans, and "however widely apart the North and South may have been in the late bloody strife, still, upon this one matter, among thinking men, there has been at heart no difference."[161] Participating in the overthrow of an imperial monarchy in Mexico was therefore an opportunity for former Confederates to prove their abiding love of republicanism, and in so doing erect a "bridge of reconciliation between the North and South" based on their "common hatred of France."[162] The *Missouri Republican* similarly argued that a joint invasion of Mexico would allow Southerners to "prove to their countrymen how truly they loved the government that they mistakenly were aiding to destroy."[163] More than this, fighting together on the battlefields of Mexico would help Union and Confederate veterans forgive one another for what they had done to each other over the past four years. "Soon we should see the press of the South lauding the valor of our Northern troops and the North that of the South," the newspaper optimistically predicted; "soon the hates and heartburnings [*sic*] would be forgotten in the united effort to save our weak neighbor from her foreign enemy."[164]

When they turned their thoughts to the more distant future, these publications saw other ways that an intervention in Mexico could aid sectional reconciliation in the United States. For example, the *Houston Telegraph* predicted that, once US troops had seated "Juarez upon the Presidential chair," the restored president, overcome with gratitude, would invite the United States to "annex the Northern States of that Republic, if not the whole of Mexico to the Union."[165] It was a remarkable prediction, not least because it presumed that the United States would accept such a gift while still in the tentative early stages of national reunion. After all, the issue of territorial expansion had been a significant point of contention between North and South before the Civil War. Moreover, as has been discussed, most major Republican newspapers at this time believed that the United States should exchange the territorial expansionism of the antebellum era for the pursuit of pacific commercial and financial relationships across the hemisphere. These Democratic organs, by contrast, expressed no objection to the imperialist agendas of previous administrations, except for the fact that they had often been thwarted or otherwise complicated by sectional tensions. Indeed, these newspapers anticipated that, now freed from its association with the slavery issue, the quest to acquire more land could become a source of cross-sectional collaboration. A "demonstration of 'Manifest Destiny,'" the *Missouri Republican* insisted in June 1865, would "revive the days of Polk and Dallas, and give the American Eagle a fresh foot hold upon the Sierra Madre."[166] Far from condemning antebellum expansionism, the *Republican* deliberately invoked the language of the old Jacksonian Democrats and their notion that, properly understood, the territorial enlargement of the US republic was a national endeavor that ought to transcend transitory sectional rivalries. It was, the newspaper averred, the "manifest DESTINY" of every US citizen "to see the North American continent under ONE Free Government."[167]

While the *Missouri Republican* spoke in general terms about the unifying power of territorial expansion, other publications tied this idea to the specific issues of postwar reunion and Reconstruction. A letter to the editor of the *Cincinnati Enquirer* published in December 1865 offers a useful example of this. Reflecting on how President Lincoln had stretched executive authority during the war, the writer insisted that US Americans must now "hasten to repair that error and free ourselves from centralizing tendencies by restoring each part of our Union to all of its local rights," including "restoring the Southern States to all their Constitutional rights and relations to the Federal Government" as soon as possible.[168] The author believed that a US intervention in Mexico would give white Southerners an opportunity to demonstrate their fealty to the Union, thereby negating the need to ensure their obedience through punitive measures such as military occupation and "Negro rule." Battling European monarchism would furthermore remind citizens from every region of certain ideals—democracy, federalism, individual liberty—that they all cherished. Thus, the writer imagined, US troops would "go to the aid of the Mexican Republic with the motto on our banners: "No centralization at home—no interference from abroad."[169] In this author's view a military venture in Mexico would, somewhat ironically, help to walk back the United States' recent slide toward militarization and centralization.

As 1866 progressed, such calls appeared with less frequency in the Northern Democratic press than in the months immediately following Appomattox. In part this was a response to the way in which congressional Republicans intensified their own politicking on the Mexican Question during this time. Reflecting on the series of pro-Juarist resolutions recently submitted in

Congress, for example, the *New York Herald* concluded in late 1866 that the Republicans in that body aimed to complicate the Johnson administration's relations with France in order to undermine public confidence in the president's "abilities as a statesman."[170] The *Herald* also suspected—not entirely without reason—that Radical Republicans submitted these resolutions primarily because it gave them opportunities to deliver speeches in the House and Senate reminding their supporters of the Confederacy's wartime associations with the French Intervention. In this way, Republicans' treatment of the Mexican Question could be understood as another form of waving the bloody shirt—a rhetorical tactic designed to rehash Confederates' wartime crimes against the Union in order to, as the *Herald* put it, keep "sectional questions . . . above all others in importance" in the postwar public mind.[171] The Baltimore *Sun* shared this concern. By continually "harping on the Monroe doctrine," the newspaper surmised, Republicans hoped to feed popular anxieties regarding a possible attack on the United States by Confederate exiles in Mexico while fueling Northerners' distrust of white Southerners inside their own borders.[172]

Suspecting that Republicans sought to harness popular pro-Juarist sympathies behind their Reconstruction agenda, Democratic organs began to rethink their previous support for a US intervention in Mexico. Other aspects of the Republicans' Southern plan, meanwhile, led them to reconsider their support for the Juarist cause entirely. During the Civil War the *New York Herald* had come to regard the Mexican Liberals and their supporters with a certain fraternal affection. As the newspaper had pronounced in 1863, "the people of Mexico are as effectually fighting our battles, in their heroic resistance against foreign intervention, as we, in putting down the rebellion, are fighting theirs," since each were battling for the "security of republican institutions on this continent."[173] By April 1866, however, the *Herald* was satisfied that the United States' slavocatic enemy had been destroyed. Indeed, by this time the newspaper was convinced that a new menace had arisen within the US body politic to take the Slave Power's place. As the *Herald* explained to its readers, Republicans had now shown their intention to place "whites and blacks in this country not only on a basis of political but social equality."[174] The result would be "an indiscriminate social admixture and general decay" across US society similar to what had occurred "in Mexico and the South American States" over past decades, condemning US Americans to a condition analogous to that of the "undesirable mongrels of Mexico."[175] Having survived one crisis of national integrity, the *Herald* feared, the United States was in danger of plunging headfirst into another.

This reference to the "mongrels of Mexico" harkened back to stereotypes about that country that had frequently appeared on the *Herald*'s pages prior to the French Intervention. As congressional Reconstruction unfolded, more and more Northern Democratic organs resuscitated similar racialized images of the Mexican population in order to make analogies with what they saw as a dangerous move toward racial equality now underway in the postwar United States. In January 1867, Congress granted Black men in the District of Columbia the right to vote. Two months later it passed the Reconstruction Act, which required all voters and would-be officeholders in the former Confederacy to take an oath of loyalty to the United States. The disenfranchisement of white Southerners coupled with the advance of Black suffrage provoked outrage among Northern Democratic publications. "The negro is absolutely incapable of self-government," the *Louisville Daily Courier* fumed in August 1867.[176] For proof, the newspaper referred its readers to "Mexico, the South American republics, Hayti, Jamaica," which "all afford the most convincing evidences of the negro's unfitness for participation, much less control, in public affairs."[177] The *Ohio Daily Statesman* made the same point in July. The reason why republican Mexico had "no stability in its Government," the *Statesman* explained, was because "in Mexico . . . Negro Suffrage is in full bloom."[178] Ignorant voters elected inept leaders, while the eradication of racial hierarchies meant that the country was in a constant state of confusion and strife. Apparently, the same state of affairs awaited the United States under Republican rule, "As it is in Mexico so will it be in the United States, when this, our boasted Republic, is governed by a population in which the different races of men are amalgamated as they are in Mexico. . . . The United States, will re-enact the scenes that has made the Mexican name a by-word and a reproach among the nations of the earth, and popular government in that ill-fated land a mere unmeaning phrase."[179]

These analogies with Mexico were centered on the specific issue of racial demoralization and its wider societal effects. At times, however, Democratic organs deployed terms such as "Mexican anarchy" and "Mexicanization" to refer to any form of social discord that created instability in government. As the *New York Post* explained in late summer 1866, Republicans sought to portray the South as a hotbed of rebelliousness in order to "fan the flames of hatred" toward that region among Northerners and thereby generate popular support for a punitive Reconstruction.[180] The newspaper warned that such a strategy would further entrench sectionalism in US political culture, deepening existing divides, which would eventually turn "us over to interminable disorders" and ultimately "rekindle civil war."[181] This turmoil would provide

Republicans with the excuse they needed to then enact the final phase of their plot: to "subvert the Constitution, and set up over our heads a despotism" first across the South, and then the entire nation.[182] Thus, the *Post* concluded, congressional Reconstruction "will Mexicanize the country; it will destroy liberty here at once and forever, as well as peace and prosperity."[183]

Here the *Post* revealed some of the complexities embedded in the concept of Mexicanization in Northern Democratic discourse at this time. In this context, Mexicanization was usually attributed to one of two causes: racial disorder or excessive sectionalism. It should be noted, however, that according to this logic both of these ills were to be feared because of the profound social and political instability they supposedly created. Northern Democratic publications were also in agreement that either method of Mexicanization would have one of two ultimate consequences: anarchy or despotism. In the abstract, these two conditions were opposites; in postbellum Northern Democratic discourse, however, they were closely related, with the former weakening society until it became powerless to prevent the imposition of the latter. Finally, Northern Democratic organs agreed that there was only one way to avert either form of Mexicanization. As the *Post* advised, citizens must reject both the politicians advocating "extreme measures" promoting racial equality and those employing "inflammatory appeals whose only object and effect is still further to irritate the people of one section against the other."[184]

As Northern Democrats' concerns about the United States' impending Mexicanization grew, their sympathy for the Juarists in Mexico cooled. In part this was because Radical Reconstruction conjured up images of racial mixing and subsequent social and political decline that Democrats had long associated with Mexican republicanism. Though suppressed during the Civil War, these negative associations with Mexico were brought to the forefront of Northern Democratic discourse as anxieties about the changing character of the postwar United States intensified. Moreover, with the Confederacy defeated there was no longer a common cause to bind Northern Democratic editors and journalists to their erstwhile Mexican allies. As such, they increasingly felt at liberty to resurrect old stereotypes of Mexican misgovernment and disorder in their efforts to outline the horrors awaiting the United States under Republican rule. Even those Democratic politicians and publicists who did not reject the Juarist cause jettisoned the idea of US intervention in the Franco-Mexican conflict, wary of how congressional Republicans were using the Mexican Question to aggravate sectional tensions in the United States. In short, Northern Democrats' turn away from the Juarist cause was in large part driven by their concerns about the current and future integrity of the postwar US republic.

The Fall of the Maximilian Regime

As congressional Reconstruction gained pace in the United States, Maximilian's position in Mexico deteriorated. As has been discussed, faced with rising opposition to the war at home, Louis-Napoleon announced a three-stage withdrawal of French troops from Mexico to begin on May 31, 1866. By late summer of that year, French soldiers were gone from Monterrey and Saltillo, and by November they had vacated the states of Sonora and Mazatlán. On February 5, 1867, French forces evacuated Mexico City, leaving Maximilian to rely on the Austro-Belgian Volunteer Corps and any Mexican soldiers he could rally to his defense. This proved to be a challenge; some of the emperor's domestic policies, including his land reforms and lukewarm support of the Catholic Church, had alienated many of his former Conservative Mexican allies. Maximilian's efforts to shore up his regime by cultivating loyal Confederate colonies, meanwhile, failed to bear fruit; though a number of settlements continued to draw in immigrants throughout the early months of 1866, these settlers had to contend with formidable challenges, including insufficient capital, difficult and unfamiliar terrain, and the threat of attack by either Juarist troops or hostile Native tribes. The result was that throughout 1867 most of the fledgling ex-Confederate colonies collapsed. A reverse migration then commenced as these self-exiled Southerners picked up their remaining possessions and began the long journey back over the border to the United States.[185]

As Maximilian's military effort faltered, the Juarists persevered. Capitalizing on the staggered withdrawal of French forces, Liberal troops won a series of victories between March and November 1866 that saw them take possession of Chihuahua, Matamoros, Tampico, and Acapulco. By January 1867 they had consolidated their hold over Oaxaca, Zacatecas, San Luis Potosí, and Guanajuato, forcing Maximilian to flee Mexico City in February 1867 and head to Querétaro. Juarist forces began a siege on that city in March that lasted for the better part of two months. Finally, on May 11, 1867, Maximilian attempted to escape the city through enemy lines; he was captured on May 15 and held prisoner awaiting court-martial. The following month the remaining Imperial troops surrendered the capital, and in July President Juárez made a triumphant return to Mexico City. The Mexican Empire had fallen; the Mexican republic was restored.

In the United States press, this news was met with mixed responses. Republican organs were jubilant. "With what energy and trustfulness, with what unpausing vigor the little Republic fought the French," the *New York Tribune* enthused before heaping praise on President Juárez, whom it described as "the leading spirit in the war" and the "ablest of the Mexican chiefs"—a model of "what perseverance combined with courage may do."[186] The mood among many Southern and Northern Democratic organs was rather different. The *Brooklyn Daily Eagle* reminded readers that the contest at the heart of the French Intervention "was not between one form of government or another; it was between a possible government and no government at all."[187] Having squandered their opportunity to be ruled by a benign, forward-thinking monarch, Mexicans had condemned themselves to be "turned over to anarchy" once again, and thus continued to bring "shame on Republicanism."[188]

These conflicting reactions were an indication of how US Americans at this time tended to view events in Mexico through the prism of their own domestic political considerations. In the months and years immediately following Appomattox, many prominent Republican politicians, editors, and journalists found it expedient to maintain a public position of sympathy with the Mexican republican cause, and to urge the US public to do the same. In doing so, they hoped to convince US Americans that, Confederate surrender notwithstanding, the fight to defend free government on the continent continued. There was still work to be done, they insisted, to fully subdue the Slave Power in the United States and so prevent it from combining with allies elsewhere in North America. By using the Mexican Question in this way, Republican-leaning organs aimed to depict Radical Reconstruction as a continuation of the Union war effort, the final front in the larger fight to protect republicanism against its antidemocratic assailants both at home and across the continent.

Republican organs hoped that this framing would hold together the wartime Union coalition behind congressional Reconstruction. As Republicans gained control over reunion policy, however, they lost valuable allies from among certain portions of the national press. Large numbers of Northern Democratic publications were appalled by the Republicans' plans to rework the Southern political order, a legislative agenda that they believed went far beyond the original aims of the Union war effort. They also doubted Republicans' claims that rebel elements were still intriguing against the US republic, whether in the South or in Mexico. The Slave Power had been vanquished, many Northern Democratic organs countered, and Republicans simply wished to keep the slavocratic ghost alive in order to terrify, divide, and thereby render pliant voters in the United States.

Such was the extent of these newspapers' concern that they rapidly came to view Republican Radicals, rather than rebel Southerners, as the chief threat facing the postwar US republic. One writer to the Louisville *Courier-Journal* summed up this sentiment well in September 1867. Describing himself as a Union veteran, the author insisted that fanaticism rather than slavery was now the principal force that was "Mexicanizing . . . our great country."[189] Whether it came in the form of a second civil war or a "consolidated tyranny," he continued, the ultimate result of this new Mexicanizing assault would be "far more pernicious than if the secession traitors had succeeded in separating the Union."[190] This writer therefore agreed with Republicans that the post–Civil War United States was still imperiled by a menace from within. The writer's view of what that menace was, however, more closely aligned to that of most white-run newspapers in the South at this time. And so, though alliances had shifted and the issues had changed since the Civil War, voices from all quarters of the United States continued to worry that their supposedly exceptional republic remained in a state of precarious fragility.

CHAPTER FOUR

Mexicanization and the End of Reconstruction, 1867–1881

Matías Romero was good at his job; he did not, however, always enjoy it. The weather in Washington, DC, did not suit him, he said, and he found it difficult to be away from his country as it struggled through such perilous times.[1] Therefore, the minister was perhaps relieved when, in the fall of 1867, President Juárez summoned him back to Mexico City to take up the role of secretary of finance. Still, the many friends Romero had cultivated during his tenure in the United States were sorry to see him go, and they insisted on marking his departure with one last banquet at Delmonico's.

The farewell dinner took place on an October evening, with all the pomp and ceremony typical of such occasions. At nine o'clock, as the wait staff cleared the tables of empty plates, journalist and poet William Cullen Bryant rose to his feet and began the customary round of toasts. Romero's "constancy is at last rewarded," Bryant happily announced, as was that of his allies in the United States.[2] The Confederacy and the Maximilian regime had been part of the same effort to "engraft European absolutism upon the institutions of our Continent."[3] It was for this reason, Bryant explained, that he and so many of his countrymen were now celebrating the Juarists' victory as if it were their own.

Only a single cloud darkened the brightening horizon of Mexico's future. As Bryant noted, in recent weeks the noble "Mexican patriots" had been "greatly maligned" in certain portions of the US press for their decision to execute Maximillian.[4] The emperor had been captured in May while attempting to escape through enemy lines at Santiago de Querétaro. Governments of the leading European nations had appealed to President Juárez to spare the Austrian prince's life on the grounds that he had been a naïve but well-intentioned pawn on Louis-Napoleon's chessboard. Juárez, however, was adamant that a message be sent to other would-be invaders around the world that intrigues against the Mexican republic would be severely punished. And so, on June 19, Maximilian, along with Conservative generals Miguel Miramón and Tomás Mejía, was marched up the Cerro de las Campanas in Querétaro City, stood before a firing squad, and shot dead.

The reaction in the United States was mixed. "MAXIMILIAN has been shot as though he had been a dog," the *Edgefield Advertiser* shuddered, a fate that this "amiable and humane prince" did not deserve.[5] This was not an act of justice, the newspaper continued, but of gratuitous violence, meant "only to appease the beastly and revengeful instincts of a nation of mongrels."[6] The *Charleston Courier* condemned Maximilian's execution in similar terms: carried out "in cold-blood" under the orders of "the Indian Juarez," the execution was "contrary to the laws of all civilized people" and revealed that at the core of the Mexican character was a "ferocity and lawlessness utterly at war with any appreciation of the principles of true liberty."[7] Maximilian's death therefore demonstrated that Mexicans—a "despised and rejected . . . mixed race"—were "unable to rule themselves" and would "submit to no law but that of license, and no freedom but that of anarchy."[8] The *Charleston Mercury* likewise took the occasion to pontificate on the future of democracy in Mexico. The Liberals' decision to execute Maximilian was emblematic of the fact that the "people of Mexico, are capable of no other government than that of an imperial or monarchical despotism," the newspaper explained; "No other can protect them, from the natural disorder of the profound barbarism, into which they have sunk."[9] Mexicans had spurned Maximilian's offer of such a government, and so had doomed their country to lapse back into violence and disorder.

A handful of US newspapers took the opposite view. Washington, DC's *Forney's Chronicle*, for example, insisted that Juárez's execution order should be understood in a context larger than that of a single man's life. "Monarchs who attempt to overthrow republics are now warned of the fate that awaits them," the newspaper explained, adding that "Mexico, by this act of signal justice, has elevated itself into the high attitude of defender of Republics."[10] Still, most publications that were otherwise supportive of Juárez struggled to defend the president's decision in this instance. "The expulsion of the invaders gains little for Mexico, unless the nation makes worthy use of its victory," the *New York Tribune* advised in August.[11] All nations that survived civil war found themselves at a crossroads upon the termination of conflict, forced to choose between punishing or forgiving those who had attempted to break apart the country. In the United States, former Confederates had received certain punishments, including property confiscation and the suspension of their voting rights. Federal authorities had not sought the trial and execution of rebels, however, reasoning that treating them with mercy would allow for a more peaceful national reunification.[12] Mexico, by contrast, seemed to have chosen revenge over grace, which the *Tribune* worried would do little to heal the fractured republic going forward. As the newspaper reminded its readers, throughout Mexican history "the sequel of every victory had been the birth of a new struggle; war has arisen out of war."[13] Friends of the Mexican republic would feel "profound regret," the *Tribune* concluded, if the "triumph of Republicanism" in that country "should also be the triumph of Barbarism" and if "the first act of the Liberals should be the proclamation of a Reign of Terror throughout the unhappy land."[14]

The *New York Tribune*'s disappointment was a sign of things to come. During the years that followed the fall of the Maximilian regime in 1867, newspapers in the United States that had previously professed undying support for republican Mexico became disenchanted with President Juárez and his government. This was a trying period for what was commonly called the Restored Republic of Mexico. Having defeated their imperial usurpers, Juárez and his fellow Liberals had to grapple with some serious challenges, including an enormous public debt, a national economy ravaged by war, and a still profoundly divided population. The last issue was particularly fraught. Having vanquished their common enemy, Liberal leaders began to clash over personal rivalries and ideological disagreements. Across the wider population, meanwhile, the absence of war saw old ethnic, socioeconomic, and regional fissures resurface. During the French Intervention, sympathetic US Americans, with the encouragement of Juarist agents in the United States, had learned to blame the Catholic Church for Mexico's chronic political turmoil. After 1867, however, this explanation was no longer satisfactory. The clerical-monarchical assault had been defeated, so why was Mexican politics still plagued by coups, corruption, and uprisings?

This cooling of popular affection toward the Mexican republic was accelerated by the fact that the fall of the Maximilian regime also brought an end to the Juárez government's propaganda campaign in the United States. With the departure of Romero and other Juarist agents, there was no network of Mexicans in the country dedicated to supplying the US press with positive information about the latest goings-on south of the border. With the clerics, Conservatives, and Imperialists now vanquished, moreover, there was no longer a villain threatening the Mexican republic that US Americans could clearly identify and rally against. As a consequence, when seeking to explain the return of violence and instability to Mexican politics in the late 1860s, commentators in the United States increasingly fell back into habits of thought that had been prevalent among them before the French Intervention and that centered on identifying apparent flaws in the Mexican character.

Some, for example, dusted off old theories regarding the supposed biological inferiority of the so-called Mexican race. Others considered the influence of experience and habit. Was it possible, they wondered, that decades of relentless internal strife had cultivated a culture of conflict in Mexican politics, which was now so embedded that it might never be unlearned?

This second explanation gained particular traction in the United States during the late 1860s and early 1870s. In large part, this was because it echoed certain concerns that some US Americans harbored about their own society as it struggled through its process of postwar reunification. During President Grant's first term (1868–1872), certain portions of the Northern press expressed reservations about congressional Republicans' Reconstruction policies. Convinced that the Slave Power had now been eradicated, moderate Republican and independent organs came to suspect that Reconstruction had been hijacked by opportunistic office seekers within the Republican Party who wished to deceive Northern voters into believing that the Southern rebel was still a credible threat to the nation. These increasingly skeptical portions of the Republican coalition found it troubling that large swathes of the US public seemed to believe this erroneous notion. The persistence of Northerners' distrust toward the South, they thought, was proof that years of internecine strife had left a stain of factionalism on US politics that might never be removed. By the late 1860s, these formerly Republican-supporting editors, journalists, and politicians had started to refer to this process as *Mexicanization*, by which they meant a form of political degeneration whereby a population, having been exposed to years of civil discord, was inured to factionalism as it became a feature of everyday political life and so were rendered incapable of living harmoniously together under a democratic form of government.

This concept of Mexicanization stemmed from deep-seated doubts about the condition of the post–Civil War US republic. During 1866 and 1867, Republican leaders had promised that their version of Reconstruction constituted the final push that would cleanse the United States of domestic enemies and reunify its population once and for all. But by late 1867, political violence was endemic across the Southern states and the tone of debate in national politics was as fiery as it had been in the years leading up to Southern secession. The old Slave Power had been a tangible foe; it could be seen, debated against in the halls of government, and even fired at with bullets on the battlefield. The affliction of Mexicanization that apparently gripped the postwar United States, however, was far more insidious—it involved a shift in the attitudes and habits of voters who had seemingly lost their ability to cooperate with their political opponents in order to govern the country.

Though the language of Mexicanization emerged as a distinctive feature of political discourse during this period, the practice of drawing cross-border comparisons was nothing new. As we have seen, since the Secession Crisis US Americans had openly worried that sectional conflict would see their country join the ranks of the New World's failed republics. Since that time, comparisons with Mexico had functioned as a barometer by which they could measure the integrity of US political institutions and culture. This chapter shows that this practice continued well into the 1870s. It also demonstrates how, by highlighting certain ills plaguing national politics, these cross-border parallels were used to simultaneously unsettle and galvanize the US public. In the years immediately following Appomattox, the fear that the United States was spiraling downward into a condition like Mexico's had helped to convince many Northerners to embrace the Republicans' revolutionary Reconstruction program. From the late 1860s onward, it pulled them in the opposite direction; in order to reverse the nation's Mexicanization, they concluded, Reconstruction must end.

Scholarly studies typically separate the era of Reconstruction from that of the Gilded Age, which began in the mid-to-late 1870s. The logic for doing so is that these two periods were defined by distinct sets of national issues: the former by the politics of slavery and sectionalism, and the latter by the politics of corruption and reform. The separation also implies evolution; by the mid-to-late 1870s, it suggests, most US Americans were ready to put the debates of the Civil War era behind them and engage with fresh issues facing their country. Thus, the advent of the Gilded Age marks a stage of national recovery, a point at which the scars of the Civil War had faded to a degree sufficient enough to enable most US Americans to look ahead and think in new ways about the next stage of their nation's development.[15] Phases of transition, however, are rarely so neat or complete. Indeed, by following the persistent use of analogies with Mexico in US discourse, and specifically the rise of the language of Mexicanization, this chapter identifies a current of insecurity regarding the internal condition of the US republic that persisted from the Reconstruction era into the early Gilded Age. To be sure, contemporaries in the United States did not worry about the survival of their country with the same intensity as they had done during either the Civil War or certain particularly tumultuous phases of Reconstruction. Still, a shadow of self-doubt hung over the nation, which scholars should acknowledge before attempting to compartmentalize the postwar years into discrete periods, and which also must be considered in order to fully understand the concerns that weighed upon US Americans as they entered the supposedly new politics of the Gilded Age.

Mexico's Restored Republic Falls Short

President Juárez's triumphant reentry into Mexico City in July 1867 received widespread press coverage in the United States. A jubilant *San Francisco Chronicle* declared that Mexicans were now free to "prove themselves capable of maintaining a stable and well-ordered government."[16] Over the following months, Mexico's prospects did indeed seem bright. Juárez called a presidential election for October 6, which he then resoundingly won, receiving 72 percent of the 10,371 electoral votes cast. Armed with a mandate to reunify the nation as he saw fit, Juárez initially opted for reconciliation. "The Government does not wish, had never wished, especially now, in the hour of the complete triumph of the Republic—to allow itself to be inspired by any sentiment of passion against the enemies that it has fought," an official presidential proclamation assured the Mexican people.[17] Certainly, an example had been made of Maximilian, but this was as far as the government's punishment of its erstwhile enemies would go. Indeed, Juárez announced amnesty for all Mexicans who had aided the French Intervention, except for those who had held the highest positions in the Maximilian Empire. The president hoped that this show of mercy would encourage his countrymen, "taught by the prolonged and dolorous experience of the calamities of war," that henceforth they must "cooperate for the well-being and prosperity of the nation."[18]

Juárez combined magnanimity toward Conservatives with the rigorous pursuit of various aspects of the Liberals' long-held reform agenda. Broadly put, the restored Juárez administration aimed to break up the power of colonial-era monopolies such as the Church and the military and replace them with rationalized bureaucratic political and economic apparatuses. With this goal in mind, Juárez demobilized the army, reducing its active reserves from 60,000 to 20,000. He also made significant advances toward the secularization of education in Mexico by replacing the old model in which schools were run by priests and nuns with a nationwide government-administered elementary public school system. As part of this effort, Liberal legislators passed laws obliging all towns with over 500 residents to establish a primary school. They also put together an educational reform commission tasked with preparing a new uniform preparatory curriculum for students in the Federal District.[19]

The central government's progress in other parts of its reform agenda, however, was slow. One problem legislators continually ran up against was a lack of revenue. The war against Maximilian's Empire had drained government coffers, driven up the national debt, and devastated many of Mexico's key industries. The Juárez administration therefore struggled to raise the funds necessary to underwrite some of its core initiatives, such as improving roads and building new railroads. In the spirit of conciliation, moreover, the federal government chose to return land confiscated from disloyal Conservatives during the French Intervention to its former owners rather than redistribute it to landless laborers. It simultaneously launched an effort to break up the Indian system of communal landholding (*ejidos*), which Liberals considered another archaic relic of the colonial era. When this land was put on the market, it was quickly gobbled up by politically powerful landowners, Liberal and Conservative alike. Thousands of dispossessed Indigenous peoples and Mexican laborers, whom Liberals had promised economic autonomy and social mobility, therefore found themselves continuing to work the land of rich *hacendados*. Popular discontent rose, and throughout 1868 and 1869 a series of antigovernment rebellions broke out across Nuevo León, Zacatecas, and Durango.[20]

Ideological differences within the Liberal ranks were also an issue. Although party members had long disagreed over critical questions such as the proper distribution of power at the federal, state, and local levels of government, these arguments had been largely suppressed during the French Intervention. After Maximilian's fall, however, they rose once again to the surface of national politics. As a radical or *puro* Liberal, Juárez viewed broad executive authority as the most effective means to coordinate national consolidation and development. In August 1867, a month after his reentry into Mexico City, he therefore issued a raft of executive decrees (named the *Convocatoria*), which proposed certain amendments to the Constitution of 1857 that would strengthen the executive branch. Pushback from both allies and opponents temporarily forced the president to back down. Following his impressive election victory in October, however, Juárez was emboldened to try again. Over the following months, he initiated a series of government reforms that, among other things, created a new Senate chamber to dilute the power of Congress and established a presidential veto over congressional legislation. Unnerved, local and state politicians of all party stripes lent varying degrees of support to the popular uprisings then breaking out across the nation, hoping that these disturbances would inhibit the federal administration's ability to implement its centralizing agenda.

News that Mexico's Restored Republic was running into difficulties reached the United States through a messy network of channels. Minister Romero had helped to usher in an unprecedented era in US-Mexican communications; never before had news from south of the border been so reliable, regular, and enthusiastically consumed by readers in the United States. When the Mexican Empire fell, however, Romero returned home, as did scores of other Juarist agents who had been operating in the United States. Romero's replacement was Ignacio Mariscal, formerly the secretary of the Mexican Legation in Washington, DC. Soon after his appointment, however, Mariscal was recalled to Mexico, apparently by his own request, due to "domestic" matters. He would not officially take up his position in the United States until June 1869. For the almost two years following Romero's departure, therefore, the Juárez administration had no formal representative in Washington, DC, to monitor and shape the information US Americans received about events south of the border.[21]

And so, US editors turned to other sources for their Mexican news. Though many US journalists departed Mexico once the excitement of the French Intervention was over, a handful did remain. The *New York Herald*, for example, maintained correspondents in Mexico City and a few other major cities who kept readers abreast of how the reestablished Juárez administration was faring. On the whole, they had little positive news to relay. "The lookout from the halls of the Montezumas is somewhat dismal," one such journalist stated in February 1868.[22] The national government had recently put down a revolt in Yucatán, only to find that "several Mexican generals had pronounced against the powers that be" at Veracruz and that "rebels held possession of the city" of Tampico.[23] The correspondent concluded this depressing report by asking, "with all these fighting factions and military aspirants out at the elbows. . . . What security is there for law and order under Juarez, or for the continuance of his administration til next Christmas?"[24] Five months later another *Herald* reporter, this time based in Veracruz, painted a similarly disheartening picture. "*Pronunciamientos* are the order," the journalist explained, before reeling off a long list of prominent military and political leaders who had recently declared against the government, including former chief justice Jesús González Ortega and Liberal generals Aureliano Rivera, Ramón Corona, and Porfirio Díaz.[25]

These *pronunciamientos* made for compelling reading and were often circulated widely in the US press. A copy of one, issued by Rivera in May 1868 and later printed in the *New York Herald*, provides an illustration of the impression these declarations created of the Juárez government. "A few months since," Rivera's address began, "the heroic Mexican people were struggling against the French invasion in order to assert their independence."[26] Now they were facing another foe, this time one that had emerged from within their own ranks. "Don Benito Juarez," the supposed hero of the Mexican republic, had amassed "supreme power in his hands, without counterpose, without giving account of its exercise and without other limitation to his will or his ambition."[27] Falsely claiming that he needed such powers in order to stabilize the country, Rivera's declaration concluded, the president had deprived "the worthy Mexican people of their rights and of those faculties that politicians call "inalienable" and "unperishable."[28]

Fed by such reports, pessimism among US newspapers regarding the future prospects of the reestablished Juárez government grew. It was expressed first and most strongly by Democratic organs in both the North and South. Of course, many of these publications had a long history of disparaging Mexico's republican project. Still, the intensity of their horror at the Restored Republic was notable and due in part to their belief that certain deleterious trends that were evident in Mexico were also emerging in US politics at this time. "Having murdered Maximilian and cast from them their only hope of a stable and well-regulated government," the *San Francisco Examiner* noted in early 1868, the Mexican Liberals were now "illustrating the beauties of Mongrel Republicanism."[29] The newspaper then pointed out that what Liberals were doing in Mexico, Republicans had "been working diligently for the past two years to bring about in the United States."[30] Both factions sought to take advantage of postwar uncertainty to centralize and militarize their respective governments. Both, furthermore, aimed to facilitate this process by enacting policies to advance social leveling, racial amalgamation, and other radical agendas, which they knew would plunge their countries into anarchy. For an example, the *Examiner* directed its readers' attention to Radical Reconstruction, which the newspaper presented as a Mexican-inspired type of social reform:

> [Republicans] have been seeking to mongrelize the Southern States—to force into equality those whom God has made unequal—to coerce by bayonets the white race to amalgamate with negroes. They have been trying to Mexicanize ten States of the Union, so that when they shall become hopelessly imbruted by political and social miscegenation, they can be used and controlled as a balance of power against the whites—the laboring masses of the Northern and Western States. Read the account of the proceedings of the Black-and-Tan Convention in Florida, indeed read the proceedings of those mumbo-jumbo reconstruction mobs in all of the Southern States, and it is enough to make the heart sicken.[31]

Such comparisons with Mexico appeared with increasing regularity in Democratic newspapers during the following months as controversy over

Reconstruction grew. Republican victory in the 1866–1867 midterm elections had set the stage for an almighty battle between the legislative and executive branches of the US federal government over national reunification. Making liberal use of his presidential veto, Johnson refused to put his signature on a series of Reconstruction legislation passed by Congress, forcing that body to override him with a two-thirds majority vote. Tensions reached a breaking point in August 1867 when the president suspended Secretary of War Edwin Stanton, a Lincoln-appointed Republican, and removed army district commanders in the South who had been enforcing the Reconstruction acts. In response, the Judiciary Committee of the House of Representatives launched an investigation to determine whether the president might have committed high crimes and misdemeanors worthy of impeachment. Two moderate Republican members of the committee thought not. In a minority report issued after the investigation, both James F. Wilson of Iowa and Frederick E. Woodbridge of Vermont argued that, while the president had betrayed the expectations of his Republican supporters, there was not enough evidence to sustain the charge that he had criminally violated his oath of office. Given that he was guilty of political crimes only, therefore, his case ought to be judged by voters at the ballot box, not by trial in the Senate. Wilson and Woodbridge's report finished with the pointed observation that wielding the institutions of government for political ends echoed the "Mexican experience," in which "almost every election" was followed by an attempt to overturn it through such machinations that were usually then "productive of a revolution."[32]

These objections were not enough to sway the rest of the House Judiciary Committee, however, which in November 1867 issued a majority report recommending the impeachment of the president. The case then moved to the Senate, where on March 5, 1868, the first presidential impeachment trial in US history began. As senators listened to witness testimony, in the public realm the president's supporters rallied to his defense. Some, such as Maryland Democratic representative James Brooks, drew parallels between Radical congressmen and Juarist Liberals in order to discredit Republicans as power-hungry extremists who had no respect for the rule of law or the authority of precedent in matters of governance. "We have had many parties," Brooks said of the Republicans in a speech he delivered on the floor of the House, "but this is the first that has ruined and abandoned the institutions of this nation . . . they are not content to Africanize the ten Southern States; but they intend to Mexicanize the government."[33] Democratic congressman from Indiana William E. Niblack expressed much the same sentiment during a discussion regarding the impeachment trial that took place in the House that March.

Congressional Republicans, he charged, had "first attempted to Africanize the institutions of the country . . . and now were ready to Mexicanize them" by using the courts "for the purpose of getting rid of a President who was distasteful to them."[34]

On May 26, 1868, thirty-five senators voted to convict President Johnson on articles two and three of the impeachment charges; nineteen of their colleagues voted for acquittal. This left the final vote one short of the two-thirds majority necessary to remove the president from office. The Baltimore *Sun*'s relief was palpable. "The great State trial of this country and of this age came to a close," the newspaper sighed.[35] From the start, the effort to impeach Johnson had been "simply a political trial for political offences"—a flagrant abuse of Congress's constitutional prerogatives that would besmirch the annals of the US republican experiment.[36] "What its consequences might have been, if successful," the newspaper shuddered, "what new and even more revolutionary measures might have followed it—what a Mexicanizor [*sic*] of government, fatal to law, liberty and peace, order and prosperity—who can tell?"[37]

The *Sun* could not revel in this victory for long, however. Hot on the heels of Johnson's impeachment trial was the 1868 presidential election. Republicans put up war hero General Ulysses S. Grant and pledged to continue congressional Reconstruction. Democrats nominated former New York governor Horatio Seymour, who campaigned on an anti-Black platform promising to end federal meddling in Southern politics. As they fell in line behind their candidate, Democratic organs occasionally deployed analogies with Mexico to highlight the alleged amalgamating and centralizing dimensions of the Republicans' Reconstruction agenda. "Mexico may be compared to a big kettle under which the fires of revolution are perpetually blazing," began one article in a Virginia newspaper in May 1868, which by its example "tells us that the experiment of equality among mixed and unequal races can never succeed."[38] According to this newspaper, the central question of the coming election was whether the United States would fan the flames of its own fire and so "go the way of Mexico and all the other Spanish American Republics."[39] Meanwhile, Tennessee's *Bolivar Bulletin* warned that "Radical tyrants" wished to enfranchise Black Americans because without these voters the Republican Party would "not be able to carry a single State beyond the limits of New England."[40] If the Republicans won the upcoming election through the "instrumentality of the Southern negroes," the *Bulletin* continued, the party would extend military rule beyond the South until it had managed to "Mexicanize the whole country from Maine to Oregon."[41]

Most US voters did not heed the Democrats' warnings. In November 1868 General Ulysses S. Grant won the Electoral College vote by a solid margin that included all the Reconstructed Southern states except Louisiana and Georgia. In North and South, the opponents of congressional Reconstruction braced for four more years of Republican rule. A writer for the Democratic *New York World* captured their pessimistic mood well. The Republicans were bent on "Mexicanizing the politics" of the United States, the author declared, clarifying that their use of this phrase was not intended as "a complimentary word to 'our sister republic.'"[42] Rather, it referred to the phenomenon whereby "like our own radical politicians, Mexican leaders recognize only two levers for moving the popular action—the lever of passion and the lever of fear."[43] The writer predicted that, over the course of Grant's second term, Republicans would foment chaos by agitating "ignorant negroes" and white Northerners "into a fury of race against the whites" of the South.[44] This would "keep alive the bitterest memories of the civil war . . . inflame the lust of vengeance in the popular heart," and thereby generate public support for maintaining federal military control over the South.[45] A year later, the *Wilmington Journal* believed that such predictions were being realized. Reflecting on how the United States and Mexico had so far fared in their respective postwar recoveries, the newspaper concluded that "both of these Republics are despotisms" that "condemn and trample on their organic constitutions—both govern by the sword—and the representatives of both tickle each other over their wine as the apostles of human liberty."[46]

Democrats were not the only ones interested in how Mexico's Restored Republic was progressing; Republican-leaning newspapers also followed events south of the border after the fall of the Maximilian regime. To do so, they relied on many of the same news sources that Democratic publications made use of, including certain Democratic-leaning organs themselves; indeed, it's worth emphasizing here that one of the few US newspapers that maintained correspondents in Mexico after 1867 was the *New York Herald*, giving this publication outsized influence over the tone and content of Mexican news circulating through the US press during this time. Perhaps unsurprisingly, then, many Republican newspapers were as unimpressed with the reported trajectory of Juárez's government after its restoration in 1867 as were their Democratic counterparts. While the latter typically turned to arguments of racial inferiority to explain this situation, however, Republican organs struggled to agree on a reason why unrest continued in Mexico even though the country's monarchical and clerical agitators had been defeated. Various theories were put forward—from structural issues in the country's financial apparatuses to the emergence of a resurgent Conservative movement aimed at unseating the Liberal administration—all of them plausible, none of them entirely satisfactory.[47]

Amidst this confusion, a small number of Republican-leaning publications coalesced around one theory in particular. By February 1870 the *Chicago Tribune* had decided that Mexico's underlying problem was the character of its political leaders. Throughout Mexican history, the *Tribune* explained, the towering specter of the Church had united Liberals. The Juarist triumph in 1867, however, had seen their common foe defeated once and for all, creating an ideological void in Mexican politics into which personal ambition had flowed. Thus, the country's politicians were drawn into camps by the promise of patronage rather than by deeply felt political beliefs. Meanwhile election campaigns, nominally forums for earnest ideological discussion, had become petty competitions "between the 'ins' and 'outs' of political power."[48] The result was that the Juárez administration was continually disturbed by "cliques of disappointed office-seekers, or discharged military officers" looking to advance their careers at the cost of party unity and national peace.[49] In another article, the newspaper explained how the self-serving nature of Mexico's political classes created a rot that had now seeped into every level of the country's governing system. South of the border candidates for political office frequently "refuse to accept defeat" after losing an election, one writer for the organ noted in the summer of 1869.[50] No sooner was a result announced than the disappointed office seeker rallied together a band of armed supporters and "a civil war, of greater or less proportions, is declared."[51] The *Tribune* conceded that sometimes the losing candidate's claims were justified, given that corruption was indeed endemic in Mexican politics. More often though, their accusations of foul play were exaggerated at best, fabrications at worst. Whatever their merit, the loser's objections were likely to be believed by their supporters, who had long since lost confidence in the integrity of their nation's electoral system. Another writer for the newspaper echoed much of this analysis, adding that President Juárez had used this degeneration of electoral politics to facilitate his recent turn toward authoritarianism. Pointing to rising instability in the government and across the country, the president had called on the Mexican Congress to grant him additional executive powers in order to secure the public peace, powers he had then used to shut down opposition newspapers and imprison political opponents. Thus, the administration in Mexico City had "morphed into a dictatorship," while beneath it local and state legislatures across the country were sick with a "plague of corruption."[52]

Although they held Mexican politicians largely responsible for this state of affairs, these newspapers also apportioned some blame to what they saw as a culture of factionalism among the wider Mexican electorate. The *Chicago Tribune*, for example, believed that the citizens of that country had become so accustomed to living in dread of the hated Church Party that they readily believed Juárez when he portrayed his "petty quarrels with rivals" as existential battles against a resurgent priesthood.[53] The *Nation*, a popular journal in the urban centers of the United States' northeastern seaboard, thought similarly. The foundation of a successful democracy, the journal mused, lay in its citizenry's "habit of obedience to the law."[54] Historically, Mexico's electoral contests had consisted of cataclysmic struggles between the republic's defenders and its avowed enemies. With the stakes of elections so high, Mexican voters had learned to tolerate all kinds of criminal behavior on the part of their representatives in order to keep the Church Party out of office. And although the clerical opposition had now been effectively eradicated, the damage was already done; Mexicans uncritically accepted corruption, chicanery, and violence as routine features of their national politics, meaning that a candidate need only accuse his opponent of collusion with the priesthood for the public to grant him the right to lie, bribe, or force his way into office. Respect for the law was the lifeblood of a democracy, the *Nation* concluded, and "if a people once loses it . . . the result, as we see in Mexico, is anarchy."[55]

Much like their Democratic counterparts, these Republican-leaning publications were projecting onto Mexico concerns that they harbored about their own postwar republic. Editor of the *New York Tribune* Horace Greeley had been born into what one historian describes as a socioeconomically "downwardly mobile" Protestant family in New Hampshire.[56] From a young age he had shown an aptitude for reading and writing, and in the 1830s he entered into the turbulent world of midcentury US journalism. After working for various New York publications, Greeley founded the *New York Tribune* in 1841. A Whig at the time, he grew the *Tribune* into one of the most widely read publications in the antebellum United States and an influential mouthpiece for feminism, pacifism, socialism, and antislavery ideas. In the 1860 election campaign, the *Tribune* had called upon its 300,000 subscribers (and many more readers) to vote the Republican Party ticket; during the subsequent war, it steadfastly supported the Union cause.[57] Following Appomattox, Greeley was an early endorser of congressional Reconstruction, an important intervention that bolstered popular support for the program just as it was getting off the ground. "Ex-Rebels," Greeley had told his readers in October 1867, hoped to take advantage of President Johnson's lenient method of reunion to bring about "an aristocratic restoration" in the South, which could eventually lead to another rebellion.[58] By contrast, Republicans' plans to "organize the Southern States on a truly democratic basis" would enable Black voters in the region to resist the resurgence of the master class and therefore "see our long strife ended, all States back in their proper places in the Union, and the whole land quiet, busy and prosperously pursuing the arts of Peace!"[59] It is important to point out that Greeley always insisted that the unprecedented use of federal power for the purposes of reunion would be temporary. "If the Republicans succeed," he vowed, "all the military machinery, Freedmen's Bureau, &c., will be swept away as mere scaffolding, and the States restored to self-government, including representation in Congress, within the next few months."[60]

Yet as the months turned into years, Greeley's faith in Reconstruction wavered. By the second half of Grant's first term, the *New York Tribune* was raising serious questions about the Republicans' Southern project. Greeley found the president's liberal use of executive authority troubling, as he did the growing number of reports in the national press detailing rampant corruption in Republican-run Southern legislatures. Underpinning all of this was the newspaperman's mounting concern that federal interference in Southern politics was doing harm to the wider effort to emotionally and spiritually reconcile the people of the North and South. In the summer of 1871 Greeley toured the former Confederate states. As he traveled he wrote letters, later published in the *Tribune*, describing the contrition and goodwill he encountered among white Southerners along the way. "I am entirely confident," read one dispatch sent from Tennessee, that "none know better than the great body of the Southern Whites that the reenslavement [*sic*] of the Freedman is a moral impossibility."[61] The trip confirmed Greeley's suspicion that Republicans had been exaggerating the degree to which disloyal sentiments persisted in the South in order to justify continuing to hold the former Confederate states under military rule. Any hostility that white Southerners did harbor toward the government, the editor believed, was an understandable response to the ignominy of living under the rule of corrupt Reconstruction legislators backed up by federal soldiers. "Thousands hate the 'carpetbaggers,'" Greeley surmised, but they "do not hate the Union."[62] In his mind, by humiliating and villainizing white Southerners, Reconstruction was now inflaming unrest in the South rather than suppressing it.

Properly understood, Greeley's shift on the Reconstruction Question was a change in tactic rather than in strategy. As one of his biographers, James M. Lundberg, notes, from the program's inception Greely had maintained with "unwavering consistency" that the purpose of Reconstruction was to reunify the United States in such a way as to safeguard the country against future civil wars.[63] Central to this task, the editor believed, was the revival of affective bonds of shared identity among citizens from the sundered sections of the Union. Patriotic unity was an intangible goal, but to Greeley a profoundly important one that could be achieved only if the right approach was taken. He was adamant that most white Southerners had been duped into supporting secession and that dormant within their hearts was an abiding love for the US republic. While he initially supported Republicans' plans to reform the South, Greeley had therefore always been clear that the program must only go as far as was necessary to break the old Slave Power's hold over the region's economic and political apparatuses. Lundberg explains that Greeley believed that any "harsh, unreasoned retribution" against white Southerners, such as imprisonment, confiscation, or disenfranchisement, would "have little effect beyond perpetuating the enmity that had led to the war in the first place."[64] By the end of the 1860s, confident that the old slaveholding class had been disempowered and sensing that federal intervention was now exacerbating rather than soothing antigovernment sentiment in the South, Greeley withdrew his support from Reconstruction.

He was not the only editor to do so. Between 1868 and 1870 several prominent newspapermen, including Samuel Bowles of the *Springfield Republican* and editor of the *Chicago Tribune* Horace White, rescinded their endorsement of Reconstruction. They did so in large part because they, like Greeley, believed that the project was undermining national reconciliation. It is no coincidence that many of these editors belonged to the upper echelons of northeastern society. Most had attended the best universities in the antebellum United States, where they had received a traditional education in Roman and classical political philosophy, among other things. The trauma of the Civil War had intensified these well-heeled editors' appreciation for certain classic republican-inspired theories, especially the notion that the citizens of a self-governing country ought to approach public affairs with a spirit of cooperation rather than factional self-interest. This teaching resonated with them even more strongly during the late 1860s as they witnessed political violence and criminality erupt across the Reconstruction South—depressing proof, they believed, of what a lack of trust, unity, and public-mindedness in a democratic society could lead to.

Finding themselves increasingly at odds with the Republican Party's Southern agenda, these editors needed a new political home. They found one in 1871 when a group of similarly alienated Republican and Democratic politicians, journalists, and reformers launched a challenge to President Grant's reelection campaign. Uniting under the banner of the Liberal Republican Party, members of this diverse group disagreed on many fundamental issues, including tariffs and free trade. All of them, however, were adamant that Reconstruction must be brought to an immediate and long overdue end. It is important to note that Liberals did not propose to reverse Reconstruction's achievements. Rather, they argued that the federal government should hand over the duty of protecting freed people's rights to state authorities administered by patriotic, civic-minded Black and white Southerners. Doing this, Liberals reasoned, would cleanse the South of corrupt carpet-bagger legislators while showing white Southerners that the federal government valued them as trusted citizens of the republic. Southern goodwill toward the Union would then grow, thereby strengthening the bonds of national unity and ensuring lasting civic peace in the country.[65]

Both the *Springfield Republican* and the *Chicago Tribune* endorsed the third-party movement, as did Edwin Godkin's *Nation*. Horace Greeley's support, meanwhile, would extend further than this. In May 1872 the Liberal Republicans met for their convention in Cincinnati. The initial frontrunner for the party's presidential nomination was Charles Francis Adams of Massachusetts. Though he won the first five rounds of voting, Adams's margins were not large enough for him to take the nomination. On the sixth ballot, delegates broke the stalemate by nominating Horace Greeley. It was an improbable choice that bemused many contemporaries at the time and historians since. Greeley was known for his eccentric temperament, a quality not traditionally desirable in a presidential candidate. He was, furthermore, a protectionist and therefore at odds with his party's large number of free trade adherents. Still, there was some logic to the nomination. Black voters would likely remember the editor's career-long battle against slavery. Somewhat paradoxically, Greeley might also garner the support of some white Southerners thanks to the fact that, ever since the Civil War, he had been calling for the federal government to treat former Confederates with mercy and respect. This gamble paid off in July when the regular Democratic Party, lacking a viable candidate of its own, also nominated Greeley to head a fusion ticket on an anti-Reconstruction platform.[66]

During the 1872 election campaign Liberal Republicans took their message about the perils of factionalism under continued Reconstruction to the people. Interestingly, they found in Mexico a topical example of the kind of dangers they were warning against. In June 1871, President Juárez had won reelection by a narrow plurality of the vote. The result provoked a rebellion led by renowned war hero General Porfirio Díaz, who accused the president of violating the 1857 Constitution's single-term presidency clause along with a host of other supposed abuses of power. The La Noria Rebellion lasted only a few months and ultimately never grew beyond a series of minor uprisings.[67] Nevertheless, it was enough to rattle the already precarious Juárez administration. It also drew the attention of the US press, which, viewing the crisis from a distance, occasionally speculated that it might spell the end of the Juárez administration.[68]

The interest that Liberal Republican organs exhibited toward the La Noria Rebellion primarily stemmed from the fact that it was a useful example of what could come from the ruinous symbiosis of popular factionalism, political criminality, and government tyranny. The *Chicago Tribune*, for example, pointed out to readers that President Grant's efforts to secure the passage of the 1871 Ku Klux Klan Act were the "same thing in principle" to the manner in which Juárez had pressured the Mexican Congress to grant him "ample powers" to suppress the uprising.[69] "Like Juarez in Mexico," Grant had supposedly abused this power to "silence all opposition by arrest, without trial . . . all persons who may oppose him."[70] The newspaper even claimed that several members of Grant's cabinet had expressed their "delight at the mode of making laws" in Mexico, where the president could "make laws by decree," and had praised Juárez for taking a "judicious step in cutting the Gordian knot" of constitutional restraint.[71] Apparently the admiration went both ways. "Juarez is sustained in his course of dictatorship by the example of Grant," the *New York Tribune* asserted, to whom the Mexican president would point whenever he was accused of abusing his executive power.[72] How could his conduct be wrong, Juárez supposedly asked his critics, if the US president administered his government in a similar manner? Thus, the *Tribune* lamented, "the baleful example of the 'model Republic'" was having a "most deleterious influence" south of the border.[73]

These newspapers insisted that a Greeley administration would correct this perversion of the United States' symbolic role on the continent. In August, a journalist based in Mexico City informed readers of the *New York Tribune* that "there is considerable anxiety expressed among the Mexicans on the subject of the Presidential election in the United States."[74] Each person to whom the reporter had talked had apparently expressed "the highest hopes" for Greeley's election in November.[75] Their keen interest in the US presidential contest, the writer explained, was due to their belief that Juárez had been "sustained in his course of dictatorship by the example of Grant."[76] Evidently these Mexicans understood something that many US Americans appeared to have forgotten—that the integrity of the United States' electoral processes were of concern to all peoples around the world who needed proof that democratic republicanism was superior to all other forms of government. The *Chicago Tribune* made a similar point in October 1872 when it contended that in recent years the United States had slipped from its "proper role as the model of democracy" by "permitting vice and venality to pollute its institutions."[77] Greeley's election, however, would restore harmony, virtue, and order to the nation's politics, regenerating the country's image as a successful republic to which Mexicans and all other admirers of free government could aspire.

Liberal Republicans would not get the opportunity to attempt to fulfill these promises. On November 5, 1871, Grant won the popular vote by an impressive majority. Two weeks later, before all of the electoral votes had been cast, Greeley died. Grant was left to capture 286 electoral votes in total.[78] The *Springfield Republican* interpreted the election's outcome as a triumph for the forces of factionalism in US society. The "perpetuation of the divisions and the animosities" that had plagued the United States since the close of the Civil War, the newspaper gloomily predicted, would continue to corrode its politics.[79] Over the course of Grant's second term, other former Liberal organs pointed to signs that this prophecy was being realized. "There has developed in the South . . . a pattern of tit-for-tat," the *Nation* observed in 1874, whereby "one party's wrongdoing . . . is taken as license for the other to do the same."[80] Republicans in control of the region's local and state electoral apparatuses routinely tampered with voting returns, the journal claimed. In response, Southern Democrats employed extralegal and often violent methods to depress the Republican vote in order to give their party a fighting chance at the polls. Republicans allegedly then used this violence to ease their consciences regarding the frauds that they themselves had committed. Thus, the two parties were locked in a spiral of corruption, which was rapidly escalating beyond control. "The next step in this devil's logic," the *Springfield Republican* foretold, "will be for the party so counted out to refuse to peacefully submit—then we shall have come to Mexicanization and anarchy."[81]

For supporters of the Liberal Republican movement, the fundamental problem facing the United States in the early 1870s was the fact that, although the Slave Power had been eradicated, the country remained as fractured as it had been immediately following the Civil War. They therefore reasoned that some new enemy must be perpetuating division and distrust in US politics. Liberal newspapers frequently held up the image of the craven office seeker to explain what was ailing their country's politics. However, they also emphasized that this villain was only able to operate thanks to the wider culture of factionalism that had seeped into the electorate. In this way, it was the habits of individual citizens that now hindered national stabilization—arguably an enemy far more difficult to uproot than the Slave Power had been.

Liberals' sense of the enormity of this challenge was apparent in their use of analogies with Mexico to describe this new national threat. During the Civil War, when they had compared Southern rebels to French imperialists, these publications had echoed the rousing sentiments of continental fraternity and stridently predicted the eventual triumph of free government in North America. By the early 1870s, however, having watched reunion on both sides of the border devolve into yet more conflict and discord, these same organs described the US-Mexican relationship as akin to a death pact, a mutual descent into dissolution and decay. The outcome of the 1872 presidential contest suggested that the Liberals' warnings had failed to resonate with the majority of US voters. The election that came four years later, however, would bring home to many people in the United States the seriousness of the threat that factionalism posed to the integrity of their supposedly exceptional republic.

The Contested Elections of 1876

Over the course of Grant's second term, the US press's interest in Mexican current affairs waned. In 1872, President Juárez died of a heart attack. In accordance with the provisions of the Mexican Constitution, he was replaced by president of the Supreme Court Sebastián Lerdo de Tejada. That October, Lerdo consolidated his position by holding and then winning a general election. In the United States, many observers had high hopes for Lerdo, an experienced politician who had some name recognition north of the border due to his time as Mexico's Secretary of Foreign Affairs between 1863 and 1871. Early in the first Lerdo administration articles appeared in the press written by US journalists stationed in Mexico that suggested Mexico's fortunes might be taking a positive turn. Soon after the election, for example, the *Burlington Free Press* printed a letter from one such correspondent explaining that the Lerdo government had issued a declaration of amnesty to all those previously in arms against the Juárez government. Apparently, the measure had been effective. "Porfirio Diaz and Donato Guerra are the only rebels of note who have not accepted the amnesty," the journalist explained, and across the country government forces were reassuming control of areas previously in rebellion.[82] Overall, the writer concluded, "the political situation is improving, and it is thought that the administration of Lerdo Tejada will be successful."[83] The following year, US Minister to Mexico Thomas H. Nelson assured readers of the *New York Herald* that Lerdo was "one of the profoundest statesmen of the age," adding that his "elevation to the Presidency brought about a confidence throughout the country which had long been wanting."[84] Not only had Lerdo earned his title peacefully through constitutional means, Nelson explained, but he also intended to pursue certain reforms that would augur well for the country. These included establishing an income tax to ensure the national government some financial stability, reviewing customs laws to root out corrupt practices, and cracking down on smuggling across the US-Mexico border.

Lerdo's time basking in rays of approval from the US press was short-lived, however. Within a year or so it had become clear to most observers in the United States that the new administration in Mexico City did not constitute the sharp break with the Juárez era they had anticipated and hoped for. Lerdo kept much of Juárez's cabinet in their positions, for example. He also pushed ahead with many of his predecessor's anticlerical reforms and, more worryingly, proved willing to make use of a broad range of extraordinary executive powers. Finally, Lerdo struggled to make headway with his promised financial and commercial reforms, partly because of widespread infighting within the Liberal Party. With the national government struggling, unrest across Mexican society grew once again. By 1873, the country's politics appeared to have slipped back into its well-established pattern of *pronunciamientos* and uprisings, a dynamic so familiar to US readers as to be mundane. While most major US newspapers continued to follow events south of the border, they increasingly relegated Mexican news items to short columns that appeared on the back pages of their issues. Between 1873 and 1875, Mexico typically made front-page news in the United States only when issues arose regarding the US-Mexican border such as smuggling and especially raiding, the latter surging at this time as Kickapoo tribe members sought vengeance against white communities in southern Texas for alleged assaults previously made against them. For their part, newspapers in the United States characterized the Mexican authorities as either unable to suppress these activities or unwilling to do so because of kickbacks they received from those who participated in these nefarious trades.[85]

By this time, Mexico finally had a minister in place in Washington, DC. However, Ignacio Mariscal would undercut his own effectiveness as a spokesman for the Lerdo administration early in his tenure by insisting whenever he was quizzed on the subject by US journalists that Washington, DC, and Mexico City were equally responsible for the situation in the borderlands. Then in 1875, Mariscal made a damaging misstep when he suggested that some of the raids were in fact being committed by US citizens in Texas. Across the United States, publications rallied to the Texans' defense. "Mariscal, the 'greaser' minister at Washington, tells our government that the Texans do more stealing than his people," the *Oklahoma Star* fumed in December 1875.[86] The *Chicago Tribune* was also disturbed that "the Mexican Minister at Washington is at some pains to set forth in strong colors the Greaser side of the border question."[87] The Chicago *Inter-Ocean*'s response was similar. "The people of Texas have made no raid upon those of Mexico since the treaty of Guadalupe Hidalgo in 1848," the newspaper asserted, condemning Mariscal for attempting to see to it that "the blame would be shifted from bloodthirsty, plundering Mexicans" onto upstanding US citizens.[88] The use of anti-Mexican racial slurs—common enough in the antebellum era but less frequently used during the 1860s, the so-called era of continental fraternity—is some indication of these newspapers' lack of respect both for Mariscal and the government that he represented. This included publications such as the *Chicago Tribune*, which only a few years earlier had been firm champions of the Mexican republic.

In 1876 the US press's interest in Mexico abruptly shifted from the border to Mexico City. This was thanks to the occurrence of two highly controversial elections that year, one in Mexico and the other in the United States. In January 1876 President Lerdo declared that he would run for a second term in office. Echoing the events of four years earlier, the announcement prompted General Porfirio Díaz to again raise a rebellion. This time he was successful. In November, rebel forces captured Mexico City and installed Díaz in the Palacio Nacional.[89] While Díaz was settling into his new residence, US voters went to the polls to elect a new president. Two candidates were in contention: Republican Rutherford B. Hayes and Democrat Samuel J. Tilden. The outcome following election day was not clear. The first count of the electoral vote gave 184 to Tilden against Hayes's 165. The remaining twenty votes were in dispute. Democrats and Republicans accused one another of having manipulated the returns in Oregon, Florida, South Carolina, and Louisiana. Each claimed these states for their respective candidate and sent their own set of returns to Washington to be counted by Congress. The two sides were at an impasse, and for weeks following nobody was sure how the crisis would be resolved.

Historian Gregory Downs has shown that during the election crisis of 1876, which lasted from election day in November to the following March, US Americans used the term Mexicanization to describe what they viewed as the breakdown of law and order in their nation's political system. Indeed, parallels between Mexico's latest election controversy and the one taking place in the United States were painfully apparent to members of the US press. The *Harrisburg Telegraph*'s pointed comparison between the two is worth quoting at length: "The miserable condition of Mexico is the first result of popular partisan revolt against the declared results of elections; and the present outburst is in consequence of Lerdo de Tejada, an Anti-Church President, having been elected at the last Presidential election. Thoughtless people, who talk lightly about withstanding the inauguration of Hayes, would do well to consider the inevitable consequences of rabble uprisings against the legally declared results of an election here, and then ask themselves whether they really intend to Mexicanize the government of this country?"[90]

Downs is correct to note that the use of phrases such as Mexicanization spiked in the months following the 1876 election. As we have seen, however, this language was nothing new; US Americans had been making fretful analogies between themselves and their Mexican neighbors on and off since the start of the Secession Crisis, even though the use of such rhetoric had lulled after the excitement surrounding Grant's 1872 reelection had subsided. Moreover, while Downs suggests that contemporaries used analogies with Mexico to refer to what they saw as the rise of criminality and specifically violence in US politics, it is more accurate to say that there was no single Mexicanization discourse with a fixed set of meanings attached to it. Rather, people in the United States understood the causes and nature of their country's apparent Mexicanization through the lens of their sectional and party affiliations. Democratic organs, for example, blamed Mexicanization on power-hungry, would-be authoritarian Republicans. Thus when President Grant sent "visiting statesmen" to recount the vote in the disputed states, Democratic newspaper the *Galveston Daily News* pronounced it an attempt by the federal government to tamper with the vote—a trick that resembled the "traditional way of managing elections and constructing administrations in Mexico" where the presidency was the "spoil of the party that can display sufficient military force to control State and municipal authorities, intimidate voters and command the deliberations of Congress."[91] The *Atlanta Constitution* was similarly alarmed by reports in December that President Grant had increased the number of federal troops in Washington, DC—a sign, the newspaper worried, that Grant planned to use the military to install Hayes in the White House if Congress failed to certify the Republican electors' returns. "Will the rightful candidate be prevented from taking his seat?" the *Constitution* anxiously asked, adding that if such a blatant violation of the popular will was allowed to pass, US Americans "need not pity Mexico, for it is our turn now."[92]

By contrast, Republicans tended to define Mexicanization as the corruption of electoral processes from below, rather than from above. "Nothing will Mexicanize a country so quickly as riot and tumult," Pennsylvania's *Reading Times* warned.[93] The *North American* thought the same. "Republicans have never appealed from the ballot to the sword in this country," the newspaper insisted on November 13, 1876.[94] *That* was a uniquely Democratic form of political criminality, a clear demonstration of which could be seen in the way that, ever since the close of the Civil War, Southern Democratic leaders, resentful over their loss of power in the post-emancipation era, had resorted to "fraud, force, or intimidation" to get their candidates elected.[95] Thus in the South the "right to vote" was currently determined by whoever possessed "the longest rifle or the heaviest artillery."[96] After years of localized violence, the *American* continued, these Southerners had become sufficiently emboldened as to employ these tactics in a presidential election. As such, the newspaper explained in another article, the question at the heart of the present electoral crisis was "whether a Presidential election in this Republic shall be decided by a fair and free ballot or by mounted and armed marauders."[97] In the *North American*'s view, the stakes of the matter could not be higher, for if the people of the United States chose the wrong path their country would become fully "Mexicanized."[98]

The two versions of the Mexicanization narrative outlined here ran along party lines. At the same time, many former Liberal Republican newspapers blamed Republicans and Democrats in equal measure for the 1876 electoral crisis. "No party," the *New York Tribune* surmised, "has emerged from this election well."[99] Without condoning the violence perpetrated by white Southerners at polling stations, the *Tribune* and other like-minded publications did argue that this criminality had been a reaction to efforts by Republican operatives to manipulate the vote count. They also made the point that such acts of political maleficence were only symptoms of Mexicanization, and not its cause. As the *Nation* explained, in recent years people in the United States had grown accustomed to "treating the political party opposed to [their] own as a band of criminals or conspirators against the Government."[100] In doing so they had learned to tolerate all kinds of chicanery on the part of their preferred representatives, so long as it kept the opposition out of office.[101] Thanks to the toxic divisiveness of Reconstruction, US Americans had lost their "familiarity and respect for certain forms and processes and principles" that had been fundamental to the political culture of their once well-ordered democracy.[102] The *Nation* concluded that prolonged exposure to severe domestic strife had rendered all US citizens vulnerable to Mexicanization. Thus, while the sickness had been evident "in a greater or less degree all over the South" since the Civil War, the 1876 election fiasco indicated that "the north has signs of catching the disease too."[103]

The dispute over the 1876 election dragged on for four tense months, during which US Americans worried whether their republic would survive the crisis. Indeed, if Mexico's experience was any guide, the United States could expect popular unrest and perhaps even armed domestic conflict to follow from the contested result. Ultimately, however, a peaceful resolution did come in the form of a political bargain. Republican representatives offered Democrats a series of concessions if Tilden agreed to a Republican victory, including the promise that, as president, Hayes would restore home rule to the South. The deal broke the deadlock over the election's outcome, and on March 5, 1877, Hayes was inaugurated as president. Soon after, he recalled federal troops from the South and much of the nation's press breathed a collective sigh of relief. "The country has passed through a period of great and protracted excitement," Philadelphia's *Public Ledger* declared, and though the "strain was so great that serious apprehensions filled many minds of the safety and strength of our institutions . . . the crisis has passed."[104] The *Chicago Tribune* said much the same, though with a little more drama. "*Te Deum laudamus!* At last the civil war is over," the newspaper announced, "after sixteen years of strife and commotion . . . peace again spreads their wings over the American nation" and its people could finally "rest from the turmoil of war and war politics, which the demagogues of partyism" had for too long been perpetuating in order to advance their own "personal fortunes and political ambition."[105] In the months that followed, references to Mexicanization almost entirely disappeared from national public discourse.

Though the compromise of 1877 had averted widespread civic unrest, the bargain did not sit well with everyone. From the moment Hayes entered the White House his detractors in the national press questioned the legitimacy of his presidency. Democratic newspapers dubbed him "His Fraudulency"—a title that stuck throughout Hayes's four years in office. Still, such attacks, though designed to undermine Hayes's credibility in the eyes of the public, were nothing out of the ordinary in the hurly-burly of late-nineteenth-century US politics. Just over a year into Hayes's term, however, a group of Democrats in Congress mounted a more serious challenge to his presidency. In May 1878, Representative of New York Clarkson N. Potter introduced a House resolution calling for an investigation into the 1876 election. The House's Democratic majority approved the bill and immediately formed the Potter Committee. For the next ten months the Committee held hearings on alleged wrongdoings committed by Republican operatives while recounting votes in the disputed states of Florida and Louisiana during the last presidential election. Ultimately, the results of the investigation were underwhelming; much of the evidence it uncovered was inconclusive and only served to damage the reputations of a handful of state election officials. What the Committee did succeed in doing, however, was to bring the controversy of 1876 once again to the forefront of national public discourse, and with it the concerns US Americans still harbored about certain divisive forces operating within their body politic. Interestingly, however, commentators' definitions of the causes and actors engaged in this nefarious work had undergone some subtle changes since the election crisis of 1876.

Republican-supporting press organs recognized the threat the Potter Committee posed to the Hayes administration's credibility and quickly sought to delegitimize its work. The *National Republican*, for example, pronounced the investigation an "assault upon the title of President Hayes," which had all the hallmarks of a Southern rebel conspiracy.[106] Certainly Representative Potter was a New Yorker, and most of the congressional Democrats who had approved his resolution hailed from Northern states. However, the *Republican* insisted that these congressmen, much like Copperheads during the Civil War, were stooges of the Southern slavocracy seeking to facilitate the "encroachment of Confederate power" over the country, albeit this time by overturning the 1876 election result.[107] The *Sacramento Daily Record-Union* agreed. These Democratic leaders' refusal to accept defeat, the newspaper declared, echoed the old Slave Power maxim that "the minority always rule."[108] If the Potter Committee succeeded in ousting Hayes from the White House, this doctrine would become the law of the land. "Mexicanization will prevail," the *Record-Union* warned, "all true ordered government will cease, and fraud and force will be in the ascent everywhere."[109] Thirteen years since the fall of the Confederacy, the Southern rebels had apparently still not given up their treasonous ambitions.

Some Republican-leaning publications used this reasoning to call for the reinstitution of federal oversight of Southern politics. As the Chicago *Inter-Ocean* argued, the Potter Investigation proved the "error of the President's Southern policy."[110] Hayes had removed federal troops from the South on the understanding that the region's political leaders would give up their antidemocratic chicaneries. To the *Inter-Ocean*, the machinations of Representative Potter and his cabal of congressional Democrats were evidence that the president's trust had been misplaced. The *National Republican* thought the same. The "Mexicanization schemes of the Tilden plotters," the newspaper insisted, showed that the ambition of Southern traitors to overhaul the republic was as strong as ever.[111] Such accusations were buttressed in the spring of 1878 when a wave of political violence occurred during congressional elections in South Carolina, Alabama, and Louisiana. From this the *Milwaukee Daily Sentinel* surmised that the "spirit of the Confederate Democracy" had been "inspired with new hopes" thanks to the "recent Mexicanization schemes inaugurated at the Capital."[112] "The growing lawlessness needs to be checked," the newspaper insisted, and this could "only be done by the use or menace of force."[113]

Prominent Democratic publications were alarmed at this attempt to use the Potter investigation to relaunch Reconstruction. "There is no intention of the Democratic party in any part of the country to make an attempt to oust Mr. Hayes," the *Memphis Daily Appeal* insisted in June, pointing to a pledge issued by the Committee that it would not seek the authority to overturn the decision of the 1877 Electoral Commission.[114] The investigation was not the entering wedge of a coup, the newspaper continued, but rather an effort to combat corruption in the nation's political system. A proclamation produced by the Tammany Hall organization and later republished by the *Memphis Daily Appeal* said much the same. Although the "whole world knows—or ought to know" that President Hayes was an imposter, it proclaimed, Democrats understood that there could be "no appeal except to the ballot-box in 1880."[115] Democratic organs further charged that Republicans had deliberately mischaracterized the investigation as a rebel conspiracy in order to agitate public sentiment against the South. "Radical fanatics," the *Georgia Weekly Telegraph* fumed, were turning the investigation into a "mare's nest" by depicting it as the first stage of a Southern "rebellion and revolution."[116] Kentucky's *Courier-Journal* similarly chastised Republicans for claiming that "all Democrats were rebels" who were "awaiting a fair opportunity to seize the arsenals and forts" belonging to the federal government.[117] The newspaper reminded its readers that, following the close of the Civil War, Radicals had interfered in Southern race relations in order to create social and political conflict, which had then allowed them to justify holding the South under federal military occupation. Apparently, the same strategy was in play in 1878, as evidenced by the way that Republicans coupled their warnings of impending "armed rebellion" in the South with calls for the Hayes administration to recommence Reconstruction.[118]

These accusations echoed those that Democratic-supporting newspapers had made in the aftermath of the 1876 presidential election. In 1878, however, these publications had a different understanding of what lay behind the Republicans' scheming. As the *Georgia Weekly Telegraph* explained, most of the Republican leadership opposed the Potter investigation out of concern for their own "personal fortunes."[119] Atlanta's *Daily Constitution* similarly argued that the Republicans' efforts to discredit the investigation were aimed at forcing the Committee to close its work before it could uncover the "stupendous frauds" Republican operatives had committed during the 1876 election.[120] The *Memphis Daily Appeal* agreed. Republicans were terrified that the Committee's probe would reveal the full extent of the "fraud, perjury and forgery" they had engaged in to get Hayes into office.[121] Such accusations provided opportunities for Democratic organs to make the larger point that corruption was endemic in the Republican Party. As the *Galveston Daily News* explained, since the Civil War, Radicals had "assiduously cultivated" the belief among their supporters that the Democratic Party was still the political arm of what remained of the slavocracy and should therefore be considered a "public enemy whose triumph would be the sum of all political calamities."[122] This had in turn "lent sanction to the maxim that all is fair in politics" among Republican politicians and their voters.[123] US Americans who voted for Republican Party candidates generally refused to transfer their allegiance to the Democrats even if their Republican representatives were exposed as having committed "fraud and infamy" while in office.[124] Any party that endorsed excessive partisanship—and therefore corruption—in this way would inevitably attract into its ranks those who looked upon political office as a means to fill their pockets. The *Daily News* insisted that this explained why the current Republican leadership was weighed down with "vices and profligacies."[125] The newspaper continued that, though it was ostensibly an intraparty issue, the rot within the Republican Party was in fact a national concern because it engendered criminality and instability throughout the country's political system. This, the *Daily News* concluded, was "true Mexicanization," whereby a republic degenerated through "the spread of the belief" among its citizens "that the state government can only be carried on by one party, and that if the opposition should gain the ascendency" it would destroy the country.[126]

Portraying the Republican organization as a cesspool of vice and corruption enabled these organs to then present the Democratic Party as the party of honest government. The creation of the Potter Committee had been an "able and patriotic act," the *Memphis Daily Appeal* declared, the opening salvo in Democrats' "warfare against villainy and hypocrisy" in national politics.[127]

By claiming that Republicans were seeking to revive Reconstruction in order to create opportunities to enrich themselves through political office, moreover, Democrats elevated the need to oppose this effort from the particular concern of white Southerners into a national imperative. "All who hate venal elements . . . who have infected every state house, every legislature, every congress," the *Appeal* urged, "must stand up against the Stalwart move to give these forces fresh life again in the South."[128] According to this view, the controversy surrounding the Potter investigation did not center on old wartime issues of race, disloyalty, or state sovereignty; rather, it was a contest between the forces of honesty and corruption, virtue and self-interest in public life.

As the debate over the Potter investigation rolled on, the response to it among Republicans and their supporters in the press fractured. As discussed, several major Republican publications claimed to see the hand of the Slave Power pulling the strings of the Potter Committee. However, other organs questioned this assessment. As the Chicago *Inter-Ocean* pointed out, the architects of the plot were Northerners not Southerners. Moreover, they seemed to wish to advance "the personal ambition of a disappointed man," their defeated candidate Samuel Tilden, rather than to resurrect the Southern slavocracy.[129] The Pittsburgh *Commercial Gazette* similarly noted that diehard Confederates had resorted to violence to intimidate political opponents and subvert elections. The Potter Committee, by contrast, aimed at "overturning the logically ascertained results of the election, by an illegal and extraordinary use of the powers of one branch of Government."[130] Political chicanery and legislative trickery, rather than outright force, were their preferred methods of disruption. The Potter investigation, in short, bore the hallmarks of an office-seekers' intrigue, rather than a resurgent Southern rebellion.

Based on this assessment, certain Republican-supporting newspapers argued that Reconstruction was not the appropriate weapon to wield against Potter and his conspirators. As the *Milwaukee Daily Sentinel* explained, in the past the Democratic Party had been dominated by Southerners steeped in proslavery ideology. The Potter Committee, however, signaled a new epoch in Democratic leadership spearheaded by members drawn from the "office-holding and office-seeking class" of the northeastern seaboard.[131] Unlike their predecessors, these men were largely apolitical and viewed elections, voters, and even their own party merely as "instruments for their own advancement."[132] The one strand of ideological continuity between the new party managers and their Southern forbears, as Philadelphia's *Commercial Gazette* explained, was that they all adhered to the old "Southern theory "that a warlike minority shall rule the nation."[133] Some Republican publications further argued that the new leaders of the Democratic Party would be secretly pleased to see President Hayes relaunch Reconstruction. After all, the *Milwaukee Daily Sentinel* pointed out, in recent years that party's Northern leadership had become "less and less under the control of or in sympathy" with its Southern supporters.[134] This was a problem because, as the Baltimore *Sun* explained, the party needed a "solid South" in order to remain viable in national electoral politics.[135] The party's Southern base had been further eroded thanks to Hayes's conciliatory approach toward that section, which was bringing more and more white Southerners into the Republican fold. Apparently Northern Democrats had concluded that they needed to reignite the Reconstruction Question in order re-aggravate sectional tensions and so keep their Southern supporters loyal. Hence the inauguration of the Potter investigation, which had reawakened Southern Democrats' ire over the supposedly stolen election of 1876 and consequently caused some portions of the Republican Party to reject Hayes's reconciliationist policies and call instead for the reintroduction of federal troops in the South.

These Republican publications warned that reopening the Reconstruction Question would strengthen white Southerners' loyalty to the Democratic Party, perpetuate excessive partisanship in politics, and so contribute to the further erosion of national unity. "Nothing can prevent serious results from this proposed scheme," the *Milwaukee Daily Sentinel* insisted in reference to the Potter Committee, "but the united, prompt, and vigorous opposition to it by the law-and-order element of all parties the country over."[136] White Southerners must demonstrate that "the confidence was not misplaced which President Hayes manifested in the South when he withdrew the troops from the State Houses of South Carolina and Louisiana."[137] According to the *Sun*, they could do this by rejecting their conniving Democratic leaders and banding together with Republicans to initiate a "revolt against professional politicians" of all party stripes in order to bring about a "purification of politics" in the United States.[138] No doubt aiming to impress upon its readers the seriousness of the threat that Democratic machinations posed to the republic, the *Sentinel* drew on the discourse once used by Liberal Republicans to discredit Reconstruction. Southern Democrats, it declared, must stand up to their party managers' efforts to use them as pawns in a scheme to reawaken sectional tensions and so "Mexicanize the United States."[139]

The *Sentinel*'s remarks reveal the extent to which certain Republican organs had shifted in their perception of what constituted the principal domestic threat facing the post–Civil War US republic. Certainly, some Stalwarts believed that the old master class remained a powerful presence in the South and therefore called for the return of federal oversight of the region's politics. Among other portions of the Republican press, however, the office seeker had eclipsed the slaveholder as the principal menace lurking within the US body politic. This is not to suggest that one internal enemy had neatly supplanted the other. Rather, by following the various uses of the language of Mexicanization it is possible to see that most Republican publications were in fact conscious of two threats existing in their midst simultaneously, illuminated by the 1876 electoral crisis and the 1878 Potter investigation, respectively. The turmoil surrounding Hayes's election, much of which had centered on white violence against Black voters at Southern polling stations, bore the hallmarks of the disruptive practices of unreconstructed rebels. The Potter investigation, meanwhile, more closely resembled the intrigues of office seekers. Republicans were capable of holding both perceived threats in their minds at once. However, in 1878, when presented with an opportunity to revive Reconstruction, most of them declined; the chance to punish some recalcitrant Southerners, it seemed, was not worth playing into the hands of Democratic Party managers and their efforts to further divide the nation. That this was the majority opinion within the Republican Party was confirmed in 1880 when the Stalwarts failed to get their preferred candidate, former president Ulysses S. Grant, on their party's ticket on a platform pledging to deploy the judicial, legislative, and military might of the federal government to guarantee fair elections and protect Black political and civic rights in the South.[140] Instead, thanks to the machinations of a rival faction within the party named the Half-Breeds, Republican delegates at the party's convention ultimately flocked to dark horse candidate James A Garfield. The result showed that, while the old Slave Power remained a shadowy threat, by this time most Republicans had concluded that there were far more dangerous subversive influences operating in the national body politic that needed to be combated.

An Office Seeker Turns Assassin

On July 2, 1881, for the second time in less than two decades, an assassin's gun was aimed at a sitting US president. Charles J. Guiteau acted alone when he made his attempt on President James Garfield's life at the Baltimore and Potomac Railroad Station, and during his subsequent murder trial several medical practitioners testified to his insanity. Despite the idiosyncrasies of Guiteau's crime, however, much of the US press believed the incident to be the outgrowth of a broader trend in their nation's political culture. The *New*

York Tribune attributed the assassination attempt to what it called the "gradual Mexicanization" of US public life since the Civil War, which had manifested as a "malignant, grasping and desperate spirit" among the nation's politicians.[141] Publications across the political spectrum echoed this view. "This dreadful tragedy at Washington," the Democratic newspaper the *Boston Herald* claimed, "can be traced directly to the low level of our politics."[142] The Republican *Milwaukee Daily Sentinel* agreed. Guiteau's crime was the outgrowth of the "general lawlessness" that currently reigned in US politics and was guided by the mantra that "every man shall be a law unto himself."[143] A selfish thirst for power had gripped the country's leaders, driving them to desperate and deplorable acts. Guiteau's crime was extreme, but for years politicians had been committing a thousand other lesser transgressions—fraud, intimidation, deception, bribery—to get themselves into office.[144]

The target of these newspapers' scorn was not confined to politicians alone. While Guiteau's overweening ambition had led him to pull the trigger, the *New York Tribune* explained, "there is absolutely nothing to account for this horrible deed . . . except the Mexicanization" of US society writ large.[145] By this the newspaper meant the "crazy spirit of faction" that had consumed US citizens of all ideological and regional hues.[146] Repeating a warning that it had issued continually over the past decade, the *Tribune* insisted that, because of their immovable loyalty to party and to section, voters in the United States had effectively invited their leaders to carry on their nefarious deeds without fear of being punished at the polls by their supporters. US Americans' distrust of one another, it seemed, was stronger than their concern for the integrity of their country's political and electoral apparatuses.

The use of Mexicanization rhetoric following the events of July 1881 indicates that major publications of different political stripes perceived the office seeker, and the spirit of faction upon which he fed, as the preeminent destabilizing force in US public life at that time. During the early 1870s, certain independent and moderate Republican organs had raised this concern as an argument for bringing an end to federal oversight of Southern politics. Though initially supportive of Radical Reconstruction, these publications had come to believe that the expansion of federal authority that the program required had given license to Republican leaders' worst vices—namely, a love of power and the willingness to use all legitimate and illegitimate means necessary to acquire it. Furthermore, the Reconstruction Question had itself become a tool for malignant elements within both of the country's main political parties to whip up popular sectional animosities in order to persuade their supporters to tolerate all kinds of deplorable behavior on the part of their representatives rather than voting them out of office. These moderate and independent organs did not necessarily believe that the slavocracy had been entirely expunged from Southern society. They did, however, insist that whatever threat the Slave Power still posed to the nation paled in comparison to that of the avaricious office seeker.

Throughout the 1870s, similar notions steadily gained traction across other sectors of the US press. Since the Civil War, Republican organs had pointed to the aristocratic slaveholder as the chief obstacle to peaceful reunion; Democratic publications, by contrast, had placed this blame on Radicals. Over time, however, even the most partisan press organs expressed concern over the apparent rise of the office seeker in national politics. This shift made sense as the United States moved further away from its civil war. With each year of peace, the possibility of a second Southern rebellion seemed less likely. Meanwhile it became more difficult for Democrats to paint Republicans as rabid extremists after 1877, when President Hayes held out an olive branch of conciliation to the South. Though still powerful enough to influence political discourse throughout much of the 1870s, the familiar villains of the Civil War era were losing their menacing aspect, and new enemies were moving out from the wings to take center stage. Partisan newspapers typically blamed their political opponents for first introducing the spoils system and corruption into US political life. Most agreed, however, that these trends posed a serious threat to the integrity of the republic. By the late 1870s, this common concern led large portions of both the Democratic and Republican press to agree that the resurrection of Reconstruction, supposedly a powerful weapon in the hands of divisive politicians, would further compromise national unity.

The use of the language of Mexicanization in US discourse during the late 1870s indicates how seriously politicians and publicists viewed the scourge of factionalism in their nation's political culture. The idea that Mexico's political malaise was the product of a learned culture was a worrying conclusion for them to come to; after all, the theory implied that any citizenry that was exposed to prolonged internal strife could succumb to the same fate. Some people in the United States worried that this was exactly what had happened to their society during and immediately after the Civil War. Henry Bellows, a member of the Union League Club, expressed this sentiment well in a book he wrote on the history of the League that was published in 1879. The Slave Power, Bellows wrote, had been an "open enemy, whom powder and shot could reach and overcome."[147] By contrast, the "degraded public sentiment" that years of internecine conflict had imbedded in US political culture was a "secret rot, an enemy with the invisible powers of a pestilence" and thus much harder to combat.[148] By the late 1870s, many voices in public discourse saw this form of demoralization as a threat to the stability of their institutions, and therefore to their country's standing as the exemplary American republic. Immediately following the end of the Civil War, the drive to stamp out division in politics had been powerful enough to persuade many US Americans to embrace Radical Reconstruction. Just a few years later, however, that same desire convinced significant portions of them to turn against the project. As they did so, they began to look for alternative initiatives that they hoped could finally bridge the chasms cutting across the national body politic.

CHAPTER FIVE

Reconciliation above and across the Rio Grande, 1877–1883

On March 11, 1883, a baby was baptized in Monterrey, Mexico. The child was the son of Mexican general Geronimo Treviño and his wife Roberta, daughter of US Army Commander General Edward O. C. Ord. The ceremony generated a good deal of interest in the US press. The *Chicago Tribune*, for example, printed a lengthy account of the christening of the "only child known to have been born in wedlock by the cross of Mexican upon American stock"—or rather, the first such child "whose parents had any social or political standing in the Republic of Mexico."[1] This "International Baby," the newspaper declared, symbolized the dramatic improvement that US-Mexican relations had undergone in recent years.[2] In the summer of 1877, General Ord and General Treviño had faced one another on opposite sides of the Rio Grande, their armies at their backs, while newspapers on either side of the international boundary predicted war.[3] The standoff had been triggered by President Hayes's authorization to US soldiers to enter Mexican territory in pursuit of bandits and Native American raiders, a unilateral order that Mexican officials roundly condemned as a violation of their national sovereignty. This was only the most recent in a long series of disputes between the two republics, which for years had been squabbling over trade, taxes, and territory. The fact that by 1883 Treviño and Ord were joined by familial blood reflected how, in only six years, the fraught US-Mexican relationship had transformed into an intimate partnership of exchange and investment. Better still, their grandchild's godfather was former Mexican president Porfirio Díaz, the man who many in the United States credited as having first opened Mexico's doors to US capital and enterprise.

The transformation was indeed remarkable. Notwithstanding a brief interlude of "continental fraternity" between 1862 and 1867, formal US-Mexican relations during the first two-thirds of the nineteenth century had been marred by territorial disputes, recriminations over lawlessness in the borderlands, and unpaid debts. Porfirio Díaz's ascendency to the presidency in 1876, however, marked a significant turning point in this relationship, which by the end of the nineteenth century would culminate in the United States attaining a controlling presence in the Mexican economy. Among the first significant transformations was the growth of US capital investment in Mexican infrastructure and industry, especially in the railroad sector. By 1902, US companies controlled 80 percent of Mexican railroad stock.[4] Businessmen and financiers from the United States also took advantage of the expansion of Mexico's transportation networks to open up undeveloped parts of its countryside for the cultivation and extraction of natural resources. Over the final third of the nineteenth century, US interests came to dominate Mexico's mining, utilities, and petroleum industries. By 1911 the United States would control nearly 38 percent of the aggregate foreign investment in the country, predominantly in the railroad, mining, and real estate sectors.[5]

The rise of US economic activity in Mexico during this period neatly fits within a broader story that historians often tell about the evolution of the United States' global role in the late nineteenth century. Scholars have noted that this period witnessed the country shift from landed to commercial and financial expansionism in its relations with the wider Western Hemisphere. The United States adopted an approach that some historians have termed "new imperialism," which involved extending US power over other nations primarily through the pacific influences of trade and investment. Historians have further posited that, during the late 1870s and the 1880s, Mexico served as the United States' testing ground for these new methods of foreign aggrandizement. As John Mason Hart puts it, after the Civil War US Americans ventured south of the border to develop systems of neocolonial "cultural, economic, and political hegemony," which they would later apply to "the peoples of the Caribbean, the Pacific, and Central and South America."[6]

Another way to understand the growth of cross-border capitalism during the late nineteenth century that has garnered less scholarly attention is to place it within the context of post–Civil War reconciliation. As has been alluded to previously, historians tend to assume that during the two decades following Appomattox most US Americans were too absorbed in their country's domestic troubles to take much interest in foreign policy or indeed world affairs in general. As Brian Schoen puts it, throughout the postwar period people in the United States were focused on "reconstructing the Union from within."[7] As a result, "overseas work would be left—for the most part—to America's new class of financiers and overseas men."[8] This chapter shows that the reverse was in fact closer to the truth. During the early 1870s, highly influential Northern editors withdrew their support for congressional Reconstruction. As they did so, they joined with many of their Southern counterparts in calling for the program to end to allow for meaningful reconciliation between the white sections of the North and South to take place.

At the same time, these disparate portions of the national press came to believe that a robust mission to extend US economic interests south of the Rio Grande would distract their countrymen from wrangling over old wartime issues. For much of the 1870s this theory went untested. This was largely because the unstable condition of Mexican politics meant that the country was an unappealing environment to US businessmen and investors. In 1876, however, Mexico gained a new president, Porfirio Díaz, who inaugurated a period of unprecedented calm south of the Rio Grande. The following year, the US federal government recalled its troops from the former Confederate States. What followed from these two events was a dramatic surge in US commercial and financial activity in Mexico, propelled by a US press championing sectional reconciliation through national aggrandizement.

So far, the chapters of this study have examined how the perception of widespread violence, corruption, and especially factionalism in US politics during the Civil War era led newspapers to draw analogies between the United States and what they characterized as a notoriously chaotic Mexico. The supposedly exceptional US republic, they worried, was in danger of following its neighbor into endless internal discord. To be sure, feelings of national self-doubt had never been universal nor constant across US society throughout this period. Sometimes they waxed while at other times they were subsumed by other currents in the national mood that were also characteristic of the tumultuous postwar era, such as triumph, determination, or ambition. Tracking how US Americans compared their republic to Mexico is therefore one way to follow the ebbs and flows of their insecurities regarding the integrity of their own republic.

This chapter examines a period when Mexico's function in US public discourse changed, however. Beginning most noticeably in 1876, contemporaries gradually stopped worrying about the Mexicanization of the United States and instead began to talk of the Americanization of Mexico. This transformation occurred thanks to the reconciliationist power they invested into the project of economic imperialism south of the border. Initially, US Americans poured their anxieties into this project, anxious for a method to unite the still sundered factions of their republic. But over time, US investment, business, and trade initiatives south of the Rio Grande grew, and with them a broader sense of cross-sectional cooperation within the United States, as people from all parts of the nation engaged in and benefited from these activities. Public conversations about Mexico increasingly focused on the United States' advancing influence south of the border, rather than on the divided condition of its domestic politics. Eventually, prominent US newspapers stopped invoking Mexico as a portent of national disintegration and instead began to portray that country as a protégé dutifully following the United States' example toward societal stability and economic modernization. This image assured US Americans that their nation had survived its period of internecine strife and finally resumed its role as the New World's exemplary republic.

The Question of Territorial Expansion after the Civil War

In the months immediately following Union victory in 1865, the *New York Herald* had repeatedly called for the United States to invade Mexico as a means to facilitate a speedy reunion between North and South. By the end of the year, however, with Republican legislators assuming control over the process of national reunion, the newspaper had backed away from the scheme. Still, it did not forget the idea altogether, and in 1871 a new incarnation of the invasion plan appeared on the *Herald*'s pages. By this time, the Mexican republic seemed to be on the verge of collapse. That year Juárez had eked out a victory in a closely fought presidential election contest. In response, national war hero General Porfirio Díaz launched a rebellion, hoping that mounting popular dissatisfaction with the administration would carry him into the Palacio Nacional.[9] For the *New York Herald*, which had long since given up hope for the Mexican republican experiment, the drama surrounding the 1871 election was yet more evidence that "no stable government is possible" in Mexico.[10]

However, the newspaper believed that Mexico's misery might create opportunities for the United States. The *New York Herald*'s founder James Gordon Bennett had been a longtime champion of territorial expansion south of the Rio Grande, which he understood as part of the United States' providential destiny that all US citizens ought to participate in and benefit from.[11] In 1866 Bennett stepped down from the editorship of the *New York Herald* and handed control over the newspaper to his son, James Gordon Bennett Jr. By 1871, it was clear that the younger Bennett had inherited not only his father's name and newspaper but also his enthusiasm for imperialist ventures. That year the *Herald* reported that General Díaz's La Noria Rebellion, by precipitating the breakdown of central authority in Mexico City, had led to a spike in raiding activities by Native American tribes in the US-Mexican borderlands. The newspaper insisted that President Grant order US troops to take possession of Mexico's northern frontier states to protect US citizens in the region. With US sovereignty established, the *Herald* continued, "forty millions of vigorous Americans" would then flood into these lands, sweeping away their "decaying populations" and allowing that barren and lawless space to "blossom" under the United States' "strong and progressive" influence.[12]

While ostensibly designed to safeguard US citizens living near the border, the *Herald*'s plan also aimed to address another problem facing the United States at that time. Taking aim at the then ongoing project of federal Reconstruction in the South, the newspaper suggested that instead of meddling in Southern politics, President Grant "bring . . . a sharp and decisive issue involving the annexation . . . of Mexico" before the US public.[13] It based this suggestion on the reasoning that "a new and great national issue like that of the annexation of Mexico . . . would arouse popular ambition and fervor; would put an end to sectional discord, by uniting the whole of the American people—North, South, East and West—in one common object."[14]

Certain organs in the US Southwest that had long campaigned for federal action to safeguard US communities in the border regions from raiding parties and bandits responded favorably to the *Herald*'s call.[15] The plan also piqued the interest of certain Democratic newspapers based in the North, which, much like the *Herald*, were taken with the notion that a revival of Manifest Destiny could heal the scars left on US society by years of sectional warfare.[16] Outside of these pockets of support, however, the *Herald*'s Mexican scheme failed to gain much traction in the national press. The response from Southern editors and journalists was notably cool, for example. Historians have established that notions of racial superiority, specifically as they manifested in the ideologies of Anglo-Saxonism, social Darwinism, and the so-called White Man's Burden, spurred US Americans' imperialist ventures throughout the nineteenth century. And yet Eric T. Love has helpfully shown us that in certain cases, racist beliefs could also weaken enthusiasm for extending US borders due to concerns about bringing peoples of diverse races and cultures into the nation's body politic.[17] A study of how US newspapers discussed the prospect of acquiring lands from Mexico in the late 1860s and early 1870s reveals that these exact concerns were expressed at this time by large portions of the white-run Southern press in particular. As the South was then in the grips of congressional Reconstruction, these organs worried that acquiring Mexican land would accelerate the processes of social destabilization and government militarization currently coursing through the states of the former Confederacy. Mexico's "mongrel populations," Tennessee's *Public Ledger* warned in 1871, would be "joined to the blacks and mulattoes of the Southern States" in alliance over the white population.[18] One Louisiana newspaper similarly pointed out that, while the *New York Herald*'s Northern readers might benefit from the bounties to be drawn from this Mexican territory, Southerners would suffer as "several millions of Mexican Indians" flooded into their states and joined arms with freed people and their white Republican allies to strengthen the system of "Negro domination."[19] The *Memphis Daily Appeal*, meanwhile, warned that, having taken land from Mexico, President Grant would no doubt claim that he could only control these volatile regions "through compressive and repressive force."[20] The president would then send troops south of the Rio Grande, trailed by a parade of carpetbaggers who would feast upon that defenseless land just as they had done in the postwar South.[21] The *New York Herald* had suggested that territorial expansion could replace Reconstruction; these Southern organs countered that it would in fact exacerbate the program's most harmful effects.

The press reaction was hardly more encouraging in other parts of the country, though for different reasons. The Civil War had cemented a connection between slavery, disloyalty, and territorial expansion in Northern public discourse. In 1865 many Unionist publications had therefore proclaimed that the Confederacy's fall was an opportunity to forge a new path in the United States' relationship with Spanish America. "By exterminating slavery," *Harper's Weekly* asserted, US Americans had "extirpated the cancer of 'manifest destiny'" and done away with the "infinite swagger and bluster of a slavery-propagating policy."[22] By the early 1870s, many Republican-leaning publications still held firm to this belief. As the *San Francisco Chronicle* put it in 1873, though it was disappointed by the failures of the Restored Republic under President Juárez, it was the duty of the post–Civil War United States "to assist our sister republic in the world of development, rather than to annex her."[23]

Other Northern publications opposed the idea of taking land from Mexico for less idealistic reasons. In June 1872 the *Chicago Tribune* informed its readers of a rumor that President Grant planned to "raise four regiments of troops . . . to go to the Mexican frontier" and take possession of several states in northern Mexico.[24] The *Tribune* speculated that the scheme appealed to Grant's vainglorious and militaristic tendencies. It also suspected that, if the plan worked, the president intended to fill these new territories' governments with the same class of office seekers currently occupying the Southern Reconstruction legislatures. "Let the reader imagine the horror of a carpet-bag Government erected in each of the fifty states of Mexico, each Government supported by one or two regiments of troops," the newspaper shuddered.[25] In ruinous symbiosis, then, extending Reconstruction southward would strengthen its grip at home, and thereby ensure that the United States slid deeper into factionalism.

As it turned out, President Juárez was able to put down the La Noria Rebellion. He would not, however, survive the heart attack he experienced a few months later in the summer of 1872. As we have seen, under his successor Sebastián Lerdo de Tejada the Restored Republic of Mexico continued to struggle. Meanwhile US-Mexican relations steadily soured as tensions flared over raiding activity and other forms of lawlessness on the border. Every now and then the *New York Herald* would again raise the idea that the United States take possession of Mexico's northern states in order to establish some semblance of order in the region.[26] And as in previous years, such calls were approvingly echoed by certain newspapers in the Southwest and a handful of Northern Democratic-leaning publications but failed to gain support in the wider press. By 1877 a disappointed *Herald* was forced to acknowledge that "there has not been for many years so little talk in the newspapers and on the stump about 'manifest destiny'" nor of "our noble bird of freedom spreading his wings and darting toward the distant mountains of Tamaulipas, Chihuahua, Sonora and Sinaloa."[27] While some Republican-affiliated organs argued that such plans smacked of the aggressive expansionism of the old Slave Power, by far the overriding concern among publications in both the North and South was that conquering new lands and integrating them into the Union would exacerbate dislocations in their still deeply divided society. Into the early 1870s, in short, the unfinished task of national reunification dampened popular enthusiasm for territorial expansion. At the same time, however, certain voices in the United States were beginning to discuss how alternative forms of national aggrandizement south of the Rio Grande might in fact aid reconciliation between the sections.

Southern Boosters Think Continental

The Civil War left many scars on the Southern economy: torn up railroads, neglected plantations reverted to brush, state governments deeply in debt. During the postwar period, Southern boosters, determined to repair this damage, published promotional literature, hosted holiday tours, and organized state fairs to encourage outside investors to put their money into the regeneration of Southern infrastructure and industries. As they did so, these boosters emphasized the South's abundant natural resources—its vast forests, rich soil, and warm climates, all of which, they argued, indicated the region's extraordinary productive potential. Boosters were also aware of the importance of convincing potential stakeholders—specifically Northern capitalists and legislators in Washington, DC—that the postwar South was socially and politically stable, loyal to the federal government, and therefore a secure place to put their capital.[28]

Some boosters emphasized the South's proximity to the wider Caribbean and northern Mexico as another way to highlight its economic potential to outside investors. This tactic was especially common among those operating in areas close to major waterways, coastlines, and the US-Mexican border. Despite Mexico's contiguity with the United States, its capital city was harder to reach for most US Americans than London was. The only options for travel to the country were an uncomfortable journey by horse over rough land teeming with bandits and hostile Native American tribes, or a weeks-long voyage on a British steamer that ran from New York to Veracruz via a series of Caribbean ports. This was part of the reason why, by the early 1870s, US Americans were only minor players in Mexican trade, which was otherwise dominated by British and, to a lesser extent, German, Spanish, and French merchants.[29]

This point was driven home to US audiences by certain individuals, among them US Minister to Mexico Thomas H. Nelson, who, during his time in Mexico between 1869 and 1873, became appalled by how US business and merchant activity in the country lagged behind that of European competitors. As Janice Lee Jayes has shown, Nelson "lamented that in Mexico City, the largest city of Spanish America, there were no more than two or three mercantile houses run by Americans."[30] He also bemoaned "the absence of American bank branches in the capital, crucial for providing credit in a region with generally scarce banking facilities," and the "poor quality of US consular agents, who showed little interest in surveying opportunities for American traders, seldom spoke Spanish, and were generally considered useless by both the American and Mexican business communities."[31] Hoping to rectify this, Nelson impressed upon US Americans back home that they were missing valuable opportunities for investment and trade south of the border. In an interview he gave to the *New York Herald* in October 1872, for example, the minister spoke "in enthusiastic terms of the agricultural resources of Mexico," including its potential for the production of sugar, coffee, and tobacco that would apparently rival Cuba if properly developed.[32] He also emphasized that "the development of . . . railroads" was "the first among [Mexico's] great needs," adding that the Lerdo administration was eager for US investors to help push forward this aspect of its internal improvements agenda.[33]

Projects to improve transportation connections between the United States and Mexico were therefore an underdeveloped business that could be highly attractive to farsighted investors. At least this is what promoters of the Texas and Pacific (T&P) Railroad apparently believed. In March 1871 Congress awarded a charter to this newly incorporated company to build a railroad from Marshall, Texas, to San Diego, California.[34] The following year the company published a pamphlet, *The Texas and Pacific Railway: Its Route, Progress, and Land Grants,* to advertise the road's profit-making capacity. The pamphlet listed the line's numerous anticipated advantages, many of which centered on further integrating the Southwest into the US national economy. Another named benefit was that the "giant trunk line," which would run just north of US-Mexico border, would be well-placed to "connect with lines projected in Mexico."[35] These feeder roads stretching "across [Mexico's] northern frontier" would enable Mexico's *Guardia Rural* to move swiftly throughout the region and so "effectually suppress petty revolutionists" and "terminate Indian raiding" that menaced border communities.[36] The borderlands railroad network would also penetrate "the great mineral, pastoral, and agricultural regions of . . . Sonora and other populous provinces" in northern Mexico, allowing US industrialists to open mines in these regions and carry their contents northward.[37]

The Panic of 1873 dried up the T&P Railroad's funds and brought construction on the line to a halt. The following year the company's president Thomas Scott submitted a bill to Congress requesting federal bonds to enable work to recommence. To distinguish his plea from the many others that flooded congressional railroad committees during the depression, Scott emphasized the T&P Railroad's international advantages. In the memorandum accompanying the bill, for example, he pointed out that "a system of railways, based on English capital, has been inaugurated in Mexico, the line from the city of Mexico to Vera Cruz being completed."[38] It was therefore imperative, Scott argued, that the US government support the T&P Railroad to ensure that the trade of eastern Mexico was secured to the United States, to whom "it properly belongs."[39]

Over the following months this argument was echoed by other advocates of the T&P Railroad, many of whom were based either in the US Southwest or along the Mexican Gulf and who were particularly enthusiastic about projects that would link their regions to Mexican waterways and territories. In New Orleans, for example, business communities took a keen interest in the project. The New Orleans Chamber of Commerce came out in support of Scott's bill on the grounds that his railroad would give US Americans access to the "precious metals" of the "the richest States of Mexico."[40] The T&P line would also give US merchants an advantage over their European counterparts, "who can neither employ navigable waters nor transitable highways from their ocean coast across the mountains to the rich and populous cities of interior Mexico."[41] "With such a demonstration of undeveloped values only awaiting the connubial ceremony of intermarriage," the Chamber asked in a letter sent to the US Congress, "does not your honorable body perceive that in postponing this consummation" it is "depriving the American people of the full fruits, which should not be deferred one day beyond the possibility of completion?"[42]

Newspapers in New Orleans were equally supportive of the project. In part this was because, as that city's *Times-Democrat* explained, the "material results" of this and other transportation connections between the United States and Mexico "would be beneficial . . . especially to the Southwestern States, whose commercial future is bound up in the development of relations with Mexico."[43] The *New Orleans Republican* similarly remarked that "there is a world opening to our commerce with the tropics . . . within the grasp of the United States," and that the Southern states were the key to accessing it.[44] By way of an example, the newspaper explained that it was "from New Orleans that commercial expansion must be conducted" because it was "from this port the commercial and postal steamers must depart. Here must the passengers and commodities be interchanged. Here must the results of this commerce be collected, and from this city must their distribution be made."[45] As such, it was in the interests of both "the State and federal authorities" to do all they could to develop "trade between New Orleans and the country of the mines and the Montezumas."[46]

As the above examples suggest, certain Southern newspapermen predicted that the T&P Railroad, and indeed the wider effort to develop transportation links between the United States and Mexico, would redound particularly well to the South. This benefit would not just be economic, but political too. Texas newspaper the *Weekly Democrat Statesman* had cheered when Democrats retook the state legislature in 1873. The coming months provided more cause for celebration as Texas's so-called Redemption was followed by a wave of other Democratic victories in local and state elections across the South, resulting in the party taking control of the US House of Representatives for the first time since before the Civil War. Still, the *Statesman* made a point of reminding its readers that the fight against Reconstruction was not over yet; Republican editors and journalists were bound to respond to their electoral losses by attempting to "discredit" the South, publishing reports that portrayed the section as a hotbed of seditious violence in order to sustain in the minds of Northern voters the "delusion of Southern barbarity and disloyalty."[47] The newspaper reasoned that "the people of Texas" must therefore "preserve the peace" and "suppress all illegal outbreaks and outrages" in order to deny Radical publications the fodder they needed to inflict this "injury" on the South.[48]

The *Statesman* held up the T&P Railroad as a reward white Texans would receive if they complied with this injunction. After all, once federal legislators were confident that Texas was pacified and loyal, they would be more inclined to invest in its economic development by underwriting this and similar infrastructure projects. The *Statesman* pointed out that the T&P line was especially valuable to Texans because it was destined to evolve into an "international route," which would give them direct access to "the great body of the rich Mexican trade."[49] The subsequent boom in cross-border commerce would spur the development of other lines throughout Texas that would "consolidate and unify the State . . . into one vast, indissoluble empire."[50] This, the *Statesman* asserted, would do more to "foster an ennobling State pride in the breasts of all [Texans] than even hallowed memories of early Texan history."[51] The newspaper returned to this theme in a later article, this time emphasizing that the T&P Railroad would be "used by the people of every section" of the United States and would therefore elevate Texas into "the richest, most populous and powerful [state] in the Union."[52] Northerners would quickly realize that they had more to gain from the state's prosperity than its misery, and so demand that Texas be liberated from the oppressions of Reconstruction. Once this shift in public sentiment occurred, the *Statesman* promised, Texans would be protected from undue federal interference "even if Grant rattled thunderbolts on the summit of Olympus."[53]

By the mid-1870s, certain prominent Southern politicians had picked up this message and were broadcasting it to audiences across the South. John C. Brown had been a strident opponent of Reconstruction during his time as governor of Tennessee. After leaving office in 1874, however, he moderated his position on the issue.[54] In 1876 Brown, now vice president of the T&P Railroad, gave an interview to the *Railroad Gazette* in which he professed to be "deeply troubled" by the "violence of feeling" that white Southerners frequently displayed toward the federal government.[55] The Reconstruction Amendments "are now a *fait accompli*," Brown remarked; intimidating Black voters and carpetbaggers therefore accomplished little other than to make the South "an uninviting field for investment" to outside capitalists.[56] Brown urged his fellow Southerners to "lay aside all questions of sectional political strife" and instead "address all their efforts to the improvement of their country."[57] Courting federal assistance for the T&P Railroad would be a good place for them to start. As Brown explained, the feeder lines running southward from the T&P trunk road would provide a "guarantee of peace" in the borderlands while also carrying Mexico's "semi-tropical fruits, sugar, coffee, and many other productions" into Texas and from there throughout the Southern states.[58] Thus if they exchanged political violence for strategic economic collaboration, Brown promised, Southerners would become the principal directors and chief beneficiaries of future advances in US-Mexican trade.

Brown's thinking aligned with that of the business-minded Bourbon elements of the postbellum Southern Democracy. These politicians had been at the forefront of the Redemption movement of the mid-1870s. Now that much of the South was back under Democratic control, however, many Bourbons advised that white Southerners moderate their open, often violent opposition to Reconstruction and make a public show of accepting at least some basic realities of the post-emancipation era. They reasoned that only this would convince federal legislators to cease meddling in the South's politics and social relations and instead invest in its economic modernization.[59] Some of these Democratic politicians echoed Brown in promising continental commercial hegemony as white Southerners' reward for cooperating in this strategy. James Throckmorton had been ousted from the governor's mansion in Austin in 1867 for obstructing the rollout of federal military occupation in Texas. When he returned to politics as a congressman in 1876, however, Throckmorton was calling on Southerners to collaborate with federal power. "How long will you refuse to aid yourselves . . . because of your ancient prejudices against the policy of the Federal Government?" he asked his Southern colleagues in the House.[60] They ought to reflect on what this obstinacy cost them; Mexico possessed "many of the oldest and richest mines" in the world, most of which were "unworked for want of proper machinery to exhaust the water."[61] "What a field for American enterprise and capital is here," Throckmorton remarked, and the only way to access it was through the South.[62] All that was needed was federal funding to build roads connecting Texas to the "northern states of Mexico" and the entire section would transform "into a busy hub of continental trade."[63]

Promoters of other Southern infrastructure projects similarly claimed that their particular initiatives held special advantages for opening up continental trade. For example, delegates to the 1869 Southern Pacific Railroad Convention insisted that their road, running from San Diego to central Texas via El Paso, would "attract numerous feeders from the neighboring Republic of Mexico."[64] The line therefore had the potential to open "the great mineral resources of Arizona and Sonora" to US markets while rendering "more valuable the great stock raising districts of Texas, New Mexico, and Northern Mexico."[65] Meanwhile in 1870 the Southern Commercial Convention demanded federal funds to improve the harbors of the Mexican Gulf states on the grounds that these ports were vital centers of "Mexican trade" and the gateways at which Southern exports have "always found, and must forever in the future find, [their] outlet to the sea."[66] Boosters up and down the Mississippi River also touted their respective projects' continental connections. In 1874, for example, Logan U. Reavis was busy promoting the St Louis and Iron Mountain Railway, projected to run between "Galveston, New Orleans, and Mobile" before "extending to the city of Mexico."[67] Reavis boasted that the road would bring "a unity of purpose, nature and art" to the citizens of the United States and "contribute to the destiny of our people" to hold commercial sway over the continent.[68] Of course, promoters often insisted that their particular project would provide the best access to Mexican trade. Collectively, however, they created an image of the South as the key to unlocking the abundance of resources and both trade and business opportunities awaiting US Americans just below the Rio Grande.

Meanwhile in the Southern press, writers presented continental commercial hegemony as the payment white Southerners would receive for moderating their approach to the Reconstruction Question. Sometimes this message came from Republican organs located in the South. For example, the *New Orleans Republican* asserted that the Mississippi Valley ought to be the "center of the whole tropical intercourse" of the hemisphere.[69] To achieve this, the currently underdeveloped region needed investment, and this could only be acquired if outside capitalists believed that the postwar South had been fully pacified. "The State of Louisiana," the *Republican* explained, "requires nothing more than social order and total abstinence from party politics to make her the most prosperous part of the Union."[70] Certain Southern Democratic organs, particularly those based in urban and industrial centers, made similar arguments. *De Bow's Review*, located in New Orleans at this time, for example, reasoned that outside capital was vital if Southern transportation networks were ever to reach "the trade of Mexico and . . . the southern tropics," which it noted were "among the most rapidly growing in the world."[71] Accepting financial aid from the federal government and private Northern investors was therefore a tactical move in a wider strategy to see the South "gain recognition and appreciation" as the nation's "connecting link to the trade of the hemisphere."[72]

Southerners were not the only ones looking south of the border at this time; during the early 1870s certain Northern organs were also considering the domestic political benefits of expanding US economic activity in Mexico. By 1874 the *New York Tribune* was still adamant that Reconstruction was a "foolhardy enterprise" that only served to "whip up passions and prejudices" among the people of the United States.[73] Legislators in Washington, DC, the newspaper believed, ought to focus "on the regeneration of [the South's] economy" rather than "meddling with its politics."[74] Only by doing so could they encourage former Confederates to view the federal government "not as an enemy . . . but as a generous benefactor" and from this foster a "unity of interest" among the wider US population.[75] The *Tribune* was adamant that this would do "more to restore the ancient good-will and esteem between the different sections of the Union" than federal bayonets ever could.[76] In another article, the newspaper acknowledged that some Republican Southern legislatures had directed revenue into state and local infrastructure projects, but added that typically such monies were either insufficient or misspent. Meanwhile "sectional prejudice" prohibited Northern financiers from committing funds to "any honest program for [Southern] States' improvement."[77] Instead these capitalists focused "their energies westward," the result being that the United States had a "multitude of railroads running east to west" and "hardly any . . . north to south."[78]

Evidently some impetus was needed to draw federal and private capital southward. The *Tribune* postulated that Northerners might "invest more in the Southern States" if they viewed this as part of a larger mission to "open up the commerce of the continent."[79] The same notion occurred to a writer for the *Chicago Tribune*. "What trade there is to be had from Mexico . . . is currently controlled by the Europeans," the author noted in 1873.[80] This was no exaggeration; between 1872 and 1873, Great Britain, France, and Prussia together received 56.7 percent of Mexico's exports and accounted for 64.8 percent of its imports. This compared with the United States' share of 36.1 percent and 25.7 percent, respectively.[81] The fact that Mexican trade was dominated by Europeans, the *Chicago Tribune* continued, was "against the natural law of proximity, against the sympathies inspired by similar political institutions."[82] In order to establish the United States in its rightful role as "purveyor of commerce on this continent," its citizens must invest in "the development of railroads and other means of travel in the South."[83] Furthermore, this "bold venture to assert our nation's influence on the continent" would bolster US Americans' national pride, lessening the appeal of sectional tribalism and thereby taking "political trump cards out of the hands of gambling politicians" who still played on lingering wartime divisions among the population to lever themselves into office.[84] Through foreign aggrandizement, in short, the people of the United States could finally overcome "the evils" of factionalism that had plagued their society since the Civil War.[85]

Despite growing interest among various portions of the national press, plans to expand US commercial and business activity in Mexico went largely unfulfilled throughout the first half of the 1870s. From his position in the United States, Minister Mariscal worked hard to impress upon US audiences that his government was open for business.[86] Much like Romero before him, however, Mariscal was also aware that there were some in the United States who still looked upon Mexican territory with a covetous eye. He therefore frequently coupled his calls for US business and financial cooperation with firm reminders that Mexican land was not available for purchase or conquest, and that his government would jealously guard its borders against encroachments from its northern neighbor. "Mexico has already alienated enough of its territory," the minister insisted in an 1873 public statement addressed to the people of the United States, "and she has resolved to part with no more."[87] It was not only Mariscal who thought this way; President Lerdo was also desirous of securing US capital, skills, and technology without courting a so-called peaceful invasion that would see Yankees strip Mexico of its resources and economic autonomy. He was especially wary of the development of railroad routes across the borderlands, which, as historian Richard White explains, many Mexican politicians at this time worried were "paving the way for the expansion of the United States into Mexico."[88] Lerdo's approach to relations with US business interests reflected this ambiguity. While the president attempted to advance the Liberals' long-held ambitions to expand Mexico's transportation and communication networks, he refused to support the construction of railroads that would connect directly with the United States, fearful of granting US Americans' too easy access to his country's valuable northern mining districts. The president also cancelled a number of government contracts with US business interests, including a decision in 1875 to rescind concessions to all US railroad companies seeking to build in Mexico except the New York–based Mexican National Railroad Company.[89] Throughout Lerdo's presidency, in short, mutual suspicion and old prejudices continued to hamper US-Mexican economic relations.

The Gates of Mexico Open

People in the United States breathed a sigh of relief when President Hayes was peacefully inaugurated on March 5, 1877. Their country had passed through one of its biggest electoral crises seemingly unscathed. Many were also pleased to see the president then announce the withdrawal of federal troops from the South—a promising sign, they hoped, that the fraught Reconstruction Question might soon be gone from the national political agenda. And yet there were voices in public discourse warning that simply removing sources of sectional controversy would not be enough to fully harmonize US society. As Washington, DC's *National Republican* told its readers, ending Reconstruction was just the first step in a longer journey US Americans must now take in order to "rise above the prejudices which bind them to the one side or the other."[90] The next stage was for Southerners to "act in harmony with the Republican party in building up the country and restoring the relations of good-will and accord between the sections."[91] The *Chicago Tribune* likewise cautioned that the hard work of reconciliation still lay ahead; now that formal Reconstruction was apparently over, the people of the United States needed to be reminded that they shared a "glorious future of reunited destinies and hopes" and compelled to "forget everything else but that they are Americans."[92]

At this time prospects for using economic expansion into Mexico as a way to bind together the United States looked dim. This was partly because in late 1876, as US Americans were navigating the fallout of their contested presidential election, Mexicans were experiencing a political crisis of their own. By November of that year, rebel forces had run the Lerdo government out of Mexico City and installed General Porfirio Díaz in the Palacio Nacional. Tumult in the Mexican capital precipitated a breakdown in law and order along the country's northern frontier. Raiding activities by the Kickapoo and Apache upon communities on both sides of the border surged in the early months of 1877 as a result. In the United States, pressure mounted on the newly inaugurated President Hayes to respond decisively. The cloud of doubt surrounding his claim to the presidency made it important for him to demonstrate to the US public that his administration would be strong and capable. Hayes also owed a political debt to friends in the Texas congressional delegation who had given him crucial support during the recent election controversy.[93] One way of repaying them, Hayes understood, would be to end the border depredations that terrorized their constituents in southern Texas.

With these considerations in mind, President Hayes issued a directive on June 1, 1877, which permitted US commander of the Department of Texas General Edward O. C. Ord to pursue marauders across the Rio Grande into Mexican territory. This was not the first time that US troops had crossed the border without the permission of the Mexican government.[94] Much as had occurred in these previous instances, moreover, the act caused outrage among Mexico's political leaders, who interpreted the unilateral decision as a violation of their national sovereignty and a possible prelude to a US invasion. President Díaz—who, like Hayes, was newly in office and therefore eager to demonstrate his leadership abilities—responded forcefully. Mexican troops under General Geronimo Treviño were dispatched to Piedras Negras, opposite US troops stationed near Eagle Pass, with orders to repel US troops by force if necessary. What followed was a military standoff that lasted for the remainder of the year. Interestingly, on the ground General Ord and General Treviño developed a degree of mutual trust and over time agreed on measures that allowed their troops to collaborate in patrolling the border. Despite this, diplomatic relations between the governments in Washington, DC, and Mexico City remained tense; President Díaz insisted that the United States formally recognize his government before he would agree to negotiate official arrangements for policing the border. The Hayes administration countered that it would only recognize President Díaz once he had shown his willingness to shoulder Mexico's share of responsibilities relating to border security. Most US newspapers, skeptical of Díaz's staying power, supported Hayes's firm stance in the matter. As the *New York Times* sniffed, "Díaz is President" only until "some one raises a larger and better army."[95]

But forces were already in motion that would shift public opinion in the United States toward a more favorable view of Mexico's new president. Díaz had fought alongside the Juarists during the French Intervention and generally identified with the Liberal Party. He was no ideologue, however, and his presidency would mark a decisive turn in the Mexican Liberal tradition toward pragmatic technocratic and economic-oriented reform. Much of Díaz's thinking was influenced by Positivist theories, which were gaining ground within certain political and intellectual circles across Spanish America throughout the second half of the nineteenth century.[96] Broadly speaking, Díaz and his allies attributed disparities in wealth within any given population to the relative talent and hard work of individuals, rather than to inequities embedded in wider political or social systems. Additionally, as subscribers to the teaching of racial science and Social Darwinism, they held that a person's race was a particularly accurate indicator of their ability to thrive in a modern economy. For this reason, they were also leery of broad democratic political participation, which in their view gave political power to "backward" peoples such as Native Americans, who did not possess the requisite abilities to exercise this power responsibly. Bringing such peoples into the public realm was a guarantee of political and social instability, which in turn would be a distraction from the more essential work of economic development. Indeed, Díaz and the *Científicos*, as his advisers in government were called, prized social order and economic modernity, rather than political liberty, as the hallmarks of an enlightened nation. Consequently, they jettisoned the traditional Liberal emphasis on political rights and humanistic reform in favor of economic development and commercial liberalism as the best means to promote social peace, individual opportunity, and national prosperity in Mexico.

Once in power, Díaz therefore moved to limit democratic electoral participation in Mexico, especially at the national level, while simultaneously expanding the authority of the executive. His aim was to create a muscular central state with sufficient power to suppress popular uprisings and manage national economic growth. In terms of the latter objective, Díaz focused on several key areas, including the diversification and commercialization of Mexican agriculture, the modernization of the country's productive industries such as mining, and the improvement of its transportation systems in order to facilitate the expansion of domestic and international trade. True to the *Científicos*' creed, Díaz was adamant that these measures would integrate the disparate factions of Mexican society and give employment to its indigent members, thereby deterring them from engaging in rebellions and other disruptive activities.[97]

These ambitious plans required capital—something that Mexico sorely lacked. Díaz knew that he would therefore need to enlist foreign stakeholders to help him to realize his vision. Unlike Lerdo, Díaz and his supporters were unequivocal in their public avowals that Mexico's most powerful neighbor ought to also be its closest economic partner. Indeed they insisted, somewhat paradoxically, that US capital, technology, and expertise could be harnessed to facilitate Mexico's evolution into a strong and wealthy nation able to defend itself against outside aggression, including from the United States.[98] They also argued that courting US investment, trade, and immigration would serve as a useful counterweight to the British, Spanish, and Germans who collectively dominated Mexico's commerce and extractive industries at the time.[99]

It was with these objectives in mind that, during the second half of 1877, Díaz made a series of high-profile gestures that aimed to resolve the ongoing diplomatic and military standoff between the United States and Mexico over President Hayes's Ord Order. Among these was a declaration that his administration would resume repayments on long-standing claims owed by the central government in Mexico to US residents.[100] Díaz simultaneously took decisive steps toward stabilizing the Mexican side of the borderlands by announcing the permanent expansion of patrol forces operating in the region. The Mexican president also made it known that he was willing to grant generous concessions and land grants to US railroad companies seeking to build in Mexico and to offer tax breaks and other incentives to any US businessmen who founded companies in the country. Finally, to assure would-be investors that Mexico was now a safe place to do business, Díaz pledged to provide security forces to guard any new mines, factories, railroad projects, and other foreign-run initiatives in the country.

Díaz's actions soon caught the attention of newspapers in the United States. One Texas publication described them as "auspicious signs" that Mexico's new president wished to inaugurate "a new era in the relations of the sister republics of North America."[101] The *New York Herald*, meanwhile, was impressed by Díaz's efforts to control the "border robberies and outrages" that for decades "had been systematically carried on from the Mexican States against our citizens."[102] When "President Hayes and Secretary Evarts announced in positive language that these must stop," the newspaper noted, there had been "a violent outcry on the part of the Mexicans."[103] Now, however, it was clear that these objections had emanated from the old guard of Mexican politicians who still viewed the United States with suspicion. "But Diaz," who represented a new generation of open-minded and enterprising Mexican leaders, was apparently willing to admit "the justice of [Hayes's] demands and sent an agent to arrange with General Ord for the better protection of the border."[104] "For an administration not yet six months old," the *Herald* surmised, "this is pretty well."[105]

By January 1878 the *Herald* had come to believe that the Hayes administration's refusal to recognize the Díaz administration was beginning to harm US economic interests south of the border. The newspaper was concerned, for example, by the news that "the non-recognition of [Díaz's] government is said to have caused the defeat in the Mexican Congress of the American railroad scheme . . . to build a railroad from the city of Mexico . . . to the American frontier connecting with the Texas-Pacific."[106] The *Herald* grumbled that "the subjects of the Emperor William almost monopolize the commerce of Mexico" while "there is but one American house of any prominence in [Mexico City], and probably not half a dozen in the whole Republic."[107] Clearly "the delay in the recognition of the Díaz government, which is probably now as firmly established as any Mexican government can be, is injurious to the commercial interests of American citizens."[108] Other major newspapers agreed. Mexico's new president was "in the fourteenth month of a rule which has been practically unresisted since its establishment," the *New York Times* observed in January 1878.[109] "We perceive no harm that is likely to result either to Mexico or ourselves from his complete diplomatic recognition, and we can easily see how some good may flow from it to both countries."[110] The following month calls for the United States to open formal relations with Mexico's new government were bolstered by the US Minister to Mexico James Foster. Though initially skeptical of the Díaz administration, Foster had evolved on the issue, to the point where in February 1878 he delivered a report to the House of Representatives warning that nonrecognition was preventing US Americans from gaining a foothold in what under Díaz's guidance would likely soon be a booming Mexican economy.[111] Bowing to the changing winds of public opinion, the Hayes administration relented and in April 1878 officially recognized the Díaz government.

The reopening of relations between Washington, DC, and Mexico City precipitated a surge in US investment activity south of the Rio Grande, which would continue to gain pace throughout Díaz's first term in office. Much of this activity centered on the railroad sector. Soon after assuming power Díaz had begun issuing generous land grants and subsidies to enable US railroad companies to build lines across Mexico. In Sonora, for example, a state known for its extraordinary mineral-productive potential, Díaz granted a concession to the Sonora Railway Company, a subsidy of the US Atchison, Topeka, and Santa Fe Company, to build a railroad from the border to the port of Guaymas. He also subsidized the road's construction at a rate of 9,000 pesos per kilometer of track built. Other concessions followed; between 1876 and 1881 Díaz awarded a total of five concessions to US railroad companies for over 2,500 miles of track and granted them subsidies amounting to $32 million. Many of these lines traversed Mexico's northern frontier, linking remote border towns in the northeast and northwest to central Mexico.[112] Meanwhile similar developments were taking place just north of the border in the US Southwest. In 1881, for example, the Texas and Pacific Railroad was finally connected to the Southern Pacific at Sierra Blanca, Texas. A new line from Shreveport to New Orleans was also added to the road.[113] Throughout the first four years of Díaz's presidency, in short, both the north Mexican and US southwestern railway systems were expanding at a rapid clip.

For some time, portions of the US press had been forecasting that the development of cross-border rail connections would stimulate economic integration among certain areas *within* the United States. As one New Mexico newspaper had explained in 1877, the transportation of Mexican products into and then throughout the United States would connect "the trade of the South" with the "trade of New York, Philadelphia, and Baltimore," creating bonds of "commercial and political sympathy between the people of the North and South" that would "complete the beneficial policy of reconciliation begun so successfully by President Hayes."[114] By the 1880s, these predictions were apparently being realized. "Mexico trade," one Mississippi newspaper reported in 1881, "has given a fresh impetus to business" in New Orleans and the surrounding area, which "is spreading in every direction, and sections that never patronized the city before are now buying largely from it."[115] The *Dallas Daily Herald*, meanwhile, enthused that each road connecting Texas to the "wealth of Mexico" was evolving into an international "highway" from which "the whole country can hope to reap the same great benefits" while also engaging in new projects based on cross-sectional economic collaboration.[116] For evidence the newspaper pointed to the recent creation of a congressional lobby consisting of delegates "from Louisiana, Texas, California, Colorado, Oregon and other sections interested in looking to general appropriations . . . for deepening the water on our gulf coast."[117] The *Herald* approvingly reported that "jealousies between the delegations of different States" were forgotten in recognition that their "common interest beget a Union powerful enough to accomplish its ends."[118]

The Americanization of Mexico

As these examples suggest, these newspapers believed that increased trade with Mexico created opportunities for interregional economic cooperation within the United States, which in turn encouraged US citizens to engage in more profound forms of emotional reconciliation. The basis of this method of reconciliation supposedly went beyond mere mutual economic self-interest, however. During the late 1870s and early 1880s growing economic activity in Mexico took on a deeper cultural meaning due to its associations with popular notions of the United States' national identity and hemispheric destiny. To understand how and why, it is useful to first examine how Mexico's place in US public discourse shifted during President Díaz's first term in office. In 1877 the then newly established president had dispatched agents to the United States tasked with launching a public relations campaign to improve US public opinion of Mexico. The most prominent of these agents was Mexico's minister to the United States Manuel María de Zamacona, an experienced diplomat who had briefly served as Secretary of Foreign Affairs under President Juárez. Zamacona docked in New Orleans in November 1877 before heading up the East Coast to Washington, DC. From there he traveled to New York, then inland through the Midwest via Pittsburg,

Milwaukee, St. Louis, Cincinnati, and Chicago. Along the way Zamacona seized every opportunity he could to speak to the US public. This included giving interviews to reporters and delivering speeches before chambers of commerce, workingmen's groups, and industrial associations. When he had finished his tour, Zamacona settled in Washington, DC, where he set to work hobnobbing with influential editors, politicians, and businessmen, quickly gaining a reputation among the capital's elite for his lavish dinners and warm hospitality.[119]

In certain respects, Zamacona's message to the people of the United States echoed that of his predecessor Matías Romero, who seventeen years earlier had also taken on the herculean task of improving US Americans' perceptions of their Mexican neighbors. Like Romero, Zamacona emphasized Mexico's potentially extraordinary economic value to the United States. As a correspondent for Baltimore's *Sun* reported, at a dinner in December 1878 Zamacona had treated "a meeting of leading citizens and merchants" in Baltimore to a fulsome description of "the climate and civilization of his country, of its productiveness and commercial resources, and of the encouragement which the present government of Mexico is giving to foreign commerce and commercial enterprise in the way of subsidies to steamship lines, concessions to railroads, and facilities and protection to traders."[120] Much like Romero, moreover, Zamacona stressed that the United States and Mexico were members of the same republican brotherhood. As historian Janice Jayes notes, the concept of the two nations being "sister republics" was a common motif in the pro-Mexican literature commissioned by Zamacona for distribution in the United States. Zamacona focused in particular on drawing parallels between US and Mexican history, comparing the disorderly period following Mexican independence to the Early Republic era in the United States and Mexico's War of Reform to the US Civil War.[121] As he did so, Zamacona, much like Romero before him, hoped to normalize Mexico's historic political turbulence for US Americans and encourage them to view their southern neighbors as fellow travelers on the journey toward stable self-government.

Zamacona also shared Romero's intuitive understanding of how to appeal to US Americans' national pride and ambition in ways that advanced Mexico's own interests. During the French Intervention, Romero had spoken often of the Monroe Doctrine, reminding Unionists of their self-claimed duty to aid other American republics through the trials of national consolidation. Zamacona did likewise, but with a slight difference—while Romero had depicted the proper relationship between the two North American republics as one of mutual defense, respect, and exchange, Zamacona was more willing (at least when speaking to US audiences) to portray the United States as Mexico's superior and guide. For example, he gave the United States credit for helping Mexico through the crisis of the French Intervention and thereby rescuing the Mexican republic from one of the most serious challenges to its survival in recent history. "Aided by the good advice and friendly officers of the United States," he reminded a reporter for the *New York Herald* in November 1878, "Mexico was able to hurl the invader from her shores and to overthrow the throne which the enemies of republican government had attempted to establish."[122] More generally, Zamacona was open about President Díaz's admiration of the United States and his desire to imitate its success. As he told the *New York Herald* in November 1877, though many Mexican leaders were still "bitterly opposed to any friendship between the two countries," Díaz recognized that "he must be friendly with [the United States], whose power he understands and appreciates."[123] In other interviews with the press, Zamacona took care to point out that Díaz had staffed his administration with men who had a deep understanding of the United States' system of government and economic apparatuses. As he told the *Chicago Tribune*, "Diaz requested me to come to the United States" because he knew that "I was acquainted with the country," having previously lived there for a number of years, during which he had made "a thorough study of the elements of American industries in regard to the Mexican market."[124]

According to Zamacona, Mexico's new president and his fellow *Científicos* had learned many lessons from the United States. Among these was that economic progress could be used to create social order, institutional stability, and political harmony in a democratic republic. Indeed, Zamacona asserted that the US example proved that economic development was in fact the most effective way to achieve these valuable ends. As he told the Chicago Commercial Convention in November 1878, "some republics existed which had particular regard for civil liberties."[125] While renowned as a bastion of democracy, he continued, the United States was also "acknowledged all over the world" as the model for how the "development of the commerce of the republican and Federal Governments" could produce results that benefitted "the general and moral advancement of mankind" beyond the achievements of any other republic in world history.[126] In another interview, this time with the *Chicago Tribune*, Zamacona illustrated this contention by pointing to the settlement of the US western territories after the Civil War. Zamacona professed astonishment at how quickly "railroads, cheaply constructed, built up the country" throughout the late 1860s and 1870s, crisscrossing the vast western expanses with steel roads that drew these distant regions into the national fold.[127] Zamacona proclaimed his admiration for this process not only as an extraordinary feat of technology and manpower, but also as a national endeavor that had bound US Americans in a common purpose at a time of severe domestic division, thereby helping to safely guide the country through its perilous post–Civil War period. Zamacona intimated that President Díaz had taken note of this achievement and intended to apply the same methods to Mexico, a nation that also possessed both expansive unsettled frontier regions and deep social fissures no military or political tools had yet satisfactorily healed. "I cannot understand why the same enterprises which have been successful and profitable here," Zamacona declared, "may not be productive of the same results in Mexico under the same circumstances."[128]

Other spokesmen for the Díaz government in the United States echoed Zamacona's message. As Mexican general José Mariscal told the *New York Herald* early on in the president's first term, Díaz wished to "cultivate the most friendly relations with our eldest sister, from whom we have copied many of our institutions."[129] Mariscal explained that Mexico's new president understood that after the Civil War the United States had suffered from acute political factionalism, similar to that which had plagued Mexico for decades. Díaz had therefore observed with interest and "admiration" how US Americans had overcome their "many prejudices" by channeling their energies into projects for domestic economic development, and he was determined to help Mexicans to do the same.[130]

This flattery was well-received. The *Chicago Tribune*, for example, approvingly noted that President Díaz was "a man who is familiar with the United States, who knows our greatness and resources . . . and who is familiar with our public men and public policy."[131] What most impressed the *Tribune* was that Díaz had apparently learned from the United States that economic progress, rather than political experimentation, was the surest way to unify a divided population—a lesson hard-learned by US Americans during the trials of Reconstruction. The *New York Herald* similarly praised Díaz for having gleaned from the US example that productive employment would most effectually cultivate Mexicans' "desire for stable government and steady business, instead of bad government and frequent revolutions."[132] The *Washington Post* explained this further when it described how, historically speaking, poverty had created political instability in Mexican society by encouraging its lower orders to "join in any revolutionary uprising" that promised to improve their condition.[133] Once they were recruited into the ranks of a military chieftain, the newspaper continued, these Mexicans "acquired all the habits of idleness, and the vices common to soldiers."[134] The *Post* concluded that Díaz was therefore wise to focus on economic development in order to create work for his country's malcontents, understanding that the consequent rise in prosperity and social mobility among the population would undercut the appeal of demagogues' calls for rebellion.

A substantial portion of the US press held that societal peace and economic development were the best that any federal government in Mexico could hope to achieve. Having long since concluded that Mexicans were unfit for self-government, these publications argued that it would be useless for any central administration to attempt to improve that country through the pursuit of more politically orientated goals such as widening democratic activity or extending civic and political equality across Mexican society. They therefore praised Díaz's efforts to shift popular attention from politics to industry. Some were even willing to reconcile themselves to certain authoritarian aspects of the new president's regime. By early 1878, for example, Texas's *Weekly Democratic Statesman* had come to terms with the means by which Díaz had first seized power. "The truth is that however defective the title of Díaz to the presidency, it was none of our business to investigate," the newspaper insisted.[135] The *New York Times* thought much the same, pointing out that Díaz's path to the presidency was hardly extraordinary in the context of Mexican political history. "Though Gen. DIAZ made himself President by overturning the lawful Government," the newspaper remarked, "the event was not so unprecedented in Mexico as to make us unduly sensitive about accepting it as a fully-accomplished fact."[136] The *Times* added that, "though Diaz held control of the country as dictator," his efficacy so far in terms of quashing uprisings, revolutions, and coups was unprecedented.[137] "Now and again . . . we fear of military adventurers pronouncing against the Government," the newspaper observed, but "their efforts have always ignominiously failed."[138] Díaz, in short, had offered Mexicans domestic peace in exchange for some of their democratic liberties—an eminently fair deal according to these publications.

Other newspapers in the United States that admired the Díaz administration were more reluctant to throw in the towel on Mexico's democratic republican experiment. Nevertheless, these organs were able to reconcile themselves to the undemocratic aspects of Díaz's government by reasoning that the social order brought about by the new president's economic regeneration program would pacify, unify, and harmonize Mexican society—essential foundations, they said, upon which to develop that country into a healthy democracy in the future. As the *New York Herald* explained in February 1879, "it will be impossible to secure political stability in Mexico" without first establishing "a strong government" capable of directing the country's economic modernization.[139] The newspaper pointed out that throughout history most revolutions had occurred when "illegitimate agitators" riled up "the hungry and idle for the instruments with which they hope to overturn society."[140] By contrast, citizens engaged in meaningful employment who had opportunities for economic advancement and therefore a stake in the existing order were rarely drawn into these intrigues. Thus "no workingman is a revolutionist unless his personal rights are outrageously violated."[141] The *Herald* continued that economic development also encouraged interaction across class and regional lines, fusing together fragmented sections of society and creating a sense of common purpose among the citizenry. Should this happen in Mexico, the newspaper predicted, a spirit of "national vitality" would organically emerge among the population, which would then evolve into popular adhesion to the republic's democratic institutions and the values that underpinned them.[142] Following this reasoning, the *New York Herald* asserted in a later article that Díaz's decision to prioritize economic over political progress was in fact a tactical move within a wider effort to transform his country into a successful democratic republic. "The process . . . must be slow," the newspaper informed its readers, "but that a start has been made toward securing so desirable a result is a great point gained."[143]

Efforts by US newspapers to present the Díaz regime as a stepping stone toward true democracy in Mexico were most apparent in the run-up to the 1880 Mexican presidential election. In the summer of 1879, Díaz announced that he would abide by the Mexican Constitution's single-term clause and step down from office at the end of his term the following year. The news stunned observers in the United States. "He firmly declines to serve another term," an amazed *Atlanta Constitution* reported, "even if the constitutional amendment prohibiting his re-election is repealed."[144] This was not the ordinary conduct of a Mexican president; even the Liberal hero Benito Juárez had twice run for reelection in contravention of this constitutional rule. US newspapers were further impressed with President Díaz's behavior over the following months as the election campaign got underway. The *Chicago Tribune*, for instance, approvingly noted that "President Diaz has taken firm ground against office intrigues in the coming election" and instructed "circulars to be directed to all Government employees throughout the Republic, ordering them to abstain from all participation in the election organization under a penalty of removal."[145]

The US press did catch wind of some dubious activities as election day approached. It was widely rumored that Díaz had secretly chosen his secretary of war Manuel González to be his successor, for example, and that he was quietly making arrangements to ensure that González won the election. And yet most major organs in the United States seemed remarkably unperturbed by this news. "It is true enough that Gen. GONZALEZ . . . has for some time been on terms of great intimacy with the President, and there is no doubt that the latter must view his success with peculiar satisfaction," the New York *Sun* conceded.[146] The newspaper explained that this was not necessarily a bad thing, however. After all, González was cut from the same ideological cloth as Díaz and was therefore certain to continue his predecessor's economic regeneration agenda. Moreover, given that Mexicans were still unused to carrying out the sober duties of democratic citizenship, a truly open election might well end in the masses electing a rabble-rousing demagogue who would undo all the good work of the last four years. The *Sun* insisted that what really mattered was not the reality of an entirely free presidential election in Mexico, but its appearance. Díaz had consciously adopted a public "attitude of self-repression and unswerving fidelity to the laws" of the Constitution in his management of the election so far, the newspaper explained.[147] His aim in doing so was to teach his people by example the importance of respect for the rule of law in politics. Though he may have engaged in some backroom manipulations, the *Sun* concluded, Díaz's outward-facing conduct would do much to restore Mexicans' trust in their electoral system. For this effort alone, the Mexican president ought to receive the "cordial esteem of the friends of republican institutions throughout the world."[148]

Few US observers were surprised when González won the 1880 presidential election. Far more extraordinary to them was that the following December Díaz fulfilled his pledge to relinquish the reins of power to his successor. "The populace cheered ex-President Díaz when he left the palace after delivering the executive departments to President Gonzales," the *Philadelphia Inquirer* enthused, adding that "General Gonzales is the first President under the Constitution of 1857 who has peacefully succeeded to the Chair. All his predecessors, except President Díaz, were violently deposed."[149] This in fact was not accurate; Sebastián Lerdo de Tejada had peacefully assumed the presidency after Benito Juárez, albeit due to the latter's death from natural causes. Nevertheless, the point remained that a rare peaceful transfer of power between two Mexican presidents had just taken place. It was an achievement significant enough to cement Díaz's image in the US press as a Cincinnatus-like figure who had voluntarily given up power to teach his people the importance of respect for the rule of law.

It is worth probing a little further to understand why so many newspapers in the United States were eager to excuse or even embrace the flagrantly undemocratic aspects of the Díaz government. Part of the answer lies in the fact that at this time Positivist thinking was making inroads not only among Mexico's governing classes, but throughout the Atlantic world, including in the United States. The result was a growing faith among US political and intellectual elites in the virtues of technocratic governance, of which the Díaz regime seemed to offer a good example.[150] It is also possible that some US editors and journalists simply wished to soothe their consciences as they watched US capital, manpower, and expertise flow into Díaz's Mexico. Finally, the argument that Díaz's style of governance would eventually bring about true democracy in Mexico allowed these US Americans to see this economic activity as facilitating the consummation of not only Mexico's national destiny, but the United States' as well. In November 1880, the *Chicago Tribune* recalled that in the past many US Americans had believed that the "absorption of Mexico by the American Union was inevitable."[151] Now, however, people in the United States were using different methods to advance their national interests south of the border, the most striking example of this being the "grand system of railway transportation" that now extended from the United States over "the Rio Grande . . . penetrating by various routes . . . every part of Mexico."[152] This, the *Tribune* declared, was "manifest destiny" for the modern age, whereby the United States would "strengthen Mexico, not by taking her territory and incorporating it into the American Union, but by teaching Mexico and giving her the means of strengthening herself by the introduction of trade and commerce."[153] In short, through economic collaboration the United States would "Americanize the Mexicans without denationalizing Mexico."[154]

References to Americanization were becoming increasingly common in US public discourse in the early 1880s.[155] Some publications used the term to refer to the rising numbers of US entrepreneurs, workers, and tourists migrating south of the border during this time.[156] "Now that slavery has been abolished in this country there will not be the same disposition to annex Mexico," the *Wheeling Daily Intelligencer* predicted in November 1880.[157] Instead, the "present mixture of population" in Mexico "will have its identity, so far as it has any, obliterated, and new, hardy, and progressive blood will be infused in its veins."[158] By these means Mexico would over time transform from "being a land of half-breed Indians and Spaniards" into "a mixture of the Anglo-Saxon and the Celtic blood of America and Europe."[159]

Others understood Americanization as a cultural phenomenon whereby, through the influence of its products, technologies, and capital, the United States would gradually teach Mexicans the values and habits of US civilization. This view was most common among Republican-leaning publications, which still held that the post-emancipation United States ought to extend and exert its international clout only through pacific means. It also appealed to Southern organs still concerned about the effects that acquiring territory from Mexico would have on the racial composition of US society. As the *Dallas Daily Herald* remarked, "Mexico with its old habits of life, modes of thought and methods of business, could never be a part of the United States in anything but in name."[160] "But Mexico Americanized . . . waked up to the rush of latter day enterprise, inventiveness and liberality, would even under a separate government be essentially one with this country in purpose and in destiny."[161] To these organs, this so-called new Manifest Destiny therefore offered US Americans the promise of continental hegemony without the risks of formal colonialism, as well as a means to unite Democrats and Republicans, Northerners and Southerners behind a single project of national aggrandizement.

These two methods of Americanizing Mexico—one by migration, the other by economic tutelage—were in fact not mutually exclusive. As the *Wheeling Daily Intelligencer* explained, in order to make Mexico a suitable environment for large-scale US immigration, it was first necessary for that country's current population to have undergone a degree of cultural transformation. The newspaper suggested that this would be best achieved by growing commercial and economic interactions between the United States and Mexico, which would precipitate "a vast change socially, politically and commercially" in that country as its population was gradually "assimilated to American ideas."[162] Thus, through cultural, political, and demographic change, Mexico "will become to all intents and purposes an American country" and therefore a congenial place for US immigrants to move into.[163]

By the early 1880s, a growing number of US newspapers were contemplating how Mexico could be used to launch a wider campaign to extend the United States' renovating powers further afield. "Mexico's success under American influences," the *Chicago Tribune* declared, could be repeated "throughout the southern portions of the hemisphere."[164] "Extend our commerce ever further southward," and US Americans could teach "weaker republics, modelled after our own, the benefits . . . of domestic peace and industry."[165] The *New York Herald* agreed. "The Monroe Doctrine must be readjusted to the modern times in which we live" to become "a means of spreading America's commercial influence in the name of industry, law, and order" throughout the Western Hemisphere, the newspaper insisted.[166] It should be noted that there was no consensus in the US press regarding the details of future US foreign policy in the wider hemisphere. As these enthusiastic proposals suggest, however, there was growing agreement among newspapers of all political and regional affiliations that henceforth the United States would fulfill its mission to advance republicanism in the New World primarily through economic means. "We will teach them industry," the *Chicago Tribune* declared in 1881, "and with that . . . the blessings of peace and harmony."[167] In doing so, US Americans would transform those "chaotic nations into fine republics like our own."[168]

The fact that for years many of these newspapers had insisted that Mexicans (and Spanish Americans in general) were incapable of self-government brings into question the sincerity of their claims that democracy would eventually flourish south of the Rio Grande. Nevertheless, it is significant that these publications felt the need to assure their readers that economic growth and short-term curbs on democratic participation were in fact way stations on the road to stable republicanism, both in Mexico and throughout the southern portions of the hemisphere. Doing so enabled them to present surging US economic activity south of the border as a continuation of the United States' self-claimed role as the model and champion of republican government in the New World. It was a powerful message to communicate to postwar US Americans, who for so long had been told by the press that their supposedly exceptional republic might never recover from its devastating civil war and was therefore doomed to follow the Spanish American nations into endless internecine strife. Indeed, the increasingly popular term Americanization was a stark contrast to the fears of Mexicanization that had filled the pages of US newspapers since the Civil War. This shift in public discourse was a signal to readers that the flows of influence between North America's two republics had returned to their proper direction; rather than imitating Mexico, the United States was once again the example that Mexicans sought to emulate.

Díaz Visits the United States

After attending his godson's christening in Monterrey, Mexico, in March 1883, former president Porfirio Díaz began a three-month tour of the United States. His route read like a roadmap of his host country's burgeoning postwar industrial and commercial centers. It began in New Orleans, where the city's merchants impressed their Mexican guest with a tour of warehouses filled with stock ready to be shipped into the Mexican Gulf. Díaz then boarded a special carriage provided by US railroad magnate James Sullivan, which carried him through the hub towns of Galveston, Brownsville, and Laredo where Texan trunk lines connected with branch roads running southward over the Rio Grande. Next Díaz traveled north to New York via St. Louis and Chicago to visit the factories flooding Mexican markets with finished goods. He ended his tour in Washington, DC, where the former Mexican president met with President Chester A. Arthur and received a formal welcome from the US Congress. At every stop the local press praised Díaz as a visionary and proclaimed that his visit confirmed that the United States was both the sponsor of and inspiration for the former president's remarkable achievements in bringing about the economic regeneration of the Mexican republic.[169]

This was a relatively recent notion in postbellum US public discourse. Throughout much of the post–Civil War period, many US publicists and political leaders had been troubled by the persistence of sectionalism in their nation's political culture. In their more pessimistic moments, they had invoked Mexico's image as a hopelessly anarchic republic to warn their countrymen of the condition the United States was descending toward. While this image reflected US Americans' insecurities about continued disunity in their republic, however, Mexico itself offered them a means to reverse this troubling trend. During the late 1870s newspapers and journals across the United States insisted that a common effort to extend and strengthen their nation's commercial reach over Mexico would help to unify US society. This collective endeavor, they contended, would distract US Americans from divisive domestic issues and subsume their lingering sectional antipathies in a spirit of patriotic fervor. A powerful force behind US Americans' growing interest in continental commercial aggrandizement, therefore, was widespread anxiety regarding the fragility of their post–Civil War republic.

Mexico's function as a harmonizing influence on US society was symbolic as well as literal. During Díaz's first term, significant portions of the US press insisted that, by contributing to Mexico's economic development, people in the United States were also assisting in that country's social and political stabilization. Díaz never intended his regime to become a fully democratic one. However, US publications reasoned that, by following the United States' example, Mexicans could unify the discordant elements of their society and thus create the preconditions necessary for the eventual development of a stable representative democracy. The process would be slow; Mexico's internal divisions were supposedly more deeply entrenched than those in the

United States and it would therefore take some time for economic forces to complete their work. Nevertheless, by the early 1880s US newspapers were proudly declaring that the United States was the example guiding Mexicans toward finally making a success of their republican experiment. Previously a representation of US Americans' deepest fears for their own republic, Mexico's image by this time reassured people in the United States that their nation had recovered its standing as the New World's exceptional republic.

Epilogue

By November 1883, the *Atlanta Constitution* had concluded that Mexico's current president Manuel González was a disappointment. In late 1882, González had mandated the conversion of part of Mexico's coinage from silver to nickel. The move had triggered a spike in inflation, the devaluation of the *peso,* and economic hardship throughout the population. During the months that followed, Mexican newspapers reported rumblings of unrest across the country, which would eventually culminate in a series of significant uprisings in several major cities.

Despite this, the *Constitution* was remarkably sanguine about Mexico's future, at least in the long term. After all, the newspaper pointed out, next year the country would hold a presidential election, which would likely see former president Porfirio Díaz "elected without opposition."[1] The *Constitution* explained that unlike González, Díaz was an intelligent and decisive leader. He was, moreover, a careful student of US history, who understood that "sectional differences in Mexico are similar to those of the United States."[2] For evidence the newspaper pointed out that, during his first presidential term 1876–1880, Díaz had implemented a domestic agenda that was "modelled after that of [the United States]" and that had successfully soothed social and political tensions across Mexican society by channeling popular energies into projects of national economic regeneration.[3] The *Constitution* was certain that, once he was back in office, Díaz would recommence this program and with the help of US capital, manpower, and technology complete Mexico's transformation into "one of the most progressive [nations] in the world."[4]

In this article the *Constitution* portrayed Mexico as the United States's admiring protégé—a prevalent though relatively new image in US public discourse at the time. During the antebellum period, few prominent US newspapers had been so optimistic about Mexicans' ability to stabilize and modernize their country. Since its conversion into a republic in 1824, Mexico had been gripped by what had appeared to observers in the United States to be an endless cycle of domestic upheavals, ranging from military coups and separatist rebellions to peasant uprisings. For those US Americans who cared to take notice, this endemic chaos pointed to a single truth: Mexicans, whether due to biology, culture, or religion, were incapable of self-government.

This conclusion might have troubled US Americans of the founding generation, who had been taught that the republican institutions devised by the Framers were destined to be adopted by all peoples around the world. But in the antebellum period, many in the United States took satisfaction from the notion that Spanish Americans were unable to live up to the US republican model. The first half of the nineteenth century had wrought some dramatic changes in US politics; the advent of universal white male suffrage, mass party politics, and the two-party system had all caused disquiet among certain sectors of society regarding the integrity of their system of government and the wider political culture that surrounded it. No matter their concerns, however, US Americans could look across the Rio Grande and be reassured that, at least in comparison to Mexico, the United States' political system was sturdy and well-functioning. By its failings, in short, Mexico proved the unique success of the US republic.

The outbreak of the US Civil War shattered this illusion. To be sure, the sectional crisis had been mounting for decades; during the 1850s violence had occasionally broken out, both in the halls of government and among the general population. But no matter how fractious the political climate became, antebellum US Americans could still believe that, if national peace were ever seriously imperiled, their representatives would set aside their differences and cooperate in the name of the public good. Yet the months following the 1860 presidential election exposed the fallacy of this assumption as all efforts to negotiate an agreement to keep the Southern states in the Union failed. Whether they welcomed secession or not, Northerners and Southerners were now confronted with the reality that the United States had succumbed to the kind of civil strife that many of them had previously believed was only possible in republics south of the Rio Grande.

This realization destabilized Mexico's image in wartime public discourse, North and South. For many Unionist organs, the fact that the slaveholders' rebellion was closely followed by France's invasion of Mexico was evidence that these two assaults were somehow intertwined. Northern editors, journalists, and orators therefore professed newfound sympathy for their Mexican republican neighbors, and throughout the Civil War they urged their countrymen to forget their prejudices and embrace Mexicans as co-defenders of the North American republican tradition. Interestingly, many Confederate publications also drew parallels between the Union and the Mexican republic; their purpose in doing so, however, was hardly complimentary. Casting Republicans in the United States and Liberals in Mexico as pro-miscegenationist proto-authoritarians, these organs insisted that the slaveholding Confederacy was the last bastion of true republicanism on the continent. Supporters of the Richmond government simultaneously pronounced it their nation's mission to promote political pluralism across the New World, allowing all nations to choose whatever form of government best suited the nature, interests, and capabilities of their respective populations.

The Confederacy's fall in 1865 ended the Civil War and determined that the sundered sections of the Union would be reunited. And yet throughout the late 1860s and the 1870s many US Americans continued to believe that their country remained in the grip of severe civil strife. Images of Mexico in US public discourse therefore remained in flux. The fact that ex-Confederates and many Northern Democrats were anxious about the country's condition was to be expected. Emancipation, after all, was now the law of the land while the federal government was in the hands of wild-eyed radicals. In response, following Appomattox former Confederate organs and their sympathizers in the Northern press repeated the warnings they had issued during the Civil War regarding Republicans' apparent plans to ruin the US republic—by first weakening it with anarchy, then crushing it with tyranny. To give color to these premonitions they pointed to Mexico as an example of how aspiring tyrants created chaos with policies such as universal suffrage and racial mixing to demoralize society and thereby prime it for the rollout of military despotism.

More surprising was that the Civil War's apparent victors were also worried about the republic's survival. In the heady months following Appomattox, pro-Republican leaders and newspapers were confident that a thoroughgoing program of Reconstruction would expunge the last remnants of the Slave Power from the South and thereby remove all sources of dissension from US society. Over the late 1860s and early 1870s, however, the politics of Reconstruction became marred by inflammatory rhetoric, contested elections, accusations of corruption, and bouts of paramilitary violence. In the press, some of Reconstruction's initial supporters' faith in the federal government's ability to stabilize Southern society faded. Certain newspapers even wondered whether the Civil War had left a stain of factionalism on US society that might never be removed. As their concerns grew, these publications' view of Mexico darkened. During the Civil War they had praised the Juarists as the Union's noble allies; in the postwar period, these same organs increasingly invoked republican Mexico's image as a warning of the interminable disorder that awaited the United States if it did not find a way to reunite the discordant elements of its still deeply divided society.

It was not until the early 1880s that warnings that the United States was sliding into a condition analogous to chaotic Mexico substantially declined in nationwide public discourse. Having concluded that Reconstruction had not only failed to reunite North and South but was in fact creating new sources of dissension between the sections, many previously pro-Republican editors, writers, and orators publicly rejected the program. Some of them began to consider how the pursuit of economic opportunities south of the Rio Grande might be a more effective way to heal the nation by distracting US Americans from wrangling over the legacies of the Civil War and encouraging them to instead subsume their sectional antipathies in a collaborative project of national commercial aggrandizement. In 1876 Mexico's new president Porfirio Díaz opened his country's doors to US capital, emigration, and enterprise and so gave US Americans the opportunity to put this new plan for reconciliation into action.

At the same time the Díaz administration launched a public relations effort that aimed to convince US Americans that Mexico's new leaders admired the United States and wished to implement the lessons of its example in their own quest to harmonize Mexican society. These platitudes were well received among US newspapermen, many of whom had spent the past decade tortured by the thought that the United States was failing to live up to its self-claimed title as the world's exemplary republic. Readily taking their Mexican flatterers at their word, publications from across the political spectrum in the United States crafted a new image that depicted Mexico as their country's pupil. The subtext was that every step that Mexico took toward stabilization and modernization was evidence of the transformative power of the US example. And so, by the early 1880s, the portrayal of Mexico gaining traction in US public discourse was one designed to assure people in the United States that their country had finally overcome its domestic difficulties and reclaimed its providential role as the New World's model republic.

People in the Civil War–era United States had a keen sense of the wider world. Advances in both domestic and global communication throughout the first half of the nineteenth century meant that they were better informed about international affairs than any generation that had preceded them. As a result, they had a wealth of foreign models to draw upon as they navigated the challenges of civil war and reunion. Of course, certain international examples were more appropriate than others, depending on the social or political issue at hand. Jamaica, for instance, offered lessons in how emancipation might play out in the United States. Meanwhile US Americans seeking instructions for how to create a modern nation from a disparate collection of individual states could look to the Italian Risorgimento or later to German unification. Not every foreign example offered a model of success; US Americans often invoked a foreign nation's experience to illuminate pathways to avoid as well as ones to follow. Either way, contemporaries in the United States understood that, while certain aspects of their sectional conflict were distinctly homemade, most of the issues it raised had been grappled with before in one form or another by other peoples around the world.

Scholarly awareness of nineteenth-century US Americans' vast and varied understanding of the wider world is growing. Nevertheless, most existing studies in this vein primarily focus on Northerners' and Southerners' engagement with European experiences by tracing, for example, how each used the language of Atlantic nationalism to communicate the meaning of their respective war efforts to European audiences during the Civil War. The authors of these studies have found that, once they had put down the Confederate rebellion, Unionists boldly declared themselves the rightful heirs to the international cause of modern nation-state formation. Throughout the postwar period Republican leaders in particular invoked this transatlantic discourse to make the case for their version of Reconstruction. The plan to rework the South, they insisted, was part of the post-emancipation United States' duty to provide the world with an example of how a modern democratic nation-state could bring security, opportunity, and liberty to its citizens.

There is no question that many contemporary US writers, orators, and politicians drew connections between the Civil War and the European nationalist tradition. However, our understanding of the Civil War's international dimensions will always be incomplete if we concentrate on one (albeit influential) transnational discourse while ignoring others. Throughout the wartime and postwar eras, both Northerners and Southerners used the experiences of numerous other countries to help them find answers to the difficult questions arising from disunion and reunion. In the realm of public discourse, moreover, a politician's or editor's decision to reference a certain international model was typically strategic, since they knew that each model was associated with a particular set of values or concerns in the minds of their audiences. Both Northerners and Southerners also used different international discourses to give voice to the various emotions—fear, hope, triumph, despair—that they experienced during wartime and the postwar period. What all of this means is that no single international discourse can tell us everything about how contemporaries experienced the Civil War era; only by considering each as one element within a wider kaleidoscope of international narratives and frameworks can we begin to appreciate the full array of concerns, ambitions, and agendas that actuated people in the United States during this period.

This book has illuminated an as-yet understudied international discourse utilized by US Americans during this time that placed their civil war in a distinctly hemispheric context. It was a discourse that was also notably pessimistic in its view of the United States' future. This is especially true when it is compared to the inspiring visions of national progress, righteousness, and glory that both Unionists and Confederates sought to invoke when they presented their respective war efforts as continuations of the European fight for liberal nationalism. The touchstones of the hemispheric discourse, by contrast, were those problems arising from postcolonial nation-building that for years had plagued the Spanish American republics. These issues included a deeply divided polity, excessive factionalism in the political realm, and the prevalence of corruption, coercion, and extralegal violence at all levels of the political system.

Most antebellum US Americans were familiar with republican Spanish America's turbulent history, at least in terms of its broad outlines. When the Civil War began, therefore, they were quick to see parallels between their internecine contest and the conflicts that had roiled the southern portions of the hemisphere over previous decades. No doubt during the Civil War both Unionists and Confederates preferred to think optimistically, to ponder the blessings of peace, prosperity, and prestige that awaited their country should its war effort be successful. And yet they could not entirely ignore the lessons that Mexico and the other Spanish American republics had taught them: that there was a chance that their fratricidal war would pull their society into a spiral of civil disorders, meaning the end of domestic peace for themselves and their descendants for generations to come. Though not always the dominant international framework, the specter of Spanish American dissolution was a constant feature in both Northern and Southern discourse, an ever-present undercurrent as people in both sections grappled with the challenges of disunion, reunion, and reconciliation.

This study has traced the development of this discourse up to the early 1880s, when the heat of Reconstruction politics had finally subsided. To be sure, other ruptures would challenge US society over the course of the rest of the century. Most of these, however, had their origins in industrialization, immigration, or imperialism—new issues, in short, which were not directly related to the old sectional contest. Indeed, as US Americans moved further away from their civil war, the effect of that conflict's aftershocks on the national psyche diminished. Twenty or so years after Appomattox, the possibility that a second sectional rebellion would follow on the heels of the first seemed remote. It was around this time that US Americans therefore grew confident enough in their nation's internal cohesion to turn their minds away from postwar recovery and toward foreign aggrandizement. Meanwhile Díaz's Mexico was rapidly becoming the United States' most favored hemispheric partner, a place where US entrepreneurs did business, US manufacturers sent their products, and US capital was coming to dominate almost every major industry. In this climate, Mexico's image in US public discourse—so unsettled throughout the 1860s and 1870s—took on a more fixed form as that of a pliant neighbor bending to the United States' influence.

This was the prevailing view of Mexico in the United States up until the early twentieth century, at which point US Americans' perceptions of their southern neighbors underwent yet another shift. As it happened, Díaz would renege on his pledge in 1876 to serve just one term in office. In 1884, he returned to the presidency, after which he tightened his grip on Mexico's electoral system, closely managing national elections to ensure that he and his allies remained at the helm of government. From the early days of Díaz's first administration, newspapers in the United States had praised the Mexican leader for manipulating election outcomes in ways that supposedly benefitted the public good even while they subverted the popular will. In 1910, however, Díaz's hold slipped; his victory in that year's presidential election was vociferously disputed by defeated candidate Francisco I. Madero, who then launched a rebellion. Able to draw to his side large swathes of those portions of Mexican society that had been displaced, dispossessed, and disempowered by the Porfiriato, Madero expanded his revolt into a sustained, countrywide revolution. A ten-year civil war followed that eventually saw the Díaz regime, so admired in the US press for its fortress-like stability, crumble.

The Mexican Revolution ended US Americans' view of Mexico as a well-managed, docile country awaiting the renovating touch of US civilization. Though there were US journalists in the field trailing the armies of Pancho Villa and other warriors, the war was difficult for audiences in the United States to follow. The conflict consisted of numerous warring factions and saw multiple heads of state take power only to be deposed in quick succession. In addition to this, news that some of these factions subscribed to socialist and other radical political beliefs gave the contest an air of dangerous exoticism for many US observers. And finally, there was the simple fact that the Mexican Revolution dragged on for roughly a decade. This meant that for the best part of ten years, US readers taking in the latest news from Mexico were presented with descriptions of upturned governments, bloody guerilla fighting, and widespread social dislocation. Little wonder that by the time the Revolution ended in 1920, Mexico's image in the US imagination bore strong resemblance to what it had been in the antebellum era: a troubled country wracked by ceaseless political turmoil and violence.[5]

In the years that followed the Revolution, developments in US-Mexican relations did little to improve US Americans' opinion of their southern neighbor. Trade, finance, and business had brought the two nations together during the last third of the nineteenth century; from the 1940s onward, however, their diplomatic interactions increasingly consisted of disputes over immigration, border security, and narcotics. The dynamics of these interactions also shifted; while previously US businessmen, financiers, and other fortune seekers had moved into Mexico, from the mid-twentieth century onward large numbers of people and huge amounts of illegal goods flooded into the United States from south of the border. As a result, Mexico frequently appeared on the pages of US newspapers and on TV screens as the progenitor of a whole host of social ills—undocumented immigrants, illegal drugs, cartel violence—that threatened to pollute the United States should they manage to cross the border. Much like before the Civil War, then, by the late twentieth century popular US perceptions of Mexico suggested a fundamental difference between the two North American republics, with the border marking the line between poverty and chaos in the south and prosperity and peace in the north.

Historians—and the histories they write—are the products of the times in which they live. It is no surprise, therefore, that prevailing stereotypes of Mexico have had some influence on how scholars approach the history of US-Mexican relations. In the case of historians of the United States in particular, there is a tendency to assume that the relationship between the two nations has been defined by a fixed binary wherein a strong, virile United States stood alongside a weak and disorderly Mexico, a dynamic supposedly established around the time of the Texas Revolution that has not changed much since. This notion often leads scholars to assume that historically, US Americans only turned their thoughts to Mexico when they wished to take something from their weaker neighbor or punish it for some supposed transgression. Unsurprisingly, scholars find that during such times, US Americans voiced sweeping generalizations about Mexico's supposed inferiorities, which they then compared to the United States' apparent strengths. In doing so, historians produce studies that reaffirm the notion that the dynamics of the

US-Mexican relationship have remained locked in this uneven dichotomy throughout US history.

There is still more to learn about what lay beneath US Americans' disdainful condemnations of their Mexican neighbors over the centuries. Indeed, scholars could go much further to probe these proclamations of repulsion to see if they masked any hints of familiarity or affinity, perhaps even sympathy. This line of inquiry has enormous potential given that, at least until the mid-nineteenth century, the United States and Mexico shared much in common. Prior to the US-Mexican War (1846–1848), for example, the two countries were comparable in both population and geographic size. Each possessed predominantly agrarian economies, practiced variations of both free and unfree labor, and was inhabited by polyglot populations composed of the descendants of European immigrants, enslaved Africans, and Native Americans. Throughout the nineteenth century, moreover, both the United States and Mexico had to deal with similar challenges arising from the process of transforming their colonies into self-governing republics, including reconciling diverse populations, setting the boundaries of democratic citizenship, and determining the nature and scope of federal power.

When surveying this history from the vantage point of the twenty-first century, it is easy to forget that it was not always clear to midcentury US Americans which (if either) of the two North American republics would survive. Certainly, their confidence in the US system of government grew as the nineteenth century progressed. Nevertheless, neither Mexico nor the United States grappled with the growing pains of nation-building without provoking serious domestic unrest. Each country experienced popular rebellions, clashes between settlers and Indigenous populations, various forms of racial and ethnic tension, and serious challenges to federal power from local and state authorities. And finally, both populations understood that gaining independence was only the beginning of their fight to create lasting republics, and that whether either country would ultimately succeed in that goal was still an open question.

The materials produced by those who advocated expanding US borders, markets, and business activity south of the border tell us much about nineteenth-century US Americans' imperialistic fervor and nationalist pretensions. They are not the sources to consult, however, if we wish to know whether contemporaries in the United States ever thought about the difficult experiences they shared in common with their Mexican neighbors as fellow travelers on the road toward national consolidation. To answer that question, we must instead look to periods of prolonged uncertainty and disruption in the United States, such as the Civil War, when flaws in the country's republican system were laid bare. And yet scholars have largely failed to ask whether Civil War–era US Americans saw parallels between their conflict and those that had disturbed Mexico and other Spanish American republics throughout the nineteenth century. Indeed, in the existing scholarship the Civil War sits apart from that ignominious hemispheric tradition, apparently the region's only internecine contest that demonstrated the resilience rather than the weakness of its country's institutions, and that had a regenerative rather than destructive effect on its society.

In tracing how Civil War–era US Americans imagined Mexico, this study has attempted to rethink certain assumptions that blinker current scholarship on the history of the US-Mexican relationship. It has done this by examining Mexico's place in US public discourse during a period of profound crisis in the US republican experiment. During this time, Mexico's image in the United States became a reflection of US Americans' usually unspoken fear that the myth of their exceptionalism might be unfounded and a representation of the future that awaited their country if this proved to be so. In this way, following Mexico's place in US public discourse gives us an index to popular concerns in the Civil War–era United States regarding the integrity of the US republic, and specifically its political institutions, systems, and culture. It is also a means to understand the Civil War as it was experienced by those who lived through it and who therefore had no way of knowing if and how the sectional conflict would end. Seen from this perspective, the Civil War loses its aura of romantic mysticism and is instead revealed as a protracted period of national crisis wrought with confusion and uncertainty.

This analysis has also shown how these anxieties could be manipulated in ways that gave them political power. The Civil War era was a time of revolutionary changes in the United States' social and political order. Successful revolutions of all kinds often require a zeal for improvement or innovation on the part of at least some portion of the population. What this study has explored, however, are the more prosaic popular impulses, which can also create the conditions needed for extraordinary changes to take place. Those studied here who crafted the narratives of Mexicanization aimed to speak to what they believed were the concerns of segments of the US public regarding the possibility of endless civil disturbances and the impact this would have on their everyday lives. They therefore presented some of the most extraordinarily transformative projects of the period—emancipation, secession, imperialism—as designed to pull the United States back from the brink of so-called Mexicanization and return the country to some imagined past era of untrammeled domestic peace.

Insecurities about their republic were not the only force that motivated people in the United States throughout this transformative phase in their nation's history. Rather, throughout the wartime and postwar periods popular concerns about the country's fragility ebbed and flowed with the tide of battles and political events, at times eclipsed by other widespread sentiments of optimism, righteousness, or determination. Nevertheless, throughout this period the troubling notion that perhaps Providence had not marked out an exceptional fate for the United States never fully disappeared from the public consciousness. It was, therefore, a period of crisis in the myth of US exceptionalism during which US Americans saw in Mexico a possible future where their once mighty republic lay in tatters, another wreck in the long list of the New World's failed republics. US Americans' efforts to avoid this fate played an important part in guiding them through their period of civil strife and it is therefore vital to understand the decisions they made as they navigated a path from disunion to reunion.

Notes

Introduction

1. "Will You or Won't You," *Weekly Wisconsin Patriot*, February 9, 1861.

2. "Will You or Won't You."

3. The term "Spanish American" will be used in this book rather than "Latin American" or "Hispanic." The reasons for this are twofold. First, the term distinguishes those countries that had been colonies of the Spanish Empire from those, such as Haiti or Brazil, that had once belonged to France, Portugal, or some other European power. This is useful because Civil War–era US Americans attributed Mexico's political ills to a particular form of *Spanish* American republican degeneration, which was apparently rooted in these republics' similar racial composition, religion, and cultures—all of which were legacies of Spanish colonialism. Second, the terms "Latin American" and "Hispanic" would be anachronistic in a study focused on the mid-nineteenth-century United States. "Latin American," for example, was first used by certain French, Mexican, and Central and South American intellectuals during the 1830s but would not enter the US lexicon until the final third of the nineteenth century (Gobat, "The Invention of Latin America," 1345–75).

4. Bethell, ed., *The Independence of Latin America*; Blanchard, *Under the Flags of Freedom*; Brown and Paquette, eds., *Connections after Colonialism*; Costeloe, *Response to Revolution*; Langley, *The Americas in the Age of Revolution, 1750–1850*; McFarlane, *War and Independence in Spanish America*; Mirow, *Latin American Constitutions*; Rodriguez O., *The Independence of Spanish America*.

5. Fitz, *Our Sister Republics*; Naish, *Silence and Slavery*.

6. Fallaw, *Religion and State Formation in Postrevolutionary Mexico*; Guardino, *Peasants, Politics, and the Formation of Mexico's National State*; Robinson, *The Mark of Rebels*; Rodríguez O., ed., *The Divine Charter*; Rodriguez O., *"We Are Now the True Spaniards."*

7. Costeloe, *The Central Republic in Mexico, 1835–1846*; Hale, *Mexican Liberalism in the Age of Mora, 1828–1853*; Shawcross, *France, Mexico and Informal Empire in Latin America, 1820–1867*; Smith, *The Roots of Conservatism in Mexico*; Stevens, *Origins of Instability in Early Republican Mexico*; Thompson with LaFrance, *Patriotism, Politics, and Popular Liberalism in Nineteenth-Century Mexico*; Wasserman, *Everyday Life and Politics in Nineteenth-Century Mexico*.

8. Fowler, ed., *Forceful Negotiations*; Fowler, *Independent Mexico*.

9. Brian Connaughton, "The Enemy Within: Catholics and Liberalism in Independent Mexico, 1821–1860," in *The Divine Charter*, ed. Rodríguez O., 183–204; O'Hara, *A Flock Divided*; Smith, *The Roots of Conservatism in Mexico*, 1–202.

10. Prescott, *The History of the Conquest of Mexico*. For more on writings about Mexico by US explorers, tourists, anthropologists, and scientists during the Jacksonian and antebellum eras, see Cabanas, *The Cultural "Other" in Nineteenth-Century Travel Narratives*; Pike, *The United States and Latin America*.

11. Johannsen, *To the Halls of the Montezumas*; Van Wagenen, *Remembering the Forgotten War*. For an interesting study of how Mexican writers remembered the conflict, see Rodríguez, *The Literatures of the US-Mexican War*. For broader examinations of how imperial ambitions shaped US Americans' perceptions of Mexico throughout the first half of the nineteenth century, see Greenberg, *Manifest Manhood and the Antebellum American Empire*; Horsman, *Race and Manifest Destiny*; Johnson, *A Hemisphere Apart*; Joseph, Legrand, and Salvatore, eds., *Close Encounters of Empire*.

12. Baumgartner, *South to Freedom*; DeLay, "Independent Indians and the US-Mexican War," 35–68; DeLay, *War of a Thousand Deserts*; Hernández, *Mexican American Colonization during the Nineteenth Century*, 1–164; St. John, *Line in the Sand*; Torget, *Seeds of Empire*.

13. Gibson, ed., *The Black Legend*.

14. Pinheiro, *Missionaries of Republicanism*.

15. Horsman, *Race and Manifest Destiny*, 3.

16. DeGuzman, *Spain's Long Shadow*; Gómez, *Manifest Destinies*; Horsman, *Race and Manifest Destiny*; Pascoe, *What Comes Naturally*.

17. Cabanas, *The Cultural "Other"*; Naish, *Silence and Slavery*; Pike, *The United States and Latin America*; Shelley Streeby, "Imagining Mexico in Love and War: Nineteenth-Century US Literature and Visual Culture," in *Mexico and Mexicans in the Making of the United States*, ed. Tutino, 110–40. Conversely, scholars of Latin America have noted that during this time people in Mexico and other Spanish American republics often used the United States as a negative reference point to their own racially hybrid and supposedly more enlightened versions of republicanism. See, for example, Gobat, "The Invention of Latin America"; Grandin, "The Liberal Traditions in the Americas," 68–91; Körner, Miller, and Smith, eds., *America Imagined*; Sanders, *The Vanguard of the Atlantic World*.

18. Bensel, *The American Ballot Box in the Nineteenth Century*; Feldberg, *The Turbulent Era*; Freeman, *The Field of Blood*; Jackson, *Force and Freedom*; Selinger, *Embracing Dissent*.

19. Cunningham, *Mexico and the Foreign Policy of Napoleon III*; Shawcross, *France, Mexico and Informal Empire in Latin America*; Thier, "The View from Paris," 627–44; Thompson with LaFrance, *Patriotism, Politics, and Popular Liberalism in Nineteenth-Century Mexico*.

20. "Mexico and the Tribune," *New York Times*, April 20, 1858.

21. "Mexico and the Tribune."

22. Speech of Hon. Thomas Corwin of Ohio, House of Representatives, *Congressional Globe*, 36th Cong., 2nd Sess., January 21, 1861, 74.

23. Speech of Hon. Corwin, 74.

24. "The Result in This State," *Weekly Standard* (Raleigh, NC), March 6, 1861.

25. "Whom the Gods Wish to Destroy, They First Make Mad," *Nashville Union and American*, February 6, 1861.

26. Downs, "Mexicanization of American Politics," 387–409.

27. "Forewarned Is Forearmed," *Harper's Weekly* quoted in *Nebraska Advertiser*, October 3, 1867.

28. "Forewarned Is Forearmed."

29. "Forewarned Is Forearmed."

30. Downs, "Mexicanization of American Politics," 388.

31. Baker, *Affairs of Party*; Ford, *Origins of Southern Radicalism*; Formasino, *The Transformation of Political Culture*; Shalhope, *John Taylor of Caroline*; Silbey, *The American Political Nation, 1838–1898*; Smith, *No Party Now*; Voss-Hubbard, *Beyond Party*.

32. Baker, *Affairs of Party*; Smith, *No Party Now*; Voss-Hubbard, *Beyond Party*.

33. This interpretation of the economic significance of the Civil War was widely accepted among historians during the early-to-mid twentieth century (Beard and Beard, *The Rise of American Civilization*; Hacker, *The Triumph of American Capitalism*). Though it has been questioned since, elements of the thesis live on in more recent scholarship. See, for example, Ayers, *The Promise of the New South*; Onuf and Onuf, *Nations, Markets, and War*; Ransom, *Conflict and Compromise*; Roger L. Ransom, "The Economic Consequences of the American Civil War," in *The Political Economy of War and Peace*, ed. Wolfson, 49–74; Ransom and Sutch, *One Kind of Freedom*; Wright, *Old South, New South*. For studies that position the Civil War era as a watershed moment in US politics when the issues of slavery and sectionalism were eclipsed by those stemming from industrialization, capitalism, and class conflict, see Butler, *Critical Americans*; Calhoun, *Conceiving a New Republic*; Cohen, *Reconstruction of American Liberalism, 1865–1914*; Ninkovich, *Global Dawn*.

34. Campbell, *The Transformation of American Foreign Relations*; LaFeber, *The New Empire*; Paolino, *The Foundations of the American Empire*; Schonberger, *Transportation to the Seaboard*. More recent studies in a similar vein include Hart, *Empire and Revolution*; Hopkins, *American Empire*; Pletcher, *The Diplomacy of Trade and Investment*; Schoonover, *The United States in Central America, 1860–1911*.

35. Lawson, *Patriot Fires*; McPherson, "Was Blood Thicker Than Water?," 102–8; Neely Jr., *Lincoln and the Triumph of the Nation*.

36. Bonner, "Slavery, Confederate Diplomacy, and the Racialist Mission of Henry Hotze," 288–316; Davis, *Secret History of Confederate Diplomacy Abroad*; Don H. Doyle, "Slavery or Independence: The Confederate Dilemma in Europe," in *The U.S. South and Europe*, ed. van Minnen and Berg, 105–24; Faust, *The Creation of Confederate Nationalism*; Fleche, *The Revolution of 1861*; Fox-Genovese and Genovese, *The Mind of the Master Class*; Gentry, "A Confederate Success in Europe," 157–88; Hubbard, *The Burden of Confederate Diplomacy*; Sexton, *Debtor Diplomacy*, 82–189; Quigley, *Shifting Grounds*; Tucker, *Newest Born of Nations*.

37. Ayers, "The American Civil War," 54–61; Clarke, "'Let All Nations See,'" 66–93; Doyle, *The Cause of All Nations*; Fleche, *The Revolution of 1861*; Nagler, Doyle, and Gräser, eds., *The Transnational Significance of the American Civil War*.

38. Doyle, *Cause of All Nations*, 7. See also Blackett, *Divided Hearts*; Crawford, *The Anglo-American Crisis of the Mid-Nineteenth Century*; Grant, *The American Civil War and the British Press*. For the role of European immigrant volunteers in the fighting of the Civil War, see Bruce, *The Harp and the Eagle*; Stephen D. Engle, "Yankee Dutchmen: Germans, the Union, and the Construction of Wartime Identity," in *Civil War Citizens*, ed. Ural, 11–55; Keller, *Chancellorsville and the Germans*; Samito, *Becoming American under Fire*.

39. Butler, *Critical Americans*; Cohen, *Reconstruction of American Liberalism*; Körner, Miller, and Smith, eds., *America Imagined*; Ninkovich, *Global Dawn*.

40. Downs, *The Second American Revolution*; Kelly, "The Lost Continent of Abraham Lincoln," 223–48; Kelly, "The North American Crisis of the 1860s," 337–68; Rothera, *Civil*

Wars and Reconstructions in the Americas. See also Azevedo, *Abolitionism in the United States and Brazil*; Bergad, *The Comparative Histories of Slavery in Brazil, Cuba, and the United States*; Enrico Dal Lago, *American Slavery, Atlantic Slavery, and Beyond*, 145–72; Link, ed., *United States Reconstruction Across the Americas*; Sanders, "Hemispheric Reconstructions," 41–62.

41. Barton Schweiger, "The Literate South," 331–59.

42. Barton Schweiger, "The Literate South," 331.

43. Andrews, "The Confederate Press and Public Morale," 447.

44. Dabney, *Richmond*, 132.

45. Copeland, *The Antebellum Era*, 15.

46. For studies this author has found useful on the relationship between the press and public opinion in the nineteenth-century United States, see Barker and Burrows, eds., *Press, Politics and the Public Sphere in Europe and North America, 1760–1820*; Jones, *Powers of the Press*; Margolis, *Fictions of Mass Democracy in Nineteenth-Century America*.

47. Rothera, *Civil Wars and Reconstructions in the Americas*, 10. See also Downs, *The Second American Revolution*; Kelly, "The North American Crisis of the 1860s," 337–68; Kelly, "The Lost Continent of Abraham Lincoln," 223–48.

48. Cabanas, *The Cultural "Other" in Nineteenth-Century Travel Narratives*; Greenberg, *Manifest Manhood and the Antebellum American Empire*; Horsman, *Race and Manifest Destiny*; Johannsen, *To the Halls of the Montezumas*; Johnson, *A Hemisphere Apart*; Joseph, Legrand, and Salvatore, eds., *Close Encounters of Empire*; Pike, *The United States and Latin America*.

Chapter One

1. Beckert, *The Monied Metropolis*, 129–31; Lawson, *Patriot Fires*, 88–120; Neely Jr., *The Boundaries of Political Culture in the Civil War Era*, 71–96.

2. *Dinner to Señor Matias Romero* (New York: Local Publication Society, 1864), 8.

3. *Dinner to Señor Matias Romero*, 8.

4. *Dinner to Señor Matias Romero*, 9.

5. *Dinner to Señor Matias Romero*, 13.

6. *Dinner to Señor Matias Romero*, 13.

7. "Speech of Mr. de Peyster," *Dinner to Señor Romero*, 38.

8. "Speech of Mr. de Peyster," 41.

9. "Speech of Mr. de Peyster," 41.

10. Kelly, "The Lost Continent of Abraham Lincoln," 228.

11. Goldwert, "Matías Romero and Congressional Opposition to Seward's Policy toward the French Intervention in Mexico," 22–40; Miller, "Arms across the Border," 1–68; Sexton, *The Monroe Doctrine*, 128–50; Van Hoy, "Mexican Exiles and the Monroe Doctrine," 39–60.

12. "Speech of Mr. de Peyster," 38.

13. Ahlstrom, *A Religious History of the American People*, 670–97; Grimsley, *The Hard Hand of War*; Harrold, *Lincoln and the Abolitionists*, 94–116; Hess, *Liberty, Virtue, and Progress*; Manning, *What This Cruel War Was Over*, 18; McPherson, *What They Fought For, 1861–1865*; Mitchell, *Civil War Soldiers*.

14. Bernstein, *The New York City Draft Riots*; Gallman, *The Cacophony of Politics*; Neely Jr., *Lincoln and the Democrats*.

15. Romero, *Mexican Lobby*, ed. and trans. Thomas D. Schoonover, 3.

16. Burden, "Reform before La Reforma," 283–316; Pani, "Law, Allegiance, and Sovereignty in Civil War Mexico, 1857–1867," 570–96; Schoonover, *Dollars over Dominion*; Sinkin, *The Mexican Reform, 1855–1876*; Thompson, "Popular Aspects of Liberalism in Mexico, 1848–1888," 265–92; Thompson with LaFrance, *Patriotism, Politics, and Popular Liberalism in Nineteenth-Century Mexico*.

17. Romero, *Mexican Lobby*, 2.

18. Romero, *Mexican Lobby*, 2. The causes of both the War of Reform and the broader conflict between Liberals and Conservatives were more complex than Romero allowed, and certainly were not the fault of clerical and Conservative factions alone. For well-rounded studies of the subject, see Sinkin, *The Mexican Reform, 1855–1876*; Thompson with LaFrance, *Patriotism, Politics, and Popular Liberalism in Nineteenth-Century Mexico*.

19. Olliff, *Reforma Mexico and the United States*, 150.

20. Romero, *Mexican Lobby*, 2.

21. Romero, *Mexican Lobby*, 2.

22. Schoonover, *Dollars over Dominion*, 1–39.

23. Seijas and Frederick, *Spanish Dollars and Sister Republics*, 135–50.

24. Romero, *Mexican Lobby*, 7–8.

25. Barker, "The French Legation in Mexico," 409–26; Cunningham, *Mexico and the Foreign Policy of Napoleon III*, esp. 1–78.

26. Romero to Seward, *Correspondence Relative to the President Condition of Mexico* (Washington, DC: Government Printing Office, 1862), 134.

27. Romero to Seward, *Correspondence*, 134.

28. Romero to Seward, *Correspondence*, 24–50.

29. Hanna and Hanna, *Napoleon III and Mexico*, 65–75.

30. "A Threatened Mexican Complication," *Philadelphia Inquirer*, December 23, 1861.

31. *London Times* quoted in "Details of the Arrangement," *New York Times*, October 12, 1861.

32. "The Allied Expedition," *New York Times*, February 14, 1861.

33. McPherson, *The Struggle for Equality*, 438.

34. "Our Perils from Abroad," *Liberator* (Boston, MA), January 3, 1862. For other articles raising questions about the French Intervention that appeared in the *Liberator* during this time, see "Gerrit Smith at Washington," *Liberator*, March 21, 1862; "France and Great Britain," *Liberator*, November 21, 1862.

35. "Our Perils from Abroad."

36. Brennan, *The Making of an Abolitionist*; Mayer, *All on Fire*.

37. Dal Lago, *American Slavery, Atlantic Slavery, and Beyond*; Dal Lago, *William Lloyd Garrison and Giuseppe Mazzini*; McDaniel, *The Problem of Democracy in the Age of Slavery*.

38. Roberts, *Distant Revolutions*, 83–88.

39. "Revolution Less Dangerous Than Unresisted Despotism," *Liberator*, March 5, 1858.

40. See, for example, "News of the Week," *Burlington Free Press* (VT), November 22, 1861; "News of the Week," *Burlington Free Press*, February 7, 1862; "The 22nd in Burlington," *Burlington Free Press*, February 28, 1862; "The French in Mexico," *North Star* (Rochester, NY), November 15, 1862.

41. "Louis Napoleon," *Liberator*, February 27, 1863.

42. "Louis Napoleon."

43. Shawcross, *France, Mexico and Informal Empire in Latin America, 1820–1867*, 119–56.

44. McGreevy, *Catholicism and American Freedom*, 49–56; John McGreevy, "Catholicism and Abolition: A Historical (and Theological) Problem," in *Figures in the Carpet*, ed. McClay, 418–22; McIlhenny, *To Preach Deliverance to the Captives*.

45. Aaron W. Marrs, "The Civil War Origins of the *FRUS* Series, 1861–1868," in *Toward "Thorough, Accurate, and Reliable,"* ed. McAllister, Botts, Cozzens, and Marrs, 19–20.

46. Marrs, "The Civil War Origins of the *FRUS* Series, 1861–1868," 19–20.

47. "Our Washington Letter. History of the Allied Invasion of Mexico," *Chicago Tribune*, May 1, 1862.

48. "Our Washington Letter."

49. "Our Washington Letter."

50. "Official History of the Mexican Invasion," *New York Tribune*, May 5, 1862.

51. Malespine, "Solution of the Mexican Question," 274.

52. Cunningham, *Mexico and the Foreign Policy of Napoleon III*, 108–31.

53. "Mexico," *New York Tribune*, July 25, 1863.

54. "A Threatened Mexican Complication," *Philadelphia Inquirer*, December 23, 1861.

55. "About Mexico and the Monroe Doctrine," *Philadelphia Inquirer*, July 29, 1863.

56. "The Mexican Empire," *Charles City Republican Intelligencer* (IA), August 6, 1863.

57. "The French in Mexico—Necessity of Their Immediate Departure," *New York Herald*, September 19, 1863.

58. Doyle, "Reconstruction and Anti-Imperialism: The United States and Mexico," in *United States Reconstruction across the Americas*, 59.

59. Doyle, "Reconstruction and Anti-Imperialism," 59.

60. McInerney, *The Fortunate Heirs of Freedom*, esp. 7–26 and 107–26.

61. "Treason against Republicanism," *Liberator*, October 16, 1863.

62. "South America and the Slaveholders' Rebellion," *New York Tribune*, July 24, 1863.

63. Martin Crawford, "Davis and the Confederacy," in *Themes of the American Civil War*, ed. Grant and Reid, 159; Faust, *The Creation of Confederate Nationalism*, esp. 1–40; Rubin, *A Shattered Nation*, esp. 11–49.

64. "South America and the Slaveholders' Rebellion," *New York Tribune*, July 24, 1863.

65. Klement, *The Limits of Dissent*; Silbey, *A Respectable Minority*; Matthew Warshauer, "Connecticut Copperhead Constitutionalism: A Study of Peace Democratic Political Ideology During the Civil War," in *Contested Loyalty*, ed. Sandow; Weber, *Copperheads*. For more on the Knights of the Golden Circle, see Keehn, *Knights of the Golden Circle*.

66. "The Monroe Doctrine," *Chicago Tribune*, January 29, 1863.

67. "The Monroe Doctrine and Copperhead Fault-Finding," *Evansville Daily Journal* (IN), May 26, 1864.

68. "Arrival of Gen. Sigel—His Enthusiastic Reception and Speech at the McClure House," *Wheeling Daily Intelligencer* (WV), October 15, 1863.

69. "Important from Mexico," *New York Times*, December 29, 1862.

70. "Important from Mexico."

71. "Washington," *Chicago Tribune*, February 11, 1863.

72. "Mexican Advices in Washington," *New York Herald*, January 26, 1863.

73. *New York Times* quoted in "From Mexico," *Chicago Tribune*, October 3, 1863.

74. "From Mexico."

75. "An Encouraging Example," *Washington Chronicle* (DC) quoted in *Wheeling Daily Intelligencer* (WV), May 30, 1863.

76. "An Encouraging Example."

77. No title, *Boston Daily Advertiser*, June 16, 1863. This view was commonplace in the mid-nineteenth-century United States. It was based in part on myths US Americans told themselves about how easily their forces had defeated the Mexican Army in the US-Mexican War, 1846–48. As scholars have shown, however, at the time of fighting US troops viewed their Mexican counterparts as formidable opponents who were prepared to fiercely defend their country (Johannsen, *To the Halls of the Montezumas*; Van Wagenen, *Remembering the Forgotten War*, 1–40).

78. No title, *Boston Daily Advertiser*, June 16, 1863. For more examples of Union newspapers remarking on the courage of Juarist fighters, see "Mexico," *Charles City Republican Intelligencer* (IA), October 8, 1863; "A Mexican Version of the Story," from the *North American* (Philadelphia, PA), printed in the *Indiana Progress* (PA), November 18, 1863; "The French in Mexico," *Chicago Tribune*, February 26, 1863; "Important from Mexico," *New York Times*, May 14, 1863; "Heroism of the Mexicans, and French Barbarities," *Philadelphia Inquirer*, August 20, 1863; "The French in Mexico," *Brooklyn Evening Star*, June 13, 1863; "Important from Mexico," *New York Herald*, April 27, 1863; "The French War in Mexico," *National Republican* (Washington, DC), April 27, 1863.

79. Horsman, *Race and Manifest Destiny*, 7–62.

80. Ninkovich, *Global Dawn*, 163.

81. "The Mexican Events and Their Future," *New York Times*, August 3, 1863.

82. "The Mexican Events and Their Future."

83. "The Mexican Events and Their Future."

84. No title, *Chicago Tribune*, September 26, 1864.

85. No title, *Chicago Tribune*, September 26, 1864.

86. Seward to Dayton, September 26, 1863, *Papers Relative to Mexico*, 469. For press coverage of the dispatch, see "Secretary Seward and the Monroe Doctrine," *Albany Evening Journal* (NY), January 22, 1864; "The Mexican Monarchy Question," *Chicago Tribune*, April 12, 1864; "A Hasty Accusation," *National Intelligencer* (Washington, DC), January 28, 1864.

87. Miller, "Arms across the Border," esp. 16–23; Miller, "Matías Romero," 234–37.

88. Romero to Seward, *Correspondence*, June 2, 1862, 75.

89. James Monroe, "President's Annual Message to Congress," December 2, 1823, *Annals of Congress*, 18th Cong., 1st Sess., 12.

90. Monroe, "President's Annual Message to Congress," 22.

91. Sexton, *The Monroe Doctrine*, 3–158.

92. For instances in which Romero emphasized this point in his dealings with Union politicians, see Romero, *Mexican Lobby*, 12–18.

93. "Mexico and the Monroe Doctrine," *Buffalo Courier* (NY), July 31, 1863; "The Navy Expenses," *Chicago Tribune*, January 20, 1864; "A Hasty Accusation," *Weekly National Intelligencer* (DC), 28 January 1864; "Mr Seward and the Monroe Doctrine," *Pittsburgh Gazette*, January 26, 1864; "The Monroe Doctrine and Copperhead Fault-Finding," *Evansville Daily*

Journal (IN), May 26, 1864; "War with France," *Brooklyn Daily Eagle*, September 8, 163; "France in America," *Boston Evening Transcript*, September 9, 1863.

94. "Will You or Won't You," *Weekly Wisconsin Patriot*, February 9, 1861.

95. "Will You or Won't You."

96. "Will You or Won't You."

97. "Stand by the Government—A Warning," *Milwaukee Daily Sentinel*, September 18, 1862.

98. "Our Foreign Diplomacy," *National Intelligencer* (Washington, DC), November 2, 1864.

99. "Mexico—Monroe," *New York Tribune*, July 29, 1863.

100. "Mexico—Monroe."

101. "Mexico—Monroe."

102. "Important Proceedings from Congress: Mr. Seward's Speech," *New York Times*, January 14, 1861.

103. "Mr. Seward's Speech."

104. "Mr. Seward's Speech."

105. "Mr. Seward's Speech."

106. "The Diplomacy of Great Britain," *Daily Democrat and News* (Davenport, IA), February 15, 1862.

107. "The Diplomacy of Great Britain." For more on the *Trent* affair and the fear it engendered among Northerners over possible British intervention in the Civil War, see Jones, *Blue and Gray Diplomacy*, 47–112; Mahin, *One War at a Time*, 60–85.

108. "Members of the Cabinet Threatening to Array the Citizens against Their Own Government," *Ohio Democrat*, September 25, 1863.

109. "Members of the Cabinet Threatening to Array the Citizens against Their Own Government."

110. Sainlaude, *France and the American Civil War*, 28–59; Shawcross, *France, Mexico, and Informal Empire in Latin America, 1820–1867*, 37–65, 197–219.

111. Spiridon [pseud.], "French Designs on California," *Saturday Evening Gazette* (Boston, MA) quoted in *Placer Herald* (CA), June 11, 1864.

112. Spiridon [pseud.], "French Designs on California."

113. Spiridon [pseud.], "French Designs on California."

114. Harrold, *Lincoln and the Abolitionists*, 94–116; Noll, *The Civil War as a Theological Crisis*; Rable, *God's Almost Chosen Peoples.*

115. Bernstein, *The New York City Draft Riots*; Gallman, *The Cacophony of Politics*; Neely Jr., *Lincoln and the Democrats*.

116. Browne, *An Address Delivered before the Union League, May 9, 1863*, 6–7.

117. Browne, *An Address Delivered before the Union League, May 9, 1863*, 6–7.

118. Anderson, *The Cause of the War*, 11.

119. Anderson, *The Cause of the War*, 11.

120. Anderson, *The Cause of the War*, 4.

121. Joshua Leavitt, "The Monroe Doctrine," *Pamphlets Issued by the Loyal Publication Society*, 16–17. Leavitt has received relatively little attention from historians. His only biographer, Hugh Davis, primarily focuses on his antebellum career as an evangelical minister, reformer, and antislavery campaigner (Davis, *Joshua Leavitt*).

122. Leavitt, "The Monroe Doctrine," 16–17.
123. Leavitt, "The Monroe Doctrine," 29.
124. Leavitt, "The Monroe Doctrine," 27.
125. Leavitt, "The Monroe Doctrine," 47.
126. Leavitt, "The Monroe Doctrine," 47–48.
127. Leavitt, "The Monroe Doctrine," 47–48.
128. Leavitt, "The Monroe Doctrine," 47–48.
129. Leavitt, "The Monroe Doctrine," 47.
130. No title, *Cleveland Morning Leader*, December 19, 1863.
131. "The Monroe Doctrine," *Burlington Weekly Hawk-Eye* (IA), December 26, 1863.
132. "France in Mexico," *New York Tribune*, September 8, 1863.
133. "Mexico," *Chicago Tribune*, November 1, 1864.
134. "After the War," *Milwaukee Daily Sentinel*, September 27, 1864.
135. "Mexico—Monroe," *New York Tribune*, July 29, 1863. For more examples of wartime Northern newspapers condemning the imperialism of antebellum US slaveholders, see "A Balance of Power Question," *Chicago Tribune*, March 19, 1861; "Intervention in Mexican Affairs," *Brooklyn Daily Eagle*, November 6, 1861; "The Duty of the Hour," *Liberator*, October 17, 1862; "South America and the Slaveholders' Rebellion," *New York Tribune*, July 24, 1863.
136. "Mexico—Monroe," *New York Tribune*, July 29, 1863.
137. Joshua Leavitt, "The Key of the Continent," *The New Englander*.
138. Leavitt, "The Key of the Continent."
139. Romero, *A Mexican View of America in the 1860s*, ed. and trans. Schoonover, 13.
140. "Our New York Letter," *Philadelphia Inquirer*, October 22, 1863.
141. "Our New York Letter."
142. "Our New York Letter."
143. Romero, *Mexican Lobby*, 28.
144. *US Senate Journal*, 37th Cong., 3rd sess., January 19, 1863, 120.
145. James McDougall, "Speech of Hon. J. A. McDougall, of California, in the Senate of the United States, February 3, 1863," 37th Cong., 3rd sess., 98. McDougall's speech was also published as a pamphlet. See McDougall, *French Interference in Mexico*.
146. McDougall, "Speech of Hon. J. A. McDougall," 100.
147. McDougall, "Speech of Hon. J. A. McDougall," 100.
148. McDougall, "Speech of Hon. J. A. McDougall," 28.
149. "The News from Mexico—The Mexican Question in Congress," *New York Herald*, January 26, 1863.
150. "The News from Mexico."
151. Gallagher, *Three Days at Gettysburg*; Sears, *Gettysburg*.
152. "The Grandeur of President Lincoln's Position—Will He Restore the Union?" *New York Herald*, July 9.
153. "The Grandeur of President Lincoln's Position."
154. "The Grandeur of President Lincoln's Position."
155. "The Grandeur of President Lincoln's Position."
156. "The Grandeur of President Lincoln's Position."
157. "The Grandeur of President Lincoln's Position."

158. "European Intervention in American Affairs—Its Consequences," *New York Herald,* September 11, 1863.

159. "The Crisis of the Rebellion—Future Views North and South," *New York Herald,* September 11, 1863.

160. "The Crisis of the Rebellion."

161. "The Crisis of the Rebellion."

162. "The Crisis of the Rebellion."

163. "The Crisis of the Rebellion."

164. "Special Correspondence of *The Chicago Times,*" *New Oregon Plaindealer* (IA), March 25, 1864; "Mexico and the Monroe Doctrine," *Pittsburgh Daily Post,* April 11, 1864; "Sympathy (?) for Mexico," *Placer Herald* (CA), April 16, 1864; "National Life vs. the Administration," *Daily State Sentinel* (Indianapolis, IN), April 29, 1864.

165. For examples of press reports on the California Legislature's censure of McDougall, see "Senator Benton on 'Instructing,'" *Sacramento Bee,* February 5, 1864; No title, *Los Angeles Daily News,* February 15, 1864.

166. Frank Pixley, "Something to be Proud Of," *Sacramento Bee,* May 21, 1864. For more on McDougall's fall from grace, see Goldwert, "Matías Romero," 26–27.

167. Sexton, *The Monroe Doctrine,* 152–53.

168. "The French-Mexican Question," *New York Times,* 5 April 1864.

169. *US House Journal,* 38th Cong., 1st sess., April 4, 1864, 464.

170. No title, *Boston Daily Advertiser,* June 10, 1864.

171. "The Monroe Pill Abroad," *Albany Evening Journal* (NY), May 9, 1864.

172. "The Anti-Mexican Resolution Passed by the House of Representatives," *Chicago Tribune,* May 21, 1864.

173. "The Monroe Doctrine," *Philadelphia Inquirer,* April 5, 1864.

174. "Editor's Easy Chair," *Harper's New Monthly Magazine,* June–November 1864.

175. Shawcross, *France, Mexico and Informal Empire in Latin America, 1820–1867,* 197–236.

176. Romero, *Mexican Lobby,* 39.

177. Romero, *Mexican Lobby,* 39–40.

178. Romero, *Mexican Lobby,* 39–48.

179. No title, *Daily Ohio Statesman,* July 12, 1864. Various incarnations of this joke made the rounds among Democratic publications throughout the summer and fall of 1864. See, for example, No title, *Times-Democrat* (Lima, OH), July 13, 1864; No title, *North Branch Democrat* (Tunkhannock, PA), August 10, 1864; "Pointed," *The Mountain Democrat* (Placerville, CA), August 27, 1864.

180. "The Radical Republican Protest against Mr. Lincoln's Re-nomination—An Arraignment of His Course," *New York New Nation* quoted in *Indiana State Sentinel,* May 30, 1864.

181. "Copperhead Zeal for the Monroe Doctrine," *Chicago Tribune,* June 2, 1864.

182. "Copperhead Zeal for the Monroe Doctrine."

183. "Copperhead Zeal for the Monroe Doctrine."

184. White, *Emancipation, the Union Army, and the Reelection of Abraham.*

185. Joshua Leavitt, "Speech of Joshua Leavitt," in *Proceedings of a Meeting of Citizens of New York,* 7–8.

186. Leavitt, "Speech of Joshua Leavitt," 7–8.

Chapter Two

1. Andre M. Fleche, "Race and Revolution: The Confederacy, Mexico, and the Problem of Southern Nationalism," in *The Transnational Significance of the American Civil War*, ed. Nagler, Doyle, and Gräser, 189–203; Hubbard, *The Burden of Confederate Diplomacy*, 46–47.

2. Kelly, "The North American Crisis of the 1860s," 343.

3. Kelly, "The North American Crisis of the 1860s," 344.

4. Kelly, "The North American Crisis of the 1860s," 344.

5. "From Northern Mexico," *Evening Bulletin* (Charlotte, NC), August 17, 1861.

6. Tyler, "Santiago Vidaurri and the Confederacy," 66–76. For more on the Confederacy's military and trading relationships with various actors in the borderlands, see Arenson and Graybill, eds., *Civil War Wests*; Blackshear and Ely, *Confederates and Comancheros*; Masich, *Civil War in the Southwest Borderlands, 1861–1867*.

7. "Correspondence of the Confederate State Department," in *Papers Relating to Foreign Affairs, Accompanying the Annual Message of the President to the Second Session Thirty-Eighth Congress, Part 1*. Washington, DC: Government Printing Office, 1864.

8. Slidell, "Memorandum of an Interview of Mr. Slidell with the Emperor at St. Cloud on Tuesday, October 28, 1862," in *A Compilation of Messages and Papers of the Confederacy*, ed. Richardson, 349.

9. "Recognition of the Southern Confederacy by France," *Georgia Weekly Telegraph*, June 13, 1862; "Reported Recognition of the Southern Confederacy by France," *Troy Messenger* (AL), June 25, 1862; "M. Mercier's Visit to Richmond," *Charleston Daily Courier*, May 1862; "American Affairs in France," *Memphis Daily Appeal*, September 6, 1862; "The Mediation Scheme of the French Emperor," *Nashville Daily Union*, December 13, 1862; "Reported Recognition of the Southern Confederacy by France," *Yorkville Enquirer* (SC), June 19, 1862.

10. "Recognition of the Southern Confederacy by France," *Georgia Weekly Telegraph*, June 13, 1862; "Reported Recognition of the Southern Confederacy by France," *Troy Messenger* (AL), June 25, 1862; "M. Mercier's Visit to Richmond," *Charleston Daily Courier*, May 1862; "American Affairs in France," *Memphis Daily Appeal*, September 6, 1862; "The Mediation Scheme of the French Emperor," *Nashville Daily Union*, December 13, 1862; "Reported Recognition of the Southern Confederacy by France," *Yorkville Enquirer* (SC), June 19, 1862.

11. Baumgartner, *South to Freedom*; Lavender, "Confederate Cuba," 821–45; May, *Slavery, Race, and Conquest in the Tropics*; May, *The Southern Dream of a Caribbean Empire, 1854–1861*.

12. Brettle, *Colossal Ambitions*.

13. May, "The Irony of Confederate Diplomacy," 74.

14. "Letters from Richmond," *Charleston Mercury*, February 10, 1863.

15. "General Walker," *Wilmington Journal*, September 13, 1860.

16. No title, *Richmond Examiner*, June 18, 1861.

17. No title, *Richmond Examiner*, June 18, 1861.

18. Slidell to Thouvenel, *Official Records of the Union and Confederate Navies in the War of Rebellion*, 475.

19. Slidell to Thouvenel, *Official Records of the Union and Confederate Navies*, 475.

20. Slidell to Thouvenel, *Official Records of the Union and Confederate Navies*, 475.

21. "Mr. Conway's Terms of Peace," *Weekly Advertiser* (Montgomery, AL), March 4, 1863.

22. "Mr. Conway's Terms of Peace."

23. "Richmond News and Gossip," *Charleston Mercury*, February 3, 1862.

24. No title, *Richmond Daily Dispatch*, November 30, 1864.

25. No title, *Richmond Daily Dispatch*, November 30, 1864.

26. No title, *Richmond Daily Dispatch*, November 30, 1864.

27. No title, *Richmond Daily Dispatch*, November 30, 1864.

28. No title, *Richmond Daily Dispatch*, November 30, 1864.

29. "France and the United States," *Fayetteville Semi-Weekly Observer* (NC), June 23, 1864.

30. "Emperor Napoleon's Position," *Memphis Bulletin*, September 25, 1863.

31. "Emperor Napoleon's Position."

32. "Secession—Letter from Hon. J. D. Phelan," *Weekly Advertiser* (Montgomery, AL) quoted in *Montgomery Daily Mail*, November 14, 1860.

33. "Secession—Letter from Hon. J. D. Phelan."

34. "Secession—Letter from Hon. J. D. Phelan."

35. *Mexican Extraordinary* quoted in "Interesting from Mexico," *Charleston Mercury*, January 7, 1862.

36. *Richmond Sentinel* quoted in "Very Important from Mexico," *Memphis Daily Appeal*, July 28, 1863.

37. "A Monarchy in Mexico," *Richmond Sentinel* quoted in *Charleston Daily Courier*, July 31, 1863.

38. "France in Mexico," *Richmond Enquirer*, July 28, 1863.

39. Zvengrowski, *Jefferson Davis, Napoleonic France, and the Nature of Confederate Ideology, 1815–1897*, 125–45.

40. Sainlaude, *France and the American Civil War*, 79–128.

41. "France in Mexico," *Richmond Enquirer*, July 28, 1863.

42. "France in Mexico."

43. "France in Mexico."

44. "Mexico," *Memphis Daily Appeal*, April 22, 1862; "Probable Transference of the Papal See to Mexico," *Abingdon Virginian*, July 17, 1863; "Catholic Influence and the Confederacy—Singular Coincidences," *Richmond Whig*, August 27, 1863; "Mexican Officers—The Clergy and the French," *Nashville Daily Union*, March 3, 1864.

45. Python [pseud.], "Peace between the Sections, or War to the World," *De Bow's Review* quoted in *Wilmington Journal*, March 19, 1863.

46. Python [pseud.], "Peace between the Sections, or War to the World."

47. "Maximilian and Mexico," *Richmond Daily Dispatch*, November 2, 1863.

48. Karp, *This Vast Southern Empire*.

49. "The Mexican Empire," *Richmond Daily Dispatch*, August 4, 1863.

50. "The Mexican Empire."

51. "Maximilian and Mexico," *Richmond Daily Dispatch*, November 2, 1863.

52. However, historians have uncovered some elements of pro-monarchist thinking among Southern intellectual and political circles during the Civil War era. See, for example, Heath, "'Let the Empire Come,'" 152–89; Tucker, *Newest Born of Nations*, 129–33.

53. "France in Mexico," *Richmond Enquirer*, July 28, 1863.

54. "France in Mexico."

55. Michael Chevalier, *France, Mexico, and the Confederate States* (New York: C. B. Richardson, 1863), 3.

56. "European News," *New York Herald*, September 15, 1863; "The Mexican Question," *Philadelphia Inquirer*, September 22, 1863.

57. "A Significant Pamphlet," *Wilmington Journal*, October 1, 1863.

58. "Prospects of the War," *Richmond Daily Dispatch*, October 13, 1863. See also "The New French Pamphlet," *Charleston Daily Courier*, October 3, 1863; "A Significant Pamphlet," *Richmond Daily Dispatch*, September 25, 1863; "A Significant Pamphlet," *Hillsborough Recorder* (NC), October 7, 1863; "M. Michael Chevalier," *American Citizen* (Butler, PA), October 17, 1863; "The New French Pamphlet 'France, Mexico and the Confederate States,'" *Richmond Whig*, September 30, 1863.

59. Chevalier, *France, Mexico, and the Confederate States*, 15.

60. Chevalier, *France, Mexico, and the Confederate States*, 7.

61. Chevalier, *France, Mexico, and the Confederate States*, 8.

62. Chevalier, *France, Mexico, and the Confederate States*, 8.

63. Chevalier, *France, Mexico, and the Confederate States*, 8.

64. Chevalier, *France, Mexico, and the Confederate States*, 6.

65. Chevalier, *France, Mexico, and the Confederate States*, 8.

66. Saragoza, *The Monterrey Elite and the Mexican State, 1880–1940*, 22.

67. "The Mexican Empire," *Richmond Daily Dispatch*, August 4, 1863.

68. "The Mexican Empire."

69. "The Mexican Empire."

70. Chevalier, *France, Mexico, and the Confederate States*, 9.

71. Chevalier, *France, Mexico, and the Confederate States*, 9.

72. Kushner, "Visions of the Northwest Coast," 295–306.

73. "Maximilian's Secession Nobility," *Richmond Whig*, April 7, 1864; "Later from Mexico," *Richmond Daily Dispatch*, January 31, 1865; "Mexico," *Richmond Whig*, February 1, 1865; No title, *Soldier's Journal* (Richmond, VA), February 1, 1865; "San Francisco," *Dallas Weekly Herald*, March 2, 1865.

74. Chevalier, *France, Mexico, and the Confederate States*, 13.

75. "A Significant Pamphlet," *Hillsborough Recorder* (NC), October 7, 1863.

76. "French Policy," *Yorkville Enquirer* (SC), March 4, 1863.

77. "French Policy."

78. "Our Present Confederate States," *De Bow's Review*, July 1862.

79. "The Monroe Doctrine," *De Bow's Review*, January 1864.

80. "General Houston's Speech," *Memphis Daily Appeal*, April 16, 1863.

81. Karp, *This Vast Southern Empire*, 8.

82. "Mexico," *Atlanta Confederacy* quoted in *Camden Daily Journal* (SC), July 9, 1864.

83. "Political Alliances," *Memphis Daily Appeal*, November 9, 1863.

84. "Political Alliances," *Memphis Daily Appeal*, November 9, 1863.

85. Maj. John Tyler, "Our Present Confederate Status, Foreign and Domestic," *De Bow's Review*, vol. XXXIV.

86. Tyler, "Our Present Confederate Status."

87. Tyler, "Our Present Confederate Status."

88. "Maximilian and Mexico," *Richmond Daily Dispatch*, November 2, 1863.
89. "Maximilian and Mexico."
90. "Maximilian and Mexico."
91. "Maximilian and Mexico."
92. "Arguments for Slavery," *Yorkville Enquirer* (SC), March 14, 1861.
93. "Arguments for Slavery."
94. "Arguments for Slavery."
95. "Arguments for Slavery."
96. "Hope On—Hope Ever," *Memphis Daily Appeal*, June 10, 1864.
97. Rugemer, "The Southern Response to British Abolitionism," 221–48; Rugemer, "Robert Monroe Harrison, British Abolition, Southern Anglophobia and Texas Annexation," 169–91.
98. "The Monroe Doctrine," *Richmond Daily Dispatch*, April 12, 1864.
99. "French Policy in Mexico," *Richmond Daily Dispatch*, July 27, 1864.
100. No title, *Wilmington Journal*, January 28, 1864. See also, "Hope On—Hope Ever," *Memphis Daily Appeal*, 10 June 1864.
101. "The United States and Mexico," *Richmond Daily Dispatch*, September 5, 1863.
102. "The United States and Mexico."
103. "The United States and Mexico."
104. "France and the United States," *Fayetteville Observer* (NC) quoted in *The Daily Rebel* (Chattanooga, TN), June 29, 1864.
105. No title, *Richmond Enquirer*, November 26, 1864.
106. "Mexico," *Weekly Standard* (Raleigh, NC), August 12, 1863.
107. "Mexico."
108. "For the Standard," *Weekly Standard* (Raleigh, NC), August 19, 1863.
109. "For the Standard."
110. Hubbard, *The Burden of Confederate Diplomacy*, 164; Sainlaude, *France and the American Civil War*, 110–83.
111. No title, *Richmond Examiner*, June 1, 1864.
112. "For the Standard. Fellow-Citizens of the Third Congressional District of North Carolina," *Semi-Weekly Standard* (Raleigh, NC), July 1, 1864.
113. No title, *Daily Progress* (Raleigh, NC), April 14, 1864.
114. Bernath, "The Confederacy as a Moment of Possibility," 300.
115. Bernath, "The Confederacy as a Moment of Possibility," 300.
116. Neely Jr., *Southern Rights*.
117. Harris, *William Woods Holden*, 1–74.
118. Mobley, "Zebulon B. Vance," 434–54; Raper, "William W. Holden and the Peace Movement in North Carolina," 493–516.
119. "Speech of Hon. T. C. Fuller," *Weekly Standard* (Raleigh, NC), July 20, 1864.
120. "Speech of Hon. T. C. Fuller."
121. "Speech of Hon. T. C. Fuller."
122. "Speech of Hon. T. C. Fuller."
123. No title, *Weekly Standard* (Raleigh, NC), July 27, 1864.
124. No title, *Weekly Standard* (Raleigh, NC), July 27, 1864.
125. No title, *Weekly Standard* (Raleigh, NC), July 27, 1864.

126. No title, *Weekly Standard* (Raleigh, NC), July 15, 1864.
127. No title, *Weekly Standard* (Raleigh, NC), July 15, 1864.
128. "Mexico," *Weekly Standard* (Raleigh, NC), August 12, 1863.
129. "Mexico."
130. "Tell Us Moore—Are We to Have a King?" *Weekly Standard* (Raleigh, NC), July 6, 1864.
131. Brown, *Message of His Excellency Joseph E. Brown, to the Extra Session of the Legislature*, 12.
132. Brown, *Message of His Excellency Joseph E. Brown*, 24–25.
133. Unnamed Georgia newspaper quoted in "Georgia. Adjournment of the Legislature—Protest against the Suspension of Habeas Corpus—Voice of the Press," *Daily Progress* (Raleigh, NC), March 20, 1864.
134. "Georgia. Adjournment of the Legislature—Protest against the Suspension of Habeas Corpus—Voice of the Press."
135. *Selma Daily Reporter* (AL) quoted in *Daily Progress* (Raleigh, NC), April 29, 1864.
136. *Weekly Mississippian* quoted in "A Turning Point," *Daily Progress* (Raleigh, NC), April 29, 1864.
137. "A Turning Point."
138. "A Turning Point."
139. "A Turning Point."
140. The resolution, submitted in late November 1864, was referred to the House Committee on Foreign Relations, where it languished until the end of the war (Henry S. Foote, "Resolution, November 30, 1864," in *Journal of the Congress of the Confederate States of America* VII, 312–13).
141. "News from Rebel Sources," *Nashville Daily Union*, November 9, 1864.
142. "News from Rebel Sources."
143. "News from Rebel Sources."
144. "The Rebel Congress," *The Sun* (Baltimore, MD), November 14, 1864.
145. "Speech for Stopping the War," *Daily Chattanooga Rebel* (TN), February 18, 1863; "An Abolitionist for Peace," *Yorkville Enquirer* (SC), February 25, 1863; "Reunion," *Richmond Enquirer*, July 24, 1863; "Treason in North Carolina," *Daily Selma Reporter* (AL), August 29, 1863.
146. Prior to Blair's meeting with Davis, Romero had agreed that the Confederate president would be "invited to lead an army of 20,000 men," which would consist of two divisions, one composed of Union troops, the other of Confederates. Contrary to what Blair suggested to Davis, however, the Mexican minister had not acquiesced to Mexican lands being used to pay Davis and his compatriots for this service (Romero, *Mexican Lobby*, 51–52).
147. Patrick Kelly, "The Cat's Paw: Confederate Ambitions in Latin America," in *American Civil Wars*, ed. Doyle, 76–77; Sanders Jr., "Jefferson Davis and the Hampton Roads Peace Conference," 804.
148. No title, *Daily Dispatch* (Richmond, VA), November 30, 1864.
149. "For the Observer," *Fayetteville Weekly Observer* (NC), February 6, 1865.
150. "For the Observer."
151. "The Monroe Doctrine," *Weekly Con* (Aberdeen, MS), February 8, 1865.

152. No title, *Daily Confederate* (Raleigh, NC), January 31, 1865.
153. No title, *Daily Confederate* (Raleigh, NC), January 31, 1865.
154. No title, *Daily Dispatch* (Richmond, VA), January 7, 1865.
155. No title, *Daily Dispatch* (Richmond, VA), January 7, 1865.
156. No title, *Daily Dispatch* (Richmond, VA), February 25, 1865.
157. No title, *Daily Dispatch* (Richmond, VA), January 7, 1865.
158. No title, *Daily Dispatch* (Richmond, VA), January 7, 1865.

Chapter Three

1. Cutrer, *Theater of a Separate War*; Hess, *The Civil War in the West*; Nelson, *Three-Cornered War*; Shea, "The War We Have Lost," 100–108.
2. Rolle, *The Lost Cause*, 38–49.
3. Downs, *After Appomattox*.
4. Downs, *After Appomattox*, 246.
5. Harter, *The Lost Colony of the Confederacy*; Marcus, *Confederate Exodus*; Strom and Weaver, *Confederates in the Tropics*; Wahlstrom, *The Southern Exodus to Mexico*.
6. Grady, *Matthew Fontaine Maury, Father of Oceanography*, 247–60.
7. President Juárez to Romero, May 11, 1865, in *The Assassination of Abraham Lincoln*, 627.
8. Savage, *The Life and Public Services of Andrew Johnson*, 297.
9. Romero, *Mexican Lobby*, 56.
10. Romero, *Mexican Lobby*, 56–57.
11. General Philip Sheridan to General Ulysses S. Grant, June 28, 1865, *The Papers of Ulysses S. Grant*, ed. Simon, 163.
12. Sheridan to Grant, June 28, 1865, 163.
13. Sheridan to Grant, June 28, 1865, 163.
14. Sheridan to Grant, June 28, 1865, 163.
15. Rolle, *The Lost Cause*, 55.
16. Grant to President Andrew Johnson, June 19, 1865, *The Papers of Ulysses S. Grant*, 156.
17. Grant to Johnson, June 19, 1865, 157.
18. Grant to Johnson, June 19, 1865, 156–57.
19. Grant to Johnson, June 19, 1865, 158.
20. Grant to Johnson, June 19, 1865, 158.
21. Grant to Johnson, June 19, 1865, 158.
22. Romero, *Mexican Lobby*, 73.
23. Romero, *Mexican Lobby*, 82.
24. Grant to Secretary Edwin Stanton, July 25, 1865, *The Papers of Ulysses S. Grant*, 265.
25. Grant to Sheridan, July 25, 1865, *The Papers of Ulysses S. Grant*, 285.
26. *St. Louis Republican* quoted in "The Exodus to Mexico Exaggerated," *Fairfield News and Herald* (Winnsboro, SC), August 26, 1865; "Failure of Maximilian's Agents to Induce the British Government to Change Its Policy towards Mexico," *Wheeling Daily Intelligencer* (WV), August 4, 1865.
27. "The Exodus to Mexico Exaggerated."
28. "The Exodus to Mexico Exaggerated."
29. Miller, "Arms across the Border," 13.

30. McMahon and Zeiler, eds., *Guide to US Foreign Policy*, 48.

31. Miller, "Arms across the Border," 1–68.

32. *Philadelphia Press* quoted in "Emigration to Mexico—A Mysterious Movement," *Times-Picayune* (New Orleans), May 21, 1865.

33. "Emigration to Mexico—A Mysterious Movement."

34. "Mexico," *New York Tribune*, May 25, 1865.

35. Miller, "Arms across the Border," 8–16; Miller, "Matías Romero," 228–45.

36. Romero, *Mexican Lobby*, 59–61.

37. "Meeting of the United States Service Club," *New York Tribune*, July 9, 1865; "From California," *Chicago Tribune*, July 20, 1865.

38. *Proceedings of a Meeting of Citizens of New York, July 19, 1865*, 3.

39. *Proceedings of a Meeting of Citizens of New York, July 19, 1865*, 8–10.

40. *Proceedings of a Meeting of Citizens of New York, July 19, 1865*, 10.

41. "The Monroe Doctrine in Mexico," *Courier-Journal* (Louisville, KY), July 29, 1865.

42. "Mexican Affairs," *Albany Democrat*, August 28, 1865.

43. "The Monroe Doctrine," *Perry County Democrat* (New Bloomfield, PA), August 10, 1865.

44. "The Monroe Doctrine."

45. Romero, *Mexican Lobby*, 63.

46. Romero, *Mexican Lobby*, 63.

47. Romero, *Mexican Lobby*, 63–64.

48. "A Prospect for Mexico," *Wilkies' Spirit of the Times* (New York, NY), December 23, 1865.

49. Goldwert, "Matías Romero," 36.

50. Romero, *Mexican Lobby*, 90.

51. Romero, *Mexican Lobby*, 90.

52. Romero, *Mexican Lobby*, 90.

53. President Schneider, "Debate on the Amendment to the Address about Mexico, April 11, 1865," *Papers Relating to Foreign Affairs*, 258.

54. Fry, *Lincoln, Seward, and U.S. Foreign Relations in the Civil War Era*, 154–86.

55. For examples of information provided by Romero to the press emphasizing the continued strength of the Juarist war effort, see "Important from Mexico," *Evening Star* (Washington, DC), November 30, 1865; "The News," *Chicago Tribune*," December 1, 1865. For similarly encouraging articles supplied by other representatives of the Mexican republic, see "Our Mexican Correspondence," *New York Herald*, November 3, 1865; "Liberal Successes in Mexico," *New York Herald*, November 14, 1865; "Later from Mexico," *Philadelphia Inquirer*, November 20, 1865.

56. "The Mexican Empire Established," *Dayton Daily Empire* (OH), October 17, 1865.

57. "From Europe," *Detroit Free Press*, August 26, 1865.

58. *New York Tribune* quoted in "Late Mexican News. The Imperial Side of the Story—French Victories, &c., &c.," *Pittsburgh Daily Commercial*, October 13, 1865.

59. No title, *Montana Post*, September 16, 1865; "Mexican Affairs," *Baltimore Daily Commercial*, December 15, 1865.

60. See, for example, "Mexico," *Chicago Tribune*, February 4, 1866; "The Mexican Question—The Republic the Last Chance for Maximilian," *New York Herald*, February 5,

1866; "The Fate of Mexico," *Pittsburgh Daily Commercial*, February 9, 1866; "Our Southern Next Door Neighbors—The Duty of the United States," *Evening Telegraph* (Philadelphia, PA), April 6, 1866.

61. "Washington Correspondence," *Georgia Weekly Telegraph* (Macon), June 4, 1866.

62. "Washington Correspondence."

63. "Washington Correspondence."

64. "Washington Correspondence."

65. "The French in Mexico," *Cleveland Daily Leader*, January 15, 1866; "Napoleon's Speech—The Withdrawal of French Troops from Mexico," *Cincinnati Enquirer*, February 9, 1866; "Napoleon on Mexican Affairs," *Hartford Daily Courant*, February 9, 1866; "The Mexican Question," *Chicago Evening Post*, February 19, 1866; "Foreign Troops for Mexico," *Chico Weekly Chronicle-Record* (CA), February 24, 1866; "The Mexican Correspondence," *Chicago Tribune*, April 27, 1866; "Mr. Seward's Mexican Diplomacy—Strange Reports from Washington," *New York Herald*, June 27, 1866.

66. "Latest News," *Daily Progress* (NC), May 25, 1865. For a similar perspective from a former Unionist Southern publication, see "Exit of Rebels into Mexico," *Nashville Daily Union*, July 16, 1865.

67. Slap, *Reconstructing Appalachia*, 108–9.

68. "Platforms," *New Berne Times* (NC), September 20, 1865.

69. "Platforms."

70. "Mexico," *Daily Standard* (Raleigh, NC), August 14, 1865.

71. "Mexico."

72. "Rumors Concerning Mexico," *Daily Progress* (Raleigh, NC), September 30, 1865.

73. "Mexico and the United States—The Monroe Doctrine," *Nashville Daily Union*, November 3, 1865.

74. "Mexico and the United States."

75. "Mexico and the United States."

76. "Our Account with England and France," *Montgomery Daily Mail*, June 5, 1866.

77. "Our Account with England and France."

78. "The Local Column," *Daily Progress* (Raleigh, NC), May 19, 1865.

79. "Mexico," *Daily Standard* (Raleigh, NC), September 26, 1865.

80. "Mexico."

81. "Our Foreign Relations," *Nashville Daily Union*, January 19, 1866.

82. "Our Foreign Relations."

83. "Mexico," *Daily Standard* (Raleigh, NC), August 14, 1865.

84. "France and the United States," *Daily Progress* (Raleigh, NC), November 22, 1865.

85. "France and the United States."

86. "Testimony before the Reconstruction Committee," *Cleveland Daily Leader*, March 7, 1866.

87. "Testimony before the Reconstruction Committee."

88. "Testimony before the Reconstruction Committee."

89. "Testimony before the Reconstruction Committee."

90. Neely Jr., *The Civil War and the Limits of Destruction*, 72–108. For more on ex-Confederates' attempts to establish slavery and slavery-like systems in Mexico, see Foster, *Ghosts of the Confederacy*, 14–20; Wahlstrom, *The Southern Exodus to Mexico*, 83–129.

91. Romero, *Mexican Lobby*, 101.

92. Romero, *Mexican Lobby*, 108.

93. "Maximilian and Slavery," *South Carolina Ledger*, November 25, 1865.

94. "Mexico and Slavery," *Hartford Daily Courant*, October 19, 1865.

95. "Slavery in Mexico," *New York Tribune*, January 6, 1866.

96. "The Confederate Enterprise in Mexico—Cheap Defense for Maximilian against the United States," *New York Herald*, January 28, 1866.

97. "The Confederate Enterprise in Mexico."

98. "The Confederate Enterprise in Mexico."

99. "Peonage in Mexico," *New York Tribune*, January 4, 1866.

100. "Peonage in Mexico." See also "Designs of Southern Men against Mexico," *Weekly Standard* (Raleigh, NC), February 7, 1866; "The Rebel Emigration in Mexico," *Smyrna Times* (DE), May 2, 1866; "The Disturbance of the Confederate Settlements in Mexico," *Daily Union and American* (Nashville, TN), June 28, 1866.

101. "Testimony before the Reconstruction Committee," *Cleveland Daily Leader*, March 7, 1866.

102. "Testimony before the Reconstruction Committee."

103. Tom Bingham, "The *Alabama* Claims Arbitration"; Jones, *Union in Peril*, 221–30; Long, *In the Shadows of the Alabama*; Mahin, *One War at a Time*, 286–300.

104. "Testimony before the Reconstruction Committee," *Cleveland Daily Leader*, March 7, 1866.

105. "From California," *Chicago Tribune*, June 2, 1865.

106. Joint Committee on Reconstruction, *Report of the Joint Committee on Reconstruction*, XVIII.

107. Henry Winter Davis, "Lessons of the War—The American Continent Republican—Security for the Future, and Self-Government by Law, with Liberty Guarded by Power," Speech Delivered at a Chicago Civic Celebration on July 4, 1865, in *Speeches and Addresses Delivered in the Congress of the United States*, 582–83.

108. Davis, "Lessons of the War," 582–83.

109. "The North and the South: Their Future Relations," *New York Times*, December 28, 1865.

110. "The North and the South."

111. "Suffrage," *Chicago Tribune*, May 2, 1866.

112. Other scholars have noted how certain Republican leaders highlighted the conservative and restorative—rather than the radical and transformative—elements of their Reconstruction agenda to the public. See, for example, Calhoun, *Conceiving a New Republic*. My emphasis on how US Americans' fear of further national fragmentations was an important factor in driving popular support for congressional Reconstruction has also been put forward, albeit in different ways, by other scholars. See, for example, Les Benedict, "Preserving the Constitution," 65–90; LaWanda Cox, "Reflections on the Limits of the Possible," in *Freedom, Racism, and Reconstruction*, ed. Nieman, 243–48; Summers, *The Ordeal of Reunion*.

113. *New York Herald* quoted in No title, *Montana Post*, May 27, 1865.

114. *New York Herald* quoted in No title, *Montana Post*, May 27, 1865.

115. "England and France," *Chicago Tribune*, February 22, 1866.

116. "Mexico and Maximilian," *Hartford Daily Courant*, November 18, 1865.
117. "Mexico and Maximilian."
118. "Cowell Lending a Hand," *Harper's Weekly*, March 25, 1865.
119. "The Second Life of Washington," *Harper's New Monthly Magazine*, December 1865–May 1866.
120. "The Second Life of Washington."
121. "The Second Life of Washington."
122. "Prospect of Another War," *Western Democrat* (Charlotte, NC), August 8, 1865.
123. "Prospect of Another War."
124. "Prospect of Another War."
125. "Prospect of Another War."
126. "Mutterings of War," *Staunton Spectator* (VA), November 7, 1865.
127. "From the City of Mexico," *Memphis Daily Appeal*, December 6, 1865.
128. "From the City of Mexico."
129. "The United States, Mexico, France and England," *Times-Picayune* (New Orleans, LA), December 21, 1865.
130. "The United States, Mexico, France and England."
131. "The Military Chieftains and Politicians at Issue," *Times-Picayune* (New Orleans, LA), August 18, 1865.
132. "The Military Chieftains and Politicians at Issue."
133. "The Military Chieftains and Politicians at Issue."
134. "The Military Chieftains and Politicians at Issue."
135. "Mexican News," *Daily Intelligencer* (Atlanta, GA), June 23, 1865. Historians have found that the ex-Confederate migration to Mexico was fueled by a variety of motivations. The *Daily Intelligencer* was quite right to argue that some ex-rebels ran to escape punishment at the hands of federal authorities. Others, primarily former planters, were hoping to rebuild something of their lost status and fortunes south of the border. There were also a number of migrants from the middling and lower rungs of Southern society who were seeking work and cheap land (Wahlstrom, *The Southern Exodus to Mexico*, 1–48).
136. "Mexican News," *Daily Intelligencer* (Atlanta, GA), June 23, 1865.
137. No title, *Western Democrat* (Charlotte, NC), October 24, 1865.
138. No title, *Western Democrat* (Charlotte, NC), October 24, 1865.
139. "Summary of Villainies," *Mobile Daily Times* (AL), April 20, 1866.
140. "Summary of Villainies."
141. "The Radical Ultimatum," *Daily South-Western* (Shreveport, LA), May 16, 1866.
142. "The Radical Ultimatum."
143. "The Mexican Question," *Times-Democrat* (New Orleans, LA), November 17, 1866.
144. "New York Juarists," *Times-Picayune* (New Orleans, LA), January 25, 1866.
145. "New York Juarists."
146. "Mexico—The US Eagle Hovering Over Her," *Richmond Daily Dispatch* (VA), August 4, 1866.
147. "Mexico—The US Eagle Hovering Over Her."
148. "New York Juarists."
149. "New York Juarists."
150. "New York Juarists."

151. Crouthamel, *Bennett's* New York Herald *and the Rise of the Popular Press*; Seybold, "Destroyer of *Confidence*," 83–106.

152. "Mexico Fighting Our Battles," *New York Herald*, February 2, 1863.

153. "Extraordinary Developments of the Designs of Napoleon against Mexico and the United States," *New York Herald*, February 3, 1863.

154. "The French in Mexico," *New York Herald*, June 11, 1863.

155. A good example of this is the *Herald*'s enthusiastic call following the Battle of Gettysburg for the Union to bring an end to the Civil War by launching an invasion of Mexico. See "The Grandeur of President Lincoln's Position—Will He Restore the Union?" *New York Herald*, July 9, 1863.

156. "The Peace Question," *New York Herald*, March 25, 1865.

157. "The Peace Question."

158. "The Peace Question."

159. "Political Conventions and the Monroe Doctrine," *New York Herald*, September 11, 1865.

160. *Houston Telegraph* quoted in No title, *Daily South-Western* (Shreveport, LA), June 14, 1865.

161. No title, *Daily South-Western* (Shreveport, LA), June 14, 1865.

162. No title, *Daily South-Western* (Shreveport, LA), June 14, 1865.

163. "War," *Missouri Republican*, June 8, 1865.

164. "War."

165. *Houston Telegraph* quoted in No title, *Daily South-Western* (Shreveport, LA), June 14, 1865.

166. "War."

167. "War."

168. "M. de Lamartine's Defense of the French-Mexican Policy," *Cincinnati Enquirer*, December 23, 1865.

169. "M. de Lamartine's Defense of the French-Mexican Policy."

170. "Congress and the Mexican Muddle," *New York Herald*, December 2, 1866.

171. "Congress and the Mexican Muddle."

172. "Our Mexican Neighbors," *The Sun* (Baltimore, MD), January 10, 1866.

173. "Mexico Fighting Our Battles," *New York Herald*, February 2, 1863.

174. "Senator Trumbull on the Civil Rights Bill—He Falls Short of the Real Issue," *New York Herald*, April 6, 1866.

175. "Senator Trumbull on the Civil Rights Bill."

176. "The Suffrage Question," *Louisville Daily Courier* (KY), August 8, 1867.

177. "The Suffrage Question."

178. "How to Make the United States a Second Mexico," *Ohio Daily Statesman*, July 27, 1867.

179. "How to Make the United States a Second Mexico."

180. *New York Post* quoted in "Are We to Have Civil War?" *Courier-Journal* (Louisville, KY), August 28, 1866.

181. "Are We to Have Civil War?"

182. "Are We to Have Civil War?"

183. "Are We to Have Civil War?"

184. "Are We to Have Civil War?"

185. Wahlstrom, *The Southern Exodus to Mexico*, 83–134.

186. "The Execution of Maximilian," *New York Tribune*, July 1, 1867. For just a few of the many examples of US newspapers responding with jubilation to the news that Maximilian's forces had surrendered, see "What Will Juarez Do?" *Evening Telegraph* (Philadelphia, PA), May 22, 1867; "Mexico," *Weekly Ottumwa Courier* (IA), May 30, 1867; "The Situation in Mexico," *Carson Daily Appeal* (NV), June 9, 1867; "President Juarez," *Ellsworth American* (ME), June 14, 1867; "Mexico—Scenes and Incidents of the Siege of Queretaro," *Courier-Journal* (Louisville, KY), June 21, 1867; "Maximilian's Fall" *Pittsburgh Daily Commercial*, June 29, 1867; "The Fate of Maximilian," *Vernon County Censor* (WI), July 10, 1867; "The United States and Mexico," *Chicago Evening Post*, July 13, 1867; "The Fate of Usurpers," *Santa Cruz Weekly Sentinel* (CA), July 20, 1867; "Maximilian and the Black Flag," *Mineral Point Weekly Tribune* (WI), July 31, 1867; "Italy and Mexico—Their Present States," *Boston Evening Transcript*, November 8, 1867.

187. "Maximilian," *Brooklyn Daily Eagle*, July 3, 1867.

188. "Maximilian." For more examples of US newspapers condemning the execution of Maximilian, see "Mexico—Special Correspondence of the Herald," *New York Herald*, June 4, 1867; "Maximilian," *Daily Ohio Statesman*, July 3, 1867; "Murder and Manifest Destiny," *Norfolk Virginian*, July 4, 1867; "Responsible," *Public Ledger* (Memphis, TN), July 6, 1867; "The Execution of Maximilian," *Edgefield Advertiser* (SC), July 10, 1867; "The Mexican Protectorate," *Daily South-Western* (Shreveport, LA), July 10, 1867; "The Late Inhuman Tragedy in Mexico," *Tri-Weekly Gazette & Comet* (Baton Rouge, LA), July 11, 1867; "The Tragedy in Mexico," *Chicago Tribune*, July 24, 1867; "Maximilian—Monarchy in Mexico," *American Citizen* (Butler, PA), July 31, 1867; "Mexico," *Dallas Weekly Herald*, August 10, 1867.

189. "Northern Traitors and Southern Traitors Compared," *Courier-Journal* (Louisville, KY), September 14, 1867.

190. "Northern Traitors and Southern Traitors Compared."

Chapter Four

1. Romero, *Mexican Lobby*, 150–66.

2. *Banquet to Señor Matías Romero, October 2, 1867*, 29.

3. *Banquet to Señor Matías Romero, October 2, 1867*, 29.

4. *Banquet to Señor Matías Romero, October 2, 1867*, 29–30.

5. "The Unhappy Condition of Mexico and the Hapless Fate of Maximilian," *Edgefield Advertiser* (SC), July 10, 1867.

6. "The Unhappy Condition of Mexico."

7. *Charleston Courier* quoted in "The Execution of Maximilian," *Edgefield Advertiser* (SC), July 10, 1867.

8. *Charleston Courier* quoted in "The Execution of Maximilian," *Edgefield Advertiser* (SC), July 10, 1867.

9. "Mexico," *Charleston Mercury*, July 4, 1867.

10. *Forney's Chronicle* quoted in "Mexico," *Kansas Radical*, July 13, 1867.

11. *New York Tribune* quoted in "The Reign of Terror in Mexico," *Belmont Chronicle* (OH), August 1, 1867.

12. Blair, *With Malice Towards Some*, 234–303.

13. "The Reign of Terror in Mexico."

14. "The Reign of Terror in Mexico."

15. Jay Sexton provides a useful discussion of how these assumptions have shaped the scholarship of nineteenth-century foreign relations in "Toward a Synthesis of Foreign Relations in the Civil War Era, 1848–1877," 50–73.

16. "Juarez in Mexico City," *San Francisco Chronicle*, August 23, 1867.

17. Benito Juárez, "The Triumph of the Republic," in *The Mexico Reader*, ed. Joseph and Henderson, 272.

18. Juárez, "The Triumph of the Republic," 272.

19. For more on Liberals' efforts to reform Mexico's education system in the years following the French Intervention, see Hale, *The Transformation of Liberalism in Late Nineteenth-Century Mexico*, esp. 3–24 and 139–204.

20. Hammett, "Liberalism Divided," 659–89; McNamara, *Sons of the Sierra*, 67–92; Thompson with LaFrance, *Patriotism, Politics, and Popular Liberalism in Nineteenth-Century Mexico*, 201–10.

21. For US press coverage of Mariscal's movements between 1867 and 1869, see "The Mexican Legation," *Philadelphia Inquirer*, December 23, 1867; "Mexican Affairs," *The Sun* (Baltimore, MD), December 23, 1867; "News from Mexico," *Times-Picayune* (New Orleans, LA), May 3, 1868; "From Mexico," *Alexandria Gazette* (VA), June 26, 1868; "Mexico: The Ministerial Crisis—Battle between the National Troops and the Revolutionists—Reception of Negrete at Teleta," *Burlington Weekly Sentinel* (VT), July 3, 1868; "Mexico," *New York Herald*, August 11, 1868.

22. "Mexican Affairs—Inside Revolutionists and Outside Adventurers," *New York Herald*, February 9, 1868.

23. "Mexican Affairs."

24. "Mexican Affairs."

25. "Mexico," *New York Herald*, June 15, 1868.

26. "Mexico."

27. "Mexico."

28. "Mexico."

29. "Alas: Poor Mexico," *San Francisco Examiner*, February 11, 1868.

30. "Alas: Poor Mexico."

31. "Alas: Poor Mexico."

32. "Minority Report," *Pittsburgh Gazette*, November 26, 1867.

33. "The National Issues," *The Sun* (Baltimore, MD), March 5, 1868.

34. "XLth Congress—Second Session," *Portland Daily Press* (ME), March 3, 1868.

35. "End of the Impeachment Trial—The President Acquitted and the Court Dissolved," *The Sun* (Baltimore, MD), May 27, 1868.

36. "End of the Impeachment Trial."

37. "End of the Impeachment Trial." For similar uses of Mexicanization rhetoric in the Democratic press before, during, and after Johnson's impeachment trial, see "Three Judiciary Reports on Impeachment," *Salt Lake Daily Telegraph and Commercial Advertiser*, November 28, 1867; "The Impeachment Scheme," *Argus and Patriot* (Montpelier, VT), December 5, 1867; "Mr. Chase as a Democratic Candidate," *Brooklyn Daily Eagle*, March 27, 1868; "Radical Conspiracies," *Norfolk Virginian*, September 22, 1868.

38. "A Story with a Moral," *Norfolk Virginian*, May 16, 1868.

39. "A Story with a Moral."

40. "The Next Civil War—How to Avert It," *Bolivar Bulletin* (TN), March 21, 1868.

41. "The Next Civil War." For other examples of Democratic publications drawing analogies between Radical Republicans and Mexican Liberals in the run-up to the 1868 presidential election, see "Our Sister Republic," *The Tennessean*, March 11, 1868; "Mexico," *Louisville Daily Courier* (KY), June 24, 1868.

42. *New York World* quoted in "The Mexicanizing Radicals," *Evening Telegraph* (Philadelphia, PA), November 5, 1868.

43. "The Mexicanizing Radicals."

44. "The Mexicanizing Radicals."

45. "The Mexicanizing Radicals."

46. "A Nice Tea-Party among Traitors to Liberty," *Wilmington Journal* (NC), December 31, 1869.

47. For an example of one Republican organ offering all of these theories and more in a single article, see "Mexican Anarchy. The Desperate Condition of Affairs throughout the Country," *New York Times*, March 27, 1869.

48. "Present Condition of Mexico," *Chicago Tribune*, February 10, 1870.

49. "Present Condition of Mexico."

50. "Affairs in Mexico," *Chicago Tribune*, July 27, 1869.

51. "Affairs in Mexico."

52. "Poor Mexico," *Chicago Tribune*, January 7, 1871.

53. "Mexico," *Chicago Tribune*, July 10, 1871.

54. Godkin, "Commercial Immorality and Political Corruption," *North American Review*, 1868.

55. "Commercial Immorality and Political Corruption."

56. Lundberg, *Horace Greeley*, 20.

57. This figure is James M. Lundberg's estimate (Lundberg, *Horace Greeley*, 2). For more on Greeley's newspaper career before the Civil War, see Lundberg, *Horace Greeley*, 1–112; Tuchinsky, *Horace Greeley's* New York Tribune, 1–164.

58. "The Issue," *New York Tribune*, October 25, 1867.

59. "The Issue."

60. "The Issue."

61. Greeley, *Mr. Greeley's Letters from Texas and the Lower Mississippi*, 38.

62. Greeley, *Mr. Greeley's Letters from Texas and the Lower Mississippi*, 41.

63. Lundberg, *Horace Greeley*, 147. See also Tuchinsky, *Horace Greeley's* New York Tribune, 212–42; Williams, *Horace Greeley*, 258–92.

64. Lundberg, *Horace Greeley*, 147–48.

65. Burg, "Amnesty, Civil Rights, and the Meaning of Liberal Republicanism, 1862–1872," 29–60; Gillette, *Retreat from Reconstruction, 1869–1879*; Lang, "Republicanism, Race, and Reconstruction," 559–89; Richardson, *The Death of Reconstruction*; Slap, *The Doom of Reconstruction*. All of these works draw attention to Liberal Republicans' sincere ideological and political values. In doing so, they differ from older studies, which tended to characterize the Liberal Republicans as an anti-Grant movement with no discernible agenda other than to prevent the former president's reelection. See, for example, Sproat, *"The Best Men."*

66. Snay, *Horace Greeley and the Politics of Reform in Nineteenth-Century America*, 155–82.

67. McNamara, *Sons of the Sierra*, 67–92.

68. "Another Mexican Revolution," *Philadelphia Inquirer*, June 19, 1871; "Rebellion in Mexico," *New Orleans Republican*, December 9, 1871; "The War in Mexico," *New York Herald*, December 25, 1871.

69. "The Military Interference Act," *Chicago Tribune*, May 29, 1872.

70. "The Military Interference Act."

71. "What Are We Coming To?" *Chicago Tribune*, May 7, 1872.

72. "Mexico: Signs of Revival," *New York Tribune*, August 21, 1872.

73. "Mexico: Signs of Revival."

74. "Mexico: Signs of Revival."

75. "Mexico: Signs of Revival."

76. "Mexico: Signs of Revival."

77. "The Presidential Campaign," *Chicago Tribune*, October 19, 1872.

78. Slap, *The Doom of Reconstruction*, 164–98.

79. *Springfield Republican* (MA) quoted in the *Chicago Tribune*, November 9, 1872.

80. "The South Today," *The Nation*, July 8, 1874.

81. No title, *Springfield Republican* (MA) quoted in George S. Merriam, *The Life and Times of Samuel Bowles* (New York: The Century Company, 1885), 287.

82. "Affairs in Mexico," *Burlington Free Press* (VT), October 24, 1872.

83. "Affairs in Mexico."

84. "Mexico," *New York Herald*, October 18, 1872. Nelson's interview was also published in "Mexico," *Memphis Daily Appeal*, October 25, 1872.

85. "The Border War," *New York Herald*, May 24, 1873; "The Mexican Border Trouble," *The Sun* (Baltimore, MD), May 31, 1873.

86. "Border Cattle Thieves," *Oklahoma Star*, December 28, 1875.

87. No title, *Chicago Tribune*, December 8, 1871.

88. "The Mexican Raids," *Inter-Ocean* (Chicago, IL), April 26, 1875.

89. This second uprising led by Díaz is known as the Tuxtepec rebellion. For a useful overview of its history, see McNamara, *Sons of the Sierra*, 87–92.

90. No title, *Harrisburg Telegraph* (PA), November 25, 1876.

91. "Hayes by the Light of Chandler," *Galveston Daily News*, December 15, 1876.

92. "Mr. Edmund's Resolution," *Atlanta Constitution*, December 12, 1876.

93. No title, *Reading Times* (PA), July 26, 1877.

94. "Some Differences," *North American* (Philadelphia, PA), November 13, 1876.

95. "Some Differences."

96. "Some Differences."

97. No title, *North American* (Philadelphia, PA), November 7, 1876.

98. No title, *North American* (Philadelphia, PA), November 7, 1876.

99. "The Presidential Election," *New York Tribune*, November 23, 1876.

100. "What Is Mexicanization," *The Nation* (NY), December 21, 1876.

101. "What Is Mexicanization."

102. "What Is Mexicanization."

103. "What is Mexicanization."

104. No title, *Public Ledger* (Philadelphia, PA), March 1, 1877.

105. *Chicago Tribune* quoted in "Ended at Last," *New Orleans Daily Democrat*, April 26, 1877.

106. No title, *National Republican* (Washington, DC) quoted in "Grant in 1880," *St. Louis Globe-Democrat*, July 11, 1878.

107. "Grant in 1880."

108. "The Fundamental Issue," *Sacramento Daily Record-Union*, September 11, 1880.

109. "The Fundamental Issue."

110. "Calling a Halt," *Inter-Ocean* (Chicago, IL), May 30, 1878.

111. "Grant in 1880."

112. No title, *Milwaukee Daily Sentinel*, May 24, 1878. For a useful look at the persistence of violence against Black Republican voters in the South after 1877, see Xi, *The Trial of Democracy*, 80–125.

113. No title, *Milwaukee Daily Sentinel*, May 24, 1878.

114. "Tammany Hall and the Presidency," *Memphis Daily Appeal*, June 12, 1878.

115. "Tammany Hall and the Presidency."

116. "The Attitude of Mr. Stephens," *Georgia Weekly Telegraph*, June 11, 1878.

117. No title, *Courier-Journal* (Louisville, KY) quoted in "Sherman's Girl," *Daily Arkansas Gazette*, July 2, 1878.

118. "Sherman's Girl."

119. "Personal Politics—Mexicanization," *Georgia Weekly Telegraph*, April 9, 1880.

120. "The Squeak of the Organs," *Daily Constitution* (Atlanta, GA), June 22, 1878.

121. "The Squeak of the Organs."

122. "Mexicanization and Party Spirit," *Galveston Daily News*, June 23, 1878.

123. "Mexicanization and Party Spirit."

124. "Mexicanization and Party Spirit."

125. "Mexicanization and Party Spirit."

126. "Mexicanization and Party Spirit."

127. "Winona," *Memphis Daily Appeal*, June 12, 1878.

128. "Winona."

129. "Results of Democratic Policy," *Inter-Ocean* (Chicago, IL), May 25, 1878.

130. No title, *Commercial Gazette* (Philadelphia, PA) quoted in "Mexicanization," *Chicago Tribune*, May 22, 1878.

131. "The Democratic Plot," *Milwaukee Daily Sentinel*, May 20, 1878.

132. "The Democratic Plot."

133. No Title, *Commercial Gazette* (Philadelphia, PA) quoted in "Mexicanization, *Chicago Tribune*, May 22, 1878, 3.

134. "The Democratic Plot."

135. "The Political Campaign," *The Sun* (Baltimore, MD), May 29, 1878.

136. "The Proposed Revolution," *Milwaukee Daily Sentinel*, May 30, 1878.

137. "The Proposed Revolution."

138. "The Political Campaign," *The Sun* (Baltimore, MD), May 29, 1878.

139. "The Democratic Plot," *Milwaukee Daily Sentinel*, May 20, 1878.

140. Summers, *Rum, Romanism, and Rebellion*, 65–70.

141. "Faction's Latest Crime," *New York Tribune*, July 3, 1881.

142. "Lift the Level," *Boston Herald*, July 5, 1881.

143. "The Fourth," *Milwaukee Daily Sentinel*, July 4, 1881.

144. For more examples of newspapers across the political spectrum using the language of Mexicanization in response to Garfield's assassination, see *New York Evening Post*, quoted in "Press Comments," *Portland Daily Press* (ME), July 4, 1881; "Lift the Level," *Boston Herald*, July 5, 1881; "Commercial Record. Finance and Trade," *Boston Post*, July 5, 1881; "Dongola Letter," *Cairo Bulletin* (IL), July 7, 1881; No title, *The Independent-Record* (Helena, MT), October 21, 1881.

145. "Faction's Latest Crime." *New York Tribune*, July 3, 1881.

146. "Faction's Latest Crime."

147. Bellows, *Historical Sketch of the Union League Club of New York*, 123.

148. Bellows, *Historical Sketch of the Union League Club of New York*, 123.

Chapter Five

1. "Mexican Scenes: The International Baby and the Part It Plays in Mexican Politics," *Chicago Tribune*, March 11, 1883.

2. "Mexican Scenes."

3. See, for example, "Indignant Mexico: The Orders to Ord Makes the Blood of the Greasers Boil," *Daily Constitution* (Atlanta, GA), July 7, 1877; "Mexico Hostile: Not to Help Order," *New York Tribune*, July 17, 1877; "Mexico: Threatening Condition of Affairs," *Chicago Tribune*, November 25, 1877.

4. Lorey, *The U.S.-Mexican Border in the Twentieth Century*, 40.

5. Raat and Brescia, *Mexico and the United States*, 82–83.

6. Hart, *Empire and Revolution*, 2. See also Jayes, *The Illusion of Ignorance*; Pletcher, *The Diplomacy of Trade and Investment*, 80–113; Schell Jr., *Integral Outsiders*.

7. Schoen, "The Fates of Republics and Empires Hang in the Balance," 45.

8. Schoen, "The Fates of Republics and Empires Hang in the Balance," 45. See also Sexton, "Toward a Synthesis of Foreign Relations in the Civil War Era, 1848–1877," 50–73.

9. Thompson with LaFrance, *Patriotism, Politics, and Popular Liberalism in Nineteenth-Century Mexico*, 183–200.

10. "More Mexican Anarchy and Depredations—The Duty and Opportunity of General Grant," *New York Herald*, June 5, 1872.

11. Crouthamel, *Bennett's* New York Herald *and the Rise of the Popular Press*, 56–68.

12. "Mexico and the United States," *New York Herald*, July 5, 1867.

13. "Cuba and Mexico, or Either—General Grant's Great Opportunity," *New York Herald*, January 10, 1872.

14. "General Grant's Position and Opportunity—Territorial and Commercial Expansion the Policy," *New York Herald*, December 18, 1871.

15. "The Mexican Protectorate," *Galveston Daily News*, April 7, 1872; "Let Our Eagle Spread His Wings," *Weekly Arizona Miner*, February 17, 1872.

16. No title, *Pittsburgh Daily Commercial*, August 1, 1871; "The Annexation Bug Bear," *Reading Times* (PA), November 28, 1872; No title, *Democrat and Chronicle* (Rochester, NY), March 19, 1872.

17. Love, *Race Over Empire*.

18. "Mongrel Progress," *Public Ledger* (Memphis, TN), December 8, 1871.

19. “Mexico,” *Bossier Banner* (LA), September 14, 1872.

20. No title, *Memphis Daily Appeal*, August 12, 1872.

21. No title, *Memphis Daily Appeal*, August 12, 1872.

22. “Cowell Lending a Hand,” *Harper’s Weekly*, March 25, 1865.

23. “Mexico and Annexation,” *San Francisco Chronicle*, July 11, 1873.

24. “Another Mexican War,” *Chicago Tribune*, June 28, 1872.

25. “Another Mexican War.”

26. “The Border War,” *New York Herald*, May 24, 1873.

27. “The Mexican Mystery,” *New York Herald*, July 3, 1877.

28. Ayers, *The Promise of the New South*; Hillyer, *Designing Dixie*; Link, *Atlanta, Cradle of the New South*; Prince, *Stories of the South*, 97–166.

29. Jayes, *The Illusion of Ignorance*, 9–21.

30. Jayes, *The Illusion of Ignorance*, 15.

31. Jayes, *The Illusion of Ignorance*, 15.

32. “Mexico,” *New York Herald*, October 18, 1872. See also “Our Relations with Mexico,” *Chicago Tribune*, November 21, 1872.

33. “Mexico,” *New York Herald*, October 18, 1872.

34. Mercer, *Railroads and Land Grant Policy*, 43.

35. *The Texas and Pacific Railway* (New York: Office of the Texas and Pacific Railway, 1872), 4.

36. *The Texas and Pacific Railway*, 7.

37. *The Texas and Pacific Railway*, 4.

38. “Tom Scott’s Program,” *Ouachita Telegraph* (Monroe, LA), February 27, 1874.

39. “Tom Scott’s Program.”

40. “Memorial from New Orleans Chamber of Commerce,” *Memphis Daily Appeal*, March 17, 1874.

41. “Memorial from New Orleans Chamber of Commerce.”

42. “Memorial from New Orleans Chamber of Commerce.”

43. “Chamber of Commerce,” *Times-Democrat* (New Orleans, LA), January 12, 1873.

44. “Letter of Our Minister to Mexico,” *New Orleans Republican*, January 15, 1873.

45. “Letter of Our Minister to Mexico.”

46. “Letter of Our Minister to Mexico.”

47. “A Bounden Duty,” *Weekly Democratic Statesman* (Austin, TX), June 26, 1873.

48. “A Bounden Duty.”

49. “The International Road and Texan Statecraft,” *Weekly Democratic Statesman* (Austin, TX), February 11, 1875.

50. “The International Road and Texan Statecraft.”

51. “The International Road and Texan Statecraft.”

52. “Let Us Build a Monument to This Legislature,” *Weekly Democratic Statesman* (Austin, TX), March 4, 1875.

53. “Let Us Build a Monument to This Legislature.”

54. Elliott, *John C. Brown of Tennessee*.

55. “The Texas & Pacific Railroad,” *Railroad Gazette* (NY), January 25, 1876.

56. “The Texas & Pacific Railroad.”

57. “The Texas & Pacific Railroad.”

58. "The Texas & Pacific Railroad."

59. For more on the Bourbon Democrats, see Perman, *The Road to Redemption.*

60. Throckmorton, "Texas and Pacific Railway," *Speech of Hon. Jas. W. Throckmorton of Texas, in the House of Representatives, March 1, 1877,* 19.

61. Throckmorton, "Texas and Pacific Railway," 19.

62. Throckmorton, "Texas and Pacific Railway," 19.

63. Throckmorton, "Texas and Pacific Railway," 14.

64. *Minutes of the Proceedings of the Commercial Convention held in the City of Memphis, Tennessee, May, 1869* (Memphis, TN: Southwestern Publishing Company, 1869), 88.

65. *Minutes of the Proceedings of the Commercial Convention,* 88.

66. Southern Commercial Convention, *Proceedings of the Southern Commercial Convention, October 1870* (Cincinnati, OH: Committee of Arrangements of Cincinnati, 1871), 93.

67. Reavis, *Saint Louis,* 36.

68. Reavis, *Saint Louis,* 36.

69. "Our Annual Report," *New Orleans Republican,* September 1, 1876.

70. "Our Annual Report."

71. "Commerce between the Lakes and the South Seas," *De Bow's Review,* May 1869.

72. "Commerce between the Lakes and the South Seas."

73. "The Southern Question," *New York Tribune,* May 15, 1874.

74. "The Southern Question."

75. "Railroads and the South," *New York Tribune,* October 2, 1874.

76. "Railroads and the South."

77. No title, *New York Tribune,* October 12, 1872.

78. No title, *New York Tribune,* October 12, 1872.

79. No title, *New York Tribune,* October 12, 1872.

80. "Our Commerce with Mexico," *Chicago Tribune,* December 9, 1873.

81. Pletcher, *The Diplomacy of Trade and Investment,* 109.

82. "Our Commerce with Mexico."

83. "Our Commerce with Mexico."

84. "Our Commerce with Mexico."

85. "Our Commerce with Mexico."

86. "Mexico," *Times-Picayune* (New Orleans, LA), September 5, 1873.

87. "Mexico."

88. White, *Railroaded,* 51–52. White notes that Mexican leaders were right to suspect the intentions of US railroad businessmen seeking to extend their operations into Mexico during the late 1860s and 1870s, many of whom did indeed view the realization of their projects as a prelude to US annexation of portions of Mexico's northern frontier (White, *Railroaded,* 52–55).

89. Hart, *Empire and Revolution,* 60.

90. "The Northern Democracy Opposing Pacification," *National Republican* (Washington, DC), March 13, 1877.

91. "The Northern Democracy Opposing Pacification."

92. "The Northern Democracy Opposing Pacification."

93. Cool, *Salt Warriors,* 100.

94. González-Quiroga, *War and Peace on the Rio Grande Frontier, 1830–1880*, 250–75; Hatfield, *Chasing Shadows*, 18–20.

95. "The Mexican Presidents," *New York Times*, December 16, 1876.

96. See Bulmer-Thomas, *The Economic History of Latin American since Independence*, 46.

97. Bunker, *Creating Mexican Consumer Culture in the Age of Porfirio Díaz*; Hale, *The Transformation of Liberalism in Late Nineteenth-Century Mexico*, 205–45; Lear, *Workers, Neighbors, and Citizens*; Priego, *Positivism, Science, and "The Scientists" in Porfirian Mexico*; Weiner, *Race, Nation, and Market*, 49.

98. Passananti, "'Nada de Papeluchos!'" 101–28.

99. Jayes, *The Illusion of Ignorance*, 37.

100. Jayes, *The Illusion of Ignorance*, 25.

101. No title, *San Marcos Free Press* (TX), February 15, 1879.

102. "Success of a Vigorous Foreign Policy," *New York Herald*, August 7, 1877.

103. "Success of a Vigorous Foreign Policy."

104. "Success of a Vigorous Foreign Policy."

105. "Success of a Vigorous Foreign Policy."

106. "Mexico: President Díaz's Government and Its Prospects," *New York Herald*, January 6, 1878.

107. "Mexico: President Díaz's Government and Its Prospects."

108. "Mexico: President Díaz's Government and Its Prospects."

109. "The Recognition of Díaz," *New York Times*, January 12, 1878.

110. "The Recognition of Díaz."

111. Jayes, *The Illusion of Ignorance*, 40–45.

112. Hart, *Empire and Revolution*, 106–30. For more on the growth of railroads in the early Porfiriato, see Coatsworth, *Growth against Development*; Lewis, *Iron Horse Imperialism*, 15–40; Parlee, *Porfirio Díaz, Railroads, and Development in Northern Mexico*.

113. Mercer, *Railroads and Land Grant Policy*, 46.

114. "The Texas Pacific R. R.," *Mesilla Valley Independent* (NM), October 20, 1877.

115. "New Orleans Business," *Brookhaven Ledger* (MI), November 17, 1881.

116. "An Occasion for Rejoicing," *Dallas Daily Herald*, December 1, 1881.

117. "An Occasion for Rejoicing."

118. "An Occasion for Rejoicing."

119. For studies of the Díaz government's broader public relations campaign in the United States, see Gibbs, "Díaz' Executive Agents and United States Foreign Policy," 171; Guerra, *Más Allá de la Diplomacia*, 103; Smith, "Contentious Voices amid the Order."

120. "The Mexican Minister's Address," *The Sun* (Baltimore, MD), December 2, 1878.

121. Jayes, *The Illusion of Ignorance*, 104.

122. "Our Mexican Cousins," *New York Herald*, November 10, 1878.

123. "Mexico—The Arrival of Senor Zamacona at New Orleans," *New York Herald*, November 21, 1877.

124. "Mexico—An Interview with the Agent of the Mexican Republic," *Chicago Daily Tribune*, March 8, 1878.

125. "Tom Scott's Trump," *St. Louis Globe-Democrat*, November 14, 1878.

126. "Tom Scott's Trump."

127. "Mexico—A Long Interview with M. de Zamacona, the Mexican Minister," *Chicago Daily Tribune*, November 25, 1878.

128. "Mexico—A Long Interview with M. de Zamacona."

129. "Troubled Mexico," *New York Herald*, July 3, 1877.

130. "Troubled Mexico."

131. "Petty Jealousy," *Chicago Tribune*, June 8, 1883.

132. *New York Herald* quoted in "Mexico Americanized—How Commerce Is Awakened and the Spirit of Self-Government Fostered," *Milwaukee Daily Sentinel*, February 18, 1883.

133. "Justice to Mexico," *Washington Post* (DC), 13 May 1878.

134. "Justice to Mexico."

135. "Diaz Foster and Schleicher," *Weekly Democratic Statesman* (Austin, TX), 11 April 1878.

136. "The Recognition of Diaz," *New York Times*, January 12, 1878.

137. "The Recognition of Diaz."

138. "The Recognition of Diaz."

139. "Volcanic Mexico," *New York Herald*, February 10, 1879.

140. "Volcanic Mexico."

141. "Volcanic Mexico."

142. "Volcanic Mexico."

143. *New York Herald* quoted in "Mexico Americanized," *Milwaukee Daily Sentinel*.

144. "A Special Dispatch to the Constitution," *Atlanta Constitution* (GA), August 22, 1879.

145. "Mexico," *Chicago Tribune*, November 8, 1879.

146. "The News from Mexico," *The Sun* (NY), July 15, 1880.

147. "The News from Mexico."

148. "The News from Mexico."

149. "Mexico," *Philadelphia Inquirer*, December 16, 1880.

150. Harp, *Positivist Republic*.

151. "Railroads for Mexico," *Chicago Tribune*, November 20, 1880.

152. "Railroads for Mexico."

153. "Railroads for Mexico."

154. "Railroads for Mexico."

155. Gonzáles and Fernandez, *A Century of Chicano History*, 25–26.

156. This interpretation was most common among newspapers in regions of the United States that had long-standing frontier cultures, such as the Midwest and far West. See, for example, "Mexican Colonization," *Weekly Chillicothe Crisis* (MO), March 24, 1881; "Colonists for Mexico," *Sacramento Daily Record-Union*, June 11, 1881.

157. "On to Mexico," *Wheeling Daily Intelligencer* (WV), November 23, 1880.

158. "On to Mexico."

159. "On to Mexico."

160. "Mexico," *Dallas Daily Herald*, December 17, 1880.

161. "Mexico."

162. "On to Mexico."

163. "On to Mexico."

164. "The Monroe Doctrine," *Chicago Tribune*, February 17, 1881.

165. "The Monroe Doctrine."

166. "Mexico," *New York Herald*, August 17, 1879.

167. "The American Doctrine," *Chicago Tribune*, June 16, 1881.

168. "The American Doctrine."

169. "Our Distinguished Visitors. Ex-President and Party Visit the Capital of Texas on Alamo Day," *Weekly Democratic Statesman* (Austin, TX), March 8, 1883; "General Diaz—His Arrival at New Orleans—Kindly Feelings Expressed," *Indianapolis Journal*, April 30, 1883; "The Visit of Gen. Diaz," *The Sun* (NY), April 9, 1883; "General Diaz," *Omaha Daily Bee*, March 27, 1883.

Epilogue

1. "The Use of Diaz," *Atlanta Constitution* (GA), November 22, 1883.

2. "The Use of Diaz."

3. "The Use of Diaz."

4. "The Use of Diaz."

5. Britton, *Revolution and Ideology*; Dell'Orto, *American Journalism and International Relations*, 78–82; Knudson, "John Reed," 59–68.

Bibliography

Primary Sources: Newspapers and Periodicals

Abingdon Virginian
Albany Democrat
Albany Evening Journal (NY)
Alexandria Gazette (VA)
American Citizen (Butler, PA)
Argus and Patriot (Montpelier, VT)
Atlanta Confederacy
Atlanta Constitution
Austin Weekly Statesman
Baltimore Daily Commercial
Belmont Chronicle (OH)
Bolivar Bulletin (TN)
Bossier Banner (LA)
Boston Daily Advertiser
Boston Evening Transcript
Boston Herald
Boston Post
Brookhaven Ledger (MI)
Brooklyn Daily Eagle
Brooklyn Evening Star
Buffalo Courier (NY)
Burlington Free Press (VT)
Burlington Weekly Hawk-Eye (IA)
Burlington Weekly Sentinel (VT)
Cairo Bulletin (IL)
Camden Daily Journal (SC)
Carson Daily Appeal (NV)
Charles City Republican Intelligencer (IA)
Charleston Daily Courier
Charleston Mercury
Chicago Daily Tribune
Chicago Evening Post
Chicago Times
Chicago Tribune
Chico Weekly Chronicle-Record (CA)
Christian World (NY)
Cincinnati Enquirer
Cleveland Daily Leader
Cleveland Morning Leader
Commercial Bulletin (MA)
Commercial Gazette (PA)
Congressional Globe
Congressional Record
Courier-Journal (Louisville, KY)
Crisis (OH)
Daily Arkansas Gazette
Daily Chattanooga Rebel
Daily Constitution (Atlanta, GA)
Daily Democrat and News (Davenport, IA)
Daily Dispatch (Richmond, VA)
Daily Intelligencer (Atlanta, GA)
Daily Intelligencer (Washington, DC)
Daily Ohio Statesman
Daily Progress (Raleigh, NC)
Daily Rebel (Chattanooga, TN)
Daily Register (Wheeling, WV)
Daily Selma Reporter (AL)
Daily South-Western (Shreveport, LA)
Daily Standard (Raleigh, NC)
Daily State Sentinel (Indianapolis, IN)
Daily Union and American (Nashville, TN)
Dallas Daily Herald
Dallas Weekly Herald
Dayton Daily Empire (OH)
De Bow's Review
Democrat and Chronicle (Rochester, NY)
Detroit Free Press
Dollar Weekly Bulletin (KY)
Edgefield Advertiser (SC)
Elevator (CA)
Ellsworth American (ME)
Emporia News (KS)
Evansville Daily Journal (IN)
Evening Bulletin (Charlotte, NC)

Evening Star (Washington, DC)
Evening Telegraph (Philadelphia, PA)
Fairfield News and Herald (Winnsboro, SC)
Fayetteville Semi-Weekly Observer (NC)
Feliciana Sentinel (LA)
Forney's Chronicle (Philadelphia, PA)
Fort Worth Daily Gazette
Galveston Daily News
Georgia Weekly Telegraph
Hancock Jeffersonian (OH)
Harper's New Monthly Magazine
Harper's Review
Harper's Weekly
Harrisburg Telegraph (PA)
Hartford Daily Courant
Hillsborough Recorder (NC)
Houston Telegraph
Independent-Record (Helena, MT)
Indianapolis Journal
Indiana Progress (PA)
Indiana State Sentinel
Inter-Ocean (Chicago, IL)
Juliet Signal (IL)
Kansas Radical
Lewistown Gazette (PA)
Liberator (Boston, MA)
London Times
Los Angeles Daily Herald
Los Angeles Daily News
Louisville Daily Courier (KY)
Memphis Bulletin
Memphis Daily Appeal
Mesilla Valley Independent (NM)
Mexican Extraordinary (Mexico City)
Milwaukee Daily Sentinel
Mineral Point Weekly Tribune (WI)
Missouri Republican
Mobile Daily Times (AL)
Montana Post
Montgomery Daily Mail
Mountain Democrat (Placerville, CA)
Nashville Daily Union
Nashville Union and American
Nation
National Intelligencer (Washington, DC)
National Republican (Washington, DC)
Nebraska Advertiser
New Berne Times (NC)
New Englander
New Hampshire Patriot and United States Gazette
New Oregon Plaindealer (IA)
New Orleans Daily Crescent
New Orleans Daily Democrat
New Orleans Republican
New York Herald
New York New Nation
New York Post
New York Times
New York Tribune
New York World
Norfolk Virginian
North American (Philadelphia, PA)
North American Review (Boston, MA)
North Branch Democrat (Tunkhannock, PA)
North Star (Rochester, NY)
Ohio Daily Statesman
Ohio Democrat
Oklahoma Star
Old Guard (NJ)
Omaha Daily Bee
Ouachita Telegraph (Monroe, LA)
Perry County Democrat (New Bloomfield, PA)
Philadelphia Inquirer
Philadelphia Press
Pittsburgh Daily Commercial
Pittsburgh Daily Post
Pittsburgh Gazette
Placer Herald (CA)
Portland Daily Press (ME)
Public Ledger (Memphis, TN)
Public Ledger (Philadelphia, PA)
Railroad Gazette (NY)
Reading Times (PA)
Richmond Daily Dispatch
Richmond Enquirer
Richmond Examiner
Richmond Whig

Rutland Weekly Herald (VT)
Sacramento Bee
Sacramento Daily Record-Union
Salt Lake Daily Telegraph and Commercial Advertiser
San Francisco Chronicle
San Francisco Examiner
San Marcos Free Press (TX)
Santa Cruz Weekly Sentinel (CA)
Saturday Evening Gazette (Boston, MA)
Smyrna Times (DE)
Soldier's Journal (Richmond, VA)
South Carolina Ledger
Southern Banner (MS)
Southern Review (LA)
Springfield Republican (MA)
Staunton Spectator (VA)
St. Louis Globe-Democrat
St. Louis Republican (MO)
The Sun (Baltimore, MD)
Sun (NY)
Tennessean
Times-Democrat (Lima, OH)
Times-Democrat (New Orleans, LA)
Times-Picayune (New Orleans, LA)
Tri-Weekly Gazette & Comet (Baton Rouge, LA)
Troy Messenger (AL)
US Senate Journal
Vernon County Censor (WI)
Washington Chronicle (DC)
Washington Post (DC)
Washington Union (DC)
Weekly Advertiser (Montgomery, AL)
Weekly Arizona Miner
Weekly Atlanta Intelligencer
Weekly Chillicothe Crisis (MO)
Weekly Conservative (Aberdeen, MS)
Weekly Democratic Statesmen (Austin, TX)
Weekly Mississippian (MS)
Weekly Ottumwa Courier (IA)
Weekly Standard (Raleigh, NC)
Weekly Wisconsin Patriot
Western Democrat (Charlotte, NC)
Wheeling Daily Intelligencer (WV)
Wilkies' Spirit of the Times (NY)
Wilmington Journal (NC)
Winchester Daily Bulletin (TN)
Yorkville Enquirer (SC)

Primary Sources: Other Published Materials

Anderson, Charles. *The Cause of the War: Who Brought It On, and For What Purpose? Speech of Col. Charles Anderson, Late of Texas, Now of U.S. Volunteers.* New York: Loyal Publication Society, 1863.

The Assassination of Abraham Lincoln, Late President of the United States of America, and the Attempted Assassination of William H. Seward, Secretary of State, and Frederick W. Seward, Assistant Secretary, On the Evening of the 14th of April 1865. Expressions of Condolence and Sympathy Inspired by These Events. Washington, DC: Government Printing Office, 1867.

Banquet to Señor Matías Romero, Envoy Extraordinary and Minister Plenipotentiary from Mexico to the United States, by the Citizens of New York, October 2, 1867. New York: Citizens' Committee, 1867.

Bellows, Henry W. *Historical Sketch of the Union League Club of New York: Its Origins, Organization, and Work, 1863–1879.* New York: G. P. Putnam's Sons, 1879.

Brassaeux, Charles A., and Katherine Carmines Mooney, eds. *Ruined by This Miserable War: The Dispatches of Charles Prosper Fauconnet, 1863–1868.* Knoxville: University of Tennessee Press, 2012.

Brown, Joseph E. *Message of His Excellency Joseph E. Brown, to the Extra Session of the Legislature, Convened March 10th, 1864, Upon the Currency Act; Secret Session of Congress;*

the Late Conscription Act; the Unconstitutionality of the Act Suspending the Privilege of the Writ of Habeas Corpus, in Cases of Illegal Arrests Made by the President; the Causes of the War and Manner of Conducting It; and the Terms Upon Which Peace Should Be Sought, &c. Milledgeville, GA: Boughton, Nisbet, Barnes & Moore, State Printer, 1864.

Browne, Nathaniel B. *An Address Delivered before the Union League in the 24th Ward of the City of Philadelphia at Its Opening Celebration, May 9, 1863.* Philadelphia: Philadelphia Union League, 1863.

Chevalier, Michael. *France, Mexico, and the Confederate States.* New York: C. B. Richardson, 1863.

Correspondence Relative to the Present Condition of Mexico, Communicated to the House of Representatives by the Department of State. Washington, DC: Government Printing Office, 1862.

Davis, Henry Winter. *Speeches and Addresses Delivered in the Congress of the United States, and on Several Public Occasions, by Henry Winter Davis of Maryland.* New York: Harper & Brothers, 1867.

Dennett, Daniel. *Louisiana as It Is: Reliable Information for Farmers, Patrons of Husbandry, Laboring Men, Manufacturers, Capitalists, Men of Enterprise, Invalids—Any Who May Desire to Settle or Purchase Lands in the Gulf States.* New Orleans: Eureka Press, 1876.

Dinner to Señor Matias Romero, Envoy Extraordinary and Minister Plenipotentiary from Mexico, December 28, 1863. New York: Loyal Publication Society, 1864.

Edwards, John N. *Shelby's Expedition to Mexico: Unwritten Leaf of the War.* Edited by Conger Beasley Jr. Fayetteville: University of Arkansas Press, 2002.

Elliott, E. N., ed. *Cotton Is King, and Pro-Slavery Arguments: Comprising the Writings of Hammond, Harper, Christy, Hodges, Bledsoe, and Cartwright.* Augusta, GA: Pritchard, Abbott & Loomis, 1860.

Foote, Henry S. *War of the Rebellion; Or, Scylla and Charybdis, Consisting of Observations upon the Causes, Course, and Consequences of the Late Civil War in the United States.* New York: Harper & Brothers, 1866.

Greeley, Horace. *Mr. Greeley's Letters from Texas and the Lower Mississippi: To Which Are Added His Address to the Farmers of Texas and His Speech on His Return to New York.* New York: Tribune Office, 1871.

Joint Committee on Reconstruction. *Report of the Joint Committee on Reconstruction, at the First Session Thirty-Ninth Congress.* Washington, DC: Government Printing Office, 1866.

Leavitt, Joshua. *The Monroe Doctrine.* New York: Loyal Publication Society, 1864.

Malespine, A. "Solution of the Mexican Question," in *Papers Relative to Mexican Affairs. Communicated to the Senate June 16, 1864.* Washington: Government Printing Office, 1865, 268–79.

McDougall, James A. *French Interference in Mexico: Speech of Hon. J. A. McDougall of California in the U.S. Senate, February 3, 1863.* Baltimore, MD: John Murphy & Co., 1863.

McPherson, Edward. *The Political History of the United States of America, during the Period of Reconstruction.* Washington, DC: Philp & Solomons, 1871.

Merriam, George S. *The Life and Times of Samuel Bowles.* New York: The Century Company, 1885.

Minutes of the Proceedings of the Commercial Convention Held in the City of Memphis, Tennessee, May, 1869. Memphis, TN: Southwestern Publishing Company, 1869.

Murphy, D. F. *Presidential Election 1864. Proceedings of the National Union Convention Held at Baltimore, MD, June 7th and 8th, 1864*. New York: Baker & Godwin, Printers, 1864.

Official Proceedings of the Democratic National Convention, Held in 1864 at Chicago. Chicago: Times Steam Book and Job Printing Book, 1864.

Official Records of the Union and Confederate Navies in the War of Rebellion. United States Naval War Records Office. Washington DC: Government Printing Office, 1922.

Opinions of Loyalists Concerning the Great Questions of the Times: Expressed in the Speeches and Letters from Prominent Citizens of All Sections and Parties, on Occasion of the Inauguration of the Loyal National League, in Mass Meeting in Union Square, New York, 11 April 1863. New York: C. S. Westcott & Co., 1863.

Owen, Robert Dale. *The Policy of Emancipation: In Three Letters to the Secretary of War, the President of the United States, and the Secretary of the Treasury*. Philadelphia: Lippincott & Co. 1863.

———. *The Wrongs of Slavery, the Right of Emancipation and the Future of the African Race in the United States*. Philadelphia: J. B. Lippincott & Co., 1864.

Pamphlets Issued by the Loyal Publication Society, from February 1, 1863, to February 1, 1864. New York: Loyal Publication Society, 1864.

Papers Relating to Foreign Affairs, Accompanying the Annual Message of the President to the Second Session Thirty-Eighth Congress, Part 1. Washington, DC: Government Printing Office, 1864.

Papers Relating to Foreign Affairs, Accompanying the Annual Message of the President to the Second Session Thirty-Ninth Congress. Washington: Government Printing Office, 1866.

Proceedings at the Organization of the Loyal National League at the Cooper Institute, March 20, 1863. New York: C. S. Westcott & Co., 1863.

Proceedings of a Meeting of Citizens of New York, to Express Sympathy and Respect for the Mexican Republican Exiles at the Cooper Institute, July 19, 1865. New York: John A. Gray & Green, 1864.

Proceedings of a Meeting of Citizens of New York, to Express Sympathy and Respect for the Mexican Republican Exiles, Cooper Institute, July 19, 1865. New York: John A. Gray & Green, 1865.

Proceedings of the National Railroad Convention at St. Louis, MO., November 23 & 24, 1875, in Regard to the Construction of the Texas & Pacific Railway as a Southern Trans-Continental Line from the Mississippi Valley to the Pacific Ocean on the Thirty-Second Parallel of Latitude. St Louis, MO: Woodward, Tiernan & Hale, 1875.

Proceedings of the Union League of Philadelphia in Commemoration of the Eighty-Seventh Anniversary of American Independence, July 4, 1863. Philadelphia: King & Bird, 1863.

Reavis, Logan U. *An International Railway to the City of Mexico*. St Louis, MO: Woodward, Tiernan & Hale, 1879.

———. *Saint Louis: The Future Great City of the World*. St Louis: Missouri Democrat Printing House, 1870.

Richardson, James D., ed. *A Compilation of Messages and Papers of the Confederacy, Including the Diplomatic Correspondence, 1861–1865*. 2 vols. Nashville, TN: United States Publishing Company, 1906.

The Rising City of the West: San Diego, Southern California, the Pacific Terminus of the Texas Pacific Railroad, 1872. New York: Wm. Moore, 1872.

Romero, Matías. *Mexican Lobby: Matías Romero in Washington, 1861–1867*. Edited and translated by Thomas D. Schoonover. Lawrence: University of Kansas Press, 1986.

———. *A Mexican View of America in the 1860s: A Foreign Diplomat Describes the Civil War and Reconstruction*. Edited and translated by Thomas D. Schoonover. London and Toronto: Associated University Press, 1991.

Savage, John. *The Life and Public Services of Andrew Johnson, Seventeenth President of the United States. Including the State Papers, Speeches, and Addresses*. New York: Derby & Miller Publishers, 1866.

Scott, E. H., ed. *The Federalist and Other Constitutional Papers*. Chicago: Albert, Scott & Company, 1894.

Simon, John Y., ed. *The Papers of Ulysses S. Grant*. Vol. 15. Carbondale and Edwardsville: Southern Illinois University Press, 1988.

The Slavery Question a Pretext to Lead the Masses on to Revolution. Philadelphia: Union League of Philadelphia Board of Publication, 1863.

Southern Commercial Convention. *Proceedings of the Southern Commercial Convention at its Annual Session at Cincinnati, Ohio, October 1870*. Cincinnati, OH: Committee of Arrangements of Cincinnati, 1871.

Stephens, Alexander H. *A Constitutional View of the Late War Between the States: Its Causes, Character, Conduct and Results, Presented in a Series of Colloquies at Liberty Hall*. Vol. 2. Philadelphia: National Publishing Company, 1868.

The Texas and Pacific Railway: Its Route, Progress, and Land Grants. New York: Office of the Texas and Pacific Railway, 1872.

Throckmorton, James W. *Speech of Hon. Jas. W. Throckmorton of Texas, in the House of Representatives, March 1, 1877, Together with the Report of the Hon. L. Q. Lamar, of Mississippi, Chairman of the Committee on Pacific Railroads, Made to the House of Representatives, January 24, 1877*. Washington, DC: Government Printing Office, 1877.

Secondary Sources: Books and Journal Articles

Adams, John A., Jr. *Conflict and Commerce on the Rio Grande, 1775–1955*. College Station: Texas A&M University Press, 2008.

Adas, Michael. *Dominance by Design: Technological Imperatives and America's Civilizing Mission*. Cambridge, MA: Belknap Press of Harvard University Press, 2006.

Ahlstrom, Sydney E. *A Religious History of the American People*. New Haven, CT: Yale University Press, 1972.

Anderson, Benedict. *Imagined Communities: Reflections on the Origin and Spread of Nationalism*. Rev. ed. New York: Verso, 1991.

Andrews, J. Cutler. "The Confederate Press and Public Morale." *Journal of Southern History* 32, no. 4 (November 1966): 445–65.

Arenson, Adam, and Andrew R. Graybill, eds. *Civil War Wests: Testing the Limits of the United States*. Oakland: University of California Press, 2015.

Ayers, Edward L. "The American Civil War: Emancipation and Reconstruction on the World Stage." *OAH Magazine of History* 20, no. 1 (January 2006): 54–61.

———. *The Promise of the New South: Life after Reconstruction*. Oxford: Oxford University Press, 1992.

Azevedo, Celia. *Abolitionism in the United States and Brazil: A Comparative Perspective.* New York: Garland, 1995.
Bailyn, Bernard. *The Ideological Origins of the American Revolution.* Cambridge, MA: Belknap Press of Harvard University Press, 1967.
Baker, Jean. *Affairs of Party: The Political Culture of Northern Democrats in the Mid-Nineteenth Century.* Ithaca, NY: Cornell University Press, 1983.
Baldwin, Deborah J. *Protestants and the Mexican Revolution: Missionaries, Ministers, and Social Change.* Urbana and Chicago: University of Illinois Press, 1990.
Baptist, Edward. *The Half Has Never Been Told: Slavery and the Making of American Capitalism.* New York: Basic Books, 2014.
Barker, Hannah, and Simon Burrows, eds. *Press, Politics and the Public Sphere in Europe and North America, 1760–1820.* Cambridge, UK: Cambridge University Press, 2002.
Barker, Nancy N. "The French Legation in Mexico: Nexus of Interventionists." *French Historical Studies* 8, no. 3 (Spring 1974): 409–26.
Barreyre, Nicolas. "The Politics of Economic Crisis: The Panic of 1873, the End of Reconstruction, and the Realignment of American Politics." *Journal of the Gilded Age and Progressive Era* 10, no. 4 (October 2011): 403–23.
Barton Schweiger, Beth. "The Literate South: Reading before Emancipation." *Journal of the Civil War Era* 3, no. 3 (September 2013): 331–59.
Baumgartner, Alice L. *South to Freedom: Runaway Slaves to Mexico and the Road to the Civil War.* New York: Basic Books, 2020.
Beard, Charles, and Mary Beard, *The Rise of American Civilization.* 2 vols. New York: Macmillan, 1927.
Becker, William H., and Samuel F. Wells Jr., eds. *Economics & World Power: An Assessment of American Diplomacy since 1789.* New York: Columbia University Press, 1984.
Beckert, Sven. *Empire of Cotton: A Global History.* New York: Alfred A. Knopf, 2014.
———. *The Monied Metropolis: New York City and the Consolidation of the American Bourgeoisie, 1850–1896.* Cambridge, UK: Cambridge University Press, 2001.
Beckert, Sven, and Seth Rockman, eds. *Slavery's Capitalism: A New History of American Economic Development.* Philadelphia: University of Pennsylvania Press, 2016.
Bederman, Gail. *Manliness and Civilization: A Cultural History of Gender and Race in the United States, 1880–1917.* Chicago: Chicago University Press, 1995.
Belohlavek, John M. *Patriots, Prostitutes, and Spies: Women and the Mexican-American War.* Charlottesville: University of Virginia Press, 2017.
Bender, Thomas, ed. *Rethinking American History in a Global Age.* Berkeley: University of California Press, 2002.
Bensel, Richard. *The American Ballot Box in the Nineteenth Century.* Cambridge, UK: Cambridge University Press, 2004.
Bergad, Laird W. *The Comparative Histories of Slavery in Brazil, Cuba, and the United States.* Cambridge, UK: Cambridge University Press, 2007.
Bernath, Michael T. "The Confederacy as a Moment of Possibility." *Journal of Southern History* 79, no. 2 (May 2013): 299–338.
Bernstein, Iver. *The New York City Draft Riots: Their Significance for American Society and Politics in the Age of the Civil War.* Oxford: Oxford University Press, 1990.

Bethell, Leslie, ed. *The Independence of Latin America*. Cambridge, UK: Cambridge University Press, 1987.

———. *Mexico Since Independence*. Cambridge, UK: Cambridge University Press, 1991.

Billings, Dwight B. *Planters and the Making of a "New South": Class, Politics, and Development in South Carolina, 1865–1900*. Chapel Hill: The University of North Carolina Press, 1979.

Bingham, Tom. "The *Alabama* Claims Arbitration." *The International and Comparative Law Quarterly* 54, no. 1 (January 2005): 1–25.

Blackett, Richard J. M. *Divided Hearts: Britain and the American Civil War*. Baton Rouge: Louisiana State University Press, 2001.

Blackshear, James Bailey, and Glen S. Ely. *Confederates and Comancheros: Skulduggery and Double-Dealing in the Texas-New Mexico Borderlands*. Norman: Oklahoma University Press, 2021.

Blair, William. *Cities of the Dead: Contesting the Memory of the Civil War in the South, 1865–1914*. Chapel Hill: The University of North Carolina Press, 2004.

———. *With Malice towards Some: Treason and Loyalty in the Civil War Era*. Chapel Hill: The University of North Carolina Press, 2014.

Blanchard, Peter. *Under the Flags of Freedom: Slave Soldiers & the Wars of Independence in Spanish South America*. Pittsburgh, PA: University of Pittsburgh Press, 2008.

Blight, David W. *Race and Reunion: The Civil War in American Memory*. Cambridge, MA: Harvard University Press, 2001.

Blum, Edward. *Reforging the White Republic: Race, Religion, and American Nationalism, 1865–1898*. Baton Rouge: Louisiana State University Press, 2005.

Bolton, Herbert E. "The Epic of Greater America." *American Historical Review* 38, no. 3 (April 1933): 448–74.

Bonner, Robert E. "Slavery, Confederate Diplomacy, and the Racialist Mission of Henry Hotze." *Civil War History* 51, no. 3 (September 2005): 288–316.

Bortz, Jeffery L., and Stephen Haber, eds. *The Mexican Economy, 1870–1930: Essays on the Economic History of Institutions, Revolution, and Growth*. Stanford, CA: Stanford University Press, 2002.

Bottoms, D. Michael. *An Aristocracy of Color: Race and Reconstruction in California and the West, 1850–1890*. Norman: University of Oklahoma Press, 2013.

Bowden, Wayne H. *Spain and the American Civil War*. Columbia: University of Missouri Press, 2011.

Brennan, Dennis. *The Making of an Abolitionist: William Lloyd Garrison's Path to Publishing* The Liberator. Jefferson, NC: McFarland & Company, 2014.

Brettle, Adrian. *Colossal Ambitions: Confederate Planning for a post-Civil War World*. Charlottesville: University of Virginia Press, 2020.

Britton, John A. *Revolution and Ideology: Images of the Mexican Revolution in the United States*. Lexington: University Press of Kentucky, 1995.

Brown, Matthew, and Gabriel Paquette, eds. *Connections after Colonialism: Europe and Latin America in the 1820s*. Tuscaloosa: University of Alabama Press, 2013.

Bruce, Susannah U. *The Harp and the Eagle: Irish-American Volunteers and the Union Army, 1861–1865*. New York: New York University Press, 2006.

Buck, Paul H. *The Road to Reunion, 1865–1900*. Boston: Little, Brown, and Company, 1937.

Buckner, Philip. "British North America and a Continent in Dissolution: The American Civil War in the Making of Canadian Confederation." *Journal of the Civil War Era* 7, no. 4 (December 2017): 512–40.

Bulmer-Thomas, Victor. *The Economic History of Latin American since Independence*. 2nd ed. Cambridge, UK: Cambridge University Press, 2003.

Bunker, Steven B. *Creating Mexican Consumer Culture in the Age of Porfirio Díaz*. Albuquerque: New Mexico University Press, 2012.

Burden, David K. "Reform before La Reforma: Liberals, Conservatives and the Debate over Immigration, 1846–1855." *Mexican Studies/Estudios Mexicanos* 23, no. 2 (Summer 2007): 283–316.

Burg, Robert W. "Amnesty, Civil Rights, and the Meaning of Liberal Republicanism, 1862–1872." *American Nineteenth Century History* 4, no. 3 (2003): 29–60.

Butler, Leslie. *Critical Americans: Victorian Intellectuals and Transatlantic Liberal Reform*. Chapel Hill: The University of North Carolina Press, 2007.

Cabanas, Miguel A. *The Cultural "Other" in Nineteenth-Century Travel Narratives: How the United States and Latin America Described Each Other*. New York: Edwin Mellen Press, 2008.

Calhoun, Charles W. *Conceiving a New Republic: The Republican Party and the Southern Question, 1869–1900*. Lawrence: University of Kansas Press, 2006.

Campbell, Charles. *The Transformation of American Foreign Relations*. New York: Harper & Row, 1976.

Catton, Bruce. *Grant Takes Command*. Boston: Little, Brown, and Company, 1968.

Clampitt, Bradley R. *The Civil War and Reconstruction in Indian Territory*. Norman: University of Oklahoma Press, 2015.

Clarke, Frances. "'Let All Nations See': Civil War Nationalism and the Memorialization of Wartime Voluntarism." *Civil War History* 52 (March 2006): 66–93.

Clavin, Matthew J. "American Toussaints: Symbols, Subversion, and the Black Atlantic Tradition in the American Civil War." *Slavery & Abolition* 28, no. 1 (May 2007): 87–113.

———. *Toussaint Louverture and the American Civil War: The Promise and Peril of a Second Haitian Revolution*. Philadelphia: University of Pennsylvania Press, 2010.

Clayton, Nichola. "Managing the Transition to a Free Society: American Interpretations of the British West Indies during the Civil War and Reconstruction." *American Nineteenth Century History* 7, no. 1 (2006): 89–108.

Coatsworth, John H. *Growth against Development: The Economic Impact of Railroads in Porfirian Mexico*. Dekalb: Northern Illinois University Press, 1981.

Cobb, James C. *Away Down South: A History of Southern Identity*. Oxford: Oxford University Press, 2005.

Cohen, Nancy. *Reconstruction of American Liberalism, 1865–1914*. Chapel Hill: The University of North Carolina Press, 2002.

Cool, Paul. *Salt Warriors: Insurgency on the Rio Grande*. College Station: Texas A&M University Press, 2008.

Copeland, David A. *The Antebellum Era: Primary Documents on Events from 1820 to 1860*. Westport, CT: Greenwood Press, 2003.

Costeloe, Michael P. *The Central Republic in Mexico, 1835–1846:* Hombres de bien *in the Age of Santa Anna*. Cambridge, UK: Cambridge University Press, 1993.

———. *Response to Revolution: Imperial Spain and the Spanish American Revolutions, 1810–1840*. Cambridge, UK: Cambridge University Press, 1986.

Cottrol, Robert J. *The Long, Lingering Shadow: Slavery, Race, and Law in the American Hemisphere*. Athens: University of Georgia Press, 2013.

Cox, LaWanda. *Freedom, Racism, and Reconstruction: Collected Writings of LaWanda Cox*. Edited by Donald G. Nieman. Athens: University of Georgia Press, 1997.

Crawford, Martin. *The Anglo-American Crisis of the Mid-Nineteenth Century: The Times and America, 1850–1862*. Athens: University of Georgia Press, 1987.

Crook, D. P. *The North, the South, and the Powers, 1861–1865*. New York: Wiley, 1974.

Crouthamel, James L. *Bennett's* New York Herald *and the Rise of the Popular Press*. Syracuse, NY: Syracuse University Press, 1989.

Cunningham, Michele. *Mexico and the Foreign Policy of Napoleon III*. New York: Palgrave Macmillan, 2011.

Curry, Richard O. "The Union as It Was: A Critique of Recent Interpretations of the 'Copperheads.'" *Civil War History* 13, no. 1 (March 1967): 25–39.

Cutrer, Thomas W. *Theater of a Separate War: The Civil War West of the Mississippi River, 1861–1865*. Chapel Hill: The University of North Carolina Press, 2017.

Dabney, Virginius. *Richmond: The Story of a City*. Garden City, NY: Doubleday & Company, 1976.

Dal Lago, Enrico. *American Slavery, Atlantic Slavery, and Beyond: The U.S. "Peculiar Institution" in International Perspective*. New York: Routledge, 2013.

———. *William Lloyd Garrison and Giuseppe Mazzini*. Baton Rouge: Louisiana State University Press, 2013.

Dash, J. Michael. *Haiti and the United States: National Stereotypes and Literary Imagination*. New York: Palgrave Macmillan, 1998.

Davis, Harold E. "Henry Grady, the Atlanta Constitution, and the Politics of Farming in the 1880s." *Georgia Historical Quarterly* 71, no. 4 (Winter 1987): 571–600.

Davis, Hugh. *Joshua Leavitt: Evangelical Abolitionist*. Baton Rouge: Louisiana State University Press, 1990.

Davis, William C., ed. *Secret History of Confederate Diplomacy Abroad*. Lawrence: University Press of Kansas, 2005.

DeConde, Alexander. *Ethnicity, Race and American Foreign Policy: A History*. Boston: Northeastern University Press, 1992.

Degler, Carl N. "One among Many." *The Virginia Quarterly Review* 39, no. 1 (Spring 1963): 289–306.

———. "Slavery in the United States and Brazil: An Essay in Comparative History." *American Historical Association* 75, no. 4 (April 1970): 1004–28.

DeGuzman, Maria. *Spain's Long Shadow: The Black Legend, Off-Whiteness, and Anglo-American Empire*. Minneapolis: University of Minnesota Press, 2005.

DeLay, Brian. "Independent Indians and the U.S.-Mexican War." *American Historical Review* 112, no. 1 (February 2007): 35–68.

———. *War of a Thousand Deserts: Indian Raids and the U.S.-Mexican War*. New Haven, CT: Yale University Press, 2008.

Dell'Orto, Giovanna. *American Journalism and International Relations: Foreign Correspondence from the Early Republic to the Digital Era*. Cambridge, UK: Cambridge University Press, 2013.

Dicken-Garcia, Hazel. *Journalistic Standards in Nineteenth-Century America*. Madison: University of Wisconsin Press, 1989.
Downs, Gregory P. *After Appomattox: Military Occupation and the Ends of War*. Cambridge, MA: Harvard University Press, 2015.
———. "The Mexicanization of American Politics: The United States' Transnational Path from Civil War to Stabilization." *American Historical Review* 117, no. 2 (April 2012): 387–409.
———. *The Second American Revolution: The Civil War-Era Struggle over Cuba and the Rebirth of the American Republic*. Chapel Hill: The University of North Carolina Press, 2019.
Downs, Gregory P., and Kate Masur, eds. *The World the Civil War Made*. Chapel Hill: The University of North Carolina Press, 2015.
Doyle, Don H., ed. *American Civil Wars: The United States, Latin America, Europe, and the Crisis of the 1860s*. Chapel Hill: The University of North Carolina Press, 2017.
———. *The Cause of All Nations: An International History of the American Civil War*. New York: Basic Books, 2015.
Doyle, Don H., and Marco Antonio Pamplona, eds. *Nationalism in the New World*. Athens: University of Georgia Press, 2006.
Dubois, Lourent. *Haiti: The Aftershocks of History*. New York: Metropolitan Books, 2012.
Duigan, Peter J., and Lewis H. Gann. *The Spanish Speakers in the United States: A History*. Lanham, MD: University Press of America, 1998.
Duncan, Jason K. *Citizens or Papists? The Politics of Anti-Catholicism in New York, 1685–1821*. New York: Fordham University Press, 2005.
Dunning, William A. *Reconstruction, Political and Economic, 1865–1877*. New York: Harper, 1907.
Earle, Rebecca, ed. *Rumours of War: Civil Conflict in Nineteenth-Century Latin America*. London: Institute of Latin American Studies, 2000.
Edling, Max. Review for *H-Diplo Roundtable Reviews* XIV, no. 10 (2012): 7–12. https://issforum.org/roundtables/PDF/Roundtable-XIV-10.pdf (accessed February 8, 2018).
Elliott, Sam Davis. *John C. Brown of Tennessee: Rebel, Redeemer, and Railroader*. Knoxville: University of Tennessee Press, 2017.
Fallaw, Ben. *Religion and State Formation in Postrevolutionary Mexico*. Durham, NC: Duke University Press, 2013.
Farrelly, Maura Jane. *Anti-Catholicism in America, 1620–1860*. Cambridge, UK: Cambridge University Press, 2017.
Faust, Drew Gilpin. *The Creation of Confederate Nationalism: Ideology and Identity in the Civil War South*. Baton Rouge: Louisiana State University Press, 1988.
———. *James Henry Hammond and the Old South: A Design for Mastery*. Baton Rouge: Louisiana State University Press, 1982.
Feldberg, Michael. *The Turbulent Era: Riot and Disorder in Jacksonian America*. Oxford: Oxford University Press, 1980.
Fifer, J. Valerie. *United States Perceptions of Latin America, 1850–1930: A "New West" South of Capricorn?* Manchester: Manchester University Press, 1991.
Fitz, Caitlin. *Our Sister Republics: The United States in an Age of American Revolutions*. New York: W. W. Norton & Co., 2016.

Fitzgerald, Michael W. *Reconstruction in Alabama: From Civil War to Redemption in the Cotton South.* Baton Rouge: Louisiana State University Press, 2017.

———. *Splendid Failure: Postwar Reconstruction in the American South.* Chicago: Ivan R. Dee Publishers, 2007.

———. *The Union League Movement in the Deep South: Politics and Agricultural Change during Reconstruction.* Baton Rouge: Louisiana State University Press, 1989.

Fleche, Andre M. "The American Civil War in the Age of Revolution." *South Central Review* 33, no. 1 (Spring 2016): 5–20.

———. *The Revolution of 1861: The American Civil War in the Age of Nationalist Conflict.* Chapel Hill: The University of North Carolina Press, 2012.

Foner, Eric. *Free Soil, Free Labor, Free Men: The Ideology of the Republican Party before the Civil War.* Oxford: Oxford University Press, 1970.

———. *Reconstruction: America's Unfinished Revolution, 1863–1877.* New York: Harper and Row, 1988.

Foos, Paul. *A Short, Offhand, Killing Affair: Soldiers and Social Conflict during the Mexican-American War.* Chapel Hill: The University of North Carolina Press, 2002.

Ford, Lacy K. *Origins of Southern Radicalism: The South Carolina Upcountry, 1800–1860.* Oxford: Oxford University Press, 1988.

Formasino, Ronald P. *The Transformation of Political Culture: Massachusetts Parties, 1790s–1840s.* Oxford: Oxford University Press, 1983.

Forster, Stig, and Jorg Nagler, eds. *On the Road to Total War: The American Civil War and the Wars of German Unification.* Cambridge, UK: Cambridge University Press, 1997.

Foster, Gaines M. *Ghosts of the Confederacy: Defeat, the Lost Cause, and the Emergence of the New South, 1865–1913.* Oxford: Oxford University Press, 1987.

Fox-Genovese, Elizabeth, and Eugene D. Genovese. *The Mind of the Master Class: History and Faith in the Southern Slaveholders' Worldview.* Cambridge, UK: Cambridge University Press, 2005.

Fowler, Will, ed. *Forceful Negotiations: The Origins of the* Pronunciamento *in Nineteenth-Century Mexico.* Lincoln: University of Nebraska Press, 2010.

———. *Independent Mexico: The Pronunciamiento in the Age of Santa Anna, 1821–1858.* Lincoln: University of Nebraska Press, 2016.

Frederickson, George M. *The Black Image in the White Mind: The Debate on Afro-American Character and Destiny, 1817–1914.* Middletown, CT: Wesleyan University Press, 1987.

Freeman, Joanne. *The Field of Blood: Violence in Congress and the Road to the Civil War.* New York: Farrar, Straus and Giroux, 2018.

Fry, Joseph A. *Lincoln, Seward, and U.S. Foreign Relations in the Civil War Era.* Lexington: University Press of Kentucky, 2019.

Frymer, Paul D. *Building an American Empire: The Era of Territorial and Political Expansion.* Princeton, NJ: Princeton University Press, 2017.

Gallagher, Gary W. *Three Days at Gettysburg: Essays on Confederate and Union Leadership.* Kent, OH: Kent State University Press, 1999.

———. *The Union War.* Cambridge, MA: Harvard University Press, 2011.

Gallman, J. Matthew. *The Cacophony of Politics: Northern Democrats and the American Civil War.* Charlottesville: University of Virginia Press, 2021.

Gannon, Barbara A. *The Won Cause: Black and White Comradeship in the Grand Army of the Republic*. Chapel Hill: The University of North Carolina Press, 2011.

Garner, Paul. *Porfirio Diaz: Profiles in Power*. New York: Pearson Education, 2001.

Gaston, Paul M. *The New South Creed: A Study in Southern Mythmaking*. Montgomery, AL: New South Books, 2002.

Geggus, David P., ed. *The Impact of the Haitian Revolution on the Atlantic World*. Columbia: University of South Carolina Press, 2001.

Gemme, Paola. *Domesticating Foreign Struggles: The Italian Risorgimento and Antebellum American Identity*. Athens: University of Georgia Press, 2005.

Genovese, Eugene D. *Roll, Jordon, Roll: The World the Slaves Made*. New York: Pantheon Books, 1974.

Gentry, Fenner. "A Confederate Success in Europe: The Erlanger Loan." *Journal of Southern History* 36, no. 2 (May 1970): 157–88.

Gerlach, Murney. *British Liberalism and the United States: Political and Social Thought in the Late Victorian Age*. New York: Palgrave Macmillan, 2001.

Gerstle, Gary. "The Civil War and State-Building: A Reconsideration." *Journal of the Civil War Era* 7, no. 1 (March 2017). https://www.journalofthecivilwarera.org/forum-the-future-of-reconstruction-studies/the-civil-war-and-state-building/ (accessed December 5, 2017).

———. *Liberty and Coercion: The Paradox of American Government from the Founding to the Present*. Princeton, NJ: Princeton University Press, 2015.

Gibbs, William E. "Díaz' Executive Agents and United States Foreign Policy." *Journal of Interamerican Studies and World Affairs* 20, no. 2 (May 1978): 165–90.

Gibson, Charles, ed. *The Black Legend: Anti-Spanish Attitudes in the Old World and the New*. New York: Alfred A. Knopf, 1971.

Gienapp, William E. *Abraham Lincoln and Civil War America*. Oxford: Oxford University Press, 2002.

Gillette, William. *Retreat from Reconstruction, 1869–1879*. Baton Rouge: Louisiana State University Press, 1979.

Glickstein, Jonathon A. *American Exceptionalism, American Anxiety: Wages, Competition, and Degraded Labor in the Antebellum United States*. Charlottesville: University of Virginia Press, 2002.

Gobat, Michel. "The Invention of Latin America: A Transnational History of Anti-Imperialism, Democracy, and Race." *American Historical Review* 118, no. 5 (December 2013): 1347–49.

Godkin, L. "Commercial Immorality and Political Corruption." *North American Review* 248 (1868): 107.

Goldwert, Marvin. "Matías Romero and Congressional Opposition to Seward's Policy toward the French Intervention in Mexico." *The Americas* 22, no. 1 (July 1965): 22–40.

Gómez, Laura E. *Manifest Destinies: The Making of the Mexican American Race*. New York: New York University Press, 2007.

González, Gilbert G. *Culture of Empire: American Writers, Mexico, & Immigrants, 1880–1930*. Austin: University of Texas Press, 2004.

González, Gilbert G., and Raul A. Fernandez. *A Century of Chicano History: Empires, Nations, and Migration*. New York: Routledge, 2003.

González, Pablo Mijangos Y. *The Lawyer of the Church: Bishop Clemente de Jesús Munguía and the Clerical Response to the Mexican Liberal Reforma*. Lincoln: University of Nebraska Press, 2015.

González-Quiroga, Miguel A. *War and Peace on the Rio Grande Frontier, 1830–1880*. Norman: University of Oklahoma Press, 2020.

Gordon, David, ed. *Secession, State, and Liberty*. New Brunswick, NJ: Transaction Publishers, 1998.

Grady, John. *Matthew Fontaine Maury, Father of Oceanography: A Biography, 1806–1873*. Jefferson, NC: McFarland & Company, 2015.

Graham, Richard. "Slavery and Economic Development: Brazil and the U.S. in the 19th Century." *Comparative Studies in Society and History* 23, no. 4 (October 1981): 620–55.

Grandin, Greg. "The Liberal Traditions in the Americas: Rights, Sovereignty, and the Origins of Liberal Multi-Lateralism." *American Historical Review* 117, no. 1 (February 2012): 68–91.

Grant, Alfred. *The American Civil War and the British Press*. Jefferson, NC: McFarland & Company, 2000.

Grant, Susan-Mary, and Brian Holden Reid, eds. *Themes of the American Civil War: The War Between the States*. New York: Routledge, 2010.

Green, Hillary. *Educational Reconstruction: African American Schools in the Urban South, 1865–1890*. New York: Fordham University Press, 2016.

Green, Michael S. *Freedom, Union, and Power: Lincoln and His Party during the American Civil War*. New York: Fordham University Press, 2004.

Greenberg, Amy S. *Manifest Manhood and the Antebellum American Empire*. Cambridge, UK: Cambridge University Press, 2005.

———. *A Wicked War: Polk, Clay, Lincoln, and the 1846 U.S. Invasion of Mexico*. New York: Alfred A. Knopf, 2012.

Greene, Jack P. "Comparing Early Modern American Worlds: Some Reflections on the Promise of a Hemispheric Perspective." *History Compass* 1, no. 1 (January 2003). https://doi.org/10.1111/1478-0542.026 (accessed February 8, 2018).

Greenfield, Liah. *Nationalism: Five Roads to Modernity*. Cambridge, MA: Harvard University Press, 1992.

Grimsley, Mark. *The Hard Hand of War: Union Military Policy toward Southern Civilians, 1861–1865*. Cambridge, UK: Cambridge University Press, 1995.

Guardino, Peter F. *Peasants, Politics, and the Formation of Mexico's National State*. Stanford, CA: Stanford University Press, 1996.

Guerra, Rubén Ruiz. *Más Allá de la Diplomacia. Relaciones de México con Bolivia, Ecuador y Perú, 1821–1994*. México: Secretaria de Relaciones Exteriores, 2007.

Guterl, Matthew Pratt. *American Mediterranean: Southern Slaveholders in the Age of Emancipation*. Cambridge, MA: Harvard University Press, 2008.

Guyatt, Nicholas. "America's Conservatory: Race, Reconstruction, and the Santo Domingo Debate." *Journal of American History* 97, no. 4 (March 2011): 974–1000.

———. *Providence and the Intervention of the United States, 1607–1876*. Cambridge, UK: Cambridge University Press, 2007.

Hacker, Louis. *The Triumph of American Capitalism: The Development of Forces in American History to the End of the Nineteenth Century*. New York: Columbia University Press, 1940.

Hahn, Steven. "Slave Emancipation, Indian Peoples, and the Projects of a New American State." *Journal of the Civil War Era* 3, no. 3 (September 2013): 307–30.

Hale, Charles A. *Mexican Liberalism in the Age of Mora, 1828–1853*. New Haven, CT: Yale University Press, 1965.

———. *The Transformation of Liberalism in Late Nineteenth-Century Mexico*. Princeton, NJ: Princeton University Press, 1990.

Hämäläinen, Pekka. *The Comanche Empire*. New Haven, CT: Yale University Press, 2008.

Hammett, Brian R. "Liberalism Divided: Regional Polities and the National Project during the Mexican Restored Republic, 1867–1876." *Hispanic American Historical Review* 76, no. 4 (1996): 659–89.

Hanke, Lewis. *Do the Americas Have a Common History? A Critique of the Bolton Theory*. New York: Alfred A. Knopf, 1964.

Hanna, Alfred J., and Kathryn A. Hanna, *Napoleon III and Mexico: American Triumph over Monarchy*. Chapel Hill: The University of North Carolina Press, 1971.

Hard, Elizabeth S., and Winnifred F. Sullivan, eds. *Theologies of American Exceptionalism*. Urbana: University of Illinois Press, 2021.

Harp, Gillis J. *Positivist Republic: Auguste Comte and the Reconstruction of American Liberalism, 1865–1920*. University Park: Pennsylvania State University Press, 1995.

Harris, M. Keith. *Across the Bloody Chasm: The Culture of Commemoration among Civil War Veterans*. Baton Rouge: Louisiana State University Press, 2014.

Harris, William C. *William Woods Holden: Firebrand of North Carolina Politics*. Baton Rouge: Louisiana State University Press, 1987.

Harrold, Stanley. *Lincoln and the Abolitionists*. Carbondale: Southern Illinois University Press, 2018.

Hart, John Mason. *Empire and Revolution: The Americans in Mexico since the Civil War*. Berkeley: University of California Press, 2002.

Harter, Eugene C. *The Lost Colony of the Confederacy*. College Station: Texas A&M University Press, 2000.

Haselby, Sam. *The Origins of American Religious Nationalism*. Oxford: Oxford University Press, 2015.

Hatfield, Shelley Ann Bowen. *Chasing Shadows: Indians along the United States-Mexico Border, 1876–1911*. Albuquerque: University of New Mexico Press, 1998.

Heath, Andrew. "'Let the Empire Come': Imperialism and Its Critics in the Reconstruction South." *Civil War History* 60, no. 2 (June 2014): 152–89.

Henderson, Timothy J. *A Glorious Defeat: Mexico and Its War with the United States*. New York: Hill & Wang, 2007.

Hernández, José Angel. *Mexican American Colonization during the Nineteenth Century: A History of the U.S.-Mexico Borderlands*. Cambridge, UK: Cambridge University Press, 2012.

Hess, Earl J. *Civil War in the West: Victory and Defeat from the Appalachians to the Mississippi*. Chapel Hill: The University of North Carolina Press, 2012.

———. *Liberty, Virtue, and Progress: Northerners and Their War for the Union*. New York: Fordham University Press, 1997.

Hickey, Donald R. "America's Response to the Slave Revolt in Haiti, 1791–1806." *Journal of the Early Republic* 2, no. 4 (Winter 1982): 362–79.

Hietala, Thomas R. *Manifest Design: Anxious Aggrandizement in Late Jacksonian America.* Ithaca, NY: Cornell University Press, 1985.

Hillyer, Reiko. *Designing Dixie: Tourism, Memory, and Urban Space in the New South.* Charlottesville: University of Virginia Press, 2014.

Hofstadter, Richard. *The Age of Reform: From Bryan to F.D.R.* New York: Vintage Books, 1955.

Hopkins, A. G. *American Empire: A Global History*. Princeton, NJ: Princeton University Press, 2018.

Horsman, Reginald. *Race and Manifest Destiny: The Origins of American Racial Anglo-Saxonism*. Cambridge, MA: Harvard University Press, 1981.

Hubbard, Charles M. *The Burden of Confederate Diplomacy*. Knoxville: University of Tennessee Press, 1998.

Hunt, Alfred N. *Haiti's Influence on Antebellum America: Slumbering Volcano in the Caribbean*. Baton Rouge: Louisiana State University Press, 1988.

Hunt, Michael H. *Ideology and U.S. Foreign Policy*. New Haven, CT: Yale University Press, 1987.

Huston, James L. *Calculating the Value of the Union: Slavery, Property Rights, and the Economic Origins of the American Civil War*. Chapel Hill: The University of North Carolina Press, 2003.

Iriye, Akira. *Global and Transnational History: The Past, Present, and Future.* New York: Palgrave Macmillan, 2013.

Jackson, Kellie Carter. *Force and Freedom: Black Abolitionists and the Politics of Violence.* Philadelphia: University of Pennsylvania Press, 2019.

Jacobson, Matthew Frye. *Barbarian Virtues: The United States Encounters Foreign Peoples at Home and Abroad, 1876–1917*. New York: Hill & Wang, 2011.

Janney, Caroline E. *Remembering the Civil War: Reunion and the Limits of Reconciliation.* Chapel Hill: The University of North Carolina Press, 2013.

Jayes, Janice Lee. *The Illusion of Ignorance: Constructing the American Encounter with Mexico, 1877–1920*. Lanham, MD: University Press of America, 2011.

Jenkins, Brian. *Britain and the War for the Union*. 2 vols. London: McGill-Queen's University Press, 1974, 1980.

Johannsen, Robert W. *To the Halls of the Montezumas: The Mexican War in the American Imagination*. Oxford: Oxford University Press, 1985.

Johnson, John J. *A Hemisphere Apart: The Foundations of United States Policy toward Latin America*. Baltimore, MD: Johns Hopkins University Press, 1990.

Jones, Aled. *Powers of the Press*. New York: Routledge, 2016.

Jones, Howard. *Blue and Gray Diplomacy: A History of Union and Confederate Foreign Relations*. Chapel Hill: The University of North Carolina Press, 2010.

———. *Union in Peril: The Crisis over British Intervention in the Civil War*. Chapel Hill: The University of North Carolina Press, 1992.

Joseph, Gilbert M., and Timothy Henderson, eds. *The Mexico Reader: History, Culture, Politics*. Durham, NC: Duke University Press, 2002.

Joseph, Gilbert M., Catherine C. Legrand, and Ricardo D. Salvatore, eds. *Close Encounters of Empire: Writing the Cultural History of U.S.-Latin American Relations*. Durham, NC: Duke University Press, 1998.

Kaplan, Amy. *The Anarchy of Empire in the Making of U.S. Culture*. Cambridge, MA: Harvard University Press, 2002.

Kaplan, Amy, and Donald E. Pease, eds. *Cultures of United States Imperialism*. Durham, NC: Duke University Press, 1993.

Karp, Matthew. *This Vast Southern Empire: Slaveholders at the Helm of American Foreign Policy*. Cambridge, MA: Harvard University Press, 2016.

Keehn, David C. *Knights of the Golden Circle: Secret Empire, Southern Secession, Civil War*. Baton Rouge: Louisiana State University Press, 2013.

Keller, Christian B. *Chancellorsville and the Germans: Nativism, Ethnicity, and Civil War Memory*. New York: Fordham University Press, 2007.

Kelly, Patrick J. "The Lost Continent of Abraham Lincoln." *Journal of the Civil War Era* 9, no. 2 (June 2019): 223–48.

———. "The North American Crisis of the 1860s." *Journal of the Civil War Era* 2, no. 3 (September 2012): 337–68.

Kim, Young C. "The Concept of Political Culture in Comparative Politics." *Journal of Politics* 26, no. 2 (May 1964): 313–36.

Klement, Frank L. "Civil War Politics, Nationalism, and Postwar Myths." *The Historian* 38, no. 3 (May 1976): 419–38.

———. *The Limits of Dissent: Clement L. Vallandigham and the Civil War*. Lexington: University Press of Kentucky, 1970.

Knudson, Jerry W. "John Reed: A Reporter in Revolutionary Mexico." *Journalism History* 29, no. 2 (2003): 59–68.

Körner, Axel, Nicola Miller, and Adam I. P. Smith, eds. *America Imagined: Explaining the United States in Nineteenth-Century Europe and Latin America*. New York: Palgrave Macmillan, 2012.

Kramer, Paul A. "Empires, Exceptions, and Anglo-Saxons: Race and Rule between the British and the United States Empires, 1880–1910." *Journal of American History* 88, no. 4 (March 2002): 1315–53.

———. "Power and Connection: Imperial Histories of the United States in the World." *American Historical Review* 116, no. 5 (December 2011): 1348–91.

Kruman, Marc W. "The Second American Party System and the Transformation of Revolutionary Republicanism." *Journal of the Early Republic* 12 (Winter 1992): 509–37.

Kushner, Howard I. "Visions of the Northwest Coast: Gwin and Seward in the 1850s." *Western Historical Quarterly* 4, no. 3 (July 1973): 295–306.

LaFeber, Walter. *The New Empire: An Interpretation of American Expansion, 1860–1898*. Ithaca, NY: Cornell University Press, 1963.

Lang, Andrew F. "Republicanism, Race, and Reconstruction: The Ethos of Military Occupation in Civil War America." *Journal of the Civil War Era* 4, no. 4 (December 2014): 559–89.

Langley, Lester D. *The Americas in the Age of Revolution, 1750–1850*. New Haven, CT: Yale University Press, 1996.

Lause, Mark A. *Free Labor: The Civil War and the Making of an American Working Class.* Urbana: University of Illinois Press, 2015.

Lavender, Caroline. "Confederate Cuba." *American Literature* 78, no. 4 (2006): 821–45.

Lavender, Caroline F., and Robert S. Levine, eds. *Hemispheric American Studies.* New Brunswick, NJ: Rutgers University Press, 2008.

Lawson, Melinda. *Patriot Fires: Forging a New American Nationalism in the Civil War North.* Lawrence: University Press of Kansas, 2002.

Lear, John. *Workers, Neighbors, and Citizens: The Revolution in Mexico City*. Lincoln: University of Nebraska Press, 2001.

Leonard, Gerald. *The Invention of Party Politics: Federalism, Popular Sovereignty, and Constitutional Development in Jacksonian Illinois*. Chapel Hill: The University of North Carolina Press, 2002.

Les Benedict, Michael. "Preserving the Constitution: The Conservative Bias of Radical Reconstruction." *Journal of American History* 61, no. 1 (June 1974): 65–90.

Lewis, Daniel. *Iron Horse Imperialism: The Southern Pacific of Mexico, 1880–1951*. Tucson: University of Arizona Press, 2007.

Lewis, James, Jr. *The American Union and the Problem of Neighborhood: The United States and the Collapse of the Spanish Empire, 1783–1820*. Chapel Hill: The University of North Carolina Press, 1998.

Linderman, Gerald F. *Embattled Courage: The Experience of Combat in the American Civil War*. New York: The Free Press, 1987.

Linenthal, Edward Tabor. *Sacred Ground: Americans and Their Battlefields*. Urbana: University of Illinois Press, 1993.

Link, William A. *Atlanta, Cradle of the New South: Race and Remembering the Civil War's Aftermath*. Chapel Hill: The University of North Carolina Press, 2013.

———, ed. *United States Reconstruction across the Americas*. Gainesville: University of Florida Press, 2019.

Long, Renata Eley. *In the Shadows of the Alabama: The British Foreign Office and the American Civil War*. Annapolis, MD: Naval Institute Press, 2015.

Lorey, David E. *The U.S.-Mexican Border in the Twentieth Century: A History of Economic and Social Transformation*. Wilmington, DE: Scholarly Resources, 1999.

Love, Eric T. L. *Race over Empire: Racism & U.S. Imperialism, 1865–1900*. Chapel Hill: The University of North Carolina Press, 2004.

Loveman, Brian. *No Higher Law: American Foreign Policy in the Western Hemisphere since 1776*. Chapel Hill: The University of North Carolina Press, 2010.

Lundberg, James M. *Horace Greeley: Print, Politics, and the Failure of American Nationhood.* Baltimore, MD: Johns Hopkins University Press, 2019.

Mach, Thomas S. *"Gentleman George" Hunt Pendleton: Party Politics and Ideological Identity in Nineteenth-Century America*. Kent, OH: Kent State University Press, 2007.

Mahin, Dean B. *One War at a Time: The International Dimensions of the American Civil War*. Washington, DC: Brassey's, 1999.

Majewski, John. *Modernizing a Slave Economy: The Economic Vision of a Confederate Nation*. Chapel Hill: The University of North Carolina Press, 2009.

Manning, Chandra. *What This Cruel War Was Over: Soldiers, Slavery, and the Civil War.* New York: Alfred A. Knopf, 2007.

Marcus, Alan P. *Confederate Exodus: Social and Environmental Forces in the Migration of U.S. Southerners to Brazil.* Lincoln: University of Nebraska Press, 2021.

Margolis, Stacey. *Fictions of Mass Democracy in Nineteenth-Century America.* Cambridge, UK: Cambridge University Press, 2015.

Masich, Andrew E. *Civil War in the Southwest Borderlands, 1861–1867.* Norman: Oklahoma University Press, 2017.

May, Robert E. "The Irony of Confederate Diplomacy: Visions of Empire, the Monroe Doctrine, and the Quest for Nationhood." *The Journal of Southern History* 83, no. 1 (February 2017): 69–106.

———. *Slavery, Race, and Conquest in the Tropics: Lincoln, Douglas, and the Future of Latin America.* Cambridge, UK: Cambridge University Press, 2013.

———. *The Southern Dream of a Caribbean Empire, 1854–1861.* Baton Rouge: Louisiana State University Press, 1973.

Mayer, Henry. *All on Fire: William Lloyd Garrison and the Abolition of Slavery.* New York: St. Martin's Press, 1998.

McAllister, William B., Joshua Botts, Peter Cozzens, and Aaron W. Marrs, eds. *Toward "Thorough, Accurate, and Reliable": A History of the* Foreign Relations of the United States *Series.* Washington, DC: US Department of State, Office of the Historian, Bureau of Public Affairs, 2015.

McClay, Wilfred M., ed. *Figures in the Carpet: Finding the Human Person in the American Past.* Grand Rapids, MI: Eerdmans, 2006.

McCurry, Stephanie. *Masters of Small Worlds: Yeoman Households, Gender Relations, and the Political Culture of the Antebellum South Carolina Low Country.* Oxford: Oxford University Press, 1995

McDaniel, W. Caleb. *The Problem of Democracy in the Age of Slavery: Garrisonian Abolitionists and Transatlantic Reform.* Baton Rouge: Louisiana State University Press, 2013.

McFarlane, Anthony. *War and Independence in Spanish America.* New York: Routledge, 2014.

McFreely, William S. *Grant: A Biography.* New York: W. W. Norton, 1981.

McGreevy, John. *Catholicism and American Freedom.* New York: Norton, 2003.

McIlhenny, Ryan. *To Preach Deliverance to the Captives: Freedom and Slavery in the Protestant Mind of George Bourne, 1780–1845.* Baton Rouge: Louisiana State University Press, 2020.

McInerney, Daniel J. *The Fortunate Heirs of Freedom: Abolition & Republican Thought.* Lincoln: University of Nebraska Press, 1994.

McMahon, Robert J., and Thomas W. Zeiler. *Guide to U.S. Foreign Policy: A Diplomatic History.* Vol 1. Washington, DC: Q. C. Press, 2012.

McNamara, Patrick J. *Sons of the Sierra: Juárez, Díaz, and the People of Ixtlán, Oaxaca, 1855–1920.* Chapel Hill: The University of North Carolina Press, 2007.

McPherson, James M. *Abraham Lincoln and the Second American Revolution.* Oxford: Oxford University Press, 1991.

———. *The Struggle for Equality: Abolitionists and the Negro in the Civil War and Reconstruction.* Princeton, NJ: Princeton University Press, 1992.

———. "Was Blood Thicker Than Water?: Ethnic and Civic Nationalism in the American Civil War." *Proceedings of the American Philosophical Society* 143, no. 1 (March 1999): 102–8.

———. *What They Fought For, 1861–1865*. Baton Rouge: Louisiana State University Press, 1994.

Mercer, Lloyd J. *Railroads and Land Grant Policy: A Study in Government Intervention*. Washington, DC: Beard Books, 2002.

Miller, Robert Ryal. "Arms across the Border: U.S. Aid to Juarez during the French Intervention in Mexico." *Transactions of the American Philosophical Society* 63, no. 6 (December 1973): 1–68.

———. "Matías Romero: Mexican Minister to the United States During the Juárez-Maximilian Era." *Hispanic American Historical Review* 45, no. 2 (1965): 228–45.

Mintz, Steven, and John Stauffer, eds. *The Problem of Evil: Slavery, Freedom, and the Ambiguities of American Reform*. Amherst and Boston: University of Massachusetts Press, 2007.

Mirow, M. C. *Latin American Constitutions: The Constitution of Cádiz and Its Legacy in Spanish America*. Cambridge, UK: Cambridge University Press, 2015.

Mitchell, Reid. *Civil War Soldiers*. New York: Viking, 1988.

Mobley, Joe A. "Zebulon B. Vance: A Confederate Nationalism in the North Carolina Gubernatorial Election of 1864." *North Carolina Historical Review* 77, no. 4 (October 2000): 434–54.

Morrison, Michael A. "American Reaction to European Revolution, 1848–52: Sectionalism, Memory and the Revolutionary Heritage." *Civil War History* 49 (2003): 111–31.

Murphy, Gretchen. *Hemispheric Imaginings: The Monroe Doctrine and Narratives of U.S. Empire*. Durham, NC: Duke University Press, 2005.

Nagler, Jörg, Don H. Doyle, and Marcus Gräser, eds. *The Transnational Significance of the American Civil War: A Global History*. New York: Palgrave Macmillan, 2016.

Naish, Paul D. *Silence and Slavery: Latin America and the U.S. Slave Debate*. Philadelphia: University of Pennsylvania Press, 2017.

Neely, Mark E., Jr. *The Boundaries of American Political Culture in the Civil War Era*. Chapel Hill: The University of North Carolina Press, 2005.

———. *The Civil War and the Limits of Destruction*. Cambridge, MA: Harvard University Press, 2007.

———. *Lincoln and the Democrats: The Politics of Opposition in the Civil War*. Cambridge, UK: Cambridge University Press, 2017.

———. *Lincoln and the Triumph of the Nation: Constitutional Conflict in the American Civil War*. Chapel Hill: The University of North Carolina Press, 2011.

———. *Southern Rights: Political Prisoners and the Myth of Confederate Constitutionalism*. Charlottesville: University of Virginia Press, 1999.

Neff, John. *Honoring the Civil War Dead: Commemoration and the Problem of Reconciliation*. Lawrence: University of Kansas Press, 2005.

Nelson, Megan Kate. *Three-Cornered War: The Union, the Confederacy, and Native Peoples in the Fight for the West*. New York: Simon & Schuster, 2020.

Ninkovich, Frank. *Global Dawn: The Cultural Foundation of American Internationalism, 1865–1890*. Cambridge, MA: Harvard University Press, 2010.

Noll, Mark A. *The Civil War as a Theological Crisis*. Chapel Hill: The University of North Carolina Press, 2006.

Nord, David Paul. *Communities of Journalism: A History of American Newspapers and Their Readers*. Urbana and Chicago: University of Illinois Press, 2008.

Nugent, Walter. *Habits of Empire: A History of American Expansion*. New York: Alfred A. Knopf, 2008.

O'Hara, Matthew D. *A Flock Divided: Race, Religion, and Politics in Mexico, 1749–1857*. Durham, NC: Duke University Press, 2010.

Olliff, Donathon C. *Reforma Mexico and the United States: A Search for Alternatives to Annexation, 1854–1861*. Tuscaloosa: University of Alabama Press, 1981.

Onuf, Nicholas, and Peter Onuf. *Nations, Markets, and War: Modern History and the American Civil War*. Charlottesville: University of Virginia Press, 2006.

Pani, Erika. "Law, Allegiance, and Sovereignty in Civil War Mexico, 1857–1867." *Journal of the Civil War Era* 7, no. 4 (December 2017): 570–96.

Paolino, Ernest. *The Foundations of the American Empire: William Henry Seward and U.S. Foreign Policy*. Ithaca, NY: Cornell University Press, 1973.

Parlee, Lorena. *Porfirio Díaz, Railroads, and Development in Northern Mexico: A Study of Government Policy Toward the Central and Nacional Railroads, 1876–1910*. San Diego: University of California, 1981.

Pascoe, Peggy. *What Comes Naturally: Miscegenation Law and the Making of Race in America*. Oxford: Oxford University Press, 2009.

Passananti, Thomas O. "'Nada de Papeluchos!' Managing Globalization in Early Porfirian Mexico." *Latin American Research Review* 42, no. 3 (October 2007): 101–28.

Peart, Daniel, and Adam I. P. Smith, eds. *Practicing Democracy: Popular Politics in the United States from the Constitution to the Civil War*. Charlottesville: University of Virginia Press, 2015.

Perman, Michael. *The Road to Redemption: Southern Politics, 1869–1879*. Chapel Hill: The University of North Carolina Press, 1984.

Pike, Frederick B. *The United States and Latin America: Myths and Stereotypes of Civilization and Nature*. Austin: University of Texas Press, 1992.

Pinheiro, John C. *Missionaries of Republicanism: A Religious History of the Mexican-American War*. Oxford: Oxford University Press, 2014.

Pletcher, David M. *The Diplomacy of Trade and Investment: American Economic Expansion in the Hemisphere, 1865–1900*. Columbia: University of Missouri Press, 1998.

Pocock, J. G. A. *The Machiavellian Moment: Florentine Political Thought and the Atlantic Republican Tradition*. Princeton, NJ: Princeton University Press, 1975.

Prescott, William. *The History of the Conquest of Mexico*. New York: The Modern Library, 2001.

Priego, Natalia. *Positivism, Science, and "The Scientists" in Porfirian Mexico: A Reappraisal*. Liverpool: Liverpool University Press, 2016.

Priest, Andrew. "Imperial Exchange: American Views of the British Empire during the Civil War and Reconstruction." *Journal of Colonialism and Colonial History* 16, no. 1 (Spring 2015). https://doi.org/10.1353/cch.2015.0015 (accessed 8 February 2018).

Prince, K. Stephen. *Stories of the South: Race and the Reconstruction of Southern Identity, 1865–1915*. Chapel Hill: The University of North Carolina Press, 2014.

Prior, David. "Civilization, Republic, Nation: Contested Keywords, Northern Republicans, and the Forgotten Reconstruction of Mormon Utah." *Civil War History* 56, no. 3 (September 2010): 283–310.

———. "'Crete the Opening Wedge": Nationalism and International Affairs in Postbellum America." *Journal of Social History* 42, no. 4 (Summer 2009): 861–87.

Quigley, Paul. *Shifting Grounds: Nationalism and the American South, 1848–1865*. Oxford: Oxford University Press, 2010.

Raat, William D. "Ideas and Society in Don Porfirio's Mexico." *The Americas* 30, no. 1 (July 1973): 32–53.

Raat, William Dirk, and Michael M. Brescia, eds. *Mexico and the United States: Ambivalent Vistas*. Athens: University of Georgia Press, 2010.

Rable, George C. *God's Almost Chosen Peoples: A Religious History of the American Civil War*. Chapel Hill: The University of North Carolina Press, 2010.

Ransom, Roger L. *Conflict and Compromise: The Political Economy of Slavery, Emancipation, and the American Civil War*. Cambridge, UK: Cambridge University Press, 1989.

Ransom, Roger L., and Richard Sutch. *One Kind of Freedom: The Economic Consequences of Emancipation*. 2nd ed. Cambridge, UK: Cambridge University Press, 2001.

Raper, Horace W. "William W. Holden and the Peace Movement in North Carolina." *North Carolina Historical Review* 31, no. 4 (October 1954): 493–516.

Resendez, Andres. "North American Peonage." *Journal of the Civil War Era* 7, no. 4 (December 2017): 597–619.

Richardson, Heather Cox. *The Death of Reconstruction: Race Labor, and Politics in the post-Civil War North, 1865–1901*. Cambridge, MA: Harvard University Press, 2001.

Roberts, Timothy Mason. *Distant Revolutions: 1848 and the Challenge to American Exceptionalism*. Charlottesville: University of Virginia Press, 2009.

Robinson, Barry M. *The Mark of Rebels: Indios Fronterizos and Mexican Independence*. Tuscaloosa: University of Alabama Press, 2016.

Rodríguez, Jaime Javier. *The Literatures of the U.S.-Mexican War: Narrative, Time, and Identity*. Austin: University of Texas Press, 2010.

Rodríguez O., Jamie E., ed. *The Divine Charter: Constitutionalism and Liberalism in Nineteenth-Century Mexico*. Lanham, MD: Rowman & Littlefield, 2005.

———. *The Independence of Spanish America*. Cambridge, UK: Cambridge University Press, 1998.

———. *"We Are Now the True Spaniards": Sovereignty, Revolution, Independence, and the Emergence of the Federal Republic of Mexico, 1808–1824*. Stanford, CA: Stanford University Press, 2012.

Rogers, Daniel T. "Republicanism: The Career of a Concept." *Journal of American History* 79, no. 1 (June 1992): 11–38.

Rolle, Andrew F. *The Lost Cause: The Confederate Exodus to Mexico*. Norman: Oklahoma University Press, 1965.

Rothera, Evan C. *Civil Wars and Reconstructions in the Americas: The United States, Mexico, & Argentina, 1860–1880*. Baton Rouge: Louisiana State University Press, 2022.

Rubin, Anne Sarah. *A Shattered Nation: The Rise and Fall of the Confederacy, 1861–1868*. Chapel Hill: The University of North Carolina Press, 2005.

Rugemer, Edward B. "Robert Monroe Harrison, British Abolition, Southern Anglophobia and Texas Annexation." *Slavery & Abolition* 28, no. 2 (August 2007): 169–91.

———. "The Southern Response to British Abolitionism: The Maturation of Proslavery Apologetics." *Journal of Southern History* 70, no. 2 (May 2004): 221–48.

Sainlaude, Stève. *France and the American Civil War: A Diplomatic History*. Translated by Jessica Edwards. Chapel Hill: The University of North Carolina Press, 2019.

Samito, Christian G. *Becoming American under Fire: Irish Americans, African Americans, and the Politics of Citizenship during the Civil War Era*. Ithaca, NY: Cornell University Press, 2009.

Sanders, Charles W., Jr. "Jefferson Davis and the Hampton Roads Peace Conference: 'To Secure Peace to the Two Countries.'" *Journal of Southern History* 63, no. 4 (November 1997): 803–26.

Sanders, James E. "Atlantic Republicanism in Nineteenth-Century Colombia: Spanish America's Challenge to the Contours of Atlantic History." *Journal of World History* 20, no. 1 (March 2009): 131–50.

———. "Hemispheric Reconstructions: Post-Emancipation Social Movements and Capitalist Reaction in Colombia and the United States." *Journal of the Gilded Age and Progressive Era* 22 (2023): 41–62.

———. *The Vanguard of the Atlantic World: Creating Modernity, Nation and Democracy in Nineteenth-Century Latin America*. Durham, NC: Duke University Press, 2014.

Sandow, Robert M., ed. *Contested Loyalty: Debates over Patriotism in the Civil War North*. New York: Fordham University Press, 2018.

Saragoza, Alex M. *The Monterrey Elite and the Mexican State, 1880–1940*. Austin: University of Texas Press, 1988.

Schell, William, Jr. *Integral Outsiders: The American Colony in Mexico City, 1876–1911*. Wilmington, DE: Scholarly Resources, 2001.

Schoen, Brian. "The Fates of Republics and Empires Hang in the Balance: The United States and Europe during the Civil War Era." *OAH Magazine of History* 27, no. 2 (April 2013): 41–47.

Schonberger, Howard. *Transportation to the Seaboard: The "Communication Revolution" and American Foreign Policy, 1860–1900*. Westport, CT: Greenwood, 1971.

Schoonover, Thomas D. *Dollars over Dominion: The Triumph of Liberalism in Mexican-United States Relations, 1861–1867*. Baton Rouge: Louisiana State University Press, 1978.

———. *The United States in Central America, 1860–1911: Episodes of Social Imperialism and Imperial Rivalry in the World System*. Durham, NC: Duke University Press, 1991.

Scott, James C. *Seeing Like a State: How Certain Schemes to Improve the Human Condition Have Failed*. New Haven, CT: Yale University Press, 1998.

Sears, Stephen W. *Gettysburg*. New York: Houghton Mifflin, 2003.

Seijas, Tatiana, and Jake Frederick. *Spanish Dollars and Sister Republics: The Money That Made Mexico and the United States*. Lanham, MD: Rowman & Littlefield, 2017.

Selinger, Jeffrey S. *Embracing Dissent: Political Violence and Party Development in the United States*. Philadelphia: University of Pennsylvania Press, 2016.

Sexton, Jay. *Debtor Diplomacy: Finance and American Foreign Relations in the Civil War Era, 1837–1873*. Oxford: Oxford University Press, 2005.

———. *The Monroe Doctrine: Empire and Nation in Nineteenth-Century America.* New York: Hill & Wang, 2011.

———. "Toward a Synthesis of Foreign Relations in the Civil War Era, 1848–1877." *American Nineteenth Century History* 5, no. 3 (2004): 50–73.

———. "The United States, the Cuban Rebellion, and the Multilateral Initiative of 1875." *Diplomatic History* 30, no. 3 (May 2006): 335–65.

Seybold, Matt. "Destroyer of *Confidence*: James Gordon Bennett, Jacksonian Paranoia, and the Original Confidence Man." *American Studies* 56, no. 3/4 (2018): 83–106.

Shalhope, Robert E. *John Taylor of Caroline: Pastoral Republican*. Columbia: University of South Carolina Press, 1980.

———. "Thomas Jefferson's Republicanism and Antebellum Southern Thought." *Journal of Southern History* 42, no. 4 (November 1976): 529–56.

Shawcross, Edward. *France, Mexico and Informal Empire in Latin America, 1820–1867: Equilibrium in the New World*. Cham, Switzerland: Palgrave Macmillan, 2018.

Shea, William L. "The War We Have Lost." *Arkansas Historical Quarterly* 70, no. 2 (Summer 2011): 100–108.

Silbey, Joel. *The American Political Nation, 1838–1898*. Stanford, CA: Stanford University Press, 1991.

———. *A Respectable Minority: The Democratic Party in the Civil War Era, 1860–1868*. New York: W. W. Norton, 1977.

Sinha, Manisha. *The Counterrevolution of Slavery: Politics and Ideology in Antebellum South Carolina*. Chapel Hill: The University of North Carolina Press, 2000.

Sinkin, Richard N. *The Mexican Reform, 1855–1876: A Study of Liberal Nation-Building*. Austin: University of Texas Press, 1979.

Slap, Andrew L. *The Doom of Reconstruction: The Liberal Republicans in the Civil War Era*. New York: Fordham University Press, 2006.

———. *Reconstructing Appalachia: The Civil War's Aftermath*. Lexington: University Press of Kentucky, 2010.

Smith, Adam I. P. *No Party Now: Politics in the Civil War North*. Oxford: Oxford University Press, 2006.

Smith, Benjamin T. *The Roots of Conservatism in Mexico: Catholicism, Society, and Politics in the Mixteca Baja, 1750–1962*. Albuquerque: University of New Mexico Press, 2012.

Smith, Michael Thomas. *The Enemy Within: Fears of Corruption in the Civil War North*. Charlottesville: University of Virginia Press, 2011.

Smith, Phyllis L. "Contentious Voices amid the Order: The Opposition Press in Mexico City, 1876–1911." *Journalism History* 22, no. 4 (Winter 1997): 138–45.

Smith, Stacey L. "Beyond North and South: Putting the West in the Civil War and Reconstruction." *Journal of the Civil War Era* 6, no. 4 (December 2016): 566–91.

———. *Freedom's Frontier: California and the Struggle over Unfree Labor, Emancipation, and Reconstruction*. Chapel Hill: The University of North Carolina Press, 2013.

Snay, Mitchell. *Fenians, Freedman, and Southern Whites: Race and Nationality in the Era of Reconstruction*. Baton Rouge: Louisiana State University Press, 2007.

———. *Horace Greeley and the Politics of Reform in Nineteenth-Century America*. Lanham, MD: Rowman & Littlefield, 2011.

Sproat, John G. *"The Best Men": Liberal Reformers in the Gilded Age*. Oxford: Oxford University Press, 1968.

Stevens, Donald Fithian. *Origins of Instability in Early Republican Mexico*. Durham, NC: Duke University Press, 1991.

St. John, Rachel. *Line in the Sand: A History of the Western U.S.-Mexican Border*. Princeton, NJ: Princeton University Press, 2011.

Stout, Joseph A. *Schemers and Dreamers: Filibustering in Mexico, 1848–1921*. Fort Worth: Texas Christian University Press, 2002.

Strom, Sharon Hartman, and Frederick Stirton Weaver. *Confederates in the Tropics: Charles Swett's Travelogue of 1868*. Jackson: University of Mississippi Press, 2011.

Summers, Mark Wahlgren. *A Dangerous Stir: Fear, Paranoia, and the Making of Reconstruction*. Chapel Hill: The University of North Carolina Press, 2009.

———. *The Ordeal of the Reunion: A New History of Reconstruction*. Chapel Hill: The University of North Carolina Press, 2014.

———. *Railroads, Reconstruction, and the Gospel of Prosperity: Aid under the Radical Republicans, 1865–1877*. Princeton, NJ: Princeton University Press, 1984.

———. *Rum, Romanism, and Rebellion: The Making of a President, 1884*. Chapel Hill: The University of North Carolina Press, 2000.

Taylor, William R. *Cavalier & Yankee: The Old South and American National Character*. Oxford: Oxford University Press, 1993.

Thelen, David. "The Nation and Beyond: Transnational Perspectives on United States History." *Journal of American History* 86, no. 3 (December 1999): 965–75.

Thier, Maike. "The View from Paris: 'Latinity', 'Anglo-Saxonism', and the Americas, as discussed in the *Revue des Races Latines*, 1857–1864." *International History Review* 33, no. 4 (December 2011): 627–44.

Thompson, Guy P. "Popular Aspects of Liberalism in Mexico, 1848–1888." *Bulletin of Latin American Research* 10, no. 3 (1991): 265–92.

Thompson, Guy P. C., with David G. LaFrance. *Patriotism, Politics, and Popular Liberalism in Nineteenth-Century Mexico: Juan Francisco Lucas and the Puebla Sierra*. Wilmington, DE: Scholarly Resources, 1999.

Torget, Andrew J. *Seeds of Empire: Cotton, Slavery, and the Transformation of the Texas Borderlands, 1800–1850*. Chapel Hill: The University of North Carolina Press, 2015.

Tripp, Steven Elliott. *Yankee Town, Southern City: Race and Class Relations in Civil War Lynchburg*. New York: New York University Press, 1997.

Truett, Samuel. *Fugitive Landscapes: The Forgotten History of the U.S.-Mexican Borderlands*. New Haven, CT: Yale University Press, 2006.

Tuchinsky, Adam. *Horace Greeley's* New York Tribune*: Civil War–Era Socialism and the Crisis of Free Labor*. Ithaca, NY: Cornell University Press, 2009.

Tucker, Ann L. *Newest Born of Nations: European Nationalist Movements and the Making of the Confederacy*. Charlottesville: University of Virginia Press, 2020.

Tutino, John ed. *Mexico and Mexicans in the Making of the United States*. Austin: University of Texas Press, 2012.

Tyler, R. Curtis. "Santiago Vidaurri and the Confederacy." *The Americas* 26, no. 1 (July 1969): 66–76.

Tyler, Ronnie C. "Fugitive Slaves in Mexico." *Journal of Negro History* 57, no. 1 (January 1972): 1–12.

Tyrell, Ian. *Reforming the World: The Creation of America's Moral Empire*. Princeton, NJ: Princeton University Press, 2010.

———. *Transnational Nation: United States History in Global Perspective since 1789*. New York: Palgrave MacMillan, 2007.

Underwood, Rodman L. *Waters of Discord: The Union Blockade of Texas during the Civil War*. Jefferson, NC: McFarland & Company, 2003.

Ural, Susannah J., ed. *Civil War Citizens: Race, Ethnicity, and Identity in America's Bloodiest Conflict*. New York: New York University Press, 2010.

Vallenilla, Nikita Harwich. "Venezuelan Positivism and Modernity." *Hispanic American Historical Review* 70, no. 2 (1990): 327–44.

Van Hoy, Teresa. "Mexican Exiles and the Monroe Doctrine: New York and the Borderlands, 1865." *Camino Real* 7, no. 10 (2015): 39–60.

van Minnen, Cornelius A., and Manfred Berg, eds. *The U. S. South and Europe: Transatlantic Relations in the Nineteenth and Twentieth Centuries*. Lexington: University Press of Kentucky, 2013.

Van Wagenen, Michael Scott. *Remembering the Forgotten War: The Enduring Legacies of the U.S.-Mexican War*. Amherst: University of Massachusetts Press, 2013.

Voss-Hubbard, Mark. *Beyond Party: Cultures of Antipartisanship in Northern Politics before the Civil War*. Baltimore, MA: Johns Hopkins University Press, 2002.

Wahlstrom, Todd. *The Southern Exodus to Mexico: Migration across the Borderlands after the American Civil War*. Lincoln: University of Nebraska Press, 2015.

Waite, Kevin. "Jefferson Davis and Proslavery Visions of Empire in the Far West." *Journal of the Civil War Era* 6, no. 4 (December 2016): 536–65.

Wasserman, Mark. *Everyday Life and Politics in Nineteenth-Century Mexico: Men, Women, and War*. Albuquerque: University of New Mexico Press, 2000.

Watson Jr., Ritchie Devon. *Normans and Saxons: Southern Race Mythology and the Intellectual History of the American Civil War*. Baton Rouge: Louisiana State University Press, 2008.

Waugh, Joan. *U.S. Grant: American Hero, American Myth*. Chapel Hill: The University of North Carolina Press, 2009.

Weber, David J., ed. *Myth and the History of the Hispanic Southwest: Essays by David J. Weber*. Albuquerque: University of New Mexico Press, 1987.

Weber, Jennifer L. *Copperheads: The Rise and Fall of Lincoln's Opponents in the North*. Oxford: Oxford University Press, 2006.

Weinberg, Albert K. *Manifest Destiny: A Study of Nationalist Expansionism in American History*. Baltimore, MD: Johns Hopkins Press, 1935.

Weiner, Richard. *Race, Nation, and Market: Economic Culture in Porfirian Mexico*. Tucson: University of Arizona Press, 2004.

West, Elliot. "Reconstructing Race." *Western Historical Quarterly* 34, no. 1 (Spring 2003): 6–26.

Wetherington, Mark V. *The New South Comes to Wiregrass Georgia, 1860–1910*. Knoxville: University of Tennessee Press, 1994.

White, Ashi. *Encountering Revolution: Haiti and the Making of the Early Republic*. Baltimore, MD: Johns Hopkins University Press, 2010.

White, Johnathan W. *Emancipation, the Union Army, and the Reelection of Abraham Lincoln*. Baton Rouge: Louisiana State University Press, 2020.

White, Richard. *Railroaded: The Transcontinentals and the Making of Modern America*. New York: W. W. Norton & Company, 2011.

———. *The Republic for Which It Stands: The United States during Reconstruction and the Gilded Age, 1865–1896*. Oxford: Oxford University Press, 2017.

Whitman, T. Stephen. *Antietam 1862: Gateway to Emancipation*. Santa Barbara, CA: Praeger, 2012.

Wiley, Bell Irvin. *The Life of Billy Yank: The Common Soldier of the Union*. Indianapolis, IN: Bobbs-Merrill Company, 1952.

Williams, Robert C. *Horace Greeley: Champion of American Freedom*. New York: New York University Press, 2006.

Williams, William Appleman, ed. *From Colony to Empire: Essays in the History of American Foreign Relations*. New York: John Wiley & Sons, 1972.

———. *The Tragedy of American Diplomacy*. 2nd ed. New York: Dell Publishing Co., 1972.

Wolfson, M., ed. *The Political Economy of War and Peace*. Norwell, MA: Kluwer Academic Publishers, 1998.

Wood, Gordon S. "Classical Republicanism and the American Revolution." *Chicago-Kent Law Review* 66, no. 1 (April 1990): 13–38.

———. *The Creation of the American Republic, 1776–1787*. Chapel Hill: The University of North Carolina Press, 1969.

Woog, Adam. *The Emancipation Proclamation: Ending Slavery in America*. New York: Infobase Publishing, 2009.

Wright, Gavin. *Old South, New South: Revolutions in the Southern Economy since the Civil War*. New York: Basic Books, 1986.

Wrobel, David M. *Global West, American Frontier: Travel, Empire, and Exceptionalism from Manifest Destiny to the Great Depression*. Albuquerque: University of New Mexico Press, 2013.

Wynne, Ben. *The Man Who Punched Jefferson Davis: The Political Life of Henry S. Foote*. Baton Rouge: Louisiana State University Press, 2018.

Xi, Wang. *The Trial of Democracy: Black Suffrage and Northern Republicans, 1860–1910*. Athens: University of Georgia Press, 1997.

Zvengrowski, Jeffery. *Jefferson Davis, Napoleonic France, and the Nature of Confederate Ideology, 1815–1897*. Baton Rouge: Louisiana State University Press, 2019.

Index

www.ingramcontent.com/pod-product-compliance
Lightning Source LLC
Chambersburg PA
CBHW022330260225
22648CB00006B/110

* 9 7 8 1 4 6 9 6 8 5 2 1 2 *